FREE Study Skills Videos/DVD Offer

Dear Customer,

Thank you for your purchase from Mometrix! We consider it an honor and a privilege that you have purchased our product and we want to ensure your satisfaction.

As part of our ongoing effort to meet the needs of test takers, we have developed a set of Study Skills Videos that we would like to give you for FREE. These videos cover our *best practices* for getting ready for your exam, from how to use our study materials to how to best prepare for the day of the test.

All that we ask is that you email us with feedback that would describe your experience so far with our product. Good, bad, or indifferent, we want to know what you think!

To get your FREE Study Skills Videos, you can use the **QR code** below, or send us an **email** at studyvideos@mometrix.com with *FREE VIDEOS* in the subject line and the following information in the body of the email:

- The name of the product you purchased.
- Your product rating on a scale of 1-5, with 5 being the highest rating.
- Your feedback. It can be long, short, or anything in between. We just want to know your impressions and experience so far with our product. (Good feedback might include how our study material met your needs and ways we might be able to make it even better. You could highlight features that you found helpful or features that you think we should add.)

If you have any questions or concerns, please don't hesitate to contact me directly.

Thanks again!

Sincerely,

Jay Willis
Vice President
jay.willis@mometrix.com
1-800-673-8175

CLT

Secrets Study Guide

Exam Prep Book and
Practice Questions for
the Classic Learning Test

2nd Edition

Written and edited by Mometrix Test Prep

Printed in the United States of America

This paper meets the requirements of ANSI/NISO Z39.48-1992 (Permanence of Paper).

Paperback
ISBN 13: 978-1-5167-2401-7
ISBN 10: 1-5167-2401-1

Dear Future Exam Success Story

First of all, **THANK YOU** for purchasing Mometrix study materials!

Second, congratulations! You are one of the few determined test-takers who are committed to doing whatever it takes to excel on your exam. **You have come to the right place.** We developed these study materials with one goal in mind: to deliver you the information you need in a format that's concise and easy to use.

In addition to optimizing your guide for the content of the test, we've outlined our recommended steps for breaking down the preparation process into small, attainable goals so you can make sure you stay on track.

We've also analyzed the entire test-taking process, identifying the most common pitfalls and showing how you can overcome them and be ready for any curveball the test throws you.

Standardized testing is one of the biggest obstacles on your road to success, which only increases the importance of doing well in the high-pressure, high-stakes environment of test day. Your results on this test could have a significant impact on your future, and this guide provides the information and practical advice to help you achieve your full potential on test day.

Your success is our success

We would love to hear from you! If you would like to share the story of your exam success or if you have any questions or comments in regard to our products, please contact us at **800-673-8175** or **support@mometrix.com**.

Thanks again for your business and we wish you continued success!

Sincerely,
The Mometrix Test Preparation Team

Written and edited by the Mometrix Exam Secrets Test Prep Team
Printed in the United States of America

TABLE OF CONTENTS

Introduction

Thank you for purchasing this resource! You have made the choice to prepare yourself for a test that could have a huge impact on your future, and this guide is designed to help you be fully ready for test day. Obviously, it's important to have a solid understanding of the test material, but you also need to be prepared for the unique environment and stressors of the test, so that you can perform to the best of your abilities.

For this purpose, the first section that appears in this guide is the **Secret Keys**. We've devoted countless hours to meticulously researching what works and what doesn't, and we've boiled down our findings to the five most impactful steps you can take to improve your performance on the test. We start at the beginning with study planning and move through the preparation process, all the way to the testing strategies that will help you get the most out of what you know when you're finally sitting in front of the test.

We recommend that you start preparing for your test as far in advance as possible. However, if you've bought this guide as a last-minute study resource and only have a few days before your test, we recommend that you skip over the first two Secret Keys since they address a long-term study plan.

If you struggle with **test anxiety**, we strongly encourage you to check out our recommendations for how you can overcome it. Test anxiety is a formidable foe, but it can be beaten, and we want to make sure you have the tools you need to defeat it.

Review Video Directory

As you work your way through this guide, you will see numerous review video links interspersed with the written content. If you would like to access all of these review videos in one place, click on the video directory link found on the bonus page: **mometrix.com/bonus948/claslearntest**

Secret Key #1 – Plan Big, Study Small

There's a lot riding on your performance. If you want to ace this test, you're going to need to keep your skills sharp and the material fresh in your mind. You need a plan that lets you review everything you need to know while still fitting in your schedule. We'll break this strategy down into three categories.

Information Organization

Start with the information you already have: the official test outline. From this, you can make a complete list of all the concepts you need to cover before the test. Organize these concepts into groups that can be studied together, and create a list of any related vocabulary you need to learn so you can brush up on any difficult terms. You'll want to keep this vocabulary list handy once you actually start studying since you may need to add to it along the way.

Time Management

Once you have your set of study concepts, decide how to spread them out over the time you have left before the test. Break your study plan into small, clear goals so you have a manageable task for each day and know exactly what you're doing. Then just focus on one small step at a time. When you manage your time this way, you don't need to spend hours at a time studying. Studying a small block of content for a short period each day helps you retain information better and avoid stressing over how much you have left to do. You can relax knowing that you have a plan to cover everything in time. In order for this strategy to be effective though, you have to start studying early and stick to your schedule. Avoid the exhaustion and futility that comes from last-minute cramming!

Study Environment

The environment you study in has a big impact on your learning. Studying in a coffee shop, while probably more enjoyable, is not likely to be as fruitful as studying in a quiet room. It's important to keep distractions to a minimum. You're only planning to study for a short block of time, so make the most of it. Don't pause to check your phone or get up to find a snack. It's also important to **avoid multitasking**. Research has consistently shown that multitasking will make your studying dramatically less effective. Your study area should also be comfortable and well-lit so you don't have the distraction of straining your eyes or sitting on an uncomfortable chair.

The time of day you study is also important. You want to be rested and alert. Don't wait until just before bedtime. Study when you'll be most likely to comprehend and remember. Even better, if you know what time of day your test will be, set that time aside for study. That way your brain will be used to working on that subject at that specific time and you'll have a better chance of recalling information.

Finally, it can be helpful to team up with others who are studying for the same test. Your actual studying should be done in as isolated an environment as possible, but the work of organizing the information and setting up the study plan can be divided up. In between study sessions, you can discuss with your teammates the concepts that you're all studying and quiz each other on the details. Just be sure that your teammates are as serious about the test as you are. If you find that your study time is being replaced with social time, you might need to find a new team.

Secret Key #2 – Make Your Studying Count

You're devoting a lot of time and effort to preparing for this test, so you want to be absolutely certain it will pay off. This means doing more than just reading the content and hoping you can remember it on test day. It's important to make every minute of study count. There are two main areas you can focus on to make your studying count.

Retention

It doesn't matter how much time you study if you can't remember the material. You need to make sure you are retaining the concepts. To check your retention of the information you're learning, try recalling it at later times with minimal prompting. Try carrying around flashcards and glance at one or two from time to time or ask a friend who's also studying for the test to quiz you.

To enhance your retention, look for ways to put the information into practice so that you can apply it rather than simply recalling it. If you're using the information in practical ways, it will be much easier to remember. Similarly, it helps to solidify a concept in your mind if you're not only reading it to yourself but also explaining it to someone else. Ask a friend to let you teach them about a concept you're a little shaky on (or speak aloud to an imaginary audience if necessary). As you try to summarize, define, give examples, and answer your friend's questions, you'll understand the concepts better and they will stay with you longer. Finally, step back for a big picture view and ask yourself how each piece of information fits with the whole subject. When you link the different concepts together and see them working together as a whole, it's easier to remember the individual components.

Finally, practice showing your work on any multi-step problems, even if you're just studying. Writing out each step you take to solve a problem will help solidify the process in your mind, and you'll be more likely to remember it during the test.

Modality

Modality simply refers to the means or method by which you study. Choosing a study modality that fits your own individual learning style is crucial. No two people learn best in exactly the same way, so it's important to know your strengths and use them to your advantage.

For example, if you learn best by visualization, focus on visualizing a concept in your mind and draw an image or a diagram. Try color-coding your notes, illustrating them, or creating symbols that will trigger your mind to recall a learned concept. If you learn best by hearing or discussing information, find a study partner who learns the same way or read aloud to yourself. Think about how to put the information in your own words. Imagine that you are giving a lecture on the topic and record yourself so you can listen to it later.

For any learning style, flashcards can be helpful. Organize the information so you can take advantage of spare moments to review. Underline key words or phrases. Use different colors for different categories. Mnemonic devices (such as creating a short list in which every item starts with the same letter) can also help with retention. Find what works best for you and use it to store the information in your mind most effectively and easily.

Secret Key #3 – Practice the Right Way

Your success on test day depends not only on how many hours you put into preparing, but also on whether you prepared the right way. It's good to check along the way to see if your studying is paying off. One of the most effective ways to do this is by taking practice tests to evaluate your progress. Practice tests are useful because they show exactly where you need to improve. Every time you take a practice test, pay special attention to these three groups of questions:

- The questions you got wrong
- The questions you had to guess on, even if you guessed right
- The questions you found difficult or slow to work through

This will show you exactly what your weak areas are, and where you need to devote more study time. Ask yourself why each of these questions gave you trouble. Was it because you didn't understand the material? Was it because you didn't remember the vocabulary? Do you need more repetitions on this type of question to build speed and confidence? Dig into those questions and figure out how you can strengthen your weak areas as you go back to review the material.

Additionally, many practice tests have a section explaining the answer choices. It can be tempting to read the explanation and think that you now have a good understanding of the concept. However, an explanation likely only covers part of the question's broader context. Even if the explanation makes perfect sense, **go back and investigate** every concept related to the question until you're positive you have a thorough understanding.

As you go along, keep in mind that the practice test is just that: practice. Memorizing these questions and answers will not be very helpful on the actual test because it is unlikely to have any of the same exact questions. If you only know the right answers to the sample questions, you won't be prepared for the real thing. **Study the concepts** until you understand them fully, and then you'll be able to answer any question that shows up on the test.

It's important to wait on the practice tests until you're ready. If you take a test on your first day of study, you may be overwhelmed by the amount of material covered and how much you need to learn. Work up to it gradually.

On test day, you'll need to be prepared for answering questions, managing your time, and using the test-taking strategies you've learned. It's a lot to balance, like a mental marathon that will have a big impact on your future. Like training for a marathon, you'll need to start slowly and work your way up. When test day arrives, you'll be ready.

Start with the strategies you've read in the first two Secret Keys—plan your course and study in the way that works best for you. If you have time, consider using multiple study resources to get different approaches to the same concepts. It can be helpful to see difficult concepts from more than one angle. Then find a good source for practice tests. Many times, the test website will suggest potential study resources or provide sample tests.

Practice Test Strategy

If you're able to find at least three practice tests, we recommend this strategy:

Untimed and Open-Book Practice

Take the first test with no time constraints and with your notes and study guide handy. Take your time and focus on applying the strategies you've learned.

Timed and Open-Book Practice

Take the second practice test open-book as well, but set a timer and practice pacing yourself to finish in time.

Timed and Closed-Book Practice

Take any other practice tests as if it were test day. Set a timer and put away your study materials. Sit at a table or desk in a quiet room, imagine yourself at the testing center, and answer questions as quickly and accurately as possible.

Keep repeating timed and closed-book tests on a regular basis until you run out of practice tests or it's time for the actual test. Your mind will be ready for the schedule and stress of test day, and you'll be able to focus on recalling the material you've learned.

Secret Key #4 – Pace Yourself

Once you're fully prepared for the material on the test, your biggest challenge on test day will be managing your time. Just knowing that the clock is ticking can make you panic even if you have plenty of time left. Work on pacing yourself so you can build confidence against the time constraints of the exam. Pacing is a difficult skill to master, especially in a high-pressure environment, so **practice is vital**.

Set time expectations for your pace based on how much time is available. For example, if a section has 60 questions and the time limit is 30 minutes, you know you have to average 30 seconds or less per question in order to answer them all. Although 30 seconds is the hard limit, set 25 seconds per question as your goal, so you reserve extra time to spend on harder questions. When you budget extra time for the harder questions, you no longer have any reason to stress when those questions take longer to answer.

Don't let this time expectation distract you from working through the test at a calm, steady pace, but keep it in mind so you don't spend too much time on any one question. Recognize that taking extra time on one question you don't understand may keep you from answering two that you do understand later in the test. If your time limit for a question is up and you're still not sure of the answer, mark it and move on, and come back to it later if the time and the test format allow. If the testing format doesn't allow you to return to earlier questions, just make an educated guess; then put it out of your mind and move on.

On the easier questions, be careful not to rush. It may seem wise to hurry through them so you have more time for the challenging ones, but it's not worth missing one if you know the concept and just didn't take the time to read the question fully. Work efficiently but make sure you understand the question and have looked at all of the answer choices, since more than one may seem right at first.

Even if you're paying attention to the time, you may find yourself a little behind at some point. You should speed up to get back on track, but do so wisely. Don't panic; just take a few seconds less on each question until you're caught up. Don't guess without thinking, but do look through the answer choices and eliminate any you know are wrong. If you can get down to two choices, it is often worthwhile to guess from those. Once you've chosen an answer, move on and don't dwell on any that you skipped or had to hurry through. If a question was taking too long, chances are it was one of the harder ones, so you weren't as likely to get it right anyway.

On the other hand, if you find yourself getting ahead of schedule, it may be beneficial to slow down a little. The more quickly you work, the more likely you are to make a careless mistake that will affect your score. You've budgeted time for each question, so don't be afraid to spend that time. Practice an efficient but careful pace to get the most out of the time you have.

Secret Key #5 – Have a Plan for Guessing

When you're taking the test, you may find yourself stuck on a question. Some of the answer choices seem better than others, but you don't see the one answer choice that is obviously correct. What do you do?

The scenario described above is very common, yet most test takers have not effectively prepared for it. Developing and practicing a plan for guessing may be one of the single most effective uses of your time as you get ready for the exam.

In developing your plan for guessing, there are three questions to address:

- When should you start the guessing process?
- How should you narrow down the choices?
- Which answer should you choose?

When to Start the Guessing Process

Unless your plan for guessing is to select C every time (which, despite its merits, is not what we recommend), you need to leave yourself enough time to apply your answer elimination strategies. Since you have a limited amount of time for each question, that means that if you're going to give yourself the best shot at guessing correctly, you have to decide quickly whether or not you will guess.

Of course, the best-case scenario is that you don't have to guess at all, so first, see if you can answer the question based on your knowledge of the subject and basic reasoning skills. Focus on the key words in the question and try to jog your memory of related topics. Give yourself a chance to bring the knowledge to mind, but once you realize that you don't have (or you can't access) the knowledge you need to answer the question, it's time to start the guessing process.

It's almost always better to start the guessing process too early than too late. It only takes a few seconds to remember something and answer the question from knowledge. Carefully eliminating wrong answer choices takes longer. Plus, going through the process of eliminating answer choices can actually help jog your memory.

Summary: Start the guessing process as soon as you decide that you can't answer the question based on your knowledge.

How to Narrow Down the Choices

The next chapter in this book (**Test-Taking Strategies**) includes a wide range of strategies for how to approach questions and how to look for answer choices to eliminate. You will definitely want to read those carefully, practice them, and figure out which ones work best for you. Here though, we're going to address a mindset rather than a particular strategy.

Your odds of guessing an answer correctly depend on how many options you are choosing from.

Number of options left	5	4	3	2	1
Odds of guessing correctly	20%	25%	33%	50%	100%

You can see from this chart just how valuable it is to be able to eliminate incorrect answers and make an educated guess, but there are two things that many test takers do that cause them to miss out on the benefits of guessing:

- Accidentally eliminating the correct answer
- Selecting an answer based on an impression

We'll look at the first one here, and the second one in the next section.

To avoid accidentally eliminating the correct answer, we recommend a thought exercise called **the $5 challenge**. In this challenge, you only eliminate an answer choice from contention if you are willing to bet $5 on it being wrong. Why $5? Five dollars is a small but not insignificant amount of money. It's an amount you could afford to lose but wouldn't want to throw away. And while losing $5 once might not hurt too much, doing it twenty times will set you back $100. In the same way, each small decision you make—eliminating a choice here, guessing on a question there—won't by itself impact your score very much, but when you put them all together, they can make a big difference. By holding each answer choice elimination decision to a higher standard, you can reduce the risk of accidentally eliminating the correct answer.

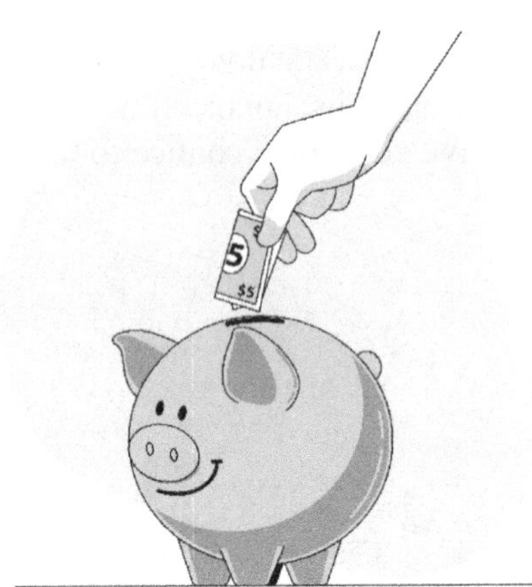

The $5 challenge can also be applied in a positive sense: If you are willing to bet $5 that an answer choice *is* correct, go ahead and mark it as correct.

Summary: Only eliminate an answer choice if you are willing to bet $5 that it is wrong.

Which Answer to Choose

You're taking the test. You've run into a hard question and decided you'll have to guess. You've eliminated all the answer choices you're willing to bet $5 on. Now you have to pick an answer. Why do we even need to talk about this? Why can't you just pick whichever one you feel like when the time comes?

The answer to these questions is that if you don't come into the test with a plan, you'll rely on your impression to select an answer choice, and if you do that, you risk falling into a trap. The test writers know that everyone who takes their test will be guessing on some of the questions, so they intentionally write wrong answer choices to seem plausible. You still have to pick an answer though, and if the wrong answer choices are designed to look right, how can you ever be sure that you're not falling for their trap? The best solution we've found to this dilemma is to take the decision out of your hands entirely. Here is the process we recommend:

Once you've eliminated any choices that you are confident (willing to bet $5) are wrong, select the first remaining choice as your answer.

Whether you choose to select the first remaining choice, the second, or the last, the important thing is that you use some preselected standard. Using this approach guarantees that you will not be enticed into selecting an answer choice that looks right, because you are not basing your decision on how the answer choices look.

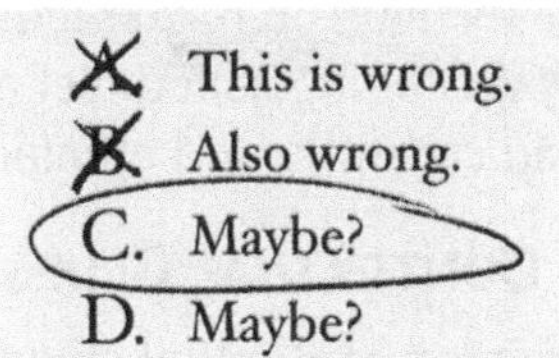

This is not meant to make you question your knowledge. Instead, it is to help you recognize the difference between your knowledge and your impressions. There's a huge difference between thinking an answer is right because of what you know, and thinking an answer is right because it looks or sounds like it should be right.

Summary: To ensure that your selection is appropriately random, make a predetermined selection from among all answer choices you have not eliminated.

Test-Taking Strategies

This section contains a list of test-taking strategies that you may find helpful as you work through the test. By taking what you know and applying logical thought, you can maximize your chances of answering any question correctly!

It is very important to realize that every question is different and every person is different: no single strategy will work on every question, and no single strategy will work for every person. That's why we've included all of them here, so you can try them out and determine which ones work best for different types of questions and which ones work best for you.

Question Strategies

✓ Read Carefully

Read the question and the answer choices carefully. Don't miss the question because you misread the terms. You have plenty of time to read each question thoroughly and make sure you understand what is being asked. Yet a happy medium must be attained, so don't waste too much time. You must read carefully and efficiently.

✓ Contextual Clues

Look for contextual clues. If the question includes a word you are not familiar with, look at the immediate context for some indication of what the word might mean. Contextual clues can often give you all the information you need to decipher the meaning of an unfamiliar word. Even if you can't determine the meaning, you may be able to narrow down the possibilities enough to make a solid guess at the answer to the question.

✓ Prefixes

If you're having trouble with a word in the question or answer choices, try dissecting it. Take advantage of every clue that the word might include. Prefixes can be a huge help. Usually, they allow you to determine a basic meaning. *Pre-* means before, *post-* means after, *pro-* is positive, *de-* is negative. From prefixes, you can get an idea of the general meaning of the word and try to put it into context.

✓ Hedge Words

Watch out for critical hedge words, such as *likely, may, can, sometimes, often, almost, mostly, usually, generally, rarely,* and *sometimes.* Question writers insert these hedge phrases to cover every possibility. Often an answer choice will be wrong simply because it leaves no room for exception. Be on guard for answer choices that have definitive words such as *exactly* and *always.*

✓ Switchback Words

Stay alert for *switchbacks.* These are the words and phrases frequently used to alert you to shifts in thought. The most common switchback words are *but, although,* and *however.* Others include *nevertheless, on the other hand, even though, while, in spite of, despite,* and *regardless of.* Switchback words are important to catch because they can change the direction of the question or an answer choice.

⊘ Face Value

When in doubt, use common sense. Accept the situation in the problem at face value. Don't read too much into it. These problems will not require you to make wild assumptions. If you have to go beyond creativity and warp time or space in order to have an answer choice fit the question, then you should move on and consider the other answer choices. These are normal problems rooted in reality. The applicable relationship or explanation may not be readily apparent, but it is there for you to figure out. Use your common sense to interpret anything that isn't clear.

Answer Choice Strategies

⊘ Answer Selection

The most thorough way to pick an answer choice is to identify and eliminate wrong answers until only one is left, then confirm it is the correct answer. Sometimes an answer choice may immediately seem right, but be careful. The test writers will usually put more than one reasonable answer choice on each question, so take a second to read all of them and make sure that the other choices are not equally obvious. As long as you have time left, it is better to read every answer choice than to pick the first one that looks right without checking the others.

⊘ Answer Choice Families

An answer choice family consists of two (in rare cases, three) answer choices that are very similar in construction and cannot all be true at the same time. If you see two answer choices that are direct opposites or parallels, one of them is usually the correct answer. For instance, if one answer choice says that quantity *x* increases and another either says that quantity *x* decreases (opposite) or says that quantity *y* increases (parallel), then those answer choices would fall into the same family. An answer choice that doesn't match the construction of the answer choice family is more likely to be incorrect. Most questions will not have answer choice families, but when they do appear, you should be prepared to recognize them.

⊘ Eliminate Answers

Eliminate answer choices as soon as you realize they are wrong, but make sure you consider all possibilities. If you are eliminating answer choices and realize that the last one you are left with is also wrong, don't panic. Start over and consider each choice again. There may be something you missed the first time that you will realize on the second pass.

⊘ Avoid Fact Traps

Don't be distracted by an answer choice that is factually true but doesn't answer the question. You are looking for the choice that answers the question. Stay focused on what the question is asking for so you don't accidentally pick an answer that is true but incorrect. Always go back to the question and make sure the answer choice you've selected actually answers the question and is not merely a true statement.

⊘ Extreme Statements

In general, you should avoid answers that put forth extreme actions as standard practice or proclaim controversial ideas as established fact. An answer choice that states the "process should be used in certain situations, if..." is much more likely to be correct than one that states the "process should be discontinued completely." The first is a calm rational statement and doesn't even make a definitive, uncompromising stance, using a hedge word *if* to provide wiggle room, whereas the second choice is far more extreme.

⊘ BENCHMARK

As you read through the answer choices and you come across one that seems to answer the question well, mentally select that answer choice. This is not your final answer, but it's the one that will help you evaluate the other answer choices. The one that you selected is your benchmark or standard for judging each of the other answer choices. Every other answer choice must be compared to your benchmark. That choice is correct until proven otherwise by another answer choice beating it. If you find a better answer, then that one becomes your new benchmark. Once you've decided that no other choice answers the question as well as your benchmark, you have your final answer.

⊘ PREDICT THE ANSWER

Before you even start looking at the answer choices, it is often best to try to predict the answer. When you come up with the answer on your own, it is easier to avoid distractions and traps because you will know exactly what to look for. The right answer choice is unlikely to be word-for-word what you came up with, but it should be a close match. Even if you are confident that you have the right answer, you should still take the time to read each option before moving on.

General Strategies

⊘ TOUGH QUESTIONS

If you are stumped on a problem or it appears too hard or too difficult, don't waste time. Move on! Remember though, if you can quickly check for obviously incorrect answer choices, your chances of guessing correctly are greatly improved. Before you completely give up, at least try to knock out a couple of possible answers. Eliminate what you can and then guess at the remaining answer choices before moving on.

⊘ CHECK YOUR WORK

Since you will probably not know every term listed and the answer to every question, it is important that you get credit for the ones that you do know. Don't miss any questions through careless mistakes. If at all possible, try to take a second to look back over your answer selection and make sure you've selected the correct answer choice and haven't made a costly careless mistake (such as marking an answer choice that you didn't mean to mark). This quick double check should more than pay for itself in caught mistakes for the time it costs.

⊘ PACE YOURSELF

It's easy to be overwhelmed when you're looking at a page full of questions; your mind is confused and full of random thoughts, and the clock is ticking down faster than you would like. Calm down and maintain the pace that you have set for yourself. Especially as you get down to the last few minutes of the test, don't let the small numbers on the clock make you panic. As long as you are on track by monitoring your pace, you are guaranteed to have time for each question.

⊘ DON'T RUSH

It is very easy to make errors when you are in a hurry. Maintaining a fast pace in answering questions is pointless if it makes you miss questions that you would have gotten right otherwise. Test writers like to include distracting information and wrong answers that seem right. Taking a little extra time to avoid careless mistakes can make all the difference in your test score. Find a pace that allows you to be confident in the answers that you select.

✅ Keep Moving

Panicking will not help you pass the test, so do your best to stay calm and keep moving. Taking deep breaths and going through the answer elimination steps you practiced can help to break through a stress barrier and keep your pace.

Final Notes

The combination of a solid foundation of content knowledge and the confidence that comes from practicing your plan for applying that knowledge is the key to maximizing your performance on test day. As your foundation of content knowledge is built up and strengthened, you'll find that the strategies included in this chapter become more and more effective in helping you quickly sift through the distractions and traps of the test to isolate the correct answer.

Now that you're preparing to move forward into the test content chapters of this book, be sure to keep your goal in mind. As you read, think about how you will be able to apply this information on the test. If you've already seen sample questions for the test and you have an idea of the question format and style, try to come up with questions of your own that you can answer based on what you're reading. This will give you valuable practice applying your knowledge in the same ways you can expect to on test day.

Good luck and good studying!

Verbal Reasoning

Transform passive reading into active learning! After immersing yourself in this chapter, put your comprehension to the test by taking a quiz. The insights you gained will stay with you longer this way. Scan the QR code to go directly to the chapter quiz interface for this study guide. If you're using a computer, simply visit the bonus page at **mometrix.com/bonus948/claslearntest** and click the Chapter Quizzes link.

Verbal Reasoning Overview

The verbal reasoning portion of the Classic Learning Test will consist of one 40-minute section. It will contain 3 single passages and one pair of passages. There will be a total of 40 questions, with 10 questions per passage.

Literature	These passages are taken from influential classic and modern prose literature. These passages are more likely to include questions on tone or a character's motives.
Scientific Thinker	These passages are often modern works about a particular scientific topic, often including social implications of a breakthrough or development in biology, physics, chemistry, Earth, or space science. These are accompanied by a graphic and a single question asking the reader to interpret data.
Philosophy/Religion	These passages are from a variety of authors from ancient times to modern philosophers and focus on common philosophical topics such as truth, ethics, and reasoning. The passages selected intentionally represent a variety of perspectives.
Historical/American Founding Documents	These passages are pairs of shorter selections that represent a pivotal historical or social concept. The test taker will be asked to compare and contrast views, as well as answer more typical reading comprehension questions about each passage.

Question Types in the Verbal Reasoning Section

Each passage will correspond to ten questions, varying in difficulty. The types of questions that will appear on your test include, but are not strictly limited to the following:

- **Main ideas** –the test-taker will need to read and understand the primary topic and focus of a passage.
- **Author's tone or position** - the test-taker will need to understand the feeling that the author conveys, as well as identify an author's own thoughts about the topic based on the type of language the author uses.
- **Characters and their motives** - the test-taker will need to distinguish between characters in the passage and understand the dynamics and varied intentions that the characters have.
- **Meanings of words or phrases in context** - the test-taker will need to find and determine the contextual meaning of a word or group of words in the passage. These questions rely heavily on context clues, but also rely on the test-taker's knowledge of vocabulary in general.

- **Passage structure** - the test-taker will need to recognize the organization, or flow of thought, of a passage and identify how a sentence or group of sentences contribute to the meaning of a passage as a whole.
- **Evidence or support for the answer to a previous question** - the test-taker will need to read through several sentences and select the one that best supports the correct answer to a previously-answered question.
- **Passage-based analogies** - the test-taker will be presented with the first half of an analogy and will have to select the choice that best completes the analogy as it pertains to the passage.
- **Inference** – the test-taker will need to draw conclusions based on something implied, but not clearly stated in the passage.

Word Roots and Prefixes and Suffixes

Affixes

Affixes in the English language are morphemes that are added to words to create related but different words. Derivational affixes form new words based on and related to the original words. For example, the affix *–ness* added to the end of the adjective *happy* forms the noun *happiness.* Inflectional affixes form different grammatical versions of words. For example, the plural affix *–s* changes the singular noun *book* to the plural noun *books,* and the past tense affix *–ed* changes the present tense verb *look* to the past tense *looked.* Prefixes are affixes placed in front of words. For example, *heat* means to make hot; *preheat* means to heat in advance. Suffixes are affixes placed at the ends of words. The *happiness* example above contains the suffix *–ness.* Circumfixes add parts both before and after words, such as how *light* becomes *enlighten* with the prefix *en-* and the suffix *–en.* Interfixes create compound words via central affixes: *speed* and *meter* become *speedometer* via the interfix *–o–.*

Review Video: Affixes
Visit mometrix.com/academy and enter code: 782422

Word Roots, Prefixes, and Suffixes to Help Determine Meanings of Words

Many English words were formed from combining multiple sources. For example, the Latin *habēre* means "to have," and the prefixes *in-* and *im-* mean a lack or prevention of something, as in *insufficient* and *imperfect.* Latin combined *in-* with *habēre* to form *inhibēre,* whose past participle was *inhibitus.* This is the origin of the English word *inhibit,* meaning to prevent from having. Hence by knowing the meanings of both the prefix and the root, one can decipher the word meaning. In Greek, the root *enkephalo-* refers to the brain. Many medical terms are based on this root, such as encephalitis and hydrocephalus. Understanding the prefix and suffix meanings (*-itis* means inflammation; *hydro-* means water) allows a person to deduce that encephalitis refers to brain inflammation and hydrocephalus refers to water (or other fluid) in the brain.

Review Video: Determining Word Meanings
Visit mometrix.com/academy and enter code: 894894

Prefixes

Knowing common prefixes is helpful for all readers as they try to determining meanings or definitions of unfamiliar words. For example, a common word used when cooking is *preheat.* Knowing that *pre-* means in advance can also inform them that *presume* means to assume in advance, that *prejudice* means advance judgment, and that this understanding can be applied to many other words beginning with *pre-*. Knowing that the prefix *dis-* indicates opposition informs the meanings of words like *disbar, disagree, disestablish,* and many more. Knowing *dys-* means bad, impaired, abnormal, or difficult informs *dyslogistic, dysfunctional, dysphagia,* and *dysplasia.*

Suffixes

In English, certain suffixes generally indicate both that a word is a noun, and that the noun represents a state of being or quality. For example, *-ness* is commonly used to change an adjective into its noun form, as with *happy* and *happiness, nice* and *niceness,* and so on. The suffix *–tion* is commonly used to transform a verb into its noun form, as with *converse* and *conversation or move* and *motion*. Thus, if readers are unfamiliar with the second form of a word, knowing the meaning of the transforming suffix can help them determine meaning.

Prefixes for Numbers

Prefix	Definition	Examples
bi-	two	bisect, biennial
mono-	one, single	monogamy, monologue
poly-	many	polymorphous, polygamous
semi-	half, partly	semicircle, semicolon
uni-	one	uniform, unity

Prefixes for Time, Direction, and Space

Prefix	Definition	Examples
a-	in, on, of, up, to	abed, afoot
ab-	from, away, off	abdicate, abjure
ad-	to, toward	advance, adventure
ante-	before, previous	antecedent, antedate
anti-	against, opposing	antipathy, antidote
cata-	down, away, thoroughly	catastrophe, cataclysm
circum-	around	circumspect, circumference
com-	with, together, very	commotion, complicate
contra-	against, opposing	contradict, contravene
de-	from	depart
dia-	through, across, apart	diameter, diagnose
dis-	away, off, down, not	dissent, disappear
epi-	upon	epilogue
ex-	out	extract, excerpt
hypo-	under, beneath	hypodermic, hypothesis
inter-	among, between	intercede, interrupt
intra-	within	intramural, intrastate
ob-	against, opposing	objection
per-	through	perceive, permit
peri-	around	periscope, perimeter
post-	after, following	postpone, postscript
pre-	before, previous	prevent, preclude
pro-	forward, in place of	propel, pronoun
retro-	back, backward	retrospect, retrograde
sub-	under, beneath	subjugate, substitute
super-	above, extra	supersede, supernumerary
trans-	across, beyond, over	transact, transport
ultra-	beyond, excessively	ultramodern, ultrasonic

Negative Prefixes

Prefix	Definition	Examples
a-	without, lacking	atheist, agnostic
in-	not, opposing	incapable, ineligible
non-	not	nonentity, nonsense
un-	not, reverse of	unhappy, unlock

Extra Prefixes

Prefix	Definition	Examples
for-	away, off, from	forget, forswear
fore-	previous	foretell, forefathers
homo-	same, equal	homogenized, homonym
hyper-	excessive, over	hypercritical, hypertension
in-	in, into	intrude, invade
mal-	bad, poorly, not	malfunction, malpractice
mis-	bad, poorly, not	misspell, misfire
neo-	new	Neolithic, neoconservative
omni-	all, everywhere	omniscient, omnivore
ortho-	right, straight	orthogonal, orthodox
over-	above	overbearing, oversight
pan-	all, entire	panorama, pandemonium
para-	beside, beyond	parallel, paradox
re-	backward, again	revoke, recur
sym-	with, together	sympathy, symphony

Below is a list of common suffixes and their meanings:

Adjective Suffixes

Suffix	Definition	Examples
-able (-ible)	capable of being	toler*able*, ed*ible*
-esque	in the style of, like	picturesque, grotesque
-ful	filled with, marked by	thankful, zestful
-ific	make, cause	terrific, beatific
-ish	suggesting, like	churlish, childish
-less	lacking, without	hopeless, countless
-ous	marked by, given to	religious, riotous

Noun Suffixes

Suffix	Definition	Examples
-acy	state, condition	accuracy, privacy
-ance	act, condition, fact	acceptance, vigilance
-ard	one that does excessively	drunkard, sluggard
-ation	action, state, result	occupation, starvation
-dom	state, rank, condition	serfdom, wisdom
-er (-or)	office, action	teach*er*, elevat*or*, hon*or*
-ess	feminine	waitress, duchess
-hood	state, condition	manhood, statehood
-ion	action, result, state	union, fusion
-ism	act, manner, doctrine	barbarism, socialism
-ist	worker, follower	monopolist, socialist
-ity (-ty)	state, quality, condition	acid*ity*, civil*ity*, twen*ty*
-ment	result, action	Refreshment
-ness	quality, state	greatness, tallness
-ship	position	internship, statesmanship
-sion (-tion)	state, result	revi*sion*, expedi*tion*
-th	act, state, quality	warmth, width
-tude	quality, state, result	magnitude, fortitude

Verb Suffixes

Suffix	Definition	Examples
-ate	having, showing	separate, desolate
-en	cause to be, become	deepen, strengthen
-fy	make, cause to have	glorify, fortify
-ize	cause to be, treat with	sterilize, mechanize

Nuance and Word Meanings

Synonyms and Antonyms

When you understand how words relate to each other, you will discover more in a passage. This is explained by understanding **synonyms** (e.g., words that mean the same thing) and **antonyms** (e.g., words that mean the opposite of one another). As an example, *dry* and *arid* are synonyms, and *dry* and *wet* are antonyms.

There are many pairs of words in English that can be considered synonyms, despite having slightly different definitions. For instance, the words *friendly* and *collegial* can both be used to describe a warm interpersonal relationship, and one would be correct to call them synonyms. However, *collegial* (kin to *colleague*) is often used in reference to professional or academic relationships, and *friendly* has no such connotation.

If the difference between the two words is too great, then they should not be called synonyms. *Hot* and *warm* are not synonyms because their meanings are too distinct. A good way to determine whether two words are synonyms is to substitute one word for the other word and verify that the meaning of the sentence has not changed. Substituting *warm* for *hot* in a sentence would convey a different meaning. Although warm and hot may seem close in meaning, warm generally means that the temperature is moderate, and hot generally means that the temperature is excessively high.

Antonyms are words with opposite meanings. *Light* and *dark*, *up* and *down*, *right* and *left*, *good* and *bad*: these are all sets of antonyms. Be careful to distinguish between antonyms and pairs of words that are simply different. *Black* and *gray*, for instance, are not antonyms because gray is not the opposite of black. *Black* and *white*, on the other hand, are antonyms.

Not every word has an antonym. For instance, many nouns do not. What would be the antonym of *chair*? During your exam, the questions related to antonyms are more likely to concern adjectives. You will recall that adjectives are words that describe a noun. Some common adjectives include *purple*, *fast*, *skinny*, and *sweet*. From those four adjectives, *purple* is the item that lacks a group of obvious antonyms.

Review Video: What Are Synonyms and Antonyms?
Visit mometrix.com/academy and enter code: 105612

Denotative vs. Connotative Meaning

The **denotative** meaning of a word is the literal meaning. The **connotative** meaning goes beyond the denotative meaning to include the emotional reaction that a word may invoke. The connotative meaning often takes the denotative meaning a step further due to associations the reader makes with the denotative meaning. Readers can differentiate between the denotative and connotative meanings by first recognizing how authors use each meaning. Most non-fiction, for example, is fact-based and authors do not use flowery, figurative language. The reader can assume that the writer is using the denotative meaning of words. In fiction, the author may use the connotative meaning. Readers can determine whether the author is using the denotative or connotative meaning of a word by implementing context clues.

Review Video: Connotation and Denotation
Visit mometrix.com/academy and enter code: 310092

Nuances of Word Meaning Relative to Connotation, Denotation, Diction, and Usage

A word's denotation is simply its objective dictionary definition. However, its connotation refers to the subjective associations, often emotional, that specific words evoke in listeners and readers. Two or more words can have the same dictionary meaning, but very different connotations. Writers use diction (word choice) to convey various nuances of thought and emotion by selecting synonyms for other words that best communicate the associations they want to trigger for readers. For example, a car engine is naturally greasy; in this sense, "greasy" is a neutral term. But when a person's smile, appearance, or clothing is described as "greasy," it has a negative connotation. Some words have even gained additional or different meanings over time. For example, *awful* used to be used to describe things that evoked a sense of awe. When *awful* is separated into its root word, awe, and suffix, -ful, it can be understood to mean "full of awe." However, the word is now commonly used to describe things that evoke repulsion, terror, or another intense, negative reaction.

Review Video: Word Usage in Sentences
Visit mometrix.com/academy and enter code: 197863

Using Context to Determine Meaning

Context Clues

Readers of all levels will encounter words that they have either never seen or have encountered only on a limited basis. The best way to define a word in **context** is to look for nearby words that can assist in revealing the meaning of the word. For instance, unfamiliar nouns are often accompanied by examples that provide a definition. Consider the following sentence: *Dave arrived at the party in hilarious garb: a leopard-print shirt, buckskin trousers, and bright green sneakers.* If a reader was unfamiliar with the meaning of garb, he or she could read the examples (i.e., a leopard-print shirt, buckskin trousers, and high heels) and quickly determine that the word means *clothing.* Examples will not always be this obvious. Consider this sentence: *Parsley, lemon, and flowers were just a few of the items he used as garnishes.* Here, the word *garnishes* is exemplified by parsley, lemon, and flowers. Readers who have eaten in a variety of restaurants will probably be able to identify a garnish as something used to decorate a plate.

Review Video: Reading Comprehension: Using Context Clues
Visit mometrix.com/academy and enter code: 613660

Using Contrast in Context Clues

In addition to looking at the context of a passage, readers can use contrast to define an unfamiliar word in context. In many sentences, the author will not describe the unfamiliar word directly; instead, he or she will describe the opposite of the unfamiliar word. Thus, you are provided with some information that will bring you closer to defining the word. Consider the following example: *Despite his intelligence, Hector's low brow and bad posture made him look obtuse.* The author writes that Hector's appearance does not convey intelligence. Therefore, *obtuse* must mean unintelligent. Here is another example: *Despite the horrible weather, we were beatific about our trip to Alaska.* The word *despite* indicates that the speaker's feelings were at odds with the weather. Since the weather is described as *horrible*, then *beatific* must mean something positive.

Substitution to Find Meaning

In some cases, there will be very few contextual clues to help a reader define the meaning of an unfamiliar word. When this happens, one strategy that readers may employ is **substitution**. A good reader will brainstorm some possible synonyms for the given word, and he or she will substitute these words into the sentence. If the sentence and the surrounding passage continue to make sense, then the substitution has revealed at least some information about the unfamiliar word. Consider the sentence: *Frank's admonition rang in her ears as she climbed the mountain.* A reader unfamiliar with *admonition* might come up with some substitutions like *vow, promise, advice, complaint,* or *compliment.* All of these words make general sense of the sentence, though their meanings are diverse. However, this process has suggested that an admonition is some sort of message. The substitution strategy is rarely able to pinpoint a precise definition, but this process can be effective as a last resort.

Occasionally, you will be able to define an unfamiliar word by looking at the descriptive words in the context. Consider the following sentence: *Fred dragged the recalcitrant boy kicking and screaming up the stairs.* The words *dragged*, *kicking*, and *screaming* all suggest that the boy does not want to go up the stairs. The reader may assume that *recalcitrant* means something like unwilling or protesting. In this example, an unfamiliar adjective was identified.

Additionally, using description to define an unfamiliar noun is a common practice compared to unfamiliar adjectives, as in this sentence: *Don's wrinkled frown and constantly shaking fist identified him as a curmudgeon of the first order*. Don is described as having a *wrinkled frown and constantly shaking fist*, suggesting that a *curmudgeon* must be a grumpy person. Contrasts do not always provide detailed information about the unfamiliar word, but they at least give the reader some clues.

Words with Multiple Meanings

When a word has more than one meaning, readers can have difficulty determining how the word is being used in a given sentence. For instance, the verb *cleave*, can mean either *join* or *separate*. When readers come upon this word, they will have to select the definition that makes the most sense. Consider the following sentence: *Hermione's knife cleaved the bread cleanly*. Since a knife cannot join bread together, the word must indicate separation. A slightly more difficult example would be the sentence: *The birds cleaved to one another as they flew from the oak tree.* Immediately, the presence of the words *to one another* should suggest that in this sentence *cleave* is being used to mean *join*. Discovering the intent of a word with multiple meanings requires the same tricks as defining an unknown word: look for contextual clues and evaluate the substituted words.

Context Clues to Help Determine Meanings of Words

If readers simply bypass unknown words, they can reach unclear conclusions about what they read. However, looking for the definition of every unfamiliar word in the dictionary can slow their reading progress. Moreover, the dictionary may list multiple definitions for a word, so readers must search the word's context for meaning. Hence context is important to new vocabulary regardless of reader methods. Four types of context clues are examples, definitions, descriptive words, and opposites. Authors may use a certain word, and then follow it with several different examples of what it describes. Sometimes authors actually supply a definition of a word they use, which is especially true in informational and technical texts. Authors may use descriptive words that elaborate upon a vocabulary word they just used. Authors may also use opposites with negation that help define meaning.

Examples and Definitions

An author may use a word and then give examples that illustrate its meaning. Consider this text: "Teachers who do not know how to use sign language can help students who are deaf or hard of hearing understand certain instructions by using gestures instead, like pointing their fingers to indicate which direction to look or go; holding up a hand, palm outward, to indicate stopping; holding the hands flat, palms up, curling a finger toward oneself in a beckoning motion to indicate 'come here'; or curling all fingers toward oneself repeatedly to indicate 'come on', 'more', or 'continue.'" The author of this text has used the word "gestures" and then followed it with examples, so a reader unfamiliar with the word could deduce from the examples that "gestures" means "hand motions." Readers can find examples by looking for signal words "for example," "for instance," "like," "such as," and "e.g."

While readers sometimes have to look for definitions of unfamiliar words in a dictionary or do some work to determine a word's meaning from its surrounding context, at other times an author may make it easier for readers by defining certain words. For example, an author may write, "The company did not have sufficient capital, that is, available money, to continue operations." The author defined "capital" as "available money," and heralded the definition with the phrase "that is." Another way that authors supply word definitions is with appositives. Rather than being introduced by a signal phrase like "that is," "namely," or "meaning," an appositive comes after the vocabulary word it defines and is enclosed within two commas. For example, an author may write, "The Indians introduced the Pilgrims to pemmican, cakes they made of lean meat dried and mixed with fat, which proved greatly beneficial to keep settlers from starving while trapping." In this example, the appositive phrase following "pemmican" and preceding "which" defines the word "pemmican."

Descriptions

When readers encounter a word they do not recognize in a text, the author may expand on that word to illustrate it better. While the author may do this to make the prose more picturesque and vivid, the reader can also take advantage of this description to provide context clues to the meaning of the unfamiliar word. For example, an author may write, "The man sitting next to me on the airplane was obese. His shirt stretched across his vast expanse of flesh, strained almost to bursting." The descriptive second sentence elaborates on and helps to define the previous sentence's word "obese" to mean extremely fat. A reader unfamiliar with the word "repugnant" can decipher its meaning through an author's accompanying description: "The way the child grimaced and shuddered as he swallowed the medicine showed that its taste was particularly repugnant."

Opposites

Text authors sometimes introduce a contrasting or opposing idea before or after a concept they present. They may do this to emphasize or heighten the idea they present by contrasting it with something that is the reverse. However, readers can also use these context clues to understand familiar words. For example, an author may write, "Our conversation was not cheery. We sat and talked very solemnly about his experience and a number of similar events." The reader who is not familiar with the word "solemnly" can deduce by the author's preceding use of "not cheery" that "solemn" means the opposite of cheery or happy, so it must mean serious or sad. Or if someone writes, "Don't condemn his entire project because you couldn't find anything good to say about it," readers unfamiliar with "condemn" can understand from the sentence structure that it means the opposite of saying anything good, so it must mean reject, dismiss, or disapprove. "Entire" adds another context clue, meaning total or complete rejection.

Syntax to Determine Part of Speech and Meanings of Words

Syntax refers to sentence structure and word order. Suppose that a reader encounters an unfamiliar word when reading a text. To illustrate, consider an invented word like "splunch." If this word is used in a sentence like "Please splunch that ball to me," the reader can assume from syntactic context that "splunch" is a verb. We would not use a noun, adjective, adverb, or preposition with the object "that ball," and the prepositional phrase "to me" further indicates "splunch" represents an action. However, in the sentence, "Please hand that splunch to me," the reader can assume that "splunch" is a noun. Demonstrative adjectives like "that" modify nouns. Also, we hand someone some*thing*—a thing being a noun; we do not hand someone a verb, adjective, or adverb. Some sentences contain further clues. For example, from the sentence, "The princess wore the glittering splunch on her head," the reader can deduce that it is a crown, tiara, or something similar from the syntactic context, without knowing the word.

Syntax to Indicate Different Meanings of Similar Sentences

The syntax, or structure, of a sentence affords grammatical cues that aid readers in comprehending the meanings of words, phrases, and sentences in the texts that they read. Seemingly minor differences in how the words or phrases in a sentence are ordered can make major differences in meaning. For example, two sentences can use exactly the same words but have different meanings based on the word order:

- "The man with a broken arm sat in a chair."
- "The man sat in a chair with a broken arm."

While both sentences indicate that a man sat in a chair, differing syntax indicates whether the man's or chair's arm was broken.

Determining Meaning of Phrases and Paragraphs

Like unknown words, the meanings of phrases, paragraphs, and entire works can also be difficult to discern. Each of these can be better understood with added context. However, for larger groups of words, more context is needed. Unclear phrases are similar to unclear words, and the same methods can be used to understand their meaning. However, it is also important to consider how the individual words in the phrase work together. Paragraphs are a bit more complicated. Just as words must be compared to other words in a sentence, paragraphs must be compared to other paragraphs in a composition or a section.

Determining Meaning in Various Types of Compositions

To understand the meaning of an entire composition, the type of composition must be considered. **Expository writing** is generally organized so that each paragraph focuses on explaining one idea, or part of an idea, and its relevance. **Persuasive writing** uses paragraphs for different purposes to organize the parts of the argument. **Unclear paragraphs** must be read in the context of the paragraphs around them for their meaning to be fully understood. The meaning of full texts can also be unclear at times. The purpose of composition is also important for understanding the meaning of a text. To quickly understand the broad meaning of a text, look to the introductory and concluding paragraphs. Fictional texts are different. Some fictional works have implicit meanings, but some do not. The target audience must be considered for understanding texts that do have an implicit meaning, as most children's fiction will clearly state any lessons or morals. For other fiction, the application of literary theories and criticism may be helpful for understanding the text.

Main Ideas and Supporting Details

Identifying Topics and Main Ideas

One of the most important skills in reading comprehension is the identification of **topics** and **main ideas**. There is a subtle difference between these two features. The topic is the subject of a text (i.e., what the text is all about). The main idea, on the other hand, is the most important point being made by the author. The topic is usually expressed in a few words at the most while the main idea often needs a full sentence to be completely defined. As an example, a short passage might be written on the topic of penguins, and the main idea could be written as *Penguins are different from other birds in many ways.* In most nonfiction writing, the topic and the main idea will be **stated directly** and often appear in a sentence at the very beginning or end of the text. When being tested on an understanding of the author's topic, you may be able to skim the passage for the general idea by reading only the first sentence of each paragraph. A body paragraph's first sentence is often—but not always—the main **topic sentence** which gives you a summary of the content in the paragraph.

However, there are cases in which the reader must figure out an **unstated** topic or main idea. In these instances, you must read every sentence of the text and try to come up with an overarching idea that is supported by each of those sentences.

Note: The main idea should not be confused with the thesis statement. While the main idea gives a brief, general summary of a text, the thesis statement provides a **specific perspective** on an issue that the author supports with evidence.

Review Video: Topics and Main Ideas
Visit mometrix.com/academy and enter code: 407801

SUPPORTING DETAILS

Supporting details are smaller pieces of evidence that provide backing for the main point. In order to show that a main idea is correct or valid, an author must add details that prove their point. All texts contain details, but they are only classified as supporting details when they serve to reinforce some larger point. Supporting details are most commonly found in informative and persuasive texts. In some cases, they will be clearly indicated with terms like *for example* or *for instance*, or they will be enumerated with terms like *first*, *second*, and *last*. However, you need to be prepared for texts that do not contain those indicators. As a reader, you should consider whether the author's supporting details really back up his or her main point. Details can be factual and correct, yet they may not be **relevant** to the author's point. Conversely, details can be relevant, but be ineffective because they are based on opinion or assertions that cannot be proven.

Review Video: Supporting Details
Visit mometrix.com/academy and enter code: 396297

Author's Purpose

AUTHOR'S PURPOSE

Usually, identifying the author's **purpose** is easier than identifying his or her **position**. In most cases, the author has no interest in hiding his or her purpose. A text that is meant to entertain, for instance, should be written to please the reader. Most narratives, or stories, are written to entertain, though they may also inform or persuade. Informative texts are easy to identify, while the most difficult purpose of a text to identify is persuasion because the author has an interest in making this purpose hard to detect. When a reader discovers that the author is trying to persuade, he or she should be skeptical of the argument. For this reason, persuasive texts often try to establish an entertaining tone and hope to amuse the reader into agreement. On the other hand, an informative tone may be implemented to create an appearance of authority and objectivity.

An author's purpose is evident often in the **organization** of the text (e.g., section headings in bold font points to an informative text). However, you may not have such organization available to you in your exam. Instead, if the author makes his or her main idea clear from the beginning, then the likely purpose of the text is to **inform**. If the author begins by making a claim and provides various arguments to support that claim, then the purpose is probably to **persuade**. If the author tells a story or wants to gain the reader's attention more than to push a particular point or deliver information, then his or her purpose is most likely to **entertain**. As a reader, you must judge authors on how well they accomplish their purpose. In other words, you need to consider the type of passage (e.g., technical, persuasive, etc.) that the author has written and if the author has followed the requirements of the passage type.

Review Video: Understanding the Author's Intent
Visit mometrix.com/academy and enter code: 511819

Informational Texts

An **informational text** is written to educate and enlighten readers. Informational texts are almost always nonfiction and are rarely structured as a story. The intention of an informational text is to deliver information in the most comprehensible way. So, look for the structure of the text to be very clear. In an informational text, the thesis statement is one or two sentences that normally appears at the end of the first paragraph. The author may use some colorful language, but he or she is likely to put more emphasis on clarity and precision. Informational essays do not typically appeal to the emotions. They often contain facts and figures and rarely include the opinion of the author; however, readers should remain aware of the possibility for bias as those facts are presented. Sometimes a persuasive essay can resemble an informative essay, especially if the author maintains an even tone and presents his or her views as if they were established fact.

> **Review Video: Informational Text**
> Visit mometrix.com/academy and enter code: 924964

Persuasive Writing

In a persuasive essay, the author is attempting to change the reader's mind or **convince** him or her of something that he or she did not believe previously. There are several identifying characteristics of **persuasive writing**. One is **opinion presented as fact**. When authors attempt to persuade readers, they often present their opinions as if they were fact. Readers must be on guard for statements that sound factual but which cannot be subjected to research, observation, or experiment. Another characteristic of persuasive writing is **emotional language**. An author will often try to play on the emotions of readers by appealing to their sympathy or sense of morality. When an author uses colorful or evocative language with the intent of arousing the reader's passions, then the author may be attempting to persuade. Finally, in many cases, a persuasive text will give an **unfair explanation of opposing positions**, if these positions are mentioned at all.

Entertaining Texts

The success or failure of an author's intent to **entertain** is determined by those who read the author's work. Entertaining texts may be either fiction or nonfiction, and they may describe real or imagined people, places, and events. Entertaining texts are often narratives or poems. A text that is written to entertain is likely to contain **colorful language** that engages the imagination and the emotions. Such writing often features a great deal of figurative language, which typically enlivens the subject matter with images and analogies.

Though an entertaining text is not usually written to persuade or inform, authors may accomplish both of these tasks in their work. An entertaining text may *appeal to the reader's emotions* and cause him or her to think differently about a particular subject. In any case, entertaining texts tend to showcase the personality of the author more than other types of writing.

Descriptive Text

In a sense, almost all writing is descriptive, insofar as an author seeks to describe events, ideas, or people to the reader. Some texts, however, are primarily concerned with **description**. A descriptive text focuses on a particular subject and attempts to depict the subject in a way that will be clear to readers. Descriptive texts contain many adjectives and adverbs (i.e., words that give shades of meaning and create a more detailed mental picture for the reader). A descriptive text fails when it is unclear to the reader. A descriptive text will certainly be informative and may be persuasive and entertaining as well.

Review Video: Descriptive Texts
Visit mometrix.com/academy and enter code: 174903

EXPRESSION OF FEELINGS

When an author intends to **express feelings**, he or she may use **expressive and bold language**. An author may write with emotion for any number of reasons. Sometimes, authors will express feelings because they are describing a personal situation of great pain or happiness. In other situations, authors will attempt to persuade the reader and will use emotion to stir up the passions. This kind of expression is easy to identify when the writer uses phrases like *I felt* and *I sense*. However, readers may find that the author will simply describe feelings without introducing them. As a reader, you must know the importance of recognizing when an author is expressing emotion and not to become overwhelmed by sympathy or passion. Readers should maintain some **detachment** so that they can still evaluate the strength of the author's argument or the quality of the writing.

Review Video: Emotional Language in Literature
Visit mometrix.com/academy and enter code: 759390

EXPOSITORY PASSAGE

An **expository** passage aims to **inform** and enlighten readers. Expository passages are nonfiction and usually center around a simple, easily defined topic. Since the goal of exposition is to teach, such a passage should be as clear as possible. Often, an expository passage contains helpful organizing words, like *first*, *next*, *for example*, and *therefore*. These words keep the reader **oriented** in the text. Although expository passages do not need to feature colorful language and artful writing, they are often more effective with these features. For a reader, the challenge of expository passages is to maintain steady attention. Expository passages are not always about subjects that will naturally interest a reader, so the writer is often more concerned with **clarity** and **comprehensibility** than with engaging the reader. By reading actively, you can ensure a good habit of focus when reading an expository passage.

Review Video: Expository Passages
Visit mometrix.com/academy and enter code: 256515

NARRATIVE PASSAGE

A **narrative** passage is a story that can be fiction or nonfiction. However, there are a few elements that a text must have in order to be classified as a narrative. First, the text must have a **plot** (i.e., a series of events). Narratives often proceed in a clear sequence, but this is not a requirement. If the narrative is good, then these events will be interesting to readers. Second, a narrative has **characters**. These characters could be people, animals, or even inanimate objects—so long as they participate in the plot. Third, a narrative passage often contains **figurative language** which is meant to stimulate the imagination of readers by making comparisons and observations. For instance, a *metaphor*, a common piece of figurative language, is a description of one thing in terms of another. *The moon was a frosty snowball* is an example of a metaphor. In the literal sense this is obviously untrue, but the comparison suggests a certain mood for the reader.

TECHNICAL PASSAGE

A **technical** passage is written to *describe* a complex object or process. Technical writing is common in medical and technological fields, in which complex ideas of mathematics, science, and engineering need to be explained *simply* and *clearly*. To ease comprehension, a technical passage usually proceeds in a very logical order. Technical passages often have clear headings and subheadings, which are used to keep the reader oriented in the text. Additionally, you will find that these passages divide sections up with numbers or letters. Many technical passages look more like an outline than a piece of prose. The amount of **jargon** or difficult vocabulary will vary in a technical passage depending on the intended audience. As much as possible, technical passages try to avoid language that the reader will have to research in order to understand the message, yet readers will find that jargon cannot always be avoided.

Review Video: Technical Passages
Visit mometrix.com/academy and enter code: 478923

Common Organizations of Texts

Organization of the Text

The way a text is organized can help readers understand the author's intent and his or her conclusions. There are various ways to organize a text, and each one has a purpose and use. Usually, authors will organize information logically in a passage so the reader can follow and locate the information within the text. However, since not all passages are written with the same logical structure, you need to be familiar with several different types of passage structure.

Review Video: Organizational Methods to Structure Text
Visit mometrix.com/academy and enter code: 606263

Review Video: Sequence of Events in a Story
Visit mometrix.com/academy and enter code: 807512

Chronological

When using **chronological** order, the author presents information in the order that it happened. For example, biographies are typically written in chronological order. The subject's birth and childhood are presented first, followed by their adult life, and lastly the events leading up to the person's death.

Cause and Effect

One of the most common text structures is **cause and effect**. A **cause** is an act or event that makes something happen, and an **effect** is the thing that happens as a result of the cause. A cause-and-effect relationship is not always explicit, but there are some terms in English that signal causes, such as *since*, *because*, and *due to*. Furthermore, terms that signal effects include *consequently, therefore, this leads to*. As an example, consider the sentence *Because the sky was clear, Ron did not bring an umbrella*. The cause is the clear sky, and the effect is that Ron did not bring an umbrella. However, readers may find that sometimes the cause-and-effect relationship will not be clearly noted. For instance, the sentence *He was late and missed the meeting* does not contain any signaling words, but the sentence still contains a cause (he was late) and an effect (he missed the meeting).

Review Video: Cause and Effect
Visit mometrix.com/academy and enter code: 868099

Review Video: Rhetorical Strategy of Cause and Effect Analysis
Visit mometrix.com/academy and enter code: 725944

Multiple Effects

Be aware of the possibility for a single cause to have **multiple effects.** (e.g., *Single cause*: Because you left your homework on the table, your dog engulfed the assignment. *Multiple effects*: As a result, you receive a failing grade, your parents do not allow you to go out with your friends, you miss out on the new movie, and one of your classmates spoils it for you before you have another chance to watch it).

Multiple Causes

Also, there is the possibility for a single effect to have **multiple causes.** (e.g., *Single effect*: Alan has a fever. *Multiple causes*: An unexpected cold front came through the area, and Alan forgot to take his multi-vitamin to avoid getting sick.) Additionally, an effect can in turn be the cause of another effect, in what is known as a cause-and-effect chain. (e.g., As a result of her disdain for procrastination, Lynn prepared for her exam. This led to her passing her test with high marks. Hence, her resume was accepted and her application was approved.)

Cause and Effect in Persuasive Essays

Persuasive essays, in which an author tries to make a convincing argument and change the minds of readers, usually include cause-and-effect relationships. However, these relationships should not always be taken at face value. Frequently, an author will assume a cause or take an effect for granted. To read a persuasive essay effectively, readers need to judge the cause-and-effect relationships that the author is presenting. For instance, imagine an author wrote the following: *The parking deck has been unprofitable because people would prefer to ride their bikes.* The relationship is clear: the cause is that people prefer to ride their bikes, and the effect is that the parking deck has been unprofitable. However, readers should consider whether this argument is conclusive. Perhaps there are other reasons for the failure of the parking deck: a down economy, excessive fees, etc. Too often, authors present causal relationships as if they are fact rather than opinion. Readers should be on the alert for these dubious claims.

Problem-Solution

Some nonfiction texts are organized to **present a problem** followed by a solution. For this type of text, the problem is often explained before the solution is offered. In some cases, as when the problem is well known, the solution may be introduced briefly at the beginning. Other passages may focus on the solution, and the problem will be referenced only occasionally. Some texts will outline multiple solutions to a problem, leaving readers to choose among them. If the author has an interest or an allegiance to one solution, he or she may fail to mention or describe accurately some of the other solutions. Readers should be careful of the author's agenda when reading a problem-solution text. Only by understanding the author's perspective and interests can one develop a proper judgment of the proposed solution.

Compare and Contrast

Many texts follow the **compare-and-contrast** model in which the similarities and differences between two ideas or things are explored. Analysis of the similarities between ideas is called **comparison**. In an ideal comparison, the author places ideas or things in an equivalent structure, i.e., the author presents the ideas in the same way. If an author wants to show the similarities between cricket and baseball, then he or she may do so by summarizing the equipment and rules for each game. Be mindful of the similarities as they appear in the passage and take note of any differences that are mentioned. Often, these small differences will only reinforce the more general similarity.

> **Review Video: Compare and Contrast**
> Visit mometrix.com/academy and enter code: 798319

Thinking critically about ideas and conclusions can seem like a daunting task. One way to ease this task is to understand the basic elements of ideas and writing techniques. Looking at the ways different ideas relate to each other can be a good way for readers to begin their analysis. For instance, sometimes authors will write about two ideas that are in opposition to each other. Or, one author will provide his or her ideas on a topic, and another author may respond in opposition. The analysis of these opposing ideas is known as **contrast**. Contrast is often marred by the author's obvious partiality to one of the ideas. A discerning reader will be put off by an author who does not engage in a fair fight. In an analysis of opposing ideas, both ideas should be presented in clear and reasonable terms. If the author does prefer a side, you need to read carefully to determine the areas where the author shows or avoids this preference. In an analysis of opposing ideas, you should proceed through the passage by marking the major differences point by point with an eye that is looking for an explanation of each side's view. For instance, in an analysis of capitalism and communism, there is an importance in outlining each side's view on labor, markets, prices, personal responsibility, etc. Additionally, as you read through the passages, you should note whether the opposing views present each side in a similar manner.

Sequence

Readers must be able to identify a text's **sequence**, or the order in which things happen. Often, when the sequence is very important to the author, the text is indicated with signal words like *first, then, next,* and *last.* However, a sequence can be merely implied and must be noted by the reader. Consider the sentence *He walked through the garden and gave water and fertilizer to the plants.* Clearly, the man did not walk through the garden before he collected water and fertilizer for the plants. So, the implied sequence is that he first collected water, then he collected fertilizer, next he walked through the garden, and last he gave water or fertilizer as necessary to the plants. Texts do not always proceed in an orderly sequence from first to last. Sometimes they begin at the end and start over at the beginning. As a reader, you can enhance your understanding of the passage by taking brief notes to clarify the sequence.

> **Review Video: Sequence**
> Visit mometrix.com/academy and enter code: 489027

Making and Evaluating Predictions

Making Predictions

When we read literature, **making predictions** about what will happen in the writing reinforces our purpose for reading and prepares us mentally. A **prediction** is a guess about what will happen next. Readers constantly make predictions based on what they have read and what they already know. We can make predictions before we begin reading and during our reading. Consider the following sentence: *Staring at the computer screen in shock, Kim blindly reached over for the brimming glass of water on the shelf to her side.* The sentence suggests that Kim is distracted, and that she is not looking at the glass that she is going to pick up. So, a reader might predict that Kim is going to knock over the glass. Of course, not every prediction will be accurate: perhaps Kim will pick the glass up cleanly. Nevertheless, the author has certainly created the expectation that the water might be spilled.

As we read on, we can test the accuracy of our predictions, revise them in light of additional reading, and confirm or refute our predictions. Predictions are always subject to revision as the reader acquires more information. A reader can make predictions by observing the title and illustrations; noting the structure, characters, and subject; drawing on existing knowledge relative to the subject; and asking "why" and "who" questions. Connecting reading to what we already know enables us to learn new information and construct meaning. For example, before third-graders read a book about Johnny Appleseed, they may start a KWL chart—a list of what they *Know*, what they *Want* to know or learn, and what they have *Learned* after reading. Activating existing background knowledge and thinking about the text before reading improves comprehension.

Review Video: Predictive Reading
Visit mometrix.com/academy and enter code: 437248

Test-taking tip: To respond to questions requiring future predictions, your answers should be based on evidence of past or present behavior and events.

Evaluating Predictions

When making predictions, readers should be able to explain how they developed their prediction. One way readers can defend their thought process is by citing textual evidence. Textual evidence to evaluate reader predictions about literature includes specific synopses of the work, paraphrases of the work or parts of it, and direct quotations from the work. These references to the text must support the prediction by indicating, clearly or unclearly, what will happen later in the story. A text may provide these indications through literary devices such as foreshadowing. Foreshadowing is anything in a text that gives the reader a hint about what is to come by emphasizing the likelihood of an event or development. Foreshadowing can occur through descriptions, exposition, and dialogue. Foreshadowing in dialogue usually occurs when a character gives a warning or expresses a strong feeling that a certain event will occur. Foreshadowing can also occur through irony. However, unlike other forms of foreshadowing, the events that seem the most likely are the opposite of what actually happens. Instances of foreshadowing and irony can be summarized, paraphrased, or quoted to defend a reader's prediction.

Review Video: Textual Evidence for Predictions
Visit mometrix.com/academy and enter code: 261070

Making Inferences and Drawing Conclusions

Inferences are logical conclusions that readers make based on their observations and previous knowledge. An inference is based on both what is found in a passage or a story and what is known from personal experience. For instance, a story may say that a character is frightened and can hear howling in the distance. Based on both what is in the text and personal knowledge, it is a logical conclusion that the character is frightened because he hears the sound of wolves. A good inference is supported by the information in a passage.

Implicit and Explicit Information

By inferring, readers construct meanings from text that are personally relevant. By combining their own schemas or concepts and their background information pertinent to the text with what they read, readers interpret it according to both what the author has conveyed and their own unique perspectives. Inferences are different from **explicit information**, which is clearly stated in a passage. Authors do not always explicitly spell out every meaning in what they write; many meanings are implicit. Through inference, readers can comprehend implied meanings in the text, and also derive personal significance from it, making the text meaningful and memorable to them. Inference is a natural process in everyday life. When readers infer, they can draw conclusions about what the author is saying, predict what may reasonably follow, amend these predictions as they continue to read, interpret the import of themes, and analyze the characters' feelings and motivations through their actions.

Example of Drawing Conclusions from Inferences

Read the excerpt and decide why Jana finally relaxed.

> Jana loved her job, but the work was very demanding. She had trouble relaxing. She called a friend, but she still thought about work. She ordered a pizza, but eating it did not help. Then, her kitten jumped on her lap and began to purr. Jana leaned back and began to hum a little tune. She felt better.

You can draw the conclusion that Jana relaxed because her kitten jumped on her lap. The kitten purred, and Jana leaned back and hummed a tune. Then she felt better. The excerpt does not explicitly say that this is the reason why she was able to relax. The text leaves the matter unclear, but the reader can infer or make a "best guess" that this is the reason she is relaxing. This is a logical conclusion based on the information in the passage. It is the best conclusion a reader can make based on the information he or she has read. Inferences are based on the information in a passage, but they are not directly stated in the passage.

Test-taking tip: While being tested on your ability to make correct inferences, you must look for **contextual clues**. An answer can be true, but not the best or most correct answer. The contextual clues will help you find the answer that is the **best answer** out of the given choices. Be careful in your reading to understand the context in which a phrase is stated. When asked for the implied meaning of a statement made in the passage, you should immediately locate the statement and read the **context** in which the statement was made. Also, look for an answer choice that has a similar phrase to the statement in question.

Review Video: Inference
Visit mometrix.com/academy and enter code: 379203

Review Video: How to Support a Conclusion
Visit mometrix.com/academy and enter code: 281653

Critical Reading Skills

Opinions, Facts, and Fallacies

Critical thinking skills are mastered through understanding various types of writing and the different purposes of authors can have for writing different passages. Every author writes for a purpose. When you understand their purpose and how they accomplish their goal, you will be able to analyze their writing and determine whether or not you agree with their conclusions.

Readers must always be aware of the difference between fact and opinion. A **fact** can be subjected to analysis and proven to be true. An **opinion**, on the other hand, is the author's personal thoughts or feelings and may not be altered by research or evidence. If the author writes that the distance from New York City to Boston is about two hundred miles, then he or she is stating a fact. If the author writes that New York City is too crowded, then he or she is giving an opinion because there is no objective standard for overpopulation. Opinions are often supported by facts. For instance, an author might use a comparison between the population density of New York City and that of other major American cities as evidence of an overcrowded population. An opinion supported by facts tends to be more convincing. On the other hand, when authors support their opinions with other opinions, readers should employ critical thinking and approach the argument with skepticism.

Review Video: Distinguishing Fact and Opinion
Visit mometrix.com/academy and enter code: 870899

Reliable Sources

When you read an argumentative passage, you need to be sure that facts are presented to the reader from **reliable sources**. An opinion is what the author thinks about a given topic. An opinion is not common knowledge or proven by expert sources, instead the information is the personal beliefs and thoughts of the author. To distinguish between fact and opinion, a reader needs to consider the type of source that is presenting information, the information that backs-up a claim, and the author's motivation to have a certain point-of-view on a given topic. For example, if a panel of scientists has conducted multiple studies on the effectiveness of taking a certain vitamin, then the results are more likely to be factual than those of a company that is selling a vitamin and simply claims that taking the vitamin can produce positive effects. The company is motivated to sell their product, and the scientists are using the scientific method to prove a theory. Remember, if you find sentences that contain phrases such as "I think...", then the statement is an opinion.

Biases

In their attempts to persuade, writers often make mistakes in their thought processes and writing choices. These processes and choices are important to understand so you can make an informed decision about the author's credibility. Every author has a point of view, but authors demonstrate a **bias** when they ignore reasonable counterarguments or distort opposing viewpoints. A bias is evident whenever the author's claims are presented in a way that is unfair or inaccurate. Bias can be intentional or unintentional, but readers should be skeptical of the author's argument in either case. Remember that a biased author may still be correct. However, the author will be correct in spite of, not because of, his or her bias.

A **stereotype** is a bias applied specifically to a group of people or a place. Stereotyping is considered to be particularly abhorrent because it promotes negative, misleading generalizations about people. Readers should be very cautious of authors who use stereotypes in their writing. These faulty assumptions typically reveal the author's ignorance and lack of curiosity.

Review Video: Bias and Stereotype
Visit mometrix.com/academy and enter code: 644829

Persuasion and Rhetoric

Persuasive Techniques

To **appeal using reason**, writers present logical arguments, such as using "If... then... because" statements. To **appeal to emotions**, authors may ask readers how they would feel about something or to put themselves in another's place, present their argument as one that will make the audience feel good, or tell readers how they should feel. To **appeal to character**, **morality**, or **ethics**, authors present their points to readers as the right or most moral choices. Authors cite expert opinions to show readers that someone very knowledgeable about the subject or viewpoint agrees with the author's claims. **Testimonials**, usually via anecdotes or quotations regarding the author's subject, help build the audience's trust in an author's message through positive support from ordinary people. **Bandwagon appeals** claim that everybody else agrees with the author's argument and persuade readers to conform and agree, also. Authors **appeal to greed** by presenting their choice as cheaper, free, or more valuable for less cost. They **appeal to laziness** by presenting their views as more convenient, easy, or relaxing. Authors also anticipate potential objections and argue against them before audiences think of them, thereby depicting those objections as weak.

Authors can use **comparisons** like analogies, similes, and metaphors to persuade audiences. For example, a writer might represent excessive expenses as "hemorrhaging" money, which the author's recommended solution will stop. Authors can use negative word connotations to make some choices unappealing to readers, and positive word connotations to make others more appealing. Using **humor** can relax readers and garner their agreement. However, writers must take care: ridiculing opponents can be a successful strategy for appealing to readers who already agree with the author, but can backfire by angering other readers. **Rhetorical questions** need no answer, but create effect that can force agreement, such as asking the question, "Wouldn't you rather be paid more than less?" **Generalizations** persuade readers by being impossible to disagree with. Writers can easily make generalizations that appear to support their viewpoints, like saying, "We all want peace, not war" regarding more specific political arguments. **Transfer** and **association** persuade by example: if advertisements show attractive actors enjoying their products, audiences imagine they will experience the same. **Repetition** can also sometimes effectively persuade audiences.

Review Video: Using Rhetorical Strategies for Persuasion
Visit mometrix.com/academy and enter code: 302658

Classical Author Appeals

In his *On Rhetoric,* ancient Greek philosopher Aristotle defined three basic types of appeal used in writing, which he called *pathos*, *ethos*, and *logos*. ***Pathos*** means suffering or experience and refers to appeals to the emotions (the English word *pathetic* comes from this root). Writing that is meant to entertain audiences, by making them either happy, as with comedy, or sad, as with tragedy, uses *pathos*. Aristotle's *Poetics* states that evoking the emotions of terror and pity is one of the criteria for writing tragedy. ***Ethos*** means character and connotes ideology (the English word *ethics* comes from this root). Writing that appeals to credibility, based on academic, professional, or personal merit, uses *ethos*. ***Logos*** means "I say" and refers to a plea, opinion, expectation, word or speech, account, opinion, or reason (the English word *logic* comes from this root.) Aristotle used it to mean persuasion that appeals to the audience through reasoning and logic to influence their opinions.

Rhetorical Devices

- An **anecdote** is a brief story authors may relate to their argument, which can illustrate their points in a more real and relatable way.
- **Aphorisms** concisely state common beliefs and may rhyme. For example, Benjamin Franklin's "Early to bed and early to rise / Makes a man healthy, wealthy, and wise" is an aphorism.
- **Allusions** refer to literary or historical figures to impart symbolism to a thing or person and to create reader resonance. In John Steinbeck's *Of Mice and Men,* protagonist George's last name is Milton. This alludes to John Milton, who wrote *Paradise Lost,* and symbolizes George's eventual loss of his dream.

- **Satire** exaggerates, ridicules, or pokes fun at human flaws or ideas, as in the works of Jonathan Swift and Mark Twain.
- A **parody** is a form of satire that imitates another work to ridicule its topic or style.
- A **paradox** is a statement that is true despite appearing contradictory.
- **Hyperbole** is overstatement using exaggerated language.
- An **oxymoron** combines seeming contradictions, such as "deafening silence."
- **Analogies** compare two things that share common elements.
- **Similes** (stated comparisons using the words *like* or *as*) and **metaphors** (stated comparisons that do not use *like* or *as*) are considered forms of analogy.
- When using logic to reason with audiences, **syllogism** refers either to deductive reasoning or a deceptive, very sophisticated, or subtle argument.
- **Deductive reasoning** moves from general to specific, **inductive reasoning** from specific to general.
- **Diction** is author word choice that establishes tone and effect.
- **Understatement** achieves effects like contrast or irony by downplaying or describing something more subtly than warranted.
- **Chiasmus** uses parallel clauses, the second reversing the order of the first. Examples include T. S. Eliot's "Has the Church failed mankind, or has mankind failed the Church?" and John F. Kennedy's "Ask not what your country can do for you; ask what you can do for your country."
- **Anaphora** regularly repeats a word or phrase at the beginnings of consecutive clauses or phrases to add emphasis to an idea. A classic example of anaphora was Winston Churchill's emphasis of determination: "[W]e shall fight on the beaches, we shall fight on the landing grounds, we shall fight in the fields and in the streets, we shall fight in the hills; we shall never surrender..."

Reading Comprehension and Connecting with Texts

Comparing Two Stories

When presented with two different stories, there will be **similarities** and **differences** between the two. A reader needs to make a list, or other graphic organizer, of the points presented in each story. Once the reader has written down the main point and supporting points for each story, the two sets of ideas can be compared. The reader can then present each idea and show how it is the same or different in the other story. This is called **comparing and contrasting ideas**.

The reader can compare ideas by stating, for example: "In Story 1, the author believes that humankind will one day land on Mars, whereas in Story 2, the author believes that Mars is too far away for humans to ever step foot on." Note that the two viewpoints are different in each story that the reader is comparing. A reader may state that: "Both stories discussed the likelihood of humankind landing on Mars." This statement shows how the viewpoint presented in both stories is based on the same topic, rather than how each viewpoint is different. The reader will complete a comparison of two stories with a conclusion.

Review Video: How to Compare and Contrast
Visit mometrix.com/academy and enter code: 833765

Outlining a Passage

As an aid to drawing conclusions, **outlining** the information contained in the passage should be a familiar skill to readers. An effective outline will reveal the structure of the passage and will lead to solid conclusions. An effective outline will have a title that refers to the basic subject of the text, though the title does not need to restate the main idea. In most outlines, the main idea will be the first major section. Each major idea in the passage will be established as the head of a category. For instance, the most common outline format calls for the main ideas of the passage to be indicated with Roman numerals. In an effective outline of this kind, each of the main ideas will be represented by a Roman numeral and none of the Roman numerals will designate minor details or secondary ideas. Moreover, all supporting ideas and details should be placed in the appropriate place on the outline. An outline does not need to include every detail listed in the text, but it should feature all of those that are central to the argument or message. Each of these details should be listed under the corresponding main idea.

Review Video: Outlining as an Aid to Drawing Conclusions
Visit mometrix.com/academy and enter code: 584445

Using Graphic Organizers

Ideas from a text can also be organized using **graphic organizers**. A graphic organizer is a way to simplify information and take key points from the text. A graphic organizer such as a timeline may have an event listed for a corresponding date on the timeline, while an outline may have an event listed under a key point that occurs in the text. Each reader needs to create the type of graphic organizer that works the best for him or her in terms of being able to recall information from a story. Examples include a spider-map, which takes a main idea from the story and places it in a bubble with supporting points branching off the main idea. An outline is useful for diagramming the main and supporting points of the entire story, and a Venn diagram compares and contrasts characteristics of two or more ideas.

Review Video: Graphic Organizers
Visit mometrix.com/academy and enter code: 665513

Making Logical Conclusions about a Passage

A reader should always be drawing conclusions from the text. Sometimes conclusions are **implied** from written information, and other times the information is **stated directly** within the passage. One should always aim to draw conclusions from information stated within a passage, rather than to draw them from mere implications. At times an author may provide some information and then describe a counterargument. Readers should be alert for direct statements that are subsequently rejected or weakened by the author. Furthermore, you should always read through the entire passage before drawing conclusions. Many readers are trained to expect the author's conclusions at either the beginning or the end of the passage, but many texts do not adhere to this format.

Drawing conclusions from information implied within a passage requires confidence on the part of the reader. **Implications** are things that the author does not state directly, but readers can assume based on what the author does say. Consider the following passage: *I stepped outside and opened my umbrella. By the time I got to work, the cuffs of my pants were soaked.* The author never states that it is raining, but this fact is clearly implied. Conclusions based on implication must be well supported by the text. In order to draw a solid conclusion, readers should have **multiple pieces of evidence**. If readers have only one piece, they must be assured that there is no other possible explanation than their conclusion. A good reader will be able to draw many conclusions from information implied by the text, which will be a great help on the exam.

Drawing Conclusions

A common type of inference that a reader has to make is **drawing a conclusion**. The reader makes this conclusion based on the information provided within a text. Certain facts are included to help a reader come to a specific conclusion. For example, a story may open with a man trudging through the snow on a cold winter day, dragging a sled behind him. The reader can logically **infer** from the setting of the story that the man is wearing heavy winter clothes in order to stay warm. Information is implied based on the setting of a story, which is why **setting** is an important element of the text. If the same man in the example was trudging down a beach on a hot summer day, dragging a surf board behind him, the reader would assume that the man is not wearing heavy clothes. The reader makes inferences based on their own experiences and the information presented to them in the story.

Test-taking tip: When asked to identify a conclusion that may be drawn, look for critical "hedge" phrases, such as *likely*, *may*, *can*, and *will often*, among many others. When you are being tested on this knowledge, remember the question that writers insert into these hedge phrases to cover every possibility. Often an answer will be wrong simply because there is no room for exception. Extreme positive or negative answers (such as always or never) are usually not correct. When answering these questions, the reader **should not** use any outside knowledge that is not gathered directly or reasonably inferred from the passage. Correct answers can be derived straight from the passage.

Example

Read the following sentence from *Little Women* by Louisa May Alcott and draw a conclusion based upon the information presented:

> *You know the reason Mother proposed not having any presents this Christmas was because it is going to be a hard winter for everyone; and she thinks we ought not to spend money for pleasure, when our men are suffering so in the army.*

Based on the information in the sentence, the reader can conclude, or **infer**, that the men are away at war while the women are still at home. The pronoun *our* gives a clue to the reader that the character is speaking about men she knows. In addition, the reader can assume that the character is speaking to a brother or sister, since the term "Mother" is used by the character while speaking to another person. The reader can also come to the conclusion that the characters celebrate Christmas, since it is mentioned in the **context** of the sentence. In the sentence, the mother is presented as an unselfish character who is opinionated and thinks about the wellbeing of other people.

Summarizing

A helpful tool is the ability to **summarize** the information that you have read in a paragraph or passage format. This process is similar to creating an effective outline. First, a summary should accurately define the main idea of the passage, though the summary does not need to explain this main idea in exhaustive detail. The summary should continue by laying out the most important supporting details or arguments from the passage. All of the significant supporting details should be included, and none of the details included should be irrelevant or insignificant. Also, the summary should accurately report all of these details. Too often, the desire for brevity in a summary leads to the sacrifice of clarity or accuracy. Summaries are often difficult to read because they omit all of the graceful language, digressions, and asides that distinguish great writing. However, an effective summary should communicate the same overall message as the original text.

Review Video: Summarizing Text
Visit mometrix.com/academy and enter code: 172903

Paraphrasing

Paraphrasing is another method that the reader can use to aid in comprehension. When paraphrasing, one puts what they have read into their own words by rephrasing what the author has written, or one "translates" all of what the author shared into their own words by including as many details as they can.

Evaluating a Passage

It is important to understand the logical conclusion of the ideas presented in an informational text. **Identifying a logical conclusion** can help you determine whether you agree with the writer or not. Coming to this conclusion is much like making an inference: the approach requires you to combine the information given by the text with what you already know and make a logical conclusion. If the author intended for the reader to draw a certain conclusion, then you can expect the author's argumentation and detail to be leading in that direction.

One way to approach the task of drawing conclusions is to make brief **notes** of all the points made by the author. When the notes are arranged on paper, they may clarify the logical conclusion. Another way to approach conclusions is to consider whether the reasoning of the author raises any pertinent questions. Sometimes you will be able to draw several conclusions from a passage. On occasion these will be conclusions that were never imagined by the author. Therefore, be aware that these conclusions must be **supported directly by the text**.

Evaluation of Summaries

A summary of a literary passage is a condensation in the reader's own words of the passage's main points. Several guidelines can be used in evaluating a summary. The summary should be complete yet concise. It should be accurate, balanced, fair, neutral, and objective, excluding the reader's own opinions or reactions. It should reflect in similar proportion how much each point summarized was covered in the original passage. Summary writers should include tags of attribution, like "Macaulay argues that" to reference the original author whose ideas are represented in the summary. Summary writers should not overuse quotations; they should only quote central concepts or phrases they cannot precisely convey in words other than those of the original author. Another aspect of evaluating a summary is considering whether it can stand alone as a coherent, unified composition. In addition, evaluation of a summary should include whether its writer has cited the original source of the passage they have summarized so that readers can find it.

Making Connections to Enhance Comprehension

Reading involves thinking. For good comprehension, readers make **text-to-self**, **text-to-text**, and **text-to-world connections**. Making connections helps readers understand text better and predict what might occur next based on what they already know, such as how characters in the story feel or what happened in another text. Text-to-self connections with the reader's life and experiences make literature more personally relevant and meaningful to readers. Readers can make connections before, during, and after reading—including whenever the text reminds them of something similar they have encountered in life or other texts. The genre, setting, characters, plot elements, literary structure and devices, and themes an author uses allow a reader to make connections to other works of literature or to people and events in their own lives. Venn diagrams and other graphic organizers help visualize connections. Readers can also make double-entry notes: key content, ideas, events, words, and quotations on one side, and the connections with these on the other.

Comparing Two Texts

Synthesis of Multiple Texts

Synthesizing, i.e., understanding and integrating, information from multiple texts can at times be among the most challenging skills for some students to succeed with on tests and in school, and yet it is also among the most important. Students who read at the highest cognitive levels can select related material from different text sources and construct coherent arguments that account for these varied information sources. Synthesizing ideas and information from multiple texts actually combines other reading skills that students should have mastered previously in reading one text at a time, and applies them in the context of reading more than one text. For example, students are required to read texts closely, including identifying explicit and implicit meanings; use critical thinking and reading; draw inferences; assess author reasoning; analyze supporting evidence; and formulate opinions they can justify, based on more passages than one. When two paired texts represent opposing sides of the same argument, students can find analyzing them easier; but this is not always the case.

Similarities in Texts

When students are called upon to compare things two texts share in common, the most obvious commonality might be the same subject matter or specific topic. However, two texts need not be about the same thing to compare them. Some other features texts can share include structural characteristics. For example, they may both be written using a sequential format, such as narrating events or giving instructions in chronological order; listing and/or discussing subtopics by order of importance; or describing a place spatially in sequence from each point to the next. They may both use a comparison-contrast structure, identifying similarities and differences between, among, or within topics. They might both organize information by identifying cause-and-effect relationships. Texts can be similar in type, e.g., description, narration, persuasion, or exposition. They can be similar in using technical vocabulary or using formal or informal language. They may share similar tones and/or styles, e.g., humorous, satirical, serious, etc. They can share similar purposes, e.g., to alarm audiences, incite them to action, reassure them, inspire them, provoke strong emotional responses, etc.

Contrasts in Texts

When analyzing paired or multiple texts, students might observe differences in tone; for example, one text might take a serious approach while another uses a humorous one. Even within approaches or treatments, style can differ: one text may be humorous in a witty, sophisticated, clever way while another may exercise broad, "lowbrow" humor; another may employ mordant sarcasm; another may use satire, couching outrageous suggestions in a "deadpan" logical voice to lampoon social attitudes and behaviors as Jonathan Swift did in *A Modest Proposal.* Serious writing can range from darkly pessimistic to alarmist to objective and unemotional. Texts might have similar information, yet organize it using different structures. One text may support points or ideas using logical arguments, while another may seek to persuade its audience by appealing to their emotions. A very obvious difference in text is genre: for example, the same mythological or traditional stories have been told as oral folk tales, written dramas, written novels, etc.; and/or set in different times and places (e.g., Shakespeare's *Romeo and Juliet* vs. Laurents, Bernstein, and Sondheim's *West Side Story*).

Reading Informational Texts

LANGUAGE USE

LITERAL AND FIGURATIVE LANGUAGE

As in fictional literature, informational text also uses both **literal language**, which means just what it says, and **figurative language**, which imparts more than literal meaning. For example, an informational text author might use a simile or direct comparison, such as writing that a racehorse "ran like the wind." Informational text authors also use metaphors or implied comparisons, such as "the cloud of the Great Depression." Imagery may also appear in informational texts to increase the reader's understanding of ideas and concepts discussed in the text.

EXPLICIT AND IMPLICIT INFORMATION

When informational text states something explicitly, the reader is told by the author exactly what is meant, which can include the author's interpretation or perspective of events. For example, a professor writes, "I have seen students go into an absolute panic just because they weren't able to complete the exam in the time they were allotted." This explicitly tells the reader that the students were afraid, and by using the words "just because," the writer indicates their fear was exaggerated out of proportion relative to what happened. However, another professor writes, "I have had students come to me, their faces drained of all color, saying 'We weren't able to finish the exam.'" This is an example of implicit meaning: the second writer did not state explicitly that the students were panicked. Instead, he wrote a description of their faces being "drained of all color." From this description, the reader can infer that the students were so frightened that their faces paled.

Review Video: Explicit and Implicit Information
Visit mometrix.com/academy and enter code: 735771

MAKING INFERENCES ABOUT INFORMATIONAL TEXT

With informational text, reader comprehension depends not only on recalling important statements and details, but also on reader inferences based on examples and details. Readers add information from the text to what they already know to draw inferences about the text. These inferences help the readers to fill in the information that the text does not explicitly state, enabling them to understand the text better. When reading a nonfictional autobiography or biography, for example, the most appropriate inferences might concern the events in the book, the actions of the subject of the autobiography or biography, and the message the author means to convey. When reading a nonfictional expository (informational) text, the reader would best draw inferences about problems and their solutions, and causes and their effects. When reading a nonfictional persuasive text, the reader will want to infer ideas supporting the author's message and intent.

STRUCTURES OR ORGANIZATIONAL PATTERNS IN INFORMATIONAL TEXTS

Informational text can be **descriptive**, appealing to the five senses and answering the questions what, who, when, where, and why. Another method of structuring informational text is sequence and order. **Chronological** texts relate events in the sequence that they occurred, from start to finish, while how-to texts organize information into a series of instructions in the sequence in which the steps should be followed. **Comparison-contrast** structures of informational text describe various ideas to their readers by pointing out how things or ideas are similar and how they are different. **Cause and effect** structures of informational text describe events that occurred and identify the causes or reasons that those events occurred. **Problem and solution** structures of informational texts introduce and describe problems and offer one or more solutions for each problem described.

Determining an Informational Author's Purpose

Informational authors' purposes are why they write texts. Readers must determine authors' motivations and goals. Readers gain greater insight into a text by considering the author's motivation. This develops critical reading skills. Readers perceive writing as a person's voice, not simply printed words. Uncovering author motivations and purposes empowers readers to know what to expect from the text, read for relevant details, evaluate authors and their work critically, and respond effectively to the motivations and persuasions of the text. The main idea of a text is what the reader is supposed to understand from reading it; the purpose of the text is why the author has written it and what the author wants readers to do with its information. Authors state some purposes clearly, while other purposes may be unstated but equally significant. When stated purposes contradict other parts of a text, the author may have a hidden agenda. Readers can better evaluate a text's effectiveness, whether they agree or disagree with it, and why they agree or disagree through identifying unstated author purposes.

Identifying Author's Point of View or Purpose

In some informational texts, readers find it easy to identify the author's point of view and purpose, such as when the author explicitly states his or her position and reason for writing. But other texts are more difficult, either because of the content or because the authors give neutral or balanced viewpoints. This is particularly true in scientific texts, in which authors may state the purpose of their research in the report, but never state their point of view except by interpreting evidence or data.

To analyze text and identify point of view or purpose, readers should ask themselves the following four questions:

1. With what main point or idea does this author want to persuade readers to agree?
2. How does this author's word choice affect the way that readers consider this subject?
3. How do this author's choices of examples and facts affect the way that readers consider this subject?
4. What is it that this author wants to accomplish by writing this text?

Review Video: Understanding the Author's Intent
Visit mometrix.com/academy and enter code: 511819

Review Video: Author's Position
Visit mometrix.com/academy and enter code: 827954

Evaluating Arguments Made by Informational Text Writers

When evaluating an informational text, the first step is to identify the argument's conclusion. Then identify the author's premises that support the conclusion. Try to paraphrase premises for clarification and make the conclusion and premises fit. List all premises first, sequentially numbered, then finish with the conclusion. Identify any premises or assumptions not stated by the author but required for the stated premises to support the conclusion. Read word assumptions sympathetically, as the author might. Evaluate whether premises reasonably support the conclusion. For inductive reasoning, the reader should ask if the premises are true, if they support the conclusion, and if so, how strongly. For deductive reasoning, the reader should ask if the argument is valid or invalid. If all premises are true, then the argument is valid unless the conclusion can be false. If it can, then the argument is invalid. An invalid argument can be made valid through alterations such as the addition of needed premises.

Use of Rhetoric in Informational Texts

There are many ways authors can support their claims, arguments, beliefs, ideas, and reasons for writing in informational texts. For example, authors can appeal to readers' sense of **logic** by communicating their reasoning through a carefully sequenced series of logical steps to help "prove" the points made. Authors can appeal to readers' **emotions** by using descriptions and words that evoke feelings of sympathy, sadness, anger, righteous indignation, hope, happiness, or any other emotion to reinforce what they express and share with their audience. Authors may appeal to the **moral** or **ethical values** of readers by using words and descriptions that can convince readers that something is right or wrong. By relating personal anecdotes, authors can supply readers with more accessible, realistic examples of points they make, as well as appealing to their emotions. They can provide supporting evidence by reporting case studies. They can also illustrate their points by making analogies to which readers can better relate.

Technical Language

Technical Language

Technical language is more impersonal than literary and vernacular language. Passive voice makes the tone impersonal. For example, instead of writing, "We found this a central component of protein metabolism," scientists write, "This was found a central component of protein metabolism." While science professors have traditionally instructed students to avoid active voice because it leads to first-person ("I" and "we") usage, science editors today find passive voice dull and weak. Many journal articles combine both. Tone in technical science writing should be detached, concise, and professional. While one may normally write, "This chemical has to be available for proteins to be digested," professionals write technically, "The presence of this chemical is required for the enzyme to break the covalent bonds of proteins." The use of technical language appeals to both technical and non-technical audiences by displaying the author or speaker's understanding of the subject and suggesting their credibility regarding the message they are communicating.

Technical Material for Non-Technical Readers

Writing about **technical subjects** for **non-technical readers** differs from writing for colleagues because authors place more importance on delivering a critical message than on imparting the maximum technical content possible. Technical authors also must assume that non-technical audiences do not have the expertise to comprehend extremely scientific or technical messages, concepts, and terminology. They must resist the temptation to impress audiences with their scientific knowledge and expertise and remember that their primary purpose is to communicate a message that non-technical readers will understand, feel, and respond to. Non-technical and technical styles include similarities. Both should formally cite any references or other authors' work utilized in the text. Both must follow intellectual property and copyright regulations. This includes the author's protecting his or her own rights, or a public domain statement, as he or she chooses.

Review Video: Technical Passages
Visit mometrix.com/academy and enter code: 478923

Non-Technical Audiences

Writers of technical or scientific material may need to write for many non-technical audiences. Some readers have no technical or scientific background, and those who do may not be in the same field as the authors. Government and corporate policymakers and budget managers need technical information they can understand for decision-making. Citizens affected by technology or science are a different audience. Non-governmental organizations can encompass many of the preceding groups. Elementary and secondary school programs also need non-technical language for presenting technical subject matter. Additionally, technical authors will need to use non-technical language when collecting consumer responses to surveys, presenting scientific or para-scientific material to the public, writing about the history of science, and writing about science and technology in developing countries.

USE OF EVERYDAY LANGUAGE

Authors of technical information sometimes must write using non-technical language that readers outside their disciplinary fields can comprehend. They should use not only non-technical terms, but also normal, everyday language to accommodate readers whose native language is different than the language the text is written in. For example, instead of writing that "eustatic changes like thermal expansion are causing hazardous conditions in the littoral zone," an author would do better to write that "a rising sea level is threatening the coast." When technical terms cannot be avoided, authors should also define or explain them using non-technical language. Although authors must cite references and acknowledge their use of others' work, they should avoid the kinds of references or citations that they would use in scientific journals—unless they reinforce author messages. They should not use endnotes, footnotes, or any other complicated referential techniques because non-technical journal publishers usually do not accept them. Including high-resolution illustrations, photos, maps, or satellite images and incorporating multimedia into digital publications will enhance non-technical writing about technical subjects. Technical authors may publish using non-technical language in e-journals, trade journals, specialty newsletters, and daily newspapers.

Visual Information in Informational Texts

CHARTS, GRAPHS, AND VISUALS

PIE CHART

A pie chart, also known as a circle graph, is useful for depicting how a single unit or category is divided. The standard pie chart is a circle with designated wedges. Each wedge is **proportional** in size to a part of the whole. For instance, consider Shawna, a student at City College, who uses a pie chart to represent her budget. If she spends half of her money on rent, then the pie chart will represent that amount with a line through the center of the pie. If she spends a quarter of her money on food, there will be a line extending from the edge of the circle to the center at a right angle to the line depicting rent. This illustration would make it clear that the student spends twice the amount of money on rent as she does on food.

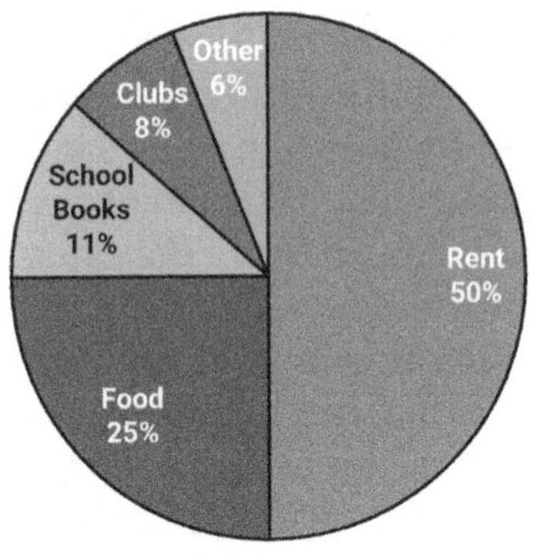

A pie chart is effective at showing how a single entity is divided into parts. They are not effective at demonstrating the relationships between parts of different wholes. For example, an unhelpful use of a pie chart would be to compare the respective amounts of state and federal spending devoted to infrastructure since these values are only meaningful in the context of the entire budget.

Bar Graph

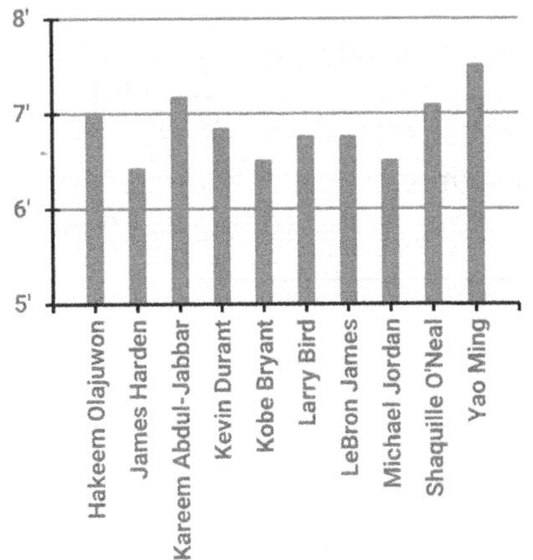

The bar graph is one of the most common visual representations of information. **Bar graphs** are used to illustrate sets of numerical **data**. The graph has a vertical axis (along which numbers are listed) and a horizontal axis (along which categories, words, or some other indicators are placed). One example of a bar graph is a depiction of the respective heights of famous basketball players: the vertical axis would contain numbers ranging from five to eight feet, and the horizontal axis would contain the names of the players. The length of the bar above the player's name would illustrate his height, and the top of the bar would stop perpendicular to the height listed along the left side. In this representation, one would see that Yao Ming is taller than Michael Jordan because Yao's bar would be higher.

Line Graph

A line graph is a type of graph that is typically used for measuring trends over time. The graph is set up along a vertical and a horizontal **axis**. The variables being measured are listed along the left side and the bottom side of the axes. Points are then plotted along the graph as they correspond with their values for each variable. For instance, consider a line graph measuring a person's income for each month of the year. If the person earned $1500 in January, there should be a point directly above January (perpendicular to the horizontal axis) and directly to the right of $1500 (perpendicular to the vertical axis). Once all of the lines are plotted, they are connected with a line from left to right. This line provides a nice visual illustration of the general **trends** of the data, if they exist. For instance, using the earlier example, if the line sloped up, then one would see that the person's income had increased over the course of the year.

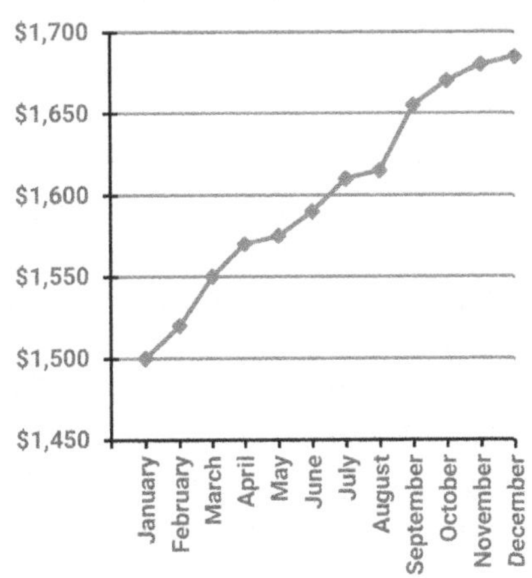

Pictographs

A **pictograph** is a graph, generally in the horizontal orientation, that uses pictures or symbols to represent the data. Each pictograph must have a key that defines the picture or symbol and gives the quantity each picture or symbol represents. Pictures or symbols on a pictograph are not always shown as whole elements. In this case, the fraction of the picture or symbol shown represents the same fraction of the quantity a whole picture or symbol stands for.

> **Review Video: Pictographs**
> Visit mometrix.com/academy and enter code: 147860

Reading Argumentative Writing

Author's Argument in Argumentative Writing

In argumentative writing, the argument is a belief, position, or opinion that the author wants to convince readers to believe as well. For the first step, readers should identify the **issue**. Some issues are controversial, meaning people disagree about them. Gun control, foreign policy, and the death penalty are all controversial issues. The next step is to determine the **author's position** on the issue. That position or viewpoint constitutes the author's argument. Readers should then identify the **author's assumptions**: things he or she accepts, believes, or takes for granted without needing proof. Inaccurate or illogical assumptions produce flawed arguments and can mislead readers. Readers should identify what kinds of **supporting evidence** the author offers, such as research results, personal observations or experiences, case studies, facts, examples, expert testimony and opinions, and comparisons. Readers should decide how relevant this support is to the argument.

Review Video: Argumentative Writing
Visit mometrix.com/academy and enter code: 561544

Evaluating an Author's Argument

The first three reader steps to **evaluate an author's argument** are to identify the **author's assumptions**, identify the **supporting evidence**, and decide **whether the evidence is relevant**. For example, if an author is not an expert on a particular topic, then that author's personal experience or opinion might not be relevant. The fourth step is to assess the **author's objectivity**. For example, consider whether the author introduces clear, understandable supporting evidence and facts to support the argument. The fifth step is evaluating whether the author's **argument is complete**. When authors give sufficient support for their arguments and also anticipate and respond effectively to opposing arguments or objections to their points, their arguments are complete. However, some authors omit information that could detract from their arguments. If instead they stated this information and refuted it, it would strengthen their arguments. The sixth step in evaluating an author's argumentative writing is to assess whether the **argument is valid**. Providing clear, logical reasoning makes an author's argument valid. Readers should ask themselves whether the author's points follow a sequence that makes sense, and whether each point leads to the next. The seventh step is to determine whether the author's **argument is credible**, meaning that it is convincing and believable. Arguments that are not valid are not credible, so step seven depends on step six. Readers should be mindful of their own biases as they evaluate and should not expect authors to conclusively prove their arguments, but rather to provide effective support and reason.

Evaluating an Author's Method of Appeal

To evaluate the effectiveness of an appeal, it is important to consider the author's purpose for writing. Any appeals an author uses in their argument must be relevant to the argument's goal. For example, a writer that argues for the reclassification of Pluto, but primarily uses appeals to emotion, will not have an effective argument. This writer should focus on using appeals to logic and support their argument with provable facts. While most arguments should include appeals to logic, emotion, and credibility, some arguments only call for one or two of these types of appeal. Evidence can support an appeal, but the evidence must be relevant to truly strengthen the appeal's effectiveness. If the writer arguing for Pluto's reclassification uses the reasons for Jupiter's classification as evidence, their argument would be weak. This information may seem relevant because it is related to the classification of planets. However, this classification is highly dependent on the size of the celestial object, and Jupiter is significantly bigger than Pluto. This use of evidence is illogical and does not support the appeal. Even when appropriate evidence and appeals are used, appeals and arguments lose their effectiveness when they create logical fallacies.

Evidence

The term **text evidence** refers to information that supports a main point or minor points and can help lead the reader to a conclusion about the text's credibility. Information used as text evidence is precise, descriptive, and factual. A main point is often followed by supporting details that provide evidence to back up a claim. For example, a passage may include the claim that winter occurs during opposite months in the Northern and Southern hemispheres. Text evidence for this claim may include examples of countries where winter occurs in opposite months. Stating that the tilt of the Earth as it rotates around the sun causes winter to occur at different times in separate hemispheres is another example of text evidence. Text evidence can come from common knowledge, but it is also valuable to include text evidence from credible, relevant outside sources.

Review Video: Textual Evidence
Visit mometrix.com/academy and enter code: 486236

Evidence that supports the thesis and additional arguments needs to be provided. Most arguments must be supported by facts or statistics. A fact is something that is known with certainty, has been verified by several independent individuals, and can be proven to be true. In addition to facts, examples and illustrations can support an argument by adding an emotional component. With this component, you persuade readers in ways that facts and statistics cannot. The emotional component is effective when used alongside objective information that can be confirmed.

Credibility

The text used to support an argument can be the argument's downfall if the text is not credible. A text is **credible**, or believable, when its author is knowledgeable and objective, or unbiased. The author's motivations for writing the text play a critical role in determining the credibility of the text and must be evaluated when assessing that credibility. Reports written about the ozone layer by an environmental scientist and a hairdresser will have a different level of credibility.

Review Video: Author Credibility
Visit mometrix.com/academy and enter code: 827257

Appeal to Emotion

Sometimes, authors will appeal to the reader's emotion in an attempt to persuade or to distract the reader from the weakness of the argument. For instance, the author may try to inspire the pity of the reader by delivering a heart-rending story. An author also might use the bandwagon approach, in which he suggests that his opinion is correct because it is held by the majority. Some authors resort to name-calling, in which insults and harsh words are delivered to the opponent in an attempt to distract. In advertising, a common appeal is the celebrity testimonial, in which a famous person endorses a product. Of course, the fact that a famous person likes something should not really mean anything to the reader. These and other emotional appeals are usually evidence of poor reasoning and a weak argument.

Review Video: Emotional Language in Literature
Visit mometrix.com/academy and enter code: 759390

Counter Arguments

When authors give both sides to the argument, they build trust with their readers. As a reader, you should start with an undecided or neutral position. If an author presents only his or her side to the argument, then they are not exhibiting credibility and are weakening their argument.

Building common ground with readers can be effective for persuading neutral, skeptical, or opposed readers. Sharing values with undecided readers can allow people to switch positions without giving up what they feel is important. People who may oppose a position need to feel that they can change their minds without betraying who they are as a person. This appeal to having an open mind can be a powerful tool in arguing a position without antagonizing other views. Objections can be countered on a point-by-point basis or in a summary paragraph. Be mindful of how an author points out flaws in counter arguments. If they are unfair to the other side of the argument, then you should lose trust with the author.

Narrator's Point of View

Point of View

Another element that impacts a text is the author's point of view. The **point of view** of a text is the perspective from which a passage is told. An author will always have a point of view about a story before he or she draws up a plot line. The author will know what events they want to take place, how they want the characters to interact, and how they want the story to resolve. An author will also have an opinion on the topic or series of events which is presented in the story that is based on their prior experience and beliefs.

The two main points of view that authors use, especially in a work of fiction, are first person and third person. If the narrator of the story is also the main character, or *protagonist*, the text is written in first-person point of view. In first person, the author writes from the perspective of *I*. Third-person point of view is probably the most common that authors use in their passages. Using third person, authors refer to each character by using *he* or *she*. In third-person omniscient, the narrator is not a character in the story and tells the story of all of the characters at the same time.

Review Video: Point of View
Visit mometrix.com/academy and enter code: 383336

First-Person Narration

First-person narratives let narrators express inner feelings and thoughts, especially when the narrator is the protagonist as Lemuel Gulliver is in Jonathan Swift's *Gulliver's Travels.* The narrator may be a close friend of the protagonist, like Dr. Watson in Sir Arthur Conan Doyle's *Sherlock Holmes.* Or, the narrator can be less involved with the main characters and plot, like Nick Carraway in F. Scott Fitzgerald's *The Great Gatsby.* When a narrator reports others' narratives, she or he is a "**frame narrator**," like the nameless narrator of Joseph Conrad's *Heart of Darkness* or Mr. Lockwood in Emily Brontë's *Wuthering Heights.* **First-person plural** is unusual but can be effective. Isaac Asimov's *I, Robot*, William Faulkner's *A Rose for Emily*, Maxim Gorky's *Twenty-Six Men and a Girl*, and Jeffrey Eugenides' *The Virgin Suicides* all use first-person plural narration. Author Kurt Vonnegut is the first-person narrator in his semi-autobiographical novel *Timequake.* Also unusual, but effective, is a **first-person omniscient** (rather than the more common third-person omniscient) narrator, like Death in Markus Zusak's *The Book Thief* and the ghost in Alice Sebold's *The Lovely Bones.*

Second-Person Narration

While **second-person** address is very commonplace in popular song lyrics, it is the least used form of narrative voice in literary works. Popular serial books of the 1980s like *Fighting Fantasy* or *Choose Your Own Adventure* employed second-person narratives. In some cases, a narrative combines both second-person and first-person voices, using the pronouns *you* and *I*. This can draw readers into the story, and it can also enable the authors to compare directly "your" and "my" feelings, thoughts, and actions. When the narrator is also a character in the story, as in Edgar Allan Poe's short story "The Tell-Tale Heart" or Jay McInerney's novel *Bright Lights, Big City,* the narrative is better defined as first-person despite it also addressing "you."

THIRD-PERSON NARRATION

Narration in the third person is the most prevalent type, as it allows authors the most flexibility. It is so common that readers simply assume without needing to be informed that the narrator is not a character in the story, or involved in its events. **Third-person singular** is used more frequently than **third-person plural**, though some authors have also effectively used plural. However, both singular and plural are most often included in stories according to which characters are being described. The third-person narrator may be either objective or subjective, and either omniscient or limited. **Objective third-person** narration does not include what the characters described are thinking or feeling, while **subjective third-person** narration does. The **third-person omniscient** narrator knows everything about all characters, including their thoughts and emotions, and all related places, times, and events. However, the **third-person limited** narrator may know everything about a particular character, but is limited to that character. In other words, the narrator cannot speak about anything that character does not know.

ALTERNATING-PERSON NARRATION

Although authors more commonly write stories from one point of view, there are also instances wherein they alternate the narrative voice within the same book. For example, they may sometimes use an omniscient third-person narrator and a more intimate first-person narrator at other times. In J. K. Rowling's series of *Harry Potter* novels, she often writes in a third-person limited narrative, but sometimes changes to narration by characters other than the protagonist. George R. R. Martin's series *A Song of Ice and Fire* changes the point of view to coincide with divisions between chapters. The same technique is used by Erin Hunter (a pseudonym for several authors of the *Warriors, Seekers,* and *Survivors* book series). Authors using first-person narrative sometimes switch to third-person to describe significant action scenes, especially those where the narrator was absent or uninvolved, as Barbara Kingsolver does in her novel *The Poisonwood Bible.*

Setting, Mood, and Tone

SETTING AND TIME FRAME

A literary text has both a setting and time frame. A **setting** is the place in which the story as a whole is set. The **time frame** is the period in which the story is set. This may refer to the historical period the story takes place in or if the story takes place over a single day. Both setting and time frame are relevant to a text's meaning because they help the reader place the story in time and space. An author uses setting and time frame to anchor a text, create a mood, and enhance its meaning. This helps a reader understand why a character acts the way he does, or why certain events in the story are important. The setting impacts the **plot** and character **motivations**, while the time frame helps place the story in **chronological context**.

EXAMPLE

Read the following excerpt from The Adventures of Huckleberry Finn by Mark Twain and analyze the relevance of setting to the text's meaning:

> We said there warn't no home like a raft, after all. Other places do seem so cramped up and smothery, but a raft don't. You feel mighty free and easy and comfortable on a raft.

This excerpt from *The Adventures of Huckleberry Finn* by Mark Twain reveals information about the **setting** of the book. By understanding that the main character, Huckleberry Finn, lives on a raft, the reader can place the story on a river, in this case, the Mississippi River in the South before the Civil War. The information about the setting also gives the reader clues about the **character** of Huck

Finn: he clearly values independence and freedom, and he likes the outdoors. The information about the setting in the quote helps the reader to better understand the rest of the text.

Syntax and Word Choice

Authors use words and **syntax**, or sentence structure, to make their texts unique, convey their own writing style, and sometimes to make a point or emphasis. They know that word choice and syntax contribute to the reader's understanding of the text as well as to the tone and mood of a text.

Review Video: What is Syntax?
Visit mometrix.com/academy and enter code: 242280

Mood and Tone

Mood is a story's atmosphere, or the feelings the reader gets from reading it. The way authors set the mood in writing is comparable to the way filmmakers use music to set the mood in movies. Instead of music, though, writers judiciously select descriptive words to evoke certain **moods**. The mood of a work may convey joy, anger, bitterness, hope, gloom, fear, apprehension, or any other emotion the author wants the reader to feel. In addition to vocabulary choices, authors also use figurative expressions, particular sentence structures, and choices of diction that project and reinforce the moods they want to create. Whereas mood is the reader's emotions evoked by reading what is written, **tone** is the emotions and attitudes of the writer that she or he expresses in the writing. Authors use the same literary techniques to establish tone as they do to establish mood. An author may use a humorous tone, an angry or sad tone, a sentimental or unsentimental tone, or something else entirely.

Mood and Tone in The Great Gatsby

To understand the difference between mood and tone, look at this excerpt from F. Scott Fitzgerald's *The Great Gatsby*. In this passage, Nick Caraway, the novel's narrator, is describing his affordable house, which sits in a neighborhood full of expensive mansions.

> "I lived at West Egg, the—well the less fashionable of the two, though this is a most superficial tag to express the bizarre and not a little sinister contrast between them. My house was at the very tip of the egg, only fifty yard from the Sound, and squeezed between two huge places that rented for twelve or fifteen thousand a season ... My own house was an eyesore, but it was a small eyesore, and it had been overlooked, so I had a view of the water, a partial view of my neighbor's lawn, and the consoling proximity of millionaires—all for eighty dollars a month."

In this description, the mood created for the reader does not match the tone created through the narrator. The mood in this passage is one of dissatisfaction and inferiority. Nick compares his home to his neighbors', saying he lives in the "less fashionable" neighborhood and that his house is "overlooked," an "eyesore," and "squeezed between two huge" mansions. He also adds that his placement allows him the "consoling proximity of millionaires." A literal reading of these details leads the reader to have negative feelings toward Nick's house and his economic inferiority to his neighbors, creating the mood.

However, Fitzgerald also conveys an opposing attitude, or tone, through Nick's description. Nick calls the distinction between the neighborhoods "superficial," showing a suspicion of the value suggested by the neighborhoods' titles, properties, and residents. Nick also undermines his critique of his own home by calling it "a small eyesore" and claiming it has "been overlooked." However, he follows these statements with a description of his surroundings, claiming that he has "a view of the water" and can see some of his wealthy neighbor's property from his home, and a comparison between the properties' rent. While the mental image created for the reader depicts a small house shoved between looming mansions, the tone suggests that Nick enjoys these qualities about his home, or at least finds it charming. He acknowledges its shortcomings, but includes the benefits of his home's unassuming appearance.

Review Video: Style, Tone, and Mood
Visit mometrix.com/academy and enter code: 416961

Historical and Social Context

Fiction that is heavily influenced by a historical or social context cannot be comprehended as the author intended if the reader does not keep this context in mind. Many important elements of the text will be influenced by any context, including symbols, allusions, settings, and plot events. These contexts, as well as the identity of the work's author, can help to inform the reader about the author's concerns and intended meanings. For example, George Orwell published his novel *1984* in the year 1949, soon after the end of World War II. At that time, following the defeat of the Nazis, the Cold War began between the Western Allied nations and the Eastern Soviet Communists. People were therefore concerned about the conflict between the freedoms afforded by Western democracies versus the oppression represented by Communism. Orwell had also previously fought in the Spanish Civil War against a Spanish regime that he and his fellows viewed as oppressive. From this information, readers can infer that Orwell was concerned about oppression by totalitarian governments. This informs *1984*'s story of Winston Smith's rebellion against the oppressive "Big Brother" government, of the fictional dictatorial state of Oceania, and his capture, torture, and ultimate conversion by that government. Some literary theories also seek to use historical and social contexts to reveal deeper meanings and implications in a text.

Character Development and Dialogue

Character Development

When depicting characters or figures in a written text, authors generally use actions, dialogue, and descriptions as characterization techniques. Characterization can occur in both fiction and nonfiction and is used to show a character or figure's personality, demeanor, and thoughts. This helps create a more engaging experience for the reader by providing a more concrete picture of a character or figure's tendencies and features. Characterizations also gives authors the opportunity to integrate elements such as dialects, activities, attire, and attitudes into their writing.

To understand the meaning of a story, it is vital to understand the characters as the author describes them. We can look for contradictions in what a character thinks, says, and does. We can notice whether the author's observations about a character differ from what other characters in the story say about that character. A character may be dynamic, meaning they change significantly during the story, or static, meaning they remain the same from beginning to end. Characters may be two-dimensional, not fully developed, or may be well developed with characteristics that stand out vividly. Characters may also symbolize universal properties. Additionally, readers can compare and contrast characters to analyze how each one developed.

A well-known example of character development can be found in Charles Dickens's *Great Expectations*. The novel's main character, Pip, is introduced as a young boy, and he is depicted as innocent, kind, and humble. However, as Pip grows up and is confronted with the social hierarchy of Victorian England, he becomes arrogant and rejects his loved ones in pursuit of his own social advancement. Once he achieves his social goals, he realizes the merits of his former lifestyle, and lives with the wisdom he gained in both environments and life stages. Dickens shows Pip's ever-changing character through his interactions with others and his inner thoughts, which evolve as his personal values and personality shift.

Review Video: Character Changes
Visit mometrix.com/academy and enter code: 408719

Dialogue

Effectively written dialogue serves at least one, but usually several, purposes. It advances the story and moves the plot, develops the characters, sheds light on the work's theme or meaning, and can, often subtly, account for the passage of time not otherwise indicated. It can alter the direction that the plot is taking, typically by introducing some new conflict or changing existing ones. **Dialogue** can establish a work's narrative voice and the characters' voices and set the tone of the story or of particular characters. When fictional characters display enlightenment or realization, dialogue can give readers an understanding of what those characters have discovered and how. Dialogue can illuminate the motivations and wishes of the story's characters. By using consistent thoughts and syntax, dialogue can support character development. Skillfully created, it can also represent real-life speech rhythms in written form. Via conflicts and ensuing action, dialogue also provides drama.

Dialogue in Fiction

In fictional works, effectively written dialogue does more than just break up or interrupt sections of narrative. While **dialogue** may supply exposition for readers, it must nonetheless be believable. Dialogue should be dynamic, not static, and it should not resemble regular prose. Authors should not use dialogue to write clever similes or metaphors, or to inject their own opinions. Nor should they use dialogue at all when narrative would be better. Most importantly, dialogue should not slow the plot movement. Dialogue must seem natural, which means careful construction of phrases rather than actually duplicating natural speech, which does not necessarily translate well to the written word. Finally, all dialogue must be pertinent to the story, rather than just added conversation.

Figurative Language

Literal and Figurative Meaning

When language is used **literally**, the words mean exactly what they say and nothing more. When language is used **figuratively**, the words mean something beyond their literal meaning. For example, "The weeping willow tree has long, trailing branches and leaves" is a literal description. But "The weeping willow tree looks as if it is bending over and crying" is a figurative description—specifically, a **simile** or stated comparison. Another figurative language form is **metaphor**, or an implied comparison. A good example is the metaphor of a city, state, or city-state as a ship, and its governance as sailing that ship. Ancient Greek lyrical poet Alcaeus is credited with first using this metaphor, and ancient Greek tragedian Aeschylus then used it in *Seven Against Thebes,* and then Plato used it in the *Republic.*

Figures of Speech

A **figure of speech** is a verbal expression whose meaning is figurative rather than literal. For example, the phrase "butterflies in the stomach" does not refer to actual butterflies in a person's stomach. It is a metaphor representing the fluttery feelings experienced when a person is nervous or excited—or when one "falls in love," which does not mean physically falling. "Hitting a sales target" does not mean physically hitting a target with arrows as in archery; it is a metaphor for meeting a sales quota. "Climbing the ladder of success" metaphorically likens advancing in one's career to ascending ladder rungs. Similes, such as "light as a feather" (meaning very light, not a feather's actual weight), and hyperbole, like "I'm starving/freezing/roasting," are also figures of speech. Figures of speech are often used and crafted for emphasis, freshness of expression, or clarity.

> **Review Video: Figures of Speech**
> Visit mometrix.com/academy and enter code: 111295

FIGURATIVE LANGUAGE

Figurative language extends past the literal meanings of words. It offers readers new insight into the people, things, events, and subjects covered in a work of literature. Figurative language also enables readers to feel they are sharing the authors' experiences. It can stimulate the reader's senses, make comparisons that readers find intriguing or even startling, and enable readers to view the world in different ways. When looking for figurative language, it is important to consider the context of the sentence or situation. Phrases that appear out of place or make little sense when read literally are likely instances of figurative language. Once figurative language has been recognized, context is also important to determining the type of figurative language being used and its function. For example, when a comparison is being made, a metaphor or simile is likely being used. This means the comparison may emphasize or create irony through the things being compared. Seven specific types of figurative language include: alliteration, onomatopoeia, personification, imagery, similes, metaphors, and hyperbole.

> **Review Video: Figurative Language**
> Visit mometrix.com/academy and enter code: 584902

ALLITERATION AND ONOMATOPOEIA

Alliteration describes a series of words beginning with the same sounds. **Onomatopoeia** uses words imitating the sounds of things they name or describe. For example, in his poem "Come Down, O Maid," Alfred Tennyson writes of "The moan of doves in immemorial elms, / And murmuring of innumerable bees." The word "moan" sounds like some sounds doves make, "murmuring" represents the sounds of bees buzzing. Onomatopoeia also includes words that are simply meant to represent sounds, such as "meow," "kaboom," and "whoosh."

> **Review Video: Alliteration in Everyday Expressions**
> Visit mometrix.com/academy and enter code: 462837

PERSONIFICATION

Another type of figurative language is **personification**. This is describing a non-human thing, like an animal or an object, as if it were human. The general intent of personification is to describe things in a manner that will be comprehensible to readers. When an author states that a tree *groans* in the wind, he or she does not mean that the tree is emitting a low, pained sound from a mouth. Instead, the author means that the tree is making a noise similar to a human groan. Of course, this personification establishes a tone of sadness or suffering. A different tone would be established if the author said that the tree was *swaying* or *dancing*. Alfred Tennyson's poem "The Eagle" uses all of these types of figurative language: "He clasps the crag with crooked hands." Tennyson used alliteration, repeating /k/ and /kr/ sounds. These hard-sounding consonants reinforce the imagery, giving visual and tactile impressions of the eagle.

Review Video: Personification Visit mometrix.com/academy and enter code: 260066

Similes and Metaphors

Similes are stated comparisons using "like" or "as." Similes can be used to stimulate readers' imaginations and appeal to their senses. Because a simile includes *like* or *as,* the device creates more space between the description and the thing being described than a metaphor does. If an author says that *a house was like a shoebox*, then the tone is different than the author saying that the house *was* a shoebox. Authors will choose between a metaphor and a simile depending on their intended tone.

Similes also help compare fictional characters to well-known objects or experiences, so the reader can better relate to them. William Wordsworth's poem about "Daffodils" begins, "I wandered lonely as a cloud." This simile compares his loneliness to that of a cloud. It is also personification, giving a cloud the human quality loneliness. In his novel *Lord Jim* (1900), Joseph Conrad writes in Chapter 33, "I would have given anything for the power to soothe her frail soul, tormenting itself in its invincible ignorance like a small bird beating about the cruel wires of a cage." Conrad uses the word "like" to compare the girl's soul to a small bird. His description of the bird beating at the cage shows the similar helplessness of the girl's soul to gain freedom.

Review Video: Similes Visit mometrix.com/academy and enter code: 642949

A **metaphor** is a type of figurative language in which the writer equates something with another thing that is not particularly similar, instead of using *like* or *as*. For instance, *the bird was an arrow arcing through the sky*. In this sentence, the arrow is serving as a metaphor for the bird. The point of a metaphor is to encourage the reader to consider the item being described in a *different way*. Let's continue with this metaphor for a flying bird. You are asked to envision the bird's flight as being similar to the arc of an arrow. So, you imagine the flight to be swift and bending. Metaphors are a way for the author to describe an item *without being direct and obvious*. This literary device is a lyrical and suggestive way of providing information. Note that the reference for a metaphor will not always be mentioned explicitly by the author. Consider the following description of a forest in winter: *Swaying skeletons reached for the sky and groaned as the wind blew through them.* In this example, the author is using *skeletons* as a metaphor for leafless trees. This metaphor creates a spooky tone while inspiring the reader's imagination.

Literary Examples of Metaphor

A **metaphor** is an implied comparison, i.e., it compares something to something else without using "like", "as", or other comparative words. For example, in "The Tyger" (1794), William Blake writes, "Tyger Tyger, burning bright, / In the forests of the night." Blake compares the tiger to a flame not by saying it is like a fire, but by simply describing it as "burning." Henry Wadsworth Longfellow's poem "O Ship of State" (1850) uses an extended metaphor by referring consistently throughout the entire poem to the state, union, or republic as a seagoing vessel, referring to its keel, mast, sail, rope, anchors, and to its braving waves, rocks, gale, tempest, and "false lights on the shore." Within the extended metaphor, Wordsworth uses a specific metaphor: "the anchors of thy hope!"

Ted Hughes' Animal Metaphors

Ted Hughes frequently used animal metaphors in his poetry. In "The Thought Fox," a model of concise, structured beauty, Hughes characterizes the poet's creative process with succinct, striking imagery of an idea entering his head like a wild fox. Repeating "loneliness" in the first two stanzas emphasizes the poet's lonely work: "Something else is alive / Beside the clock's loneliness." He treats an idea's arrival as separate from himself. Three stanzas detail in vivid images a fox's approach from the outside winter forest at starless midnight—its nose, "Cold, delicately" touching twigs and leaves; "neat" paw prints in snow; "bold" body; brilliant green eyes; and self-contained, focused progress—"Till, with a sudden sharp hot stink of fox," he metaphorically depicts poetic inspiration as the fox's physical entry into "the dark hole of the head." Hughes ends by summarizing his vision of a poet as an interior, passive idea recipient, with the outside world unchanged: "The window is starless still; the clock ticks, / The page is printed."

Review Video: Metaphors in Writing
Visit mometrix.com/academy and enter code: 133295

Metonymy

Metonymy is naming one thing with words or phrases of a closely related thing. This is similar to metaphor. However, the comparison has a close connection, unlike metaphor. An example of metonymy is to call the news media *the press*. Of course, *the press* is the machine that prints newspapers. Metonymy is a way of naming something without using the same name constantly.

Synecdoche

Synecdoche points to the whole by naming one of the parts. An example of synecdoche would be calling a construction worker a *hard hat*. Like metonymy, synecdoche is an easy way of naming something without having to overuse a name. The device allows writers to highlight pieces of the thing being described. For example, referring to businessmen as *suits* suggests professionalism and unity.

Hyperbole

Hyperbole is excessive exaggeration used for humor or emphasis rather than for literal meaning. For example, in *To Kill a Mockingbird*, Harper Lee wrote, "People moved slowly then. There was no hurry, for there was nowhere to go, nothing to buy and no money to buy it with, nothing to see outside the boundaries of Maycomb County." This was not literally true; Lee exaggerates the scarcity of these things for emphasis. In "Old Times on the Mississippi," Mark Twain wrote, "I... could have hung my hat on my eyes, they stuck out so far." This is not literal, but makes his description vivid and funny. In his poem "As I Walked Out One Evening", W. H. Auden wrote, "I'll love you, dear, I'll love you / Till China and Africa meet, / And the river jumps over the mountain / And the salmon sing in the street." He used things not literally possible to emphasize the duration of his love.

Understatement

Understatement is the opposite of hyperbole. This device discounts or downplays something. Think about someone who climbs Mount Everest. Then, they say that the journey was *a little stroll*. As with other types of figurative language, understatement has a range of uses. The device may show self-defeat or modesty as in the Mount Everest example. However, some may think of understatement as false modesty (i.e., an attempt to bring attention to you or a situation). For example, a woman is praised on her diamond engagement ring. The woman says, *Oh, this little thing?* Her understatement might be heard as stuck-up or unfeeling.

Review Video: Hyperbole and Understatement
Visit mometrix.com/academy and enter code: 308470

Chapter Quiz

Ready to see how well you retained what you just read? Scan the QR code to go directly to the chapter quiz interface for this study guide. If you're using a computer, simply visit the bonus page at **mometrix.com/bonus948/claslearntest** and click the Chapter Quizzes link.

Grammar and Writing

Transform passive reading into active learning! After immersing yourself in this chapter, put your comprehension to the test by taking a quiz. The insights you gained will stay with you longer this way. Scan the QR code to go directly to the chapter quiz interface for this study guide. If you're using a computer, simply visit the bonus page at **mometrix.com/bonus948/claslearntest** and click the Chapter Quizzes link.

Grammar/Writing Overview

The grammar/writing portion of the Classic Learning Test will consist of one 35-minute section. It will contain 4 passages of different types with 10 questions each for a total of 40 questions.

Philosophy/Religion	These passages are from a variety of authors from ancient times to modern philosophers and focus on common philosophical topics such as truth, ethics, and reasoning. The passages selected intentionally represent a variety of perspectives.
Historical Profile	These passages are short biographical pieces about key historical figures.
Science	These passages are often modern works about a particular scientific topic, often including social implications of a breakthrough or development in biology, physics, chemistry, Earth, or space science. These are accompanied by a graphic and a single question asking the reader to interpret data.
Modern/Influential Thinkers	These passages are taken from modern influential thinkers, often in realms of science, philosophy, or politics and tend to focus on modern social issues.

Question Types in the Verbal Reasoning Section

Each passage will correspond to ten questions, varying in difficulty. In most questions, the test-taker will read the passage and be presented with a specific word or phrase that may or may not need a revision. The first choice is always "no change," indicating that the original wording is correct as-is, and the other choices all consist of one or more changes that address the root problem.

The types of questions that will appear on your test include, but are not strictly limited to the following:

- **Diction** – Evaluating the choice of a word or phrase in question.
- **Punctuation** – Evaluating the punctuation in question. This can include comma placement, apostrophes, quotation marks, or other common punctuation.
- **Syntax** – Evaluating the sentence structure and how it affects clarity and meaning.
- **Flow** – Evaluating the logical progression of information in the passage. These questions often ask the reader if a sentence should be moved to a different location.
- **Logical Coherence** – Evaluating the readability of a sentence.

- **Subject/Verb Agreement** – Evaluating whether a subject and a verb agree. This type of question can consist of a variety of agreement issues, such as temporal agreement and singular/plural agreement.
- **Pronoun/Antecedent Agreement** – Evaluating pronouns and ensuring they agree with the gender and count of their antecedents.
- **Rhetorical Strength of a Revision** – These questions ask the test-taker to evaluate a proposed change and the reasoning behind the change.

Parts of Speech

Nouns

A noun is a person, place, thing, or idea. The two main types of nouns are **common** and **proper** nouns. Nouns can also be categorized as abstract (i.e., general) or concrete (i.e., specific).

Common Nouns

Common nouns are generic names for people, places, and things. Common nouns are not usually capitalized.

Examples of common nouns:

People: boy, girl, worker, manager

Places: school, bank, library, home

Things: dog, cat, truck, car

Review Video: What is a Noun?
Visit mometrix.com/academy and enter code: 344028

Proper Nouns

Proper nouns name specific people, places, or things. All proper nouns are capitalized.

Examples of proper nouns:

People: Abraham Lincoln, George Washington, Martin Luther King, Jr.

Places: Los Angeles, California; New York; Asia

Things: Statue of Liberty, Earth, Lincoln Memorial

Note: Some nouns can be either common or proper depending on their use. For example, when referring to the planet that we live on, *Earth* is a proper noun and is capitalized. When referring to the dirt, rocks, or land on our planet, *earth* is a common noun and is not capitalized.

General and Specific Nouns

General nouns are the names of conditions or ideas. **Specific nouns** name people, places, and things that are understood by using your senses.

General nouns:

Condition: beauty, strength

Idea: truth, peace

Specific nouns:

People: baby, friend, father

Places: town, park, city hall

Things: rainbow, cough, apple, silk, gasoline

Collective Nouns

Collective nouns are the names for a group of people, places, or things that may act as a whole. The following are examples of collective nouns: *class, company, dozen, group, herd, team,* and *public.* Collective nouns usually require an article, which denotes the noun as being a single unit. For instance, a choir is a group of singers. Even though there are many singers in a choir, the word choir is grammatically treated as a single unit. If we refer to the members of the group, and not the group itself, it is no longer a collective noun.

Incorrect: The *choir are* going to compete nationally this year.

Correct: The *choir is* going to compete nationally this year.

Incorrect: The *members* of the choir *is* competing nationally this year.

Correct: The *members* of the choir *are* competing nationally this year.

Pronouns

Pronouns are words that are used to stand in for nouns. A pronoun may be classified as personal, intensive, relative, interrogative, demonstrative, indefinite, and reciprocal.

Personal: *Nominative* is the case for nouns and pronouns that are the subject of a sentence. *Objective* is the case for nouns and pronouns that are an object in a sentence. *Possessive* is the case for nouns and pronouns that show possession or ownership.

Singular

	Nominative	Objective	Possessive
First Person	I	me	my, mine
Second Person	you	you	your, yours
Third Person	he, she, it	him, her, it	his, her, hers, its

Plural

	Nominative	Objective	Possessive
First Person	we	us	our, ours
Second Person	you	you	your, yours
Third Person	they	them	their, theirs

Intensive: I myself, you yourself, he himself, she herself, the (thing) itself, we ourselves, you yourselves, they themselves

Relative: which, who, whom, whose

Interrogative: what, which, who, whom, whose

Demonstrative: this, that, these, those

Indefinite: all, any, each, everyone, either/neither, one, some, several

Reciprocal: each other, one another

Review Video: Nouns and Pronouns
Visit mometrix.com/academy and enter code: 312073

VERBS

A verb is a word or group of words that indicates action or being. In other words, the verb shows something's action or state of being or the action that has been done to something. If you want to write a sentence, then you need a verb. Without a verb, you have no sentence.

TRANSITIVE AND INTRANSITIVE VERBS

A **transitive verb** is a verb whose action indicates a receiver. **Intransitive verbs** do not indicate a receiver of an action. In other words, the action of the verb does not point to an object.

Transitive: He drives a car. | She feeds the dog.

Intransitive: He runs every day. | She voted in the last election.

A dictionary will tell you whether a verb is transitive or intransitive. Some verbs can be transitive or intransitive.

ACTION VERBS AND LINKING VERBS

Action verbs show what the subject is doing. In other words, an action verb shows action. Unlike most types of words, a single action verb, in the right context, can be an entire sentence. **Linking verbs** link the subject of a sentence to a noun or pronoun, or they link a subject with an adjective. You always need a verb if you want a complete sentence. However, linking verbs on their own cannot be a complete sentence.

Common linking verbs include *appear, be, become, feel, grow, look, seem, smell, sound,* and *taste*. However, any verb that shows a condition and connects to a noun, pronoun, or adjective that describes the subject of a sentence is a linking verb.

Action: He sings. | Run! | Go! | I talk with him every day. | She reads.

Linking:

Incorrect: I am.

Correct: I am John. | The roses smell lovely. | I feel tired.

Note: Some verbs are followed by words that look like prepositions, but they are a part of the verb and a part of the verb's meaning. These are known as phrasal verbs, and examples include *call off*, *look up*, and *drop off*.

Review Video: Action Verbs and Linking Verbs
Visit mometrix.com/academy and enter code: 743142

Voice

Transitive verbs may be in active voice or passive voice. The difference between active voice and passive voice is whether the subject is acting or being acted upon. When the subject of the sentence is doing the action, the verb is in **active voice**. When the subject is being acted upon, the verb is in **passive voice**.

Active: Jon drew the picture. (The subject *Jon* is doing the action of *drawing a picture*.)

Passive: The picture is drawn by Jon. (The subject *picture* is receiving the action from Jon.)

Verb Tenses

Verb **tense** is a property of a verb that indicates when the action being described takes place (past, present, or future) and whether or not the action is completed (simple or perfect). Describing an action taking place in the present (*I talk*) requires a different verb tense than describing an action that took place in the past (*I talked*). Some verb tenses require an auxiliary (helping) verb. These helping verbs include *am, are, is* | *have, has, had* | *was, were, will* (or *shall*).

Present: I talk	Present perfect: I have talked
Past: I talked	Past perfect: I had talked
Future: I will talk	Future perfect: I will have talked

Present: The action is happening at the current time.

Example: He *walks* to the store every morning.

To show that something is happening right now, use the progressive present tense: I *am walking*.

Past: The action happened in the past.

Example: She *walked* to the store an hour ago.

Future: The action will happen later.

Example: I *will walk* to the store tomorrow.

Present perfect: The action started in the past and continues into the present or took place previously at an unspecified time.

Example: I *have walked* to the store three times today.

Past perfect: The action was completed at some point in the past. This tense is usually used to describe an action that was completed before some other reference time or event.

Example: I *had eaten* already before they arrived.

Future perfect: The action will be completed before some point in the future. This tense may be used to describe an action that has already begun or has yet to begin.

Example: The project *will have been completed* by the deadline.

Review Video: Present Perfect, Past Perfect, and Future Perfect Verb Tenses
Visit mometrix.com/academy and enter code: 269472

Conjugating Verbs

When you need to change the form of a verb, you are **conjugating** a verb. The key forms of a verb are present tense (sing/sings), past tense (sang), present participle (singing), and past participle (sung). By combining these forms with helping verbs, you can make almost any verb tense. The following table demonstrate some of the different ways to conjugate a verb:

Tense	First Person	Second Person	Third Person Singular	Third Person Plural
Simple Present	I sing	You sing	He, she, it sings	They sing
Simple Past	I sang	You sang	He, she, it sang	They sang
Simple Future	I will sing	You will sing	He, she, it will sing	They will sing
Present Progressive	I am singing	You are singing	He, she, it is singing	They are singing
Past Progressive	I was singing	You were singing	He, she, it was singing	They were singing
Present Perfect	I have sung	You have sung	He, she, it has sung	They have sung
Past Perfect	I had sung	You had sung	He, she, it had sung	They had sung

Mood

There are three **moods** in English: the indicative, the imperative, and the subjunctive.

The **indicative mood** is used for facts, opinions, and questions.

Fact: You can do this.

Opinion: I think that you can do this.

Question: Do you know that you can do this?

The **imperative** is used for orders or requests.

Order: You are going to do this!

Request: Will you do this for me?

The **subjunctive mood** is for wishes and statements that go against fact.

Wish: I wish that I were famous.

Statement against fact: If I were you, I would do this. (This goes against fact because I am not you. You have the chance to do this, and I do not have the chance.)

ADJECTIVES

An **adjective** is a word that is used to modify a noun or pronoun. An adjective answers a question: *Which one? What kind?* or *How many?* Usually, adjectives come before the words that they modify, but they may also come after a linking verb.

Which one? The *third* suit is my favorite.

What kind? This suit is *navy blue*.

How many? I am going to buy *four* pairs of socks to match the suit.

Review Video: Descriptive Text
Visit mometrix.com/academy and enter code: 174903

ARTICLES

Articles are adjectives that are used to distinguish nouns as definite or indefinite. *A*, *an*, and *the* are the only articles. **Definite** nouns are preceded by *the* and indicate a specific person, place, thing, or idea. **Indefinite** nouns are preceded by *a* or *an* and do not indicate a specific person, place, thing, or idea.

Note: *An* comes before words that start with a vowel sound. For example, "Are you going to get an **u**mbrella?"

Definite: I lost *the* bottle that belongs to me.

Indefinite: Does anyone have *a* bottle to share?

Review Video: Function of Articles in a Sentence
Visit mometrix.com/academy and enter code: 449383

COMPARISON WITH ADJECTIVES

Some adjectives are relative and other adjectives are absolute. Adjectives that are **relative** can show the comparison between things. **Absolute** adjectives can also show comparison, but they do so in a different way. Let's say that you are reading two books. You think that one book is perfect, and the other book is not exactly perfect. It is not possible for one book to be more perfect than the other. Either you think that the book is perfect, or you think that the book is imperfect. In this case, perfect and imperfect are absolute adjectives.

Relative adjectives will show the different **degrees** of something or someone to something else or someone else. The three degrees of adjectives include positive, comparative, and superlative.

The **positive** degree is the normal form of an adjective.

Example: This work is *difficult*. | She is *smart*.

The **comparative** degree compares one person or thing to another person or thing.

Example: This work is *more difficult* than your work. | She is *smarter* than me.

The **superlative** degree compares more than two people or things.

Example: This is the *most difficult* work of my life. | She is the *smartest* lady in school.

Review Video: What is an Adjective?
Visit mometrix.com/academy and enter code: 470154

Adverbs

An **adverb** is a word that is used to **modify** a verb, an adjective, or another adverb. Usually, adverbs answer one of these questions: *When? Where? How?* and *Why?* The negatives *not* and *never* are considered adverbs. Adverbs that modify adjectives or other adverbs **strengthen** or **weaken** the words that they modify.

Examples:

He walks *quickly* through the crowd.

The water flows *smoothly* on the rocks.

Note: Adverbs are usually indicated by the morpheme *-ly*, which has been added to the root word. For instance, *quick* can be made into an adverb by adding *-ly* to construct *quickly*. Some words that end in *-ly* do not follow this rule and can behave as other parts of speech. Examples of adjectives ending in *-ly* include: *early, friendly, holy, lonely, silly*, and *ugly*. To know if a word that ends in *-ly* is an adjective or adverb, check your dictionary. Also, while many adverbs end in *-ly*, you need to remember that not all adverbs end in *-ly*.

Examples:

He is *never* angry.

You are *too* irresponsible to travel alone.

Review Video: What is an Adverb?
Visit mometrix.com/academy and enter code: 713951

Review Video: Adverbs that Modify Adjectives
Visit mometrix.com/academy and enter code: 122570

Comparison with Adverbs

The rules for comparing adverbs are the same as the rules for adjectives.

The **positive** degree is the standard form of an adverb.

Example: He arrives *soon.* | She speaks *softly* to her friends.

The **comparative** degree compares one person or thing to another person or thing.

Example: He arrives *sooner* than Sarah. | She speaks *more softly* than him.

The **superlative** degree compares more than two people or things.

Example: He arrives *soonest* of the group. | She speaks the *most softly* of any of her friends.

Prepositions

A **preposition** is a word placed before a noun or pronoun that shows the relationship between that noun or pronoun and another word in the sentence.

Common prepositions:

about	before	during	on	under
after	beneath	for	over	until
against	between	from	past	up
among	beyond	in	through	with
around	by	of	to	within
at	down	off	toward	without

Examples:

The napkin is *in* the drawer.

The Earth rotates *around* the Sun.

The needle is *beneath* the haystack.

Can you find "me" *among* the words?

Review Video: Prepositions
Visit mometrix.com/academy and enter code: 946763

Conjunctions

Conjunctions join words, phrases, or clauses and they show the connection between the joined pieces. **Coordinating conjunctions** connect equal parts of sentences. **Correlative conjunctions** show the connection between pairs. **Subordinating conjunctions** join subordinate (i.e., dependent) clauses with independent clauses.

Coordinating Conjunctions

The **coordinating conjunctions** include: *and, but, yet, or, nor, for,* and *so*

Examples:

The rock was small, *but* it was heavy.

She drove in the night, *and* he drove in the day.

Correlative Conjunctions

The **correlative conjunctions** are: *either...or* | *neither...nor* | *not only...but also*

Examples:

> *Either* you are coming *or* you are staying.
>
> He *not only* ran three miles *but also* swam 200 yards.

> **Review Video: Coordinating and Correlative Conjunctions**
> Visit mometrix.com/academy and enter code: 390329
>
> **Review Video: Adverb Equal Comparisons**
> Visit mometrix.com/academy and enter code: 231291

Subordinating Conjunctions

Common **subordinating conjunctions** include:

after	since	whenever
although	so that	where
because	unless	wherever
before	until	whether
in order that	when	while

Examples:

> I am hungry *because* I did not eat breakfast.
>
> He went home *when* everyone left.

> **Review Video: Subordinating Conjunctions**
> Visit mometrix.com/academy and enter code: 958913

Interjections

Interjections are words of exclamation (i.e., audible expression of great feeling) that are used alone or as a part of a sentence. Often, they are used at the beginning of a sentence for an introduction. Sometimes, they can be used in the middle of a sentence to show a change in thought or attitude.

> Common Interjections: Hey! | Oh, | Ouch! | Please! | Wow!

Agreement and Sentence Structure

Subjects and Predicates

Subjects

The **subject** of a sentence names who or what the sentence is about. The subject may be directly stated in a sentence, or the subject may be the implied *you*. The **complete subject** includes the simple subject and all of its modifiers. To find the complete subject, ask *Who* or *What* and insert the verb to complete the question. The answer, including any modifiers (adjectives, prepositional phrases, etc.), is the complete subject. To find the **simple subject**, remove all of the modifiers in the complete subject. Being able to locate the subject of a sentence helps with many problems, such as those involving sentence fragments and subject-verb agreement.

Examples:

The small, red car is the one that he wants for Christmas.
(simple subject: car; complete subject: The small, red car)

The young artist is coming over for dinner.
(simple subject: artist; complete subject: The young artist)

Review Video: Subjects in English
Visit mometrix.com/academy and enter code: 444771

In **imperative** sentences, the verb's subject is understood (e.g., [You] Run to the store), but is not actually present in the sentence. Normally, the subject comes before the verb. However, the subject comes after the verb in sentences that begin with *There are* or *There was.*

Direct:

John knows the way to the park.	Who knows the way to the park?	John
The cookies need ten more minutes.	What needs ten minutes?	The cookies
By five o'clock, Bill will need to leave.	Who needs to leave?	Bill
There are five letters on the table for him.	What is on the table?	Five letters
There were coffee and doughnuts in the house.	What was in the house?	Coffee and doughnuts

Implied:

Go to the post office for me.	Who is going to the post office?	You
Come and sit with me, please?	Who needs to come and sit?	You

Predicates

In a sentence, you always have a predicate and a subject. The subject tells who or what the sentence is about, and the **predicate** explains or describes the subject. The predicate includes the verb or verb phrase and any direct or indirect objects of the verb, as well as any words or phrases modifying these.

Think about the sentence *He sings*. In this sentence, we have a subject (He) and a predicate (sings). This is all that is needed for a sentence to be complete. Most sentences contain more information, but if this is all the information that you are given, then you have a complete sentence.

Now, let's look at another sentence: *John and Jane sing on Tuesday nights at the dance hall.*

subject: John and Jane | predicate: sing on Tuesday nights at the dance hall.

Review Video: What is a Complete Predicate?
Visit mometrix.com/academy and enter code: 293942

Subject-Verb Agreement

Verbs must **agree** with their subjects in number and in person. To agree in number, singular subjects need singular verbs and plural subjects need plural verbs. A **singular** noun refers to **one** person, place, or thing. A **plural** noun refers to **more than one** person, place, or thing. To agree in person, the correct verb form must be chosen to match the first, second, or third person subject. The present tense ending *-s* or *-es* is used on a verb if its subject is third person singular; otherwise, the verb's ending is not modified.

Review Video: Subject-Verb Agreement
Visit mometrix.com/academy and enter code: 479190

Number Agreement Examples:

Single Subject and Verb: Dan (singular subject) calls (singular verb) home.

Dan is one person. So, the singular verb *calls* is needed.

Plural Subject and Verb: Dan and Bob (plural subject) call (plural verb) home.

More than one person needs the plural verb *call*.

Person Agreement Examples:

First Person: I *am* walking.

Second Person: You *are* walking.

Third Person: He *is* walking.

Complications with Subject-Verb Agreement

Words Between Subject and Verb

Words that come between the simple subject and the verb have no bearing on subject-verb agreement.

Examples:

The joy (singular subject) of my life returns (singular verb) home tonight.

The phrase *of my life* does not influence the verb *returns*.

The question (singular subject) that still remains unanswered is (singular verb) "Who are you?"

Don't let the phrase *"that still remains…"* trouble you. The subject *question* goes with *is*.

Compound Subjects

A compound subject is formed when two or more nouns joined by *and*, *or*, or *nor* jointly act as the subject of the sentence.

Joined by And

When a compound subject is joined by *and*, it is treated as a plural subject and requires a plural verb.

Examples:

You and Jon (plural subject) are (plural verb) invited to come to my house.

The pencil and paper (plural subject) belong (plural verb) to me.

Joined by Or/Nor

For a compound subject joined by *or* or *nor*, the verb must agree in number with the part of the subject that is closest to the verb (italicized in the examples below).

Examples:

Today or tomorrow (subject) is (verb) the day.

Stan or Phil (subject) wants (verb) to read the book.

Neither the pen nor the book (subject) is (verb) on the desk.

Either the blanket or pillows (subject) arrive (verb) this afternoon.

Indefinite Pronouns as Subject

An indefinite pronoun is a pronoun that does not refer to a specific noun. Some indefinite pronouns function as only singular, some function as only plural, and some can function as either singular or plural depending on how they are used.

ALWAYS SINGULAR

Pronouns such as *each*, *either*, *everybody*, *anybody*, *somebody*, and *nobody* are always singular.

Examples:

singular subject: Each of the runners / singular verb: has a different bib number.

singular verb: Is / singular subject: either of you ready for the game?

Note: The words *each* and *either* can also be used as adjectives (e.g., *each* person is unique). When one of these adjectives modifies the subject of a sentence, it is always a singular subject.

singular subject: Everybody / singular verb: grows a day older every day.

singular subject: Anybody / singular verb: is welcome to bring a tent.

ALWAYS PLURAL

Pronouns such as *both*, *several*, and *many* are always plural.

Examples:

plural subject: Both of the siblings / plural verb: were too tired to argue.

plural subject: Many / plural verb: have tried, but none have succeeded.

DEPEND ON CONTEXT

Pronouns such as *some*, *any*, *all*, *none*, *more*, and *most* can be either singular or plural depending on what they are representing in the context of the sentence.

Examples:

singular subject: All of my dog's food / singular verb: was still there in his bowl.

By the end of the night, plural subject: all of my guests / plural verb: were already excited about coming to my next party.

Other Cases Involving Plural or Irregular Form

Some nouns are **singular in meaning but plural in form**: news, mathematics, physics, and economics.

> The *news is* coming on now.
>
> *Mathematics is* my favorite class.

Some nouns are plural in form and meaning, and have **no singular equivalent**: scissors and pants.

> Do these *pants come* with a shirt?
>
> The *scissors are* for my project.

Mathematical operations are **irregular** in their construction, but are normally considered to be **singular in meaning**.

> *One plus one is* two.
>
> *Three times three is* nine.

Note: Look to your **dictionary** for help when you aren't sure whether a noun with a plural form has a singular or plural meaning.

Complements

A complement is a noun, pronoun, or adjective that is used to give more information about the subject or object in the sentence.

Direct Objects

A direct object is a noun or pronoun that tells who or what **receives** the action of the verb. A sentence will only include a direct object if the verb is a transitive verb. If the verb is an intransitive verb or a linking verb, there will be no direct object. When you are looking for a direct object, find the verb and ask *who* or *what.*

Examples:

> I took *the blanket.*
>
> Jane read *books.*

Indirect Objects

An indirect object is a noun or pronoun that indicates what or whom the action had an **influence** on. If there is an indirect object in a sentence, then there will also be a direct object. When you are looking for the indirect object, find the verb and ask *to/for whom or what.*

Examples:

We taught the old dog (indirect object) a new trick (direct object).

I gave them (indirect object) a math lesson (direct object).

Review Video: Direct and Indirect Objects
Visit mometrix.com/academy and enter code: 817385

PREDICATE NOMINATIVES AND PREDICATE ADJECTIVES

As we looked at previously, verbs may be classified as either action verbs or linking verbs. A linking verb is so named because it links the subject to words in the predicate that describe or define the subject. These words are called predicate nominatives (if nouns or pronouns) or predicate adjectives (if adjectives).

Examples:

My father (subject) is a lawyer (predicate nominative).

Your mother (subject) is patient (predicate adjective).

PRONOUN USAGE

The **antecedent** is the noun that has been replaced by a pronoun. A pronoun and its antecedent **agree** when they have the same number (singular or plural) and gender (male, female, or neutral).

Examples:

Singular agreement: John (antecedent) came into town, and he (pronoun) played for us.

Plural agreement: John and Rick (antecedent) came into town, and they (pronoun) played for us.

To determine which is the correct pronoun to use in a compound subject or object, try each pronoun **alone** in place of the compound in the sentence. Your knowledge of pronouns will tell you which one is correct.

Example:

Bob and (I, me) will be going.

Test: (1) *I will be going* or (2) *Me will be going*. The second choice cannot be correct because *me* cannot be used as the subject of a sentence. Instead, *me* is used as an object.

Answer: Bob and I will be going.

When a pronoun is used with a noun immediately following (as in "we boys"), try the sentence **without the added noun**.

Example:

(We/Us) boys played football last year.

Test: (1) *We played football last ye*ar or (2) *Us played football last year.* Again, the second choice cannot be correct because *us* cannot be used as a subject of a sentence. Instead, *us* is used as an object.

Answer: We boys played football last year.

Review Video: Pronoun Usage
Visit mometrix.com/academy and enter code: 666500

Review Video: What is Pronoun-Antecedent Agreement?
Visit mometrix.com/academy and enter code: 919704

A pronoun should point clearly to the **antecedent**. Here is how a pronoun reference can be unhelpful if it is puzzling or not directly stated.

Unhelpful: Ron and Jim (antecedent) went to the store, and he (pronoun) bought soda.

Who bought soda? Ron or Jim?

Helpful: Jim (antecedent) went to the store, and he (pronoun) bought soda.

The sentence is clear. Jim bought the soda.

Some pronouns change their form by their placement in a sentence. A pronoun that is a **subject** in a sentence comes in the **subjective case**. Pronouns that serve as **objects** appear in the **objective case**. Finally, the pronouns that are used as **possessives** appear in the **possessive case**.

Examples:

Subjective case: *He* is coming to the show.

The pronoun *He* is the subject of the sentence.

Objective case: Josh drove *him* to the airport.

The pronoun *him* is the object of the sentence.

Possessive case: The flowers are *mine*.

The pronoun *mine* shows ownership of the flowers.

The word *who* is a subjective-case pronoun that can be used as a **subject**. The word *whom* is an objective-case pronoun that can be used as an **object**. The words *who* and *whom* are common in subordinate clauses or in questions.

Examples:

He knows who (subject) wants (verb) to come.

He knows the man whom (object) we want (verb) at the party.

Clauses

A clause is a group of words that contains both a subject and a predicate (verb). There are two types of clauses: independent and dependent. An **independent clause** contains a complete thought, while a **dependent (or subordinate) clause** does not. A dependent clause includes a subject and a verb, and may also contain objects or complements, but it cannot stand as a complete thought without being joined to an independent clause. Dependent clauses function within sentences as adjectives, adverbs, or nouns.

Example:

I am running (independent clause) because I want to stay in shape. (dependent clause)

The clause *I am running* is an independent clause: it has a subject and a verb, and it gives a complete thought. The clause *because I want to stay in shape* is a dependent clause: it has a subject and a verb, but it does not express a complete thought. It adds detail to the independent clause to which it is attached.

Review Video: What is a Clause?
Visit mometrix.com/academy and enter code: 940170

Review Video: Independent and Dependent Clauses
Visit mometrix.com/academy and enter code: 556903

Types of Dependent Clauses

Adjective Clauses

An **adjective clause** is a dependent clause that modifies a noun or a pronoun. Adjective clauses begin with a relative pronoun (*who, whose, whom, which,* and *that*) or a relative adverb (*where, when,* and *why*).

Also, adjective clauses usually come immediately after the noun that the clause needs to explain or rename. This is done to ensure that it is clear which noun or pronoun the clause is modifying.

Examples:

I learned the reason (independent clause) why I won the award. (adjective clause)

This is the place (independent clause) where I started my first job. (adjective clause)

An adjective clause can be an essential or nonessential clause. An essential clause is very important to the sentence. **Essential clauses** explain or define a person or thing. **Nonessential clauses** give more information about a person or thing but are not necessary to define them. Nonessential clauses are set off with commas while essential clauses are not.

Examples:

essential clause

A person who works hard at first can often rest later in life.

nonessential clause

Neil Armstrong, who walked on the moon, is my hero.

Review Video: Adjective Clauses and Phrases
Visit mometrix.com/academy and enter code: 520888

Adverb Clauses

An **adverb clause** is a dependent clause that modifies a verb, adjective, or adverb. In sentences with multiple dependent clauses, adverb clauses are usually placed immediately before or after the independent clause. An adverb clause is introduced with words such as *after, although, as, before, because, if, since, so, unless, when, where,* and *while.*

Examples:

adverb clause

When you walked outside, I called the manager.

adverb clause

I will go with you unless you want to stay.

Noun Clauses

A **noun clause** is a dependent clause that can be used as a subject, object, or complement. Noun clauses begin with words such as *how, that, what, whether, which, who,* and *why*. These words can also come with an adjective clause. Unless the noun clause is being used as the subject of the sentence, it should come after the verb of the independent clause.

Examples:

noun clause

The real mystery is how you avoided serious injury.

noun clause

What you learn from each other depends on your honesty with others.

Subordination

When two related ideas are not of equal importance, the ideal way to combine them is to make the more important idea an independent clause and the less important idea a dependent or subordinate clause. This is called **subordination.**

Example:

Separate ideas: The team had a perfect regular season. The team lost the championship.

Subordinated: Despite having a perfect regular season, *the team lost the championship.*

PHRASES

A phrase is a group of words that functions as a single part of speech, usually a noun, adjective, or adverb. A **phrase** is not a complete thought and does not contain a subject and predicate, but it adds detail or explanation to a sentence, or renames something within the sentence.

PREPOSITIONAL PHRASES

One of the most common types of phrases is the prepositional phrase. A **prepositional phrase** begins with a preposition and ends with a noun or pronoun that is the object of the preposition. Normally, the prepositional phrase functions as an **adjective** or an **adverb** within the sentence.

Examples:

prepositional phrase

The picnic is on the blanket.

prepositional phrase

I am sick with a fever today.

prepositional phrase

Among the many flowers, John found a four-leaf clover.

VERBAL PHRASES

A **verbal** is a word or phrase that is formed from a verb but does not function as a verb. Depending on its particular form, it may be used as a noun, adjective, or adverb. A verbal does **not** replace a verb in a sentence.

Examples:

verb

Correct: Walk a mile daily.

This is a complete sentence with the implied subject *you*.

verbal

Incorrect: To walk a mile.

This is not a sentence since there is no functional verb.

There are three types of verbal: **participles**, **gerunds**, and **infinitives**. Each type of verbal has a corresponding **phrase** that consists of the verbal itself along with any complements or modifiers.

Participles

A **participle** is a type of verbal that always functions as an adjective. The present participle always ends with *-ing*. Past participles end with *-d, -ed, -n,* or *-t*. Participles are combined with helping verbs to form certain verb tenses, but a participle by itself cannot function as a verb.

Examples: dance (verb) | dancing (present participle) | danced (past participle)

Participial phrases most often come right before or right after the noun or pronoun that they modify.

Examples:

Shipwrecked on an island (participial phrase), the boys started to fish for food.

Having been seated for five hours (participial phrase), we got out of the car to stretch our legs.

Praised for their work (participial phrase), the group accepted the first-place trophy.

Gerunds

A **gerund** is a type of verbal that always functions as a **noun**. Like present participles, gerunds always end with *-ing*, but they can be easily distinguished from participles by the part of speech they represent (participles always function as adjectives). Since a gerund or gerund phrase always functions as a noun, it can be used as the subject of a sentence, the predicate nominative, or the object of a verb or preposition.

Examples:

We want to be known for teaching (gerund) the poor (object of preposition: teaching the poor).

Coaching (gerund) this team (subject: Coaching this team) is the best job of my life.

We like practicing (gerund) our songs (object of verb: practicing our songs) in the basement.

Infinitives

An **infinitive** is a type of verbal that can function as a noun, an adjective, or an adverb. An infinitive is made of the word *to* and the basic form of the verb. As with all other types of verbal phrases, an infinitive phrase includes the verbal itself and all of its complements or modifiers.

Examples:

infinitive: To join; noun: To join the team

To join the team is my goal in life.

infinitive: to eat; adjective: to eat for the night

The animals have enough food to eat for the night.

infinitive: to exercise; adverb: to exercise their muscles

People lift weights to exercise their muscles.

Review Video: Verbals
Visit mometrix.com/academy and enter code: 915480

Appositive Phrases

An **appositive** is a word or phrase that is used to explain or rename nouns or pronouns. Noun phrases, gerund phrases, and infinitive phrases can all be used as appositives.

Examples:

appositive: hunters at heart

Terriers, hunters at heart, have been dressed up to look like lap dogs.

The noun phrase *hunters at heart* renames the noun *terriers.*

appositive: to save and invest his money

His plan, to save and invest his money, was proven as a safe approach.

The infinitive phrase explains what the plan is.

Appositive phrases can be **essential** or **nonessential**. An appositive phrase is essential if the person, place, or thing being described or renamed is too general for its meaning to be understood without the appositive.

Examples:

essential: George Washington and Thomas Jefferson

Two of America's Founding Fathers, George Washington and Thomas Jefferson, served as presidents.

nonessential: two Founding Fathers

George Washington and Thomas Jefferson, two Founding Fathers, served as presidents.

Absolute Phrases

An absolute phrase is a phrase that consists of **a noun followed by a participle**. An absolute phrase provides **context** to what is being described in the sentence, but it does not modify or explain any particular word; it is essentially independent.

Examples:

noun participle
The alarm ringing, he pushed the snooze button.
absolute phrase

noun participle
The music paused, she continued to dance through the crowd.
absolute phrase

PARALLELISM

When multiple items or ideas are presented in a sentence in series, such as in a list, the items or ideas must be stated in grammatically equivalent ways. For example, if two ideas are listed in parallel and the first is stated in gerund form, the second cannot be stated in infinitive form. (e.g., *I enjoy reading and to study.* [incorrect]) An infinitive and a gerund are not grammatically equivalent. Instead, you should write *I enjoy reading and studying* OR *I like to read and to study*. In lists of more than two, all items must be parallel.

Example:

> **Incorrect**: He stopped at the office, grocery store, and the pharmacy before heading home.
>
> The first and third items in the list of places include the article *the*, so the second item needs it as well.
>
> **Correct**: He stopped at the office, *the* grocery store, and the pharmacy before heading home.

Example:

> **Incorrect**: While vacationing in Europe, she went biking, skiing, and climbed mountains.
>
> The first and second items in the list are gerunds, so the third item must be as well.
>
> **Correct**: While vacationing in Europe, she went biking, skiing, and *mountain climbing*.

Review Video: Parallel Sentence Construction
Visit mometrix.com/academy and enter code: 831988

SENTENCE PURPOSE

There are four types of sentences: declarative, imperative, interrogative, and exclamatory.

A **declarative** sentence states a fact and ends with a period.

> *The football game starts at seven o'clock.*

An **imperative** sentence tells someone to do something and generally ends with a period. An urgent command might end with an exclamation point instead.

> *Don't forget to buy your ticket.*

An **interrogative** sentence asks a question and ends with a question mark.

> *Are you going to the game on Friday?*

An **exclamatory** sentence shows strong emotion and ends with an exclamation point.

I can't believe we won the game!

SENTENCE STRUCTURE

Sentences are classified by structure based on the type and number of clauses present. The four classifications of sentence structure are the following:

Simple: A simple sentence has one independent clause with no dependent clauses. A simple sentence may have **compound elements** (i.e., compound subject or verb).

Examples:

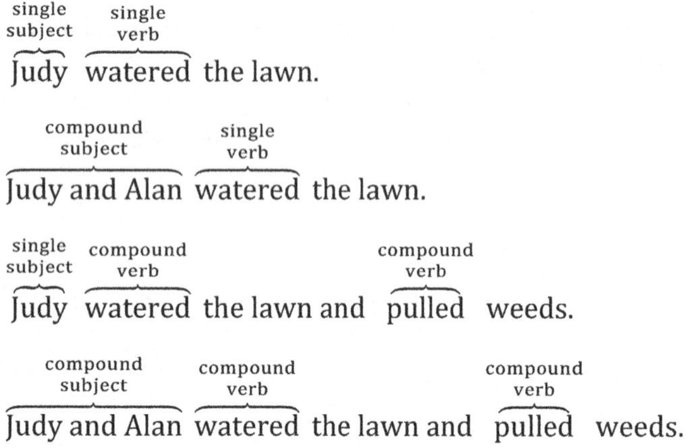

Compound: A compound sentence has two or more independent clauses with no dependent clauses. Usually, the independent clauses are joined with a comma and a coordinating conjunction or with a semicolon.

Examples:

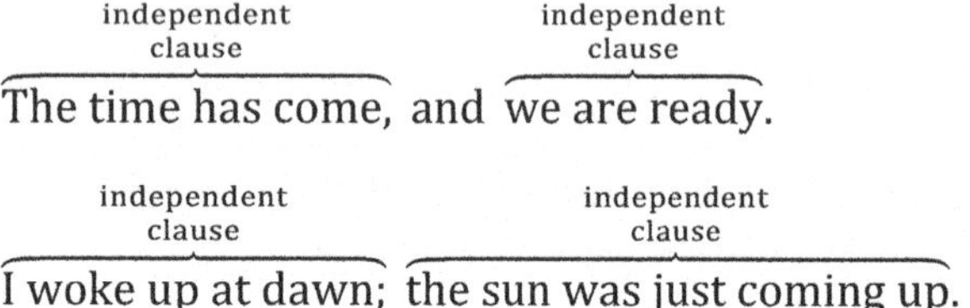

Complex: A complex sentence has one independent clause and at least one dependent clause.

Examples:

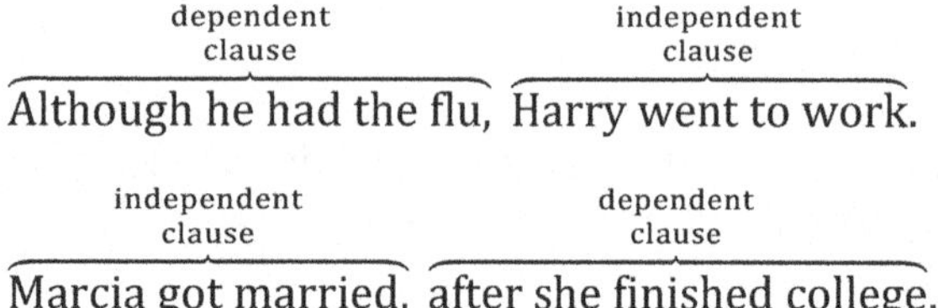

Compound-Complex: A compound-complex sentence has at least two independent clauses and at least one dependent clause.

Examples:

independent clause | dependent clause | independent clause

John is my friend who went to India, and he brought back souvenirs.

independent clause | independent clause | dependent clause

You may not realize this, but we heard the music that you played last night.

> **Review Video: Sentence Structure**
> Visit mometrix.com/academy and enter code: 700478

Sentence variety is important to consider when writing an essay or speech. A variety of sentence lengths and types creates rhythm, makes a passage more engaging, and gives writers an opportunity to demonstrate their writing style. Writing that uses the same length or type of sentence without variation can be boring or difficult to read. To evaluate a passage for effective sentence variety, it is helpful to note whether the passage contains diverse sentence structures and lengths. It is also important to pay attention to the way each sentence starts and avoid beginning with the same words or phrases.

Sentence Fragments

Recall that a group of words must contain at least one **independent clause** in order to be considered a sentence. If it doesn't contain even one independent clause, it is called a **sentence fragment**.

The appropriate process for **repairing** a sentence fragment depends on what type of fragment it is. If the fragment is a dependent clause, it can sometimes be as simple as removing a subordinating word (e.g., when, because, if) from the beginning of the fragment. Alternatively, a dependent clause can be incorporated into a closely related neighboring sentence. If the fragment is missing some required part, like a subject or a verb, the fix might be as simple as adding the missing part.

Examples:

Fragment: Because he wanted to sail the Mediterranean.

Removed subordinating word: He wanted to sail the Mediterranean.

Combined with another sentence: Because he wanted to sail the Mediterranean, he booked a Greek island cruise.

Run-on Sentences

Run-on sentences consist of multiple independent clauses that have not been joined together properly. Run-on sentences can be corrected in several different ways:

Join clauses properly: This can be done with a comma and coordinating conjunction, with a semicolon, or with a colon or dash if the second clause is explaining something in the first.

Example:

Incorrect: I went on the trip, we visited lots of castles.

Corrected: I went on the trip, and we visited lots of castles.

Split into separate sentences: This correction is most effective when the independent clauses are very long or when they are not closely related.

Example:

Incorrect: The drive to New York takes ten hours, my uncle lives in Boston.

Corrected: The drive to New York takes ten hours. My uncle lives in Boston.

Make one clause dependent: This is the easiest way to make the sentence correct and more interesting at the same time. It's often as simple as adding a subordinating word between the two clauses or before the first clause.

Example:

Incorrect: I finally made it to the store and I bought some eggs.

Corrected: When I finally made it to the store, I bought some eggs.

Reduce to one clause with a compound verb: If both clauses have the same subject, remove the subject from the second clause, and you now have just one clause with a compound verb.

Example:

Incorrect: The drive to New York takes ten hours, it makes me very tired.

Corrected: The drive to New York takes ten hours and makes me very tired.

Note: While these are the simplest ways to correct a run-on sentence, often the best way is to completely reorganize the thoughts in the sentence and rewrite it.

Review Video: Fragments and Run-on Sentences
Visit mometrix.com/academy and enter code: 541989

Dangling and Misplaced Modifiers

Dangling Modifiers

A dangling modifier is a dependent clause or verbal phrase that does not have a clear logical connection to a word in the sentence.

Example:

dangling modifier

Incorrect: Reading each magazine article, the stories caught my attention.

The word *stories* cannot be modified by *Reading each magazine article.* People can read, but stories cannot read. Therefore, the subject of the sentence must be a person.

gerund phrase

Corrected: Reading each magazine article, I was entertained by the stories.

Example:

dangling modifier

Incorrect: Ever since childhood, my grandparents have visited me for Christmas.

The speaker in this sentence can't have been visited by her grandparents when *they* were children, since she wouldn't have been born yet. Either the modifier should be clarified or the sentence should be rearranged to specify whose childhood is being referenced.

dependent clause

Clarified: Ever since I was a child, my grandparents have visited for Christmas.

adverb phrase

Rearranged: Ever since childhood, I have enjoyed my grandparents visiting for Christmas.

Misplaced Modifiers

Because modifiers are grammatically versatile, they can be put in many different places within the structure of a sentence. The danger of this versatility is that a modifier can accidentally be placed where it is modifying the wrong word or where it is not clear which word it is modifying.

Example:

modifier

Incorrect: She read the book to a crowd that was filled with beautiful pictures.

The book was filled with beautiful pictures, not the crowd.

modifier

Corrected: She read the book that was filled with beautiful pictures to a crowd.

Example:

modifier

Ambiguous: Derek saw a bus nearly hit a man on his way to work.

Was Derek on his way to work or was the other man?

modifier

Derek: On his way to work, Derek saw a bus nearly hit a man.

modifier

The other man: Derek saw a bus nearly hit a man who was on his way to work.

Split Infinitives

A split infinitive occurs when a modifying word comes between the word *to* and the verb that pairs with *to*.

Example: To *clearly* explain vs. *To explain* clearly | To *softly* sing vs. *To sing* softly

Though considered improper by some, split infinitives may provide better clarity and simplicity in some cases than the alternatives. As such, avoiding them should not be considered a universal rule.

Double Negatives

Standard English allows **two negatives** only when a **positive** meaning is intended. (e.g., The team was *not displeased* with their performance.) Double negatives to emphasize negation are not used in standard English.

Negative modifiers (e.g., never, no, and not) should not be paired with other negative modifiers or negative words (e.g., none, nobody, nothing, or neither). The modifiers *hardly, barely*, and *scarcely* are also considered negatives in standard English, so they should not be used with other negatives.

Punctuation

End Punctuation

Periods

Use a period to end all sentences except direct questions and exclamations. Periods are also used for abbreviations.

Examples: 3 p.m. | 2 a.m. | Mr. Jones | Mrs. Stevens | Dr. Smith | Bill, Jr. | Pennsylvania Ave.

Note: An abbreviation is a shortened form of a word or phrase.

Question Marks

Question marks should be used following a **direct question**. A polite request can be followed by a period instead of a question mark.

Direct Question: What is for lunch today? | How are you? | Why is that the answer?

Polite Requests: Can you please send me the item tomorrow. | Will you please walk with me on the track.

Review Video: Question Marks
Visit mometrix.com/academy and enter code: 118471

Exclamation Marks

Exclamation marks are used after a word group or sentence that shows much feeling or has special importance. Exclamation marks should not be overused. They are saved for proper **exclamatory interjections**.

Example: We're going to the finals! | You have a beautiful car! | "That's crazy!" she yelled.

Review Video: Exclamation Points
Visit mometrix.com/academy and enter code: 199367

Commas

The comma is a punctuation mark that can help you understand connections in a sentence. Not every sentence needs a comma. However, if a sentence needs a comma, you need to put it in the right place. A comma in the wrong place (or an absent comma) will make a sentence's meaning unclear.

These are some of the rules for commas:

Use Case	Example
Before a **coordinating conjunction** joining independent clauses	Bob caught three fish, and I caught two fish.
After an **introductory phrase**	After the final out, we went to a restaurant to celebrate.
After an **adverbial clause**	Studying the stars, I was awed by the beauty of the sky.
Between **items in a series**	I will bring the turkey, the pie, and the coffee.
For **interjections**	Wow, you know how to play this game.
After ***yes* and *no* responses**	No, I cannot come tomorrow.
Separate **nonessential modifiers**	John Frank, who coaches the team, was promoted today.
Separate **nonessential appositives**	Thomas Edison, an American inventor, was born in Ohio.
Separate **nouns of direct address**	You, John, are my only hope in this moment.
Separate **interrogative tags**	This is the last time, correct?
Separate **contrasts**	You are my friend, not my enemy.
Writing **dates**	July 4, 1776, is an important date to remember.
Writing **addresses**	He is meeting me at 456 Delaware Avenue, Washington, D.C., tomorrow morning.
Writing **geographical names**	Paris, France, is my favorite city.
Writing **titles**	John Smith, PhD, will be visiting your class today.
Separate **expressions like *he said***	"You can start," she said, "with an apology."

A comma is also used **between coordinate adjectives** not joined with *and*. However, not all adjectives are coordinate (i.e., equal or parallel). To determine if your adjectives are coordinate, try connecting them with *and* or reversing their order. If it still sounds right, they are coordinate.

Incorrect: The kind, brown dog followed me home.

Correct: The kind, loyal dog followed me home.

Review Video: When to Use a Comma
Visit mometrix.com/academy and enter code: 786797

Semicolons

The semicolon is used to join closely related independent clauses without the need for a coordinating conjunction. Semicolons are also used in place of commas to separate list elements that have internal commas. Some rules for semicolons include:

Use Case	Example
Between closely connected independent clauses **not connected with a coordinating conjunction**	You are right; we should go with your plan.
Between independent clauses **linked with a transitional word**	I think that we can agree on this; however, I am not sure about my friends.
Between items in a **series that has internal punctuation**	I have visited New York, New York; Augusta, Maine; and Baltimore, Maryland.

Review Video: How to Use Semicolons
Visit mometrix.com/academy and enter code: 370605

Colons

The colon is used to call attention to the words that follow it. When used in a sentence, a colon should only come at the **end** of a **complete sentence**. The rules for colons are as follows:

Use Case	Example
After an independent clause to **make a list**	I want to learn many languages: Spanish, German, and Italian.
For **explanations**	There is one thing that stands out on your resume: responsibility.
To give a **quote**	He started with an idea: "We are able to do more than we imagine."
After the **greeting in a formal letter**	To Whom It May Concern:
Show **hours and minutes**	It is 3:14 p.m.
Separate a **title and subtitle**	The essay is titled "America: A Short Introduction to a Modern Country."

Review Video: Using Colons
Visit mometrix.com/academy and enter code: 868673

Parentheses

Parentheses are used for additional information. Also, they can be used to put labels for letters or numbers in a series. Parentheses should be not be used very often. If they are overused, parentheses can be a distraction instead of a help.

Examples:

Extra Information: The rattlesnake (see Image 2) is a dangerous snake of North and South America.

Series: Include in the email (1) your name, (2) your address, and (3) your question for the author.

Review Video: Parentheses
Visit mometrix.com/academy and enter code: 947743

Quotation Marks

Use quotation marks to close off **direct quotations** of a person's spoken or written words. Do not use quotation marks around indirect quotations. An indirect quotation gives someone's message without using the person's exact words. Use **single quotation marks** to close off a quotation inside a quotation.

Direct Quote: Nancy said, "I am waiting for Henry to arrive."

Indirect Quote: Henry said that he is going to be late to the meeting.

Quote inside a Quote: The teacher asked, "Has everyone read 'The Gift of the Magi'?"

Quotation marks should be used around the titles of **short works**: newspaper and magazine articles, poems, short stories, songs, television episodes, radio programs, and subdivisions of books or websites.

Examples:

"Rip Van Winkle" (short story by Washington Irving)

"O Captain! My Captain!" (poem by Walt Whitman)

Although it is not standard usage, quotation marks are sometimes used to highlight **irony** or the use of words to mean something other than their dictionary definition. This type of usage should be employed sparingly, if at all.

Examples:

The boss warned Frank that he was walking on "thin ice."	Frank is not walking on real ice. Instead, he is being warned to avoid mistakes.
The teacher thanked the young man for his "honesty."	The quotation marks around *honesty* show that the teacher does not believe the young man's explanation.

Review Video: Quotation Marks
Visit mometrix.com/academy and enter code: 884918

Periods and commas are put **inside** quotation marks. Colons and semicolons are put **outside** the quotation marks. Question marks and exclamation points are placed inside quotation marks when they are part of a quote. When the question or exclamation mark goes with the whole sentence, the mark is left outside of the quotation marks.

Examples:

Period and comma	We read "The Gift of the Magi," "The Skylight Room," and "The Cactus."
Semicolon	They watched "The Nutcracker"; then, they went home.
Exclamation mark that is a part of a quote	The crowd cheered, "Victory!"
Question mark that goes with the whole sentence	Is your favorite short story "The Tell-Tale Heart"?

Apostrophes

An apostrophe is used to show **possession** or the **deletion of letters in contractions**. An apostrophe is not needed with the possessive pronouns *his, hers, its, ours, theirs, whose*, and *yours*.

Singular Nouns: David's car | a book's theme | my brother's board game

Plural Nouns that end with -*s*: the scissors' handle | boys' basketball

Plural Nouns that end without -*s*: Men's department | the people's adventure

Review Video: When to Use an Apostrophe
Visit mometrix.com/academy and enter code: 213068

Review Video: Punctuation Errors in Possessive Pronouns
Visit mometrix.com/academy and enter code: 221438

Hyphens

Hyphens are used to **separate compound words**. Use hyphens in the following cases:

Use Case	Example
Compound numbers from 21 to 99 when written out in words	This team needs twenty-five points to win the game.
Written-out fractions that are used as adjectives	The recipe says that we need a three-fourths cup of butter.
Compound adjectives that come before a noun	The well-fed dog took a nap.
Unusual compound words that would be hard to read or easily confused with other words	This is the best anti-itch cream on the market.

Note: This is not a complete set of the rules for hyphens. A dictionary is the best tool for knowing if a compound word needs a hyphen.

Review Video: Hyphens
Visit mometrix.com/academy and enter code: 981632

Dashes

Dashes are used to show a **break** or a **change in thought** in a sentence or to act as parentheses in a sentence. When typing, use two hyphens to make a dash. Do not put a space before or after the dash. The following are the functions of dashes:

Use Case	Example
Set off parenthetical statements or an **appositive with internal punctuation**	The three trees—oak, pine, and magnolia—are coming on a truck tomorrow.
Show a **break or change in tone or thought**	The first question—how silly of me—does not have a correct answer.

Ellipsis Marks

The ellipsis mark has **three** periods (...) to show when **words have been removed** from a quotation. If a **full sentence or more** is removed from a quoted passage, you need to use **four** periods to show the removed text and the end punctuation mark. The ellipsis mark should not be used at the beginning of a quotation. The ellipsis mark should also not be used at the end of a quotation unless some words have been deleted from the end of the final quoted sentence.

Example:

> "Then he picked up the groceries...paid for them...later he went home."

Brackets

There are two main reasons to use brackets:

Use Case	Example
Placing **parentheses inside of parentheses**	The hero of this story, Paul Revere (a silversmith and industrialist [see Ch. 4]), rode through towns of Massachusetts to warn of advancing British troops.
Adding **clarification or detail to a quotation** that is not part of the quotation	The father explained, "My children are planning to attend my alma mater [State University]."

Review Video: Brackets
Visit mometrix.com/academy and enter code: 727546

Common Usage Mistakes

Word Confusion

Which, That, and Who

The words *which, that,* and *who* can act as **relative pronouns** to help clarify or describe a noun.

Which is used for things only.

Example: Andrew's car, *which is old and rusty,* broke down last week.

That is used for people or things. *That* is usually informal when used to describe people.

Example: Is this the only book *that Louis L'Amour wrote?*

Example: Is Louis L'Amour the author *that wrote Western novels?*

Who is used for people or for animals that have an identity or personality.

Example: Mozart was the composer *who wrote those operas.*

Example: John's dog, *who is called Max,* is large and fierce.

Homophones

Homophones are words that sound alike (or similar) but have different **spellings** and **definitions**. A homophone is a type of **homonym**, which is a pair or group of words that are pronounced or spelled the same, but do not mean the same thing.

To, Too, and Two

To can be an adverb or a preposition for showing direction, purpose, and relationship. See your dictionary for the many other ways to use *to* in a sentence.

Examples: I went to the store. | I want to go with you.

Too is an adverb that means *also, as well, very,* or *in excess.*

Examples: I can walk a mile too. | You have eaten too much.

Two is a number.

Example: You have two minutes left.

There, Their, and They're

There can be an adjective, adverb, or pronoun. Often, *there* is used to show a place or to start a sentence.

Examples: I went there yesterday. | There is something in his pocket.

Their is a pronoun that is used to show ownership.

Examples: He is their father. | This is their fourth apology this week.

They're is a contraction of *they are.*

Example: Did you know that they're in town?

Knew and New

Knew is the past tense of *know.*

Example: I knew the answer.

New is an adjective that means something is current, has not been used, or is modern.

Example: This is my new phone.

Then and Than

Then is an adverb that indicates sequence or order:

Example: I'm going to run to the library and then come home.

Than is special-purpose word used only for comparisons:

Example: Susie likes chips more than candy.

Its and It's

Its is a pronoun that shows ownership.

Example: The guitar is in its case.

It's is a contraction of *it is.*

Example: It's an honor and a privilege to meet you.

Note: The *h* in honor is silent, so *honor* starts with the vowel sound *o*, which must have the article *an*.

Your and You're

Your is a pronoun that shows ownership.

Example: This is your moment to shine.

You're is a contraction of *you are.*

Example: Yes, you're correct.

Saw and Seen

Saw is the past-tense form of *see.*

Example: I saw a turtle on my walk this morning.

Seen is the past participle of *see.*

Example: I have seen this movie before.

Affect and Effect

There are two main reasons that *affect* and *effect* are so often confused: 1) both words can be used as either a noun or a verb, and 2) unlike most homophones, their usage and meanings are closely related to each other. Here is a quick rundown of the four usage options:

Affect (n): feeling, emotion, or mood that is displayed

Example: The patient had a flat *affect*. (i.e., his face showed little or no emotion)

Affect (v): to alter, to change, to influence

Example: The sunshine *affects* the plant's growth.

Effect (n): a result, a consequence

Example: What *effect* will this weather have on our schedule?

Effect (v): to bring about, to cause to be

Example: These new rules will *effect* order in the office.

The noun form of *affect* is rarely used outside of technical medical descriptions, so if a noun form is needed on the test, you can safely select *effect*. The verb form of *effect* is not as rare as the noun form of *affect*, but it's still not all that likely to show up on your test. If you need a verb and you can't decide which to use based on the definitions, choosing *affect* is your best bet.

Homographs

Homographs are words that share the same spelling, but have different meanings and sometimes different pronunciations. To figure out which meaning is being used, you should be looking for context clues. The context clues give hints to the meaning of the word. For example, the word *spot* has many meanings. It can mean "a place" or "a stain or blot." In the sentence "After my lunch, I saw a spot on my shirt," the word *spot* means "a stain or blot." The context clues of "After my lunch" and "on my shirt" guide you to this decision. A homograph is another type of homonym.

Bank

(noun): an establishment where money is held for savings or lending

(verb): to collect or pile up

Content

(noun): the topics that will be addressed within a book

(adjective): pleased or satisfied

(verb): to make someone pleased or satisfied

Fine

(noun): an amount of money that acts a penalty for an offense

(adjective): very small or thin

(adverb): in an acceptable way

(verb): to make someone pay money as a punishment

Incense

(noun): a material that is burned in religious settings and makes a pleasant aroma

(verb): to frustrate or anger

Lead

(noun): the first or highest position

(noun): a heavy metallic element

(verb): to direct a person or group of followers

(adjective): containing lead

Object

(noun): a lifeless item that can be held and observed

(verb): to disagree

Produce

(noun): fruits and vegetables

(verb): to make or create something

Refuse

(noun): garbage or debris that has been thrown away

(verb): to not allow

Subject

(noun): an area of study

(verb): to force or subdue

Tear

(noun): a fluid secreted by the eyes

(verb): to separate or pull apart

Commonly Misused Words and Phrases

A Lot

The phrase *a lot* should always be written as two words; never as *alot.*

Correct: That's a lot of chocolate!

Incorrect: He does that alot.

Can

The word *can* is used to describe things that are possible occurrences; the word *may* is used to described things that are allowed to happen.

Correct: May I have another piece of pie?

Correct: I can lift three of these bags of mulch at a time.

Incorrect: Mom said we can stay up thirty minutes later tonight.

Could Have

The phrase *could of* is often incorrectly substituted for the phrase *could have*. Similarly, *could of, may of*, and *might of* are sometimes used in place of the correct phrases *could have, may have*, and *might have*.

Correct: If I had known, I would have helped out.

Incorrect: Well, that could of gone much worse than it did.

Myself

The word *myself* is a reflexive pronoun, often incorrectly used in place of *I* or *me*.

Correct: He let me do it myself.

Incorrect: The job was given to Dave and myself.

Off

The phrase *off of* is a redundant expression that should be avoided. In most cases, it can be corrected simply by removing *of*.

Correct: My dog chased the squirrel off its perch on the fence.

Incorrect: He finally moved his plate off of the table.

Supposed To

The phrase *suppose to* is sometimes used incorrectly in place of the phrase *supposed to*.

Correct: I was supposed to go to the store this afternoon.

Incorrect: When are we suppose to get our grades?

Try To

The phrase *try and* is often used in informal writing and conversation to replace the correct phrase *try to*.

Correct: It's a good policy to try to satisfy every customer who walks in the door.

Incorrect: Don't try and do too much.

Outlining and Organizing Ideas

Essays

Essays usually focus on one topic, subject, or goal. There are several types of essays, including informative, persuasive, and narrative. An essay's structure and level of formality depend on the type of essay and its goal. While narrative essays typically do not include outside sources, other types of essays often require some research and the integration of primary and secondary sources.

The basic format of an essay typically has three major parts: the introduction, the body, and the conclusion. The body is further divided into the writer's main points. Short and simple essays may have three main points, while essays covering broader ranges and going into more depth can have almost any number of main points, depending on length.

An essay's introduction should answer three questions:

1. What is the **subject** of the essay?

   If a student writes an essay about a book, the answer would include the title and author of the book and any additional information needed—such as the subject or argument of the book.

2. How does the essay **address** the subject?

   To answer this, the writer identifies the essay's organization by briefly summarizing main points and the evidence supporting them.

3. What will the essay **prove**?

   This is the thesis statement, usually the opening paragraph's last sentence, clearly stating the writer's message.

The body elaborates on all the main points related to the thesis, introducing one main point at a time, and includes supporting evidence with each main point. Each body paragraph should state the point in a topic sentence, which is usually the first sentence in the paragraph. The paragraph should then explain the point's meaning, support it with quotations or other evidence, and then explain how this point and the evidence are related to the thesis. The writer should then repeat this procedure in a new paragraph for each additional main point.

The conclusion reiterates the content of the introduction, including the thesis, to remind the reader of the essay's main argument or subject. The essay writer may also summarize the highlights of the argument or description contained in the body of the essay, following the same sequence originally used in the body. For example, a conclusion might look like: Point 1 + Point 2 + Point 3 = Thesis, or Point 1 → Point 2 → Point 3 → Thesis Proof. Good organization makes essays easier for writers to compose and provides a guide for readers to follow. Well-organized essays hold attention better and are more likely to get readers to accept their theses as valid.

Main Ideas, Supporting Details, and Outlining a Topic

A writer often begins the first paragraph of a paper by stating the **main idea** or point, also known as the **topic sentence**. The rest of the paragraph supplies particular details that develop and support the main point. One way to visualize the relationship between the main point and supporting information is by considering a table: the tabletop is the main point, and each of the table's legs is a supporting detail or group of details. Both professional authors and students can benefit from planning their writing by first making an outline of the topic. Outlines facilitate quick identification of the main point and supporting details without having to wade through the additional language that will exist in the fully developed essay, article, or paper. Outlining can also help readers to analyze a piece of existing writing for the same reason. The outline first summarizes the main idea in one sentence. Then, below that, it summarizes the supporting details in a numbered list. Writing the paper then consists of filling in the outline with detail, writing a paragraph for each supporting point, and adding an introduction and conclusion.

Introduction

The purpose of the introduction is to capture the reader's attention and announce the essay's main idea. Normally, the introduction contains 50-80 words, or 3-5 sentences. An introduction can begin with an interesting quote, a question, or a strong opinion—something that will **engage** the reader's interest and prompt them to keep reading. If you are writing your essay to a specific prompt, your introduction should include a **restatement or summarization** of the prompt so that the reader will have some context for your essay. Finally, your introduction should briefly state your **thesis or main idea**: the primary thing you hope to communicate to the reader through your essay. Don't try to include all of the details and nuances of your thesis, or all of your reasons for it, in the introduction. That's what the rest of the essay is for!

Review Video: Introduction
Visit mometrix.com/academy and enter code: 961328

Thesis Statement

The thesis is the main idea of the essay. A temporary thesis, or working thesis, should be established early in the writing process because it will serve to keep the writer focused as ideas develop. This temporary thesis is subject to change as you continue to write.

The temporary thesis has two parts: a **topic** (i.e., the focus of your essay based on the prompt) and a **comment**. The comment makes an important point about the topic. A temporary thesis should be interesting and specific. Also, you need to limit the topic to a manageable scope. These three questions are useful tools to measure the effectiveness of any temporary thesis:

- Does the focus of my essay have enough interest to hold an audience?
- Is the focus of my essay specific enough to generate interest?
- Is the focus of my essay manageable for the time limit? Too broad? Too narrow?

The thesis should be a generalization rather than a fact because the thesis prepares readers for facts and details that support the thesis. The process of bringing the thesis into sharp focus may help in outlining major sections of the work. Once the thesis and introduction are complete, you can address the body of the work.

Review Video: Thesis Statements
Visit mometrix.com/academy and enter code: 691033

Supporting the Thesis

Throughout your essay, the thesis should be **explained clearly and supported** adequately by additional arguments. The thesis sentence needs to contain a clear statement of the purpose of your essay and a comment about the thesis. With the thesis statement, you have an opportunity to state what is noteworthy of this particular treatment of the prompt. Each sentence and paragraph should build on and support the thesis.

When you respond to the prompt, use parts of the passage to support your argument or defend your position. Using supporting evidence from the passage strengths your argument because readers can see your attention to the entire passage and your response to the details and facts within the passage. You can use facts, details, statistics, and direct quotations from the passage to uphold your position. Be sure to point out which information comes from the original passage and base your argument around that evidence.

Body

In an essay's introduction, the writer establishes the thesis and may indicate how the rest of the piece will be structured. In the body of the piece, the writer **elaborates** upon, **illustrates**, and **explains** the **thesis statement**. How writers arrange supporting details and their choices of paragraph types are development techniques. Writers may give examples of the concept introduced in the thesis statement. If the subject includes a cause-and-effect relationship, the author may explain its causality. A writer will explain or analyze the main idea of the piece throughout the body, often by presenting arguments for the veracity or credibility of the thesis statement. Writers may use development to define or clarify ambiguous terms. Paragraphs within the body may be organized using natural sequences, like space and time. Writers may employ **inductive reasoning**, using multiple details to establish a generalization or causal relationship, or **deductive reasoning**, proving a generalized hypothesis or proposition through a specific example or case.

Review Video: Drafting Body Paragraphs
Visit mometrix.com/academy and enter code: 724590

Paragraphs

After the introduction of a passage, a series of body paragraphs will carry a message through to the conclusion. Each paragraph should be **unified around a main point**. Normally, a good topic sentence summarizes the paragraph's main point. A topic sentence is a general sentence that gives an introduction to the paragraph.

The sentences that follow support the topic sentence. However, though it is usually the first sentence, the topic sentence can come as the final sentence to the paragraph if the earlier sentences give a clear explanation of the paragraph's topic. This allows the topic sentence to function as a concluding sentence. Overall, the paragraphs need to stay true to the main point. This means that any unnecessary sentences that do not advance the main point should be removed.

The main point of a paragraph requires adequate development (i.e., a substantial paragraph that covers the main point). A paragraph of two or three sentences does not cover a main point. This is especially true when the main point of the paragraph gives strong support to the argument of the thesis. An occasional short paragraph is fine as a transitional device. However, a well-developed argument will have paragraphs with more than a few sentences.

Methods of Developing Paragraphs

Common methods of adding substance to paragraphs include examples, illustrations, analogies, and cause and effect.

- **Examples** are supporting details to the main idea of a paragraph or a passage. When authors write about something that their audience may not understand, they can provide an example to show their point. When authors write about something that is not easily accepted, they can give examples to prove their point.
- **Illustrations** are extended examples that require several sentences. Well-selected illustrations can be a great way for authors to develop a point that may not be familiar to their audience.
- **Analogies** make comparisons between items that appear to have nothing in common. Analogies are employed by writers to provoke fresh thoughts about a subject. These comparisons may be used to explain the unfamiliar, to clarify an abstract point, or to argue a point. Although analogies are effective literary devices, they should be used carefully in arguments. Two things may be alike in some respects but completely different in others.
- **Cause and effect** is an excellent device to explain the connection between an action or situation and a particular result. One way that authors can use cause and effect is to state the effect in the topic sentence of a paragraph and add the causes in the body of the paragraph. This method can give an author's paragraphs structure, which always strengthens writing.

Types of Paragraphs

A **paragraph of narration** tells a story or a part of a story. Normally, the sentences are arranged in chronological order (i.e., the order that the events happened). However, flashbacks (i.e., an anecdote from an earlier time) can be included.

A **descriptive paragraph** makes a verbal portrait of a person, place, or thing. When specific details are used that appeal to one or more of the senses (i.e., sight, sound, smell, taste, and touch), authors give readers a sense of being present in the moment.

A **process paragraph** is related to time order (i.e., First, you open the bottle. Second, you pour the liquid, etc.). Usually, this describes a process or teaches readers how to perform a process.

Comparing two things draws attention to their similarities and indicates a number of differences. When authors contrast, they focus only on differences. Both comparing and contrasting may be done point-by-point, noting both the similarities and differences of each point, or in sequential paragraphs, where you discuss all the similarities and then all the differences, or vice versa.

Breaking Text into Paragraphs

For most forms of writing, you will need to use multiple paragraphs. As such, determining when to start a new paragraph is very important. Reasons for starting a new paragraph include:

- To mark off the introduction and concluding paragraphs
- To signal a shift to a new idea or topic
- To indicate an important shift in time or place
- To explain a point in additional detail
- To highlight a comparison, contrast, or cause and effect relationship

Paragraph Length

Most readers find that their comfort level for a paragraph is between 100 and 200 words. Shorter paragraphs cause too much starting and stopping and give a choppy effect. Paragraphs that are too long often test the attention span of readers. Two notable exceptions to this rule exist. In scientific or scholarly papers, longer paragraphs suggest seriousness and depth. In journalistic writing, constraints are placed on paragraph size by the narrow columns in a newspaper format.

The first and last paragraphs of a text will usually be the introduction and conclusion. These special-purpose paragraphs are likely to be shorter than paragraphs in the body of the work. Paragraphs in the body of the essay follow the subject's outline (e.g., one paragraph per point in short essays and a group of paragraphs per point in longer works). Some ideas require more development than others, so it is good for a writer to remain flexible. A paragraph of excessive length may be divided, and shorter ones may be combined.

Conclusion

Two important principles to consider when writing a conclusion are strength and closure. A strong conclusion gives the reader a sense that the author's main points are meaningful and important, and that the supporting facts and arguments are convincing, solid, and well developed. When a conclusion achieves closure, it gives the impression that the writer has stated all necessary information and points and completed the work, rather than simply stopping after a specified length. Some things to avoid when writing concluding paragraphs include:

- Introducing a completely new idea
- Beginning with obvious or unoriginal phrases like "In conclusion" or "To summarize"

- Apologizing for one's opinions or writing
- Repeating the thesis word for word rather than rephrasing it
- Believing that the conclusion must always summarize the piece

Review Video: Drafting Conclusions
Visit mometrix.com/academy and enter code: 209408

Coherence in Writing

Coherent Paragraphs

A smooth flow of sentences and paragraphs without gaps, shifts, or bumps will lead to paragraph **coherence**. Ties between old and new information can be smoothed using several methods:

- **Linking ideas clearly**, from the topic sentence to the body of the paragraph, is essential for a smooth transition. The topic sentence states the main point, and this should be followed by specific details, examples, and illustrations that support the topic sentence. The support may be direct or indirect. In **indirect support**, the illustrations and examples may support a sentence that in turn supports the topic directly.
- The **repetition of key words** adds coherence to a paragraph. To avoid dull language, variations of the key words may be used.
- **Parallel structures** are often used within sentences to emphasize the similarity of ideas and connect sentences giving similar information.
- Maintaining a **consistent verb tense** throughout the paragraph helps. Shifting tenses affects the smooth flow of words and can disrupt the coherence of the paragraph.

Review Video: How to Write a Good Paragraph
Visit mometrix.com/academy and enter code: 682127

Sequence Words and Phrases

When a paragraph opens with the topic sentence, the second sentence may begin with a phrase like *first of all*, introducing the first supporting detail or example. The writer may introduce the second supporting item with words or phrases like *also*, *in addition*, and *besides*. The writer might introduce succeeding pieces of support with wording like, *another thing*, *moreover*, *furthermore*, or *not only that, but*. The writer may introduce the last piece of support with *lastly*, *finally*, or *last but not least*. Writers get off the point by presenting off-target items not supporting the main point. For example, a main point *my dog is not smart* is supported by the statement, *he's six years old and still doesn't answer to his name*. But *he cries when I leave for school* is not supportive, as it does not indicate lack of intelligence. Writers stay on point by presenting only supportive statements that are directly relevant to and illustrative of their main point.

Review Video: Sequence
Visit mometrix.com/academy and enter code: 489027

Transitions

Transitions between sentences and paragraphs guide readers from idea to idea and indicate relationships between sentences and paragraphs. Writers should be judicious in their use of transitions, inserting them sparingly. They should also be selected to fit the author's purpose—transitions can indicate time, comparison, and conclusion, among other purposes. Tone is also important to consider when using transitional phrases, varying the tone for different audiences. For example, in a scholarly essay, *in summary* would be preferable to the more informal *in short*.

When working with transitional words and phrases, writers usually find a natural flow that indicates when a transition is needed. In reading a draft of the text, it should become apparent where the flow is disrupted. At this point, the writer can add transitional elements during the revision process. Revising can also afford an opportunity to delete transitional devices that seem heavy handed or unnecessary.

Review Video: Transitions in Writing
Visit mometrix.com/academy and enter code: 233246

TYPES OF TRANSITIONAL WORDS

Time	afterward, immediately, earlier, meanwhile, recently, lately, now, since, soon, when, then, until, before, etc.
Sequence	too, first, second, further, moreover, also, again, and, next, still, besides, finally
Comparison	similarly, in the same way, likewise, also, again, once more
Contrasting	but, although, despite, however, instead, nevertheless, on the one hand... on the other hand, regardless, yet, in contrast
Cause and Effect	because, consequently, thus, therefore, then, to this end, since, so, as a result, if... then, accordingly
Examples	for example, for instance, such as, to illustrate, indeed, in fact, specifically
Place	near, far, here, there, to the left/right, next to, above, below, beyond, opposite, beside
Concession	granted that, naturally, of course, it may appear, although it is true that
Repetition, Summary, or Conclusion	as mentioned earlier, as noted, in other words, in short, on the whole, to summarize, therefore, as a result, to conclude, in conclusion
Addition	and, also, furthermore, moreover
Generalization	in broad terms, broadly speaking, in general

Review Video: Transition Words
Visit mometrix.com/academy and enter code: 707563

Review Video: How to Effectively Connect Sentences
Visit mometrix.com/academy and enter code: 948325

Chapter Quiz

Ready to see how well you retained what you just read? Scan the QR code to go directly to the chapter quiz interface for this study guide. If you're using a computer, simply visit the bonus page at **mometrix.com/bonus948/claslearntest** and click the Chapter Quizzes link.

Essay

Transform passive reading into active learning! After immersing yourself in this chapter, put your comprehension to the test by taking a quiz. The insights you gained will stay with you longer this way. Scan the QR code to go directly to the chapter quiz interface for this study guide. If you're using a computer, simply visit the bonus page at **mometrix.com/bonus948/claslearntest** and click the Chapter Quizzes link.

Optional Essay Overview

The Classic Learning Test has an optional essay section. The essay is ungraded, but it does serve an important purpose. When an essay is written at home, there is ample opportunity to have a friend or family member help with the writing. Since there is so much room for outside resources and assistance, college boards cannot reasonably expect that this kind of essay accurately represents the applicant's skills and knowledge.

For this reason, the Classic Learning Test includes an essay portion, which allows a college or university to see an unedited sample of a student's work and to give it a fair evaluation. Students who choose to participate in the essay portion have an opportunity to show their skills in a protected environment, where time is limited and outside resources are not allowed. This is one of the few opportunities that students have to show how they truly stand out from the crowd.

In your practice test, we include a sample essay topic for you to practice on your own. We have also created a rubric that we believe will help you identify the areas that a college admissions officer will be looking for. Practice and refine your skills before test day and you can be confident that your essay will help your applications stand out.

The Writing Process

Brainstorming

Brainstorming is a technique that is used to find a creative approach to a subject. This can be accomplished by simple **free-association** with a topic. For example, with paper and pen, write every thought that you have about the topic in a word or phrase. This is done without critical thinking. You should put everything that comes to your mind about the topic on your scratch paper. Then, you need to read the list over a few times. Next, look for patterns, repetitions, and clusters of ideas. This allows a variety of fresh ideas to come as you think about the topic.

Free Writing

Free writing is a more structured form of brainstorming. The method involves taking a limited amount of time (e.g., 2 to 3 minutes) to write everything that comes to mind about the topic in complete sentences. When time expires, review everything that has been written down. Many of your sentences may make little or no sense, but the insights and observations that can come from free writing make this method a valuable approach. Usually, free writing results in a fuller expression of ideas than brainstorming because thoughts and associations are written in complete sentences. However, both techniques can be used to complement each other.

Planning

Planning is the process of organizing a piece of writing before composing a draft. Planning can include creating an outline or a graphic organizer, such as a Venn diagram, a spider-map, or a flowchart. These methods should help the writer identify their topic, main ideas, and the general organization of the composition. Preliminary research can also take place during this stage. Planning helps writers organize all of their ideas and decide if they have enough material to begin their first draft. However, writers should remember that the decisions they make during this step will likely change later in the process, so their plan does not have to be perfect.

Drafting

Writers may then use their plan, outline, or graphic organizer to compose their first draft. They may write subsequent drafts to improve their writing. Writing multiple drafts can help writers consider different ways to communicate their ideas and address errors that may be difficult to correct without rewriting a section or the whole composition. Most writers will vary in how many drafts they choose to write, as there is no "right" number of drafts. Writing drafts also takes away the pressure to write perfectly on the first try, as writers can improve with each draft they write.

Revising, Editing, and Proofreading

Once a writer completes a draft, they can move on to the revising, editing, and proofreading steps to improve their draft. These steps begin with making broad changes that may apply to large sections of a composition and then making small, specific corrections. **Revising** is the first and broadest of these steps. Revising involves ensuring that the composition addresses an appropriate audience, includes all necessary material, maintains focus throughout, and is organized logically. Revising may occur after the first draft to ensure that the following drafts improve upon errors from the first draft. Some revision should occur between each draft to avoid repeating these errors. The **editing** phase of writing is narrower than the revising phase. Editing a composition should include steps such as improving transitions between paragraphs, ensuring each paragraph is on topic, and improving the flow of the text. The editing phase may also include correcting grammatical errors that cannot be fixed without significantly altering the text. **Proofreading** involves fixing misspelled words, typos, other grammatical errors, and any remaining surface-level flaws in the composition.

Recursive Writing Process

However you approach writing, you may find comfort in knowing that the revision process can occur in any order. The **recursive writing process** is not as difficult as the phrase may make it seem. Simply put, the recursive writing process means that you may need to revisit steps after completing other steps. It also implies that the steps are not required to take place in any certain order. Indeed, you may find that planning, drafting, and revising can all take place at about the same time. The writing process involves moving back and forth between planning, drafting, and revising, followed by more planning, more drafting, and more revising until the writing is satisfactory.

Review Video: Recursive Writing Process
Visit mometrix.com/academy and enter code: 951611

Writing Style and Form

Writing Style and Linguistic Form

Linguistic form encodes the literal meanings of words and sentences. It comes from the phonological, morphological, syntactic, and semantic parts of a language. **Writing style** consists of different ways of encoding the meaning and indicating figurative and stylistic meanings. An author's writing style can also be referred to as his or her **voice**.

Writers' stylistic choices accomplish three basic effects on their audiences:

- They **communicate meanings** beyond linguistically dictated meanings,
- They communicate the **author's attitude**, such as persuasive or argumentative effects accomplished through style, and
- They communicate or **express feelings**.

Within style, component areas include:

- Narrative structure
- Viewpoint
- Focus
- Sound patterns
- Meter and rhythm
- Lexical and syntactic repetition and parallelism
- Writing genre
- Representational, realistic, and mimetic effects
- Representation of thought and speech
- Meta-representation (representing representation)
- Irony
- Metaphor and other indirect meanings
- Representation and use of historical and dialectal variations
- Gender-specific and other group-specific speech styles, both real and fictitious
- Analysis of the processes for inferring meaning from writing

TONE

Tone may be defined as the writer's **attitude** toward the topic, and to the audience. This attitude is reflected in the language used in the writing. The tone of a work should be **appropriate to the topic** and to the intended audience. While it may be fine to use slang or jargon in some pieces, other texts should not contain such terms. Tone can range from humorous to serious and any level in between. It may be more or less formal, depending on the purpose of the writing and its intended audience. All these nuances in tone can flavor the entire writing and should be kept in mind as the work evolves.

WORD SELECTION

A writer's choice of words is a signature of their style. Careful thought about the use of words can improve a piece of writing. A passage can be an exciting piece to read when attention is given to the use of vivid or specific nouns rather than general ones.

Example:

General: His kindness will never be forgotten.

Specific: His thoughtful gifts and bear hugs will never be forgotten.

ACTIVE AND PASSIVE LANGUAGE

Attention should also be given to the kind of verbs that are used in sentences. Active verbs (e.g., run, swim) are about an action. Whenever possible, an **active verb should replace a linking verb** to provide clear examples for arguments and to strengthen a passage overall. When using an active verb, one should be sure that the verb is used in the active voice instead of the passive voice. Verbs are in the active voice when the subject is the one doing the action. A verb is in the passive voice when the subject is the recipient of an action.

Example:

> Passive: The winners were called to the stage by the judges.
>
> Active: The judges called the winners to the stage.

CONCISENESS

Conciseness is writing that communicates a message in the fewest words possible. Writing concisely is valuable because short, uncluttered messages allow the reader to understand the author's message more easily and efficiently. Planning is important in writing concise messages. If you have in mind what you need to write beforehand, it will be easier to make a message short and to the point. Do not state the obvious.

Revising is also important. After the message is written, make sure you have effective, pithy sentences that efficiently get your point across. When reviewing the information, imagine a conversation taking place, and concise writing will likely result.

APPROPRIATE KINDS OF WRITING FOR DIFFERENT TASKS, PURPOSES, AND AUDIENCES

When preparing to write a composition, consider the audience and purpose to choose the best type of writing. Four common types of writing are persuasive, expository, and narrative. **Persuasive**, or argumentative writing, is used to convince the audience to take action or agree with the author's claims. **Expository** writing is meant to inform the audience of the author's observations or research on a topic. **Narrative** writing is used to tell the audience a story and often allows more room for creativity. **Descriptive** writing is when a writer provides a substantial amount of detail to the reader so he or she can visualize the topic. While task, purpose, and audience inform a writer's mode of writing, these factors also impact elements such as tone, vocabulary, and formality.

For example, students who are writing to persuade their parents to grant them some additional privilege, such as permission for a more independent activity, should use more sophisticated vocabulary and diction that sounds more mature and serious to appeal to the parental audience. However, students who are writing for younger children should use simpler vocabulary and sentence structure, as well as choose words that are more vivid and entertaining. They should treat their topics more lightly, and include humor when appropriate. Students who are writing for their classmates may use language that is more informal, as well as age-appropriate.

> **Review Video: Writing Purpose and Audience**
> Visit mometrix.com/academy and enter code: 146627

Formality in Writing

Level of Formality

The relationship between writer and reader is important in choosing a **level of formality** as most writing requires some degree of formality. **Formal writing** is for addressing a superior in a school or work environment. Business letters, textbooks, and newspapers use a moderate to high level of formality. **Informal writing** is appropriate for private letters, personal emails, and business correspondence between close associates.

For your exam, you will want to be aware of informal and formal writing. One way that this can be accomplished is to watch for shifts in point of view in the essay. For example, unless writers are using a personal example, they will rarely refer to themselves (e.g., "*I* think that *my* point is very clear.") to avoid being informal when they need to be formal.

Also, be mindful of an author who addresses his or her audience **directly** in their writing (e.g., "Readers, *like you*, will understand this argument.") as this can be a sign of informal writing. Good writers understand the need to be consistent with their level of formality. Shifts in levels of formality or point of view can confuse readers and cause them to discount the message.

Clichés

Clichés are phrases that have been **overused** to the point that the phrase has no importance or has lost the original meaning. These phrases have no originality and add very little to a passage. Therefore, most writers will avoid the use of clichés. Another option is to make changes to a cliché so that it is not predictable and empty of meaning.

Examples:

> When life gives you lemons, make lemonade.
>
> Every cloud has a silver lining.

Jargon

Jargon is **specialized vocabulary** that is used among members of a certain trade or profession. Since jargon is understood by only a small audience, writers will use jargon in passages that will only be read by a specialized audience. For example, medical jargon should be used in a medical journal but not in a New York Times article. Jargon includes exaggerated language that tries to impress rather than inform. Sentences filled with jargon are not precise and are difficult to understand.

Examples:

> "He is going to *toenail* these frames for us." (Toenail is construction jargon for nailing at an angle.)
>
> "They brought in a *kip* of material today." (Kip refers to 1000 pounds in architecture and engineering.)

Slang

Slang is an **informal** and sometimes private language that is understood by some individuals. Slang terms have some usefulness, but they can have a small audience. So, most formal writing will not include this kind of language.

Examples:

"Yes, the event was a blast!" (In this sentence, *blast* means that the event was a great experience.)

"That attempt was an epic fail." (By *epic fail*, the speaker means that his or her attempt was not a success.)

Colloquialism

A colloquialism is a word or phrase that is found in informal writing. Unlike slang, **colloquial language** will be familiar to a greater range of people. However, colloquialisms are still considered inappropriate for formal writing. Colloquial language can include some slang, but these are limited to contractions for the most part.

Examples:

"Can *y'all* come back another time?" (Y'all is a contraction of "you all.")

"Will you stop him from building this *castle in the air*?" (A "castle in the air" is an improbable or unlikely event.)

Academic Language

In educational settings, students are often expected to use academic language in their schoolwork. Academic language is also commonly found in dissertations and theses, texts published by academic journals, and other forms of academic research. Academic language conventions may vary between fields, but general academic language is free of slang, regional terminology, and noticeable grammatical errors. Specific terms may also be used in academic language, and it is important to understand their proper usage. A writer's command of academic language impacts their ability to communicate in an academic or professional context. While it is acceptable to use colloquialisms, slang, improper grammar, or other forms of informal speech in social settings or at home, it is inappropriate to practice non-academic language in academic contexts.

Preparing for an Essay Question

Brainstorm

Spend the first three to five minutes brainstorming for ideas. Write down any ideas that you might have on the topic. The purpose is to pull any helpful information from the depths of your memory. In this stage, anything goes down in a margin for notes regardless of how good or bad the idea may seem at first glance.

Strength Through Different Viewpoints

The best papers will contain several examples and mature reasoning. As you brainstorm, you should consider different perspectives. There are more than two sides to every topic. In an argument, there are countless perspectives that can be considered. On any topic, different groups are impacted and many reach the same conclusion or position. Yet, they reach the same conclusion through different paths. Before writing your essay, try to *see* the topic through as many different *eyes* as you can.

In addition, you don't have to use information on how the topic impacts others. You can draw from your own experience as you wish. If you prefer to use a personal narrative, then explain the experience and your emotions from that moment. Anything that you've seen in your community can be expanded upon to round out your position on the topic.

Once you have finished with your creative flow, you need to stop and review what you brainstormed. *Which idea allowed you to come up with the most supporting information?* Be sure to pick an angle that will allow you to have a thorough coverage of the prompt.

Every garden of ideas has weeds. The ideas that you brainstormed are going to be random pieces of information of different values. Go through the pieces carefully and pick out the ones that are the best. The best ideas are strong points that will be easy to write a paragraph in response.

Now, you have your main ideas that you will focus on. So, align them in a sequence that will flow in a smooth, sensible path from point to point. With this approach, readers will go smoothly from one idea to the next in a reasonable order. Readers want an essay that has a sense of continuity (i.e., Point 1 to Point 2 to Point 3 and so on).

Start Your Engines

Now, you have a logical flow of the main ideas for the start of your essay. Begin by expanding on the first point, then move to your second point. Pace yourself. Don't spend too much time on any one of the ideas that you are expanding on. You want to have time for all of them. Make sure that you watch your time. If you have twenty minutes left to write out your ideas and you have four ideas, then you can only use five minutes per idea. Writing so much information in so little time can be an intimidating task. Yet, when you pace yourself, you can get through all of your points. If you find that you are falling behind, then you can remove one of your weaker arguments. This will allow you to give enough support to your remaining paragraphs.

Once you finish expanding on an idea, go back to your brainstorming session where you wrote out your ideas. You can scratch through the ideas as you write about them. This will let you see what you need to write about next and what you have left to cover.

Your introductory paragraph should have several easily identifiable features.

- First, the paragraph should have a quick description or paraphrasing of the topic. Use your own words to briefly explain what the topic is about.
- Second, you should list your writing points. What are the main ideas that you came up with earlier? If someone was to read only your introduction, they should be able to get a good summary of the entire paper.
- Third, you should explain your opinion of the topic and give an explanation for why you feel that way. What is your decision or conclusion on the topic?

Each of your following paragraphs should develop one of the points listed in the main paragraph. Use your personal experience and knowledge to support each of your points. Examples should back up everything.

Once you have finished expanding on each of your main points, you need to conclude your essay. Summarize what you have written in a conclusion paragraph. Explain once more your argument on the prompt and review why you feel that way in a few sentences. At this stage, you have already backed up your statements. So, there is no need to do that again. You just need to refresh your readers on the main points that you made in your essay.

Don't Panic

Whatever you do during essay, do not panic. When you panic, you will put fewer words on the page and your ideas will be weak. Therefore, panicking is not helpful. If your mind goes blank when you see the prompt, then you need to take a deep breath. Force yourself to go through the steps listed above: brainstorm and put anything on scratch paper that comes to mind.

Also, don't get clock fever. You may be overwhelmed when you're looking at a page that is mostly blank. Your mind is full of random thoughts and feeling confused, and the clock is ticking down faster. You have already brainstormed for ideas. Therefore, you don't have to keep coming up with ideas. If you're running out of time and you have a lot of ideas that you haven't written down, then don't be afraid to make some cuts. Start picking the best ideas that you have left and expand on them. Don't feel like you have to write on all of your ideas.

A short paper that is well written and well organized is better than a long paper that is poorly written and poorly organized. Don't keep writing about a subject just to add sentences and avoid repeating a statement or idea that you have explained already. The goal is 1 to 2 pages of quality writing. That is your target, but you should not mess up your paper by trying to get there. You want to have a natural end to your work without having to cut something short. If your essay is a little long, then that isn't a problem as long as your ideas are clear and flow well from paragraph to paragraph. Remember to expand on the ideas that you identified in the brainstorming session.

Leave time at the end (at least three minutes) to go back and check over your work. Reread and make sure that everything you've written makes sense and flows well. Clean up any spelling or grammar mistakes. Also, go ahead and erase any brainstorming ideas that you weren't able to include. Then, clean up any extra information that you might have written that doesn't fit into your paper.

As you proofread, make sure that there aren't any fragments or run-ons. Check for sentences that are too short or too long. If the sentence is too short, then look to see if you have a specific subject and an active verb. If it is too long, then break up the long sentence into two sentences. Watch out for any "big words" that you may have used. Be sure that you are using difficult words correctly. Don't misunderstand; you should try to increase your vocabulary and use difficult words in your essay. However, your focus should be on developing and expressing ideas in a clear and precise way.

The Short Overview

Depending on your preferences and personality, the essay may be your hardest or your easiest section. You are required to go through the entire process of writing a paper in a limited amount of time which is very challenging.

Stay focused on each of the steps for brainstorming. Go through the process of creative flow first. You can start by generating ideas about the prompt. Next, organize those ideas into a smooth flow. Then, pick out the ideas that are the best from your list.

Create a recognizable essay structure in your paper. Start with an introduction that explains what you have decided to argue. Then, choose your main points. Use the body paragraphs to touch on those main points and have a conclusion that wraps up the topic.

Save a few moments to go back and review what you have written. Clean up any minor mistakes that you might have made and make those last few critical touches that can make a huge difference. Finally, be proud and confident of what you have written!

Chapter Quiz

Ready to see how well you retained what you just read? Scan the QR code to go directly to the chapter quiz interface for this study guide. If you're using a computer, simply visit the bonus page at **mometrix.com/bonus948/claslearntest** and click the Chapter Quizzes link.

Quantitative Reasoning

Quantitative Reasoning Overview

The quantitative reasoning portion of the Classic Learning Test will consist of one 45-minute section with 40 questions to complete. No calculator is permitted when taking this portion of the test.

Geometry	The test-taker will be expected to answer questions about a variety of geometric concepts. Test-takers are not expected to memorize formulas or to have to do complex operations that would require the use of a calculator. Instead, they expected to know how to apply formulas and geometric reasoning to solve problems. Common topics include regular and irregular shapes, area and perimeter, volume and surface area, parallel and perpendicular lines, and concepts of trigonometric formulas.	14 questions
Mathematical Reasoning	The test-taker will be expected to answer word problems that express mathematical concepts in sentence formats. These questions require the reader to apply logic and reasoning to understand what is being asked and to draw conclusions to answer the questions. These questions can have crossover with the other two categories of questions, as some questions may involve shapes or rates and proportions.	16 questions
Algebra 1 and 2	The test-taker will be expected to understand how to work with a variety of algebraic topics, including manipulating and solving equations, calculating slope, finding equivalent values, working with inequalities, and finding roots. None of these questions will require the use of a calcluator or graphing equations, but it does help to be familiar with the coordinate plane and graphing.	10 questions

Math Reasoning

Number Basics

Classifications of Numbers

Numbers are the basic building blocks of mathematics. Specific features of numbers are identified by the following terms:

Integer – any positive or negative whole number, including zero. Integers do not include fractions $\left(\frac{1}{3}\right)$, decimals (0.56), or mixed numbers $\left(7\frac{3}{4}\right)$.

Prime number – any whole number greater than 1 that has only two factors, itself and 1; that is, a number that can be divided evenly only by 1 and itself.

Composite number – any whole number greater than 1 that has more than two different factors; in other words, any whole number that is not a prime number. For example: The composite number 8 has the factors of 1, 2, 4, and 8.

Even number – any integer that can be divided by 2 without leaving a remainder. For example: 2, 4, 6, 8, and so on.

Odd number – any integer that cannot be divided evenly by 2. For example: 3, 5, 7, 9, and so on.

Decimal number – any number that uses a decimal point to show the part of the number that is less than one. Example: 1.234.

Decimal point – a symbol used to separate the ones place from the tenths place in decimals or dollars from cents in currency.

Decimal place – the position of a number to the right of the decimal point. In the decimal 0.123, the 1 is in the first place to the right of the decimal point, indicating tenths; the 2 is in the second place, indicating hundredths; and the 3 is in the third place, indicating thousandths.

The **decimal**, or base 10, system is a number system that uses ten different digits (0, 1, 2, 3, 4, 5, 6, 7, 8, 9). An example of a number system that uses something other than ten digits is the **binary**, or base 2, number system, used by computers, which uses only the numbers 0 and 1. It is thought that the decimal system originated because people had only their 10 fingers for counting.

Rational numbers include all integers, decimals, and fractions. Any terminating or repeating decimal number is a rational number.

Irrational numbers cannot be written as fractions or decimals because the number of decimal places is infinite and there is no recurring pattern of digits within the number. For example, pi (π) begins with 3.141592 and continues without terminating or repeating, so pi is an irrational number.

Real numbers are the set of all rational and irrational numbers.

Review Video: Classification of Numbers
Visit mometrix.com/academy and enter code: 461071

Review Video: Prime and Composite Numbers
Visit mometrix.com/academy and enter code: 565581

Numbers in Word Form and Place Value

When writing numbers out in word form or translating word form to numbers, it is essential to understand how a place value system works. In the decimal or base-10 system, each digit of a number represents how many of the corresponding place value—a specific factor of 10—are contained in the number being represented. To make reading numbers easier, every three digits to the left of the decimal place is preceded by a comma. The following table demonstrates some of the place values:

Power of 10	10^3	10^2	10^1	10^0	10^{-1}	10^{-2}	10^{-3}
Value	1,000	100	10	1	0.1	0.01	0.001
Place	thousands	hundreds	tens	ones	tenths	hundredths	thousandths

For example, consider the number 4,546.09, which can be separated into each place value like this:

4: thousands
5: hundreds
4: tens
6: ones
0: tenths
9: hundredths

This number in word form would be *four thousand five hundred forty-six and nine hundredths.*

Review Video: Place Value
Visit mometrix.com/academy and enter code: 205433

Rational Numbers

The term **rational** means that the number can be expressed as a ratio or fraction. That is, a number, r, is rational if and only if it can be represented by a fraction $\frac{a}{b}$ where a and b are integers and b does not equal 0. The set of rational numbers includes integers and decimals. If there is no finite way to represent a value with a fraction of integers, then the number is **irrational**. Common examples of irrational numbers include: $\sqrt{5}$, $(1+\sqrt{2})$, and π.

Review Video: Rational and Irrational Numbers
Visit mometrix.com/academy and enter code: 280645

Review Video: Ordering Rational Numbers
Visit mometrix.com/academy and enter code: 419578

Number Lines

A number line is a graph to see the distance between numbers. Basically, this graph shows the relationship between numbers. So a number line may have a point for zero and may show negative numbers on the left side of the line. Any positive numbers are placed on the right side of the line. For example, consider the points labeled on the following number line:

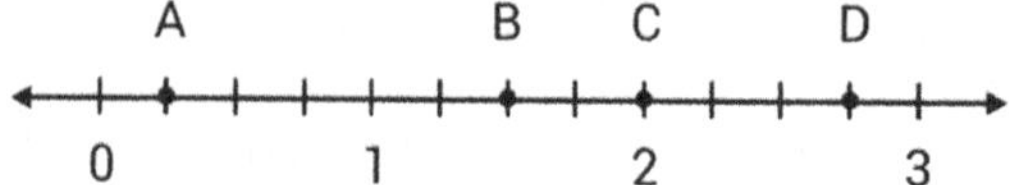

We can use the dashed lines on the number line to identify each point. Each dashed line between two whole numbers is $\frac{1}{4}$. The line halfway between two numbers is $\frac{1}{2}$.

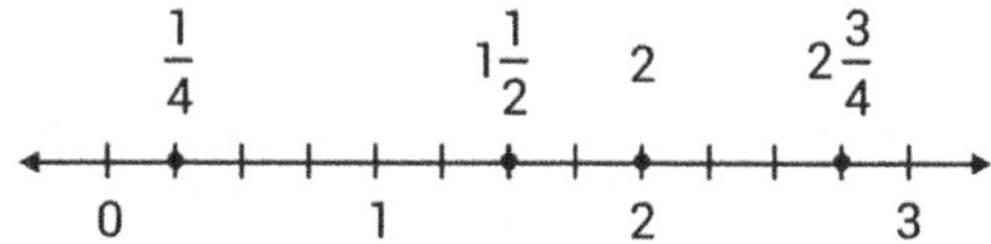

Review Video: The Number Line
Visit mometrix.com/academy and enter code: 816439

Rounding and Estimation

Rounding is reducing the digits in a number while still trying to keep the value similar. The result will be less accurate but in a simpler form and easier to use. Whole numbers can be rounded to the nearest ten, hundred, or thousand.

When you are asked to estimate the solution to a problem, you will need to provide only an approximate figure or **estimation** for your answer. In this situation, you will need to round each number in the calculation to the level indicated (nearest hundred, nearest thousand, etc.) or to a level that makes sense for the numbers involved. When estimating a sum **all numbers must be rounded to the same level**. You cannot round one number to the nearest thousand while rounding another to the nearest hundred.

Review Video: Rounding and Estimation
Visit mometrix.com/academy and enter code: 126243

Absolute Value

A precursor to working with negative numbers is understanding what **absolute values** are. A number's absolute value is simply the distance away from zero a number is on the number line. The absolute value of a number is always positive and is written $|x|$. For example, the absolute value of 3, written as $|3|$, is 3 because the distance between 0 and 3 on a number line is three units. Likewise, the absolute value of -3, written as $|-3|$, is 3 because the distance between 0 and -3 on a number line is three units. So $|3| = |-3|$.

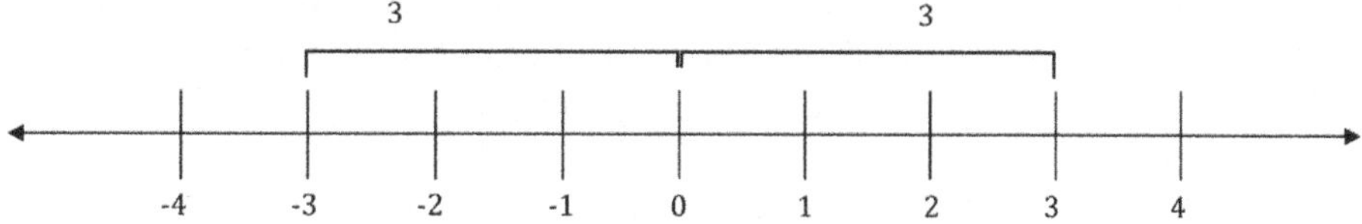

Review Video: Absolute Value
Visit mometrix.com/academy and enter code: 314669

Operations

An **operation** is simply a mathematical process that takes some value(s) as input(s) and produces an output. Elementary operations are often written in the following form: *value operation value*. For instance, in the expression $1 + 2$ the values are 1 and 2 and the operation is addition. Performing the operation gives the output of 3. In this way we can say that $1 + 2$ and 3 are equal, or $1 + 2 = 3$.

Addition

Addition increases the value of one quantity by the value of another quantity (both called **addends**). Example: $2 + 4 = 6$ or $8 + 9 = 17$. The result is called the **sum**. With addition, the order does not matter, $4 + 2 = 2 + 4$.

When adding signed numbers, if the signs are the same simply add the absolute values of the addends and apply the original sign to the sum. For example, $(+4) + (+8) = +12$ and $(-4) + (-8) = -12$. When the original signs are different, take the absolute values of the addends and subtract the smaller value from the larger value, then apply the original sign of the larger value to the difference. Example: $(+4) + (-8) = -4$ and $(-4) + (+8) = +4$.

Subtraction

Subtraction is the opposite operation to addition; it decreases the value of one quantity (the **minuend**) by the value of another quantity (the **subtrahend**). For example, $6 - 4 = 2$ or $17 - 8 = 9$. The result is called the **difference**. Note that with subtraction, the order does matter, $6 - 4 \neq 4 - 6$.

For subtracting signed numbers, change the sign of the subtrahend and then follow the same rules used for addition. Example: $(+4) - (+8) = (+4) + (-8) = -4$

Multiplication

Multiplication can be thought of as repeated addition. One number (the **multiplier**) indicates how many times to add the other number (the **multiplicand**) to itself. Example: $3 \times 2 = 2 + 2 + 2 = 6$. With multiplication, the order does not matter, $2 \times 3 = 3 \times 2$ or $3 + 3 = 2 + 2 + 2$, either way the result (the **product**) is the same.

If the signs are the same, the product is positive when multiplying signed numbers. Example: $(+4) \times (+8) = +32$ and $(-4) \times (-8) = +32$. If the signs are opposite, the product is negative. Example: $(+4) \times (-8) = -32$ and $(-4) \times (+8) = -32$. When more than two factors are multiplied together, the sign of the product is determined by how many negative factors are present. If there are an odd number of negative factors then the product is negative, whereas an even number of negative factors indicates a positive product. Example: $(+4) \times (-8) \times (-2) = +64$ and $(-4) \times (-8) \times (-2) = -64$.

Division

Division is the opposite operation to multiplication; one number (the **divisor**) tells us how many parts to divide the other number (the **dividend**) into. The result of division is called the **quotient**. Example: $20 \div 4 = 5$. If 20 is split into 4 equal parts, each part is 5. With division, the order of the numbers does matter, $20 \div 4 \neq 4 \div 20$.

The rules for dividing signed numbers are similar to multiplying signed numbers. If the dividend and divisor have the same sign, the quotient is positive. If the dividend and divisor have opposite signs, the quotient is negative. Example: $(-4) \div (+8) = -0.5$.

Review Video: Mathematical Operations
Visit mometrix.com/academy and enter code: 208095

Parentheses

Parentheses are used to designate which operations should be done first when there are multiple operations. Example: $4 - (2 + 1) = 1$; the parentheses tell us that we must add 2 and 1, and then subtract the sum from 4, rather than subtracting 2 from 4 and then adding 1 (this would give us an answer of 3).

Review Video: Mathematical Parentheses
Visit mometrix.com/academy and enter code: 978600

Exponents

An **exponent** is a superscript number placed next to another number at the top right. It indicates how many times the base number is to be multiplied by itself. Exponents provide a shorthand way to write what would be a longer mathematical expression, Example: $2^4 = 2 \times 2 \times 2 \times 2$. A number with an exponent of 2 is said to be "squared," while a number with an exponent of 3 is said to be "cubed." The value of a number raised to an exponent is called its power. So 8^4 is read as "8 to the 4th power," or "8 raised to the power of 4."

Review Video: What is an Exponent?
Visit mometrix.com/academy and enter code: 600998

Roots

A **root**, such as a square root, is another way of writing a fractional exponent. Instead of using a superscript, roots use the radical symbol ($\sqrt{\ }$) to indicate the operation. A radical will have a number underneath the bar, and may sometimes have a number in the upper left: $\sqrt[n]{a}$, read as "the nth root of a." The relationship between radical notation and exponent notation can be described by this equation:

$$\sqrt[n]{a} = a^{\frac{1}{n}}$$

The two special cases of $n = 2$ and $n = 3$ are called square roots and cube roots. If there is no number to the upper left, the radical is understood to be a square root ($n = 2$). Nearly all of the roots you encounter will be square roots. A square root is the same as a number raised to the one-half power. When we say that a is the square root of b ($a = \sqrt{b}$), we mean that a multiplied by itself equals b: ($a \times a = b$).

A **perfect square** is a number that has an integer for its square root. There are 10 perfect squares from 1 to 100: 1, 4, 9, 16, 25, 36, 49, 64, 81, 100 (the squares of integers 1 through 10).

Review Video: Roots
Visit mometrix.com/academy and enter code: 795655

Review Video: Perfect Squares and Square Roots
Visit mometrix.com/academy and enter code: 648063

Word Problems and Mathematical Symbols

When working on word problems, you must be able to translate verbal expressions or "math words" into math symbols. This chart contains several "math words" and their appropriate symbols:

Phrase	Symbol
equal, is, was, will be, has, costs, gets to, is the same as, becomes	$=$
times, of, multiplied by, product of, twice, doubles, halves, triples	$\times$
divided by, per, ratio of/to, out of	$\div$
plus, added to, sum, combined, and, more than, totals of	$+$
subtracted from, less than, decreased by, minus, difference between	$-$
what, how much, original value, how many, a number, a variable	x, n, etc.

Examples of Translated Mathematical Phrases

- The phrase four more than twice a number can be written algebraically as $2x + 4$.
- The phrase half a number decreased by six can be written algebraically as $\frac{1}{2}x - 6$.
- The phrase the sum of a number and the product of five and that number can be written algebraically as $x + 5x$.
- You may see a test question that says, "Olivia is constructing a bookcase from seven boards. Two of them are for vertical supports and five are for shelves. The height of the bookcase is twice the width of the bookcase. If the seven boards total 36 feet in length, what will be the height of Olivia's bookcase?" You would need to make a sketch and then create the equation to determine the width of the shelves. The height can be represented as double the width. (If x represents the width of the shelves in feet, then the height of the bookcase is $2x$. Since the seven boards total 36 feet, $2x + 2x + x + x + x + x + x = 36$ or $9x = 36$; $x = 4$. The height is twice the width, or 8 feet.)

Subtraction with Regrouping

A great way to make use of some of the features built into the decimal system would be regrouping when attempting longform subtraction operations. When subtracting within a place value, sometimes the minuend is smaller than the subtrahend, **regrouping** enables you to 'borrow' a unit from a place value to the left in order to get a positive difference. For example, consider subtracting 189 from 525 with regrouping.

First, set up the subtraction problem in vertical form:

$$\begin{array}{r} 525 \\ -\ 189 \\ \hline \end{array}$$

Notice that the numbers in the ones and tens columns of 525 are smaller than the numbers in the ones and tens columns of 189. This means you will need to use regrouping to perform subtraction:

$$\begin{array}{rrrr} & 5 & 2 & 5 \\ - & 1 & 8 & 9 \\ \hline \end{array}$$

To subtract 9 from 5 in the ones column you will need to borrow from the 2 in the tens columns:

$$\begin{array}{rrrr} & 5 & 1 & 15 \\ - & 1 & 8 & 9 \\ \hline & & & 6 \end{array}$$

Next, to subtract 8 from 1 in the tens column you will need to borrow from the 5 in the hundreds column:

	4	11	15
–	1	8	9
		3	6

Last, subtract the 1 from the 4 in the hundreds column:

	4	11	15
–	1	8	9
	3	3	6

Review Video: Subtracting Large Numbers
Visit mometrix.com/academy and enter code: 603350

Order of Operations

The **order of operations** is a set of rules that dictates the order in which we must perform each operation in an expression so that we will evaluate it accurately. If we have an expression that includes multiple different operations, the order of operations tells us which operations to do first. The most common mnemonic for the order of operations is **PEMDAS**, or "Please Excuse My Dear Aunt Sally." PEMDAS stands for parentheses, exponents, multiplication, division, addition, and subtraction. It is important to understand that multiplication and division have equal precedence, as do addition and subtraction, so those pairs of operations are simply worked from left to right in order.

For example, evaluating the expression $5 + 20 \div 4 \times (2 + 3)^2 - 6$ using the correct order of operations would be done like this:

- **P:** Perform the operations inside the parentheses: $(2 + 3) = 5$
- **E:** Simplify the exponents: $(5)^2 = 5 \times 5 = 25$
  - The expression now looks like this: $5 + 20 \div 4 \times 25 - 6$
- **MD:** Perform multiplication and division from left to right: $20 \div 4 = 5$; then $5 \times 25 = 125$
  - The expression now looks like this: $5 + 125 - 6$
- **AS:** Perform addition and subtraction from left to right: $5 + 125 = 130$; then $130 - 6 = 124$

Review Video: Order of Operations
Visit mometrix.com/academy and enter code: 259675

Properties of Exponents

The properties of exponents are as follows:

Property	Description
$a^1 = a$	Any number to the power of 1 is equal to itself
$1^n = 1$	The number 1 raised to any power is equal to 1
$a^0 = 1$	Any number raised to the power of 0 is equal to 1
$a^n \times a^m = a^{n+m}$	Add exponents to multiply powers of the same base number
$a^n \div a^m = a^{n-m}$	Subtract exponents to divide powers of the same base number

Property	Description
$(a^n)^m = a^{n \times m}$	When a power is raised to a power, the exponents are multiplied
$(a \times b)^n = a^n \times b^n$ $(a \div b)^n = a^n \div b^n$	Multiplication and division operations inside parentheses can be raised to a power. This is the same as each term being raised to that power.
$a^{-n} = \frac{1}{a^n}$	A negative exponent is the same as the reciprocal of a positive exponent

Note that exponents do not have to be integers. Fractional or decimal exponents follow all the rules above as well. Example: $5^{\frac{1}{4}} \times 5^{\frac{3}{4}} = 5^{\frac{1}{4}+\frac{3}{4}} = 5^1 = 5$.

Review Video: Properties of Exponents
Visit mometrix.com/academy and enter code: 532558

Factors and Multiples

Factors and Greatest Common Factor

Factors are numbers that are multiplied together to obtain a **product**. For example, in the equation $2 \times 3 = 6$, the numbers 2 and 3 are factors. A **prime number** has only two factors (1 and itself), but other numbers can have many factors.

A **common factor** is a number that divides exactly into two or more other numbers. For example, the factors of 12 are 1, 2, 3, 4, 6, and 12, while the factors of 15 are 1, 3, 5, and 15. The common factors of 12 and 15 are 1 and 3.

A **prime factor** is also a prime number. Therefore, the prime factors of 12 are 2 and 3. For 15, the prime factors are 3 and 5.

The **greatest common factor** (GCF) is the largest number that is a factor of two or more numbers. For example, the factors of 15 are 1, 3, 5, and 15; the factors of 35 are 1, 5, 7, and 35. Therefore, the greatest common factor of 15 and 35 is 5.

Review Video: Factors
Visit mometrix.com/academy and enter code: 920086

Review Video: Prime Numbers and Factorization
Visit mometrix.com/academy and enter code: 760669

Review Video: Greatest Common Factor and Least Common Multiple
Visit mometrix.com/academy and enter code: 838699

Multiples and Least Common Multiple

Often listed out in multiplication tables, **multiples** are integer increments of a given factor. In other words, dividing a multiple by the factor will result in an integer. For example, the multiples of 7 include: $1 \times 7 = 7, 2 \times 7 = 14, 3 \times 7 = 21, 4 \times 7 = 28, 5 \times 7 = 35$. Dividing 7, 14, 21, 28, or 35 by 7 will result in the integers 1, 2, 3, 4, and 5, respectively.

The least common multiple (**LCM**) is the smallest number that is a multiple of two or more numbers. For example, the multiples of 3 include 3, 6, 9, 12, 15, etc.; the multiples of 5 include 5, 10, 15, 20, etc. Therefore, the least common multiple of 3 and 5 is 15.

Review Video: Multiples
Visit mometrix.com/academy and enter code: 626738

Fractions, Decimals, and Percentages

Fractions

A **fraction** is a number that is expressed as one integer written above another integer, with a dividing line between them $\left(\frac{x}{y}\right)$. It represents the **quotient** of the two numbers "x divided by y." It can also be thought of as x out of y equal parts.

The top number of a fraction is called the **numerator**, and it represents the number of parts under consideration. The 1 in $\frac{1}{4}$ means that 1 part out of the whole is being considered in the calculation. The bottom number of a fraction is called the **denominator**, and it represents the total number of equal parts. The 4 in $\frac{1}{4}$ means that the whole consists of 4 equal parts. A fraction cannot have a denominator of zero; this is referred to as "*undefined*."

Fractions can be manipulated, without changing the value of the fraction, by multiplying or dividing (but not adding or subtracting) both the numerator and denominator by the same number. If you divide both numbers by a common factor, you are **reducing** or simplifying the fraction. Two fractions that have the same value but are expressed differently are known as **equivalent fractions**. For example, $\frac{2}{10}, \frac{3}{15}, \frac{4}{20}$, and $\frac{5}{25}$ are all equivalent fractions. They can also all be reduced or simplified to $\frac{1}{5}$.

When two fractions are manipulated so that they have the same denominator, this is known as finding a **common denominator**. The number chosen to be that common denominator should be the least common multiple of the two original denominators. Example: $\frac{3}{4}$ and $\frac{5}{6}$; the least common multiple of 4 and 6 is 12. Manipulating to achieve the common denominator: $\frac{3}{4} = \frac{9}{12}; \frac{5}{6} = \frac{10}{12}$.

Review Video: Overview of Fractions
Visit mometrix.com/academy and enter code: 262335

Proper Fractions and Mixed Numbers

A fraction whose denominator is greater than its numerator is known as a **proper fraction**, while a fraction whose numerator is greater than its denominator is known as an **improper fraction**. Proper fractions have values *less than one* and improper fractions have values *greater than one.*

A **mixed number** is a number that contains both an integer and a fraction. Any improper fraction can be rewritten as a mixed number. Example: $\frac{8}{3} = \frac{6}{3} + \frac{2}{3} = 2 + \frac{2}{3} = 2\frac{2}{3}$. Similarly, any mixed number can be rewritten as an improper fraction. Example: $1\frac{3}{5} = 1 + \frac{3}{5} = \frac{5}{5} + \frac{3}{5} = \frac{8}{5}$.

Review Video: Proper and Improper Fractions and Mixed Numbers
Visit mometrix.com/academy and enter code: 211077

ADDING AND SUBTRACTING FRACTIONS

If two fractions have a common denominator, they can be added or subtracted simply by adding or subtracting the two numerators and retaining the same denominator. If the two fractions do not already have the same denominator, one or both of them must be manipulated to achieve a common denominator before they can be added or subtracted. Example: $\frac{1}{2} + \frac{1}{4} = \frac{2}{4} + \frac{1}{4} = \frac{3}{4}$.

Review Video: Adding and Subtracting Fractions
Visit mometrix.com/academy and enter code: 378080

MULTIPLYING FRACTIONS

Two fractions can be multiplied by multiplying the two numerators to find the new numerator and the two denominators to find the new denominator. Example: $\frac{1}{3} \times \frac{2}{3} = \frac{1 \times 2}{3 \times 3} = \frac{2}{9}$.

DIVIDING FRACTIONS

Two fractions can be divided by flipping the numerator and denominator of the second fraction and then proceeding as though it were a multiplication problem. Example: $\frac{2}{3} \div \frac{3}{4} = \frac{2}{3} \times \frac{4}{3} = \frac{8}{9}$.

Review Video: Multiplying and Dividing Fractions
Visit mometrix.com/academy and enter code: 473632

MULTIPLYING A MIXED NUMBER BY A WHOLE NUMBER OR A DECIMAL

When multiplying a mixed number by something, it is usually best to convert it to an improper fraction first. Additionally, if the multiplicand is a decimal, it is most often simplest to convert it to a fraction. For instance, to multiply $4\frac{3}{8}$ by 3.5, begin by rewriting each quantity as a whole number plus a proper fraction. Remember, a mixed number is a fraction added to a whole number and a decimal is a representation of the sum of fractions, specifically tenths, hundredths, thousandths, and so on:

$$4\frac{3}{8} \times 3.5 = \left(4 + \frac{3}{8}\right) \times \left(3 + \frac{1}{2}\right)$$

Next, the quantities being added need to be expressed with the same denominator. This is achieved by multiplying and dividing the whole number by the denominator of the fraction. Recall that a whole number is equivalent to that number divided by 1:

$$= \left(\frac{4}{1} \times \frac{8}{8} + \frac{3}{8}\right) \times \left(\frac{3}{1} \times \frac{2}{2} + \frac{1}{2}\right)$$

When multiplying fractions, remember to multiply the numerators and denominators separately:

$$= \left(\frac{4 \times 8}{1 \times 8} + \frac{3}{8}\right) \times \left(\frac{3 \times 2}{1 \times 2} + \frac{1}{2}\right)$$
$$= \left(\frac{32}{8} + \frac{3}{8}\right) \times \left(\frac{6}{2} + \frac{1}{2}\right)$$

Now that the fractions have the same denominators, they can be added:

$$= \frac{35}{8} \times \frac{7}{2}$$

Finally, perform the last multiplication and then simplify:

$$= \frac{35 \times 7}{8 \times 2} = \frac{245}{16} = \frac{240}{16} + \frac{5}{16} = 15\frac{5}{16}$$

Comparing Fractions

It is important to master the ability to compare and order fractions. This skill is relevant to many real-world scenarios. For example, carpenters often compare fractional construction nail lengths when preparing for a project, and bakers often compare fractional measurements to have the correct ratio of ingredients. There are three commonly used strategies when comparing fractions. These strategies are referred to as the common denominator approach, the decimal approach, and the cross-multiplication approach.

Using a Common Denominator to Compare Fractions

The fractions $\frac{2}{3}$ and $\frac{4}{7}$ have different denominators. $\frac{2}{3}$ has a denominator of 3, and $\frac{4}{7}$ has a denominator of 7. In order to precisely compare these two fractions, it is necessary to use a common denominator. A common denominator is a common multiple that is shared by both denominators. In this case, the denominators 3 and 7 share a multiple of 21. In general, it is most efficient to select the least common multiple for the two denominators.

Rewrite each fraction with the common denominator of 21. Then, calculate the new numerators as illustrated below.

$$\frac{2}{3} \xrightarrow{\times 7} \frac{\mathbf{14}}{21} \qquad \frac{4}{7} \xrightarrow{\times 3} \frac{\mathbf{12}}{21}$$

For $\frac{2}{3}$, multiply the numerator and denominator by 7. The result is $\frac{14}{21}$.

For $\frac{4}{7}$, multiply the numerator and denominator by 3. The result is $\frac{12}{21}$.

Now that both fractions have a denominator of 21, the fractions can accurately be compared by comparing the numerators. Since 14 is greater than 12, the fraction $\frac{14}{21}$ is greater than $\frac{12}{21}$. This means that $\frac{2}{3}$ is greater than $\frac{4}{7}$.

Using decimals to compare fractions

Sometimes decimal values are easier to compare than fraction values. For example, $\frac{5}{8}$ is equivalent to 0.625 and $\frac{3}{5}$ is equivalent to 0.6. This means that the comparison of $\frac{5}{8}$ and $\frac{3}{5}$ can be determined by comparing the decimals 0.625 and 0.6. When both decimal values are extended to the thousandths place, they become 0.625 and 0.600, respectively. It becomes clear that 0.625 is greater than 0.600 because 625 thousandths is greater than 600 thousandths. In other words, $\frac{5}{8}$ is greater than $\frac{3}{5}$ because 0.625 is greater than 0.6.

Using cross-multiplication to compare fractions

Cross-multiplication is an efficient strategy for comparing fractions. This is a shortcut for the common denominator strategy. Start by writing each fraction next to one another. Multiply the numerator of the fraction on the left by the denominator of the fraction on the right. Write down the result next to the fraction on the left. Now multiply the numerator of the fraction on the right by the denominator of the fraction on the left. Write down the result next to the fraction on the right. Compare both products. The fraction with the larger result is the larger fraction.

Consider the fractions $\frac{4}{7}$ and $\frac{5}{9}$.

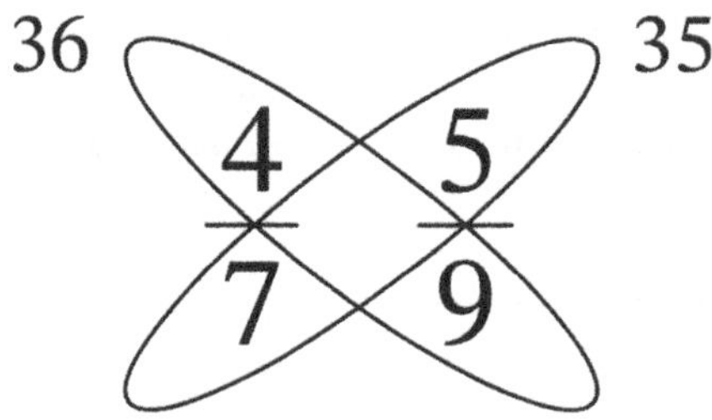

36 is greater than 35. Therefore, $\frac{4}{7}$ is greater than $\frac{5}{9}$.

Decimals

Decimals are one way to represent parts of a whole. Using the place value system, each digit to the right of a decimal point denotes the number of units of a corresponding *negative* power of ten. For example, consider the decimal 0.24. We can use a model to represent the decimal. Since a dime is worth one-tenth of a dollar and a penny is worth one-hundredth of a dollar, one possible model to represent this fraction is to have 2 dimes representing the 2 in the tenths place and 4 pennies representing the 4 in the hundredths place:

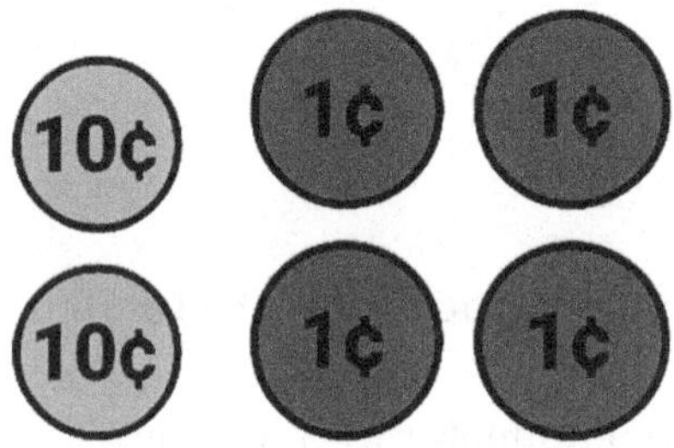

To write the decimal as a fraction, put the decimal in the numerator with 1 in the denominator. Multiply the numerator and denominator by tens until there are no more decimal places. Then simplify the fraction to lowest terms. For example, converting 0.24 to a fraction:

$$0.24 = \frac{0.24}{1} = \frac{0.24 \times 100}{1 \times 100} = \frac{24}{100} = \frac{6}{25}$$

Review Video: Decimals
Visit mometrix.com/academy and enter code: 837268

Operations with Decimals

Adding and Subtracting Decimals

When adding and subtracting decimals, the decimal points must always be aligned. Adding decimals is just like adding regular whole numbers. Example: $4.5 + 2.0 = 6.5$.

If the problem-solver does not properly align the decimal points, an incorrect answer of 4.7 may result. An easy way to add decimals is to align all of the decimal points in a vertical column visually. This will allow you to see exactly where the decimal should be placed in the final answer. Begin adding from right to left. Add each column in turn, making sure to carry the number to the left if a column adds up to more than 9. The same rules apply to the subtraction of decimals.

Review Video: Adding and Subtracting Decimals
Visit mometrix.com/academy and enter code: 381101

Multiplying Decimals

A simple multiplication problem has two components: a **multiplicand** and a **multiplier**. When multiplying decimals, work as though the numbers were whole rather than decimals. Once the final product is calculated, count the number of places to the right of the decimal in both the multiplicand and the multiplier. Then, count that number of places from the right of the product and place the decimal in that position.

For example, 12.3×2.56 has a total of three places to the right of the respective decimals. Multiply 123×256 to get 31,488. Now, beginning on the right, count three places to the left and insert the decimal. The final product will be 31.488.

Review Video: How to Multiply Decimals
Visit mometrix.com/academy and enter code: 731574

Dividing Decimals

Every division problem has a **divisor** and a **dividend**. The dividend is the number that is being divided. In the problem $14 \div 7$, 14 is the dividend and 7 is the divisor. In a division problem with decimals, the divisor must be converted into a whole number. Begin by moving the decimal in the divisor to the right until a whole number is created. Next, move the decimal in the dividend the same number of spaces to the right. For example, 4.9 into 24.5 would become 49 into 245. The decimal was moved one space to the right to create a whole number in the divisor, and then the same was done for the dividend. Once the whole numbers are created, the problem is carried out normally: $245 \div 49 = 5$.

Review Video: Dividing Decimals
Visit mometrix.com/academy and enter code: 560690

Review Video: <u>**Dividing Decimals by Whole Numbers**</u>
Visit mometrix.com/academy and enter code: 535669

PERCENTAGES

Percentages can be thought of as fractions that are based on a whole of 100; that is, one whole is equal to 100%. The word **percent** means "per hundred." Percentage problems are often presented in three main ways:

- Find what percentage of some number another number is.
  - Example: What percentage of 40 is 8?
- Find what number is some percentage of a given number.
  - Example: What number is 20% of 40?
- Find what number another number is a given percentage of.
  - Example: What number is 8 20% of?

There are three components in each of these cases: a **whole** (W), a **part** (P), and a **percentage** (%). These are related by the equation: $P = W \times \%$. This can easily be rearranged into other forms that may suit different questions better: $\% = \frac{P}{W}$ and $W = \frac{P}{\%}$. Percentage problems are often also word problems. As such, a large part of solving them is figuring out which quantities are what. For example, consider the following word problem:

In a school cafeteria, 7 students choose pizza, 9 choose hamburgers, and 4 choose tacos. What percentage of student choose tacos?

To find the whole, you must first add all of the parts: $7 + 9 + 4 = 20$. The percentage can then be found by dividing the part by the whole $\left(\% = \frac{P}{W}\right)$: $\frac{4}{20} = \frac{20}{100} = 20\%$.

Review Video: <u>**Computation with Percentages**</u>
Visit mometrix.com/academy and enter code: 693099

CONVERTING BETWEEN PERCENTAGES, FRACTIONS, AND DECIMALS

Converting decimals to percentages and percentages to decimals is as simple as moving the decimal point. To *convert from a decimal to a percentage,* move the decimal point **two places to the right**. To *convert from a percentage to a decimal,* move it **two places to the left**. It may be helpful to remember that the percentage number will always be larger than the equivalent decimal number. Example:

$$0.23 = 23\% \quad 5.34 = 534\% \quad 0.007 = 0.7\%$$
$$700\% = 7.00 \quad 86\% = 0.86 \quad 0.15\% = 0.0015$$

To convert a fraction to a decimal, simply divide the numerator by the denominator in the fraction. To convert a decimal to a fraction, put the decimal in the numerator with 1 in the denominator. Multiply the numerator and denominator by tens until there are no more decimal places. Then simplify the fraction to lowest terms. For example, converting 0.24 to a fraction:

$$0.24 = \frac{0.24}{1} = \frac{0.24 \times 100}{1 \times 100} = \frac{24}{100} = \frac{6}{25}$$

Fractions can be converted to a percentage by finding equivalent fractions with a denominator of 100. Example:

$$\frac{7}{10} = \frac{70}{100} = 70\% \quad \frac{1}{4} = \frac{25}{100} = 25\%$$

To convert a percentage to a fraction, divide the percentage number by 100 and reduce the fraction to its simplest possible terms. Example:

$$60\% = \frac{60}{100} = \frac{3}{5} \quad 96\% = \frac{96}{100} = \frac{24}{25}$$

Review Video: Converting Fractions to Percentages and Decimals
Visit mometrix.com/academy and enter code: 306233

Review Video: Converting Percentages to Decimals and Fractions
Visit mometrix.com/academy and enter code: 287297

Review Video: Converting Decimals to Fractions and Percentages
Visit mometrix.com/academy and enter code: 986765

Review Video: Converting Decimals, Improper Fractions, and Mixed Numbers
Visit mometrix.com/academy and enter code: 696924

Proportions and Ratios

Proportions

A proportion is a relationship between two quantities that dictates how one changes when the other changes. A **direct proportion** describes a relationship in which a quantity increases by a set amount for every increase in the other quantity, or decreases by that same amount for every decrease in the other quantity. Example: Assuming a constant driving speed, the time required for a car trip increases as the distance of the trip increases. The distance to be traveled and the time required to travel are directly proportional.

An **inverse proportion** is a relationship in which an increase in one quantity is accompanied by a decrease in the other, or vice versa. Example: the time required for a car trip decreases as the speed increases and increases as the speed decreases, so the time required is inversely proportional to the speed of the car.

Review Video: Proportions
Visit mometrix.com/academy and enter code: 505355

Ratios

A **ratio** is a comparison of two quantities in a particular order. Example: If there are 14 computers in a lab, and the class has 20 students, there is a student to computer ratio of 20 to 14, commonly written as 20: 14. Ratios are normally reduced to their smallest whole number representation, so 20: 14 would be reduced to 10: 7 by dividing both sides by 2.

Review Video: Ratios
Visit mometrix.com/academy and enter code: 996914

Constant of Proportionality

When two quantities have a proportional relationship, there exists a **constant of proportionality** between the quantities. The product of this constant and one of the quantities is equal to the other quantity. For example, if one lemon costs $0.25, two lemons cost $0.50, and three lemons cost $0.75, there is a proportional relationship between the total cost of lemons and the number of lemons purchased. The constant of proportionality is the **unit price**, namely $0.25/lemon. Notice that the total price of lemons, t, can be found by multiplying the unit price of lemons, p, and the number of lemons, n: $t = pn$.

Work/Unit Rate

Unit rate expresses a quantity of one thing in terms of one unit of another. For example, if you travel 30 miles every two hours, a unit rate expresses this comparison in terms of one hour: in one hour you travel 15 miles, so your unit rate is 15 miles per hour. Other examples are how much one ounce of food costs (price per ounce) or figuring out how much one egg costs out of the dozen (price per 1 egg, instead of price per 12 eggs). The denominator of a unit rate is always 1. Unit rates are used to compare different situations to solve problems. For example, to make sure you get the best deal when deciding which kind of soda to buy, you can find the unit rate of each. If soda #1 costs $1.50 for a 1-liter bottle, and soda #2 costs $2.75 for a 2-liter bottle, it would be a better deal to buy soda #2, because its unit rate is only $1.375 per 1-liter, which is cheaper than soda #1. Unit rates can also help determine the length of time a given event will take. For example, if you can paint 2 rooms in 4.5 hours, you can determine how long it will take you to paint 5 rooms by solving for the unit rate per room and then multiplying that by 5.

Review Video: Rates and Unit Rates
Visit mometrix.com/academy and enter code: 185363

Metric and Customary Measurements

Metric Measurement Prefixes

Giga-	One billion	1 *giga*watt is one billion watts
Mega-	One million	1 *mega*hertz is one million hertz
Kilo-	One thousand	1 *kilo*gram is one thousand grams
Deci-	One-tenth	1 *deci*meter is one-tenth of a meter
Centi-	One-hundredth	1 *centi*meter is one-hundredth of a meter
Milli-	One-thousandth	1 *milli*liter is one-thousandth of a liter
Micro-	One-millionth	1 *micro*gram is one-millionth of a gram

Review Video: Metric System Conversion - How the Metric System Works
Visit mometrix.com/academy and enter code: 163709

Measurement Conversion

When converting between units, the goal is to maintain the same meaning but change the way it is displayed. In order to go from a larger unit to a smaller unit, multiply the number of the known amount by the equivalent amount. When going from a smaller unit to a larger unit, divide the number of the known amount by the equivalent amount.

For complicated conversions, it may be helpful to set up conversion fractions. In these fractions, one fraction is the **conversion factor**. The other fraction has the unknown amount in the numerator. So, the known value is placed in the denominator. Sometimes, the second fraction has the known value from the problem in the numerator and the unknown in the denominator. Multiply the two fractions to get the converted measurement. Note that since the numerator and the denominator of the factor are equivalent, the value of the fraction is 1. That is why we can say that the result in the new units is equal to the result in the old units even though they have different numbers.

It can often be necessary to chain known conversion factors together. As an example, consider converting 512 square inches to square meters. We know that there are 2.54 centimeters in an inch and 100 centimeters in a meter, and we know we will need to square each of these factors to achieve the conversion we are looking for.

$$\frac{512\text{ in}^2}{1} \times \left(\frac{2.54\text{ cm}}{1\text{ in}}\right)^2 \times \left(\frac{1\text{ m}}{100\text{ cm}}\right)^2 = \frac{512\,\cancel{\text{in}^2}}{1} \times \left(\frac{6.4516\,\cancel{\text{cm}^2}}{1\,\cancel{\text{in}^2}}\right) \times \left(\frac{1\text{ m}^2}{10{,}000\,\cancel{\text{cm}^2}}\right) = 0.330\text{ m}^2$$

Review Video: Measurement Conversions
Visit mometrix.com/academy and enter code: 316703

Common Units and Equivalents

Metric Equivalents

1000 µg (microgram)	1 mg
1000 mg (milligram)	1 g
1000 g (gram)	1 kg
1000 kg (kilogram)	1 metric ton
1000 mL (milliliter)	1 L
1000 µm (micrometer)	1 mm
1000 mm (millimeter)	1 m
100 cm (centimeter)	1 m
1000 m (meter)	1 km

Distance and Area Measurement

Unit	Abbreviation	US equivalent	Metric equivalent
Inch	in	1 inch	2.54 centimeters
Foot	ft	12 inches	0.305 meters
Yard	yd	3 feet	0.914 meters
Mile	mi	5280 feet	1.609 kilometers
Acre	ac	4840 square yards	0.405 hectares
Square Mile	sq. mi. or mi.^{2}	640 acres	2.590 square kilometers

CAPACITY MEASUREMENTS

Unit	Abbreviation	US equivalent	Metric equivalent
Fluid Ounce	fl oz	8 fluid drams	29.573 milliliters
Cup	c	8 fluid ounces	0.237 liter
Pint	pt.	16 fluid ounces	0.473 liter
Quart	qt.	2 pints	0.946 liter
Gallon	gal.	4 quarts	3.785 liters
Teaspoon	t or tsp.	1 fluid dram	5 milliliters
Tablespoon	T or tbsp.	4 fluid drams	15 or 16 milliliters
Cubic Centimeter	cc or cm^3	0.271 drams	1 milliliter

WEIGHT MEASUREMENTS

Unit	Abbreviation	US equivalent	Metric equivalent
Ounce	oz	16 drams	28.35 grams
Pound	lb	16 ounces	453.6 grams
Ton	tn.	2,000 pounds	907.2 kilograms

VOLUME AND WEIGHT MEASUREMENT CLARIFICATIONS

Always be careful when using ounces and fluid ounces. They are not equivalent.

1 pint = 16 fluid ounces	1 fluid ounce ≠ 1 ounce
1 pound = 16 ounces	1 pint ≠ 1 pound

Having one pint of something does not mean you have one pound of it. In the same way, just because something weighs one pound does not mean that its volume is one pint.

In the United States, the word "ton" by itself refers to a short ton or a net ton. Do not confuse this with a long ton (also called a gross ton) or a metric ton (also spelled *tonne*), which have different measurement equivalents.

1 US ton = 2000 pounds ≠ 1 metric ton = 1000 kilograms

STATEMENTS

PREMISE AND ARGUMENT

A premise is a statement that precedes a conclusion, in an argument. It is the proposition, or assumption, of an argument. An argument will have two or more premises.

Example:

If it is hot, then I will go swimming. (Premise)
It is hot. (Premise)
Therefore, I will go swimming. (Conclusion)

SIMPLE AND COMPOUND STATEMENTS

A **statement** in propositional logic is any sentence or expression that has a truth value—that is, that may in principle be considered true or false. "Hello!", for example, is not a statement; there's no sense in which it could be considered true or false. On the other hand, "2 = 3" *is* a statement, albeit a clearly false one. A **compound statement** is a statement that contains one or more other statements, combined or modified in some way. A **simple statement**, or a **proposition**, is a statement that cannot be broken down further into smaller statements.

For example, consider the statement, "If it rains tomorrow, then the streets will be flooded and traffic will be slow." This is a compound statement, because two smaller statements are embedded within it: "it rains tomorrow" and "the streets will be flooded and traffic will be slow." the former cannot be broken down further, and is therefore a simple statement, but the latter is another compound statement, because it includes two simple statements: "the streets will be flooded" and "traffic will be slow."

Common operations used to combine and modify simple statements into compound statements include conjunction, disjunction, negation, and implication.

Types of Reasoning

Inductive Reasoning

Inductive reasoning is a method used to make a conjecture, based on patterns and observations. The conclusion of an inductive argument may be true or false.

Mathematical Example:

A cube has 6 faces, 8 vertices, and 12 edges. A square pyramid has 5 faces, 5 vertices, and 8 edges. A triangular prism has 5 faces, 6 vertices, and 9 edges. Thus, the sum of the numbers of faces and vertices, minus the number of edges, will always equal 2, for any solid.

Non-Mathematical Example:

Almost all summer days in Tucson are hot. It is a summer day in Tucson. Therefore, it will probably be hot.

Deductive Reasoning

Deductive reasoning is a method that proves a hypothesis or set of premises. The conclusion of a valid deductive argument will be true, given that the premises are true. Deductive reasoning utilizes logic to determine a conclusion. For instance, consider the following application of the chain rule:

If a ding is a dong, then a ping is a pong.	$p \rightarrow q$
If a ping is a pong, then a ring is a ting.	$q \rightarrow r$
A ding is a dong.	p
Therefore, a ring is a ting.	$\therefore r$

Formal Reasoning

Formal reasoning, in mathematics, involves justification using formal steps and processes to arrive at a conclusion. Formal reasoning is utilized when writing proofs and using logic. For example, when applying logic, validity of a conclusion is determined by truth tables. A set of premises will yield a given conclusion. This type of thinking is formal reasoning. Writing a geometric proof also employs formal reasoning. Example:

If a quadrilateral has four congruent sides, it is a rhombus.
If a shape is a rhombus, then the diagonals are perpendicular.
A quadrilateral has four congruent sides.
———
Therefore, the diagonals are perpendicular.

Informal Reasoning

Informal reasoning, in mathematics, uses patterns and observations to make conjectures. The conjecture may be true or false. Several, or even many, examples may show a certain pattern, shedding light on a possible conclusion. However, informal reasoning does not provide a justifiable conclusion. A conjecture may certainly be deemed as likely or probable. However, informal reasoning will not reveal a certain conclusion. Consider the following example:

Mathematical Idea – Given a sequence that starts with 1 and each term decreases by a factor of $\frac{1}{2}$, the limit of the sum of the sequence will be 2.

Informal Reasoning – The sum of 1 and $\frac{1}{2}$ is $1\frac{1}{2}$. The sum of 1, $\frac{1}{2}$, and $\frac{1}{4}$ is $1\frac{3}{4}$. The sum of 1, $\frac{1}{2}$, $\frac{1}{4}$, and $\frac{1}{8}$ is $1\frac{7}{8}$, Thus, it appears that as the sequence approaches infinity, the sum of the sequence approaches 2.

Algebra

Linear Expressions

Terms and Coefficients

Mathematical expressions consist of a combination of one or more values arranged in terms that are added together. As such, an expression could be just a single number, including zero. A **variable term** is the product of a real number, also called a **coefficient**, and one or more variables, each of which may be raised to an exponent. Expressions may also include numbers without a variable, called **constants** or **constant terms**. The expression $6s^2$, for example, is a single term where the coefficient is the real number 6 and the variable term is s^2. Note that if a term is written as simply a variable to some exponent, like t^2, then the coefficient is 1, because $t^2 = 1t^2$.

Linear Expressions

A **single variable linear expression** is the sum of a single variable term, where the variable has no exponent, and a constant, which may be zero. For instance, the expression $2w + 7$ has $2w$ as the variable term and 7 as the constant term. It is important to realize that terms are separated by addition or subtraction. Since an expression is a sum of terms, expressions such as $5x - 3$ can be written as $5x + (-3)$ to emphasize that the constant term is negative. A real-world example of a single variable linear expression is the perimeter of a square, four times the side length, often expressed: $4s$.

In general, a **linear expression** is the sum of any number of variable terms so long as none of the variables have an exponent. For example, $3m + 8n - \frac{1}{4}p + 5.5q - 1$ is a linear expression, but $3y^3$ is not. In the same way, the expression for the perimeter of a general triangle, the sum of the side lengths $(a + b + c)$ is considered to be linear, but the expression for the area of a square, the side length squared $(s^2)$is not.

Slope

On a graph with two points, (x_1, y_1) and (x_2, y_2), the **slope** is found with the formula $m = \frac{y_2 - y_1}{x_2 - x_1}$; where $x_1 \neq x_2$ and m stands for slope. If the value of the slope is **positive**, the line has an *upward direction* from left to right. If the value of the slope is **negative**, the line has a *downward direction* from left to right. Consider the following example:

A new book goes on sale in bookstores and online stores. In the first month, 5,000 copies of the book are sold. Over time, the book continues to grow in popularity. The data for the number of copies sold is in the table below.

# of Months on Sale	1	2	3	4	5
# of Copies Sold (In Thousands)	5	10	15	20	25

So, the number of copies that are sold and the time that the book is on sale is a proportional relationship. In this example, an equation can be used to show the data: $y = 5x$, where x is the number of months that the book is on sale. Also, y is the number of copies sold. So, the slope of the corresponding line is $\frac{\text{rise}}{\text{run}} = \frac{5}{1} = 5$.

Review Video: Finding the Slope of a Line
Visit mometrix.com/academy and enter code: 766664

Linear Equations

Equations that can be written as $ax + b = 0$, where $a \neq 0$, are referred to as **one variable linear equations**. A solution to such an equation is called a **root**. In the case where we have the equation $5x + 10 = 0$, if we solve for x we get a solution of $x = -2$. In other words, the root of the equation is -2. This is found by first subtracting 10 from both sides, which gives $5x = -10$. Next, simply divide both sides by the coefficient of the variable, in this case 5, to get $x = -2$. This can be checked by plugging -2 back into the original equation $(5)(-2) + 10 = -10 + 10 = 0$.

The **solution set** is the set of all solutions of an equation. In our example, the solution set would simply be -2. If there were more solutions (there usually are in multivariable equations) then they would also be included in the solution set. When an equation has no true solutions, it is referred to as an **empty set**. Equations with identical solution sets are **equivalent equations**. An **identity** is a term whose value or determinant is equal to 1.

Linear equations can be written many ways. Below is a list of some forms linear equations can take:

- **Standard Form**: $Ax + By = C$; the slope is $\frac{-A}{B}$ and the y-intercept is $\frac{C}{B}$
- **Slope Intercept Form**: $y = mx + b$, where m is the slope and b is the y-intercept
- **Point-Slope Form**: $y - y_1 = m(x - x_1)$, where m is the slope and (x_1, y_1) is a point on the line
- **Two-Point Form**: $\frac{y-y_1}{x-x_1} = \frac{y_2-y_1}{x_2-x_1}$, where (x_1, y_1) and (x_2, y_2) are two points on the given line
- **Intercept Form**: $\frac{x}{x_1} + \frac{y}{y_1} = 1$, where $(x_1, 0)$ is the point at which a line intersects the x-axis, and $(0, y_1)$ is the point at which the same line intersects the y-axis

Review Video: Slope-Intercept and Point-Slope Forms
Visit mometrix.com/academy and enter code: 113216

Review Video: Linear Equations Basics
Visit mometrix.com/academy and enter code: 793005

Solving Equations

Solving One-Variable Linear Equations

Multiply all terms by the lowest common denominator to eliminate any fractions. Look for addition or subtraction to undo so you can isolate the variable on one side of the equal sign. Divide both sides by the coefficient of the variable. When you have a value for the variable, substitute this value into the original equation to make sure you have a true equation. Consider the following example:

Kim's savings are represented by the table below. Represent her savings, using an equation.

X (Months)	Y (Total Savings)
2	$1,300
5	$2,050
9	$3,050
11	$3,550
16	$4,800

The table shows a function with a constant rate of change, or slope, of 250. Given the points on the table, the slopes can be calculated as $\frac{(2{,}050-1300)}{(5-2)}$, $\frac{(3{,}050-2{,}050)}{(9-5)}$, $\frac{(3{,}550-3{,}050)}{(11-9)}$, and $\frac{(4{,}800-3{,}550)}{(16-11)}$, each of which equals 250. Thus, the table shows a constant rate of change, indicating a linear function. The slope-intercept form of a linear equation is written as $y = mx + b$, where m represents the slope and b represents the y-intercept. Substituting the slope into this form gives $y = 250x + b$. Substituting corresponding x- and y-values from any point into this equation will give the y-intercept, or b. Using the point, $(2, 1{,}300)$, gives $1{,}300 = 250(2) + b$, which simplifies as $b = 800$. Thus, her savings may be represented by the equation, $y = 250x + 800$.

Rules for Manipulating Equations

Like Terms

Like terms are terms in an equation that have the same variable, regardless of whether or not they also have the same coefficient. This includes terms that *lack* a variable; all constants (i.e., numbers without variables) are considered like terms. If the equation involves terms with a variable raised to different powers, the like terms are those that have the variable raised to the same power.

For example, consider the equation $x^2 + 3x + 2 = 2x^2 + x - 7 + 2x$. In this equation, 2 and -7 are like terms; they are both constants. $3x$, x, and $2x$ are like terms, they all include the variable x raised to the first power. x^2 and $2x^2$ are like terms, they both include the variable x, raised to the second power. $2x$ and $2x^2$ are not like terms; although they both involve the variable x, the variable is not raised to the same power in both terms. The fact that they have the same coefficient, 2, is not relevant.

Review Video: Rules for Manipulating Equations
Visit mometrix.com/academy and enter code: 838871

Carrying Out the Same Operation on Both Sides of an Equation

When solving an equation, the general procedure is to carry out a series of operations on both sides of an equation, choosing operations that will tend to simplify the equation when doing so. The reason why the same operation must be carried out on both sides of the equation is because that leaves the meaning of the equation unchanged, and yields a result that is equivalent to the original equation. This would not be the case if we carried out an operation on one side of an equation and not the other. Consider what an equation means: it is a statement that two values or expressions are equal. If we carry out the same operation on both sides of the equation—add 3 to both sides, for example—then the two sides of the equation are changed in the same way, and so remain equal. If we do that to only one side of the equation—add 3 to one side but not the other—then that wouldn't be true; if we change one side of the equation but not the other then the two sides are no longer equal.

Advantage of Combining Like Terms

Combining like terms refers to adding or subtracting like terms—terms with the same variable—and therefore reducing sets of like terms to a single term. The main advantage of doing this is that it simplifies the equation. Often, combining like terms can be done as the first step in solving an equation, though it can also be done later, such as after distributing terms in a product.

For example, consider the equation $2(x + 3) + 3(2 + x + 3) = -4$. The 2 and the 3 in the second set of parentheses are like terms, and we can combine them, yielding $2(x + 3) + 3(x + 5) = -4$. Now we can carry out the multiplications implied by the parentheses, distributing the outer 2 and 3 accordingly: $2x + 6 + 3x + 15 = -4$. The $2x$ and the $3x$ are like terms, and we can add them together: $5x + 6 + 15 = -4$. Now, the constants 6, 15, and -4 are also like terms, and we can combine them as well: subtracting 6 and 15 from both sides of the equation, we get $5x = -4 - 6 - 15$, or $5x = -25$, which simplifies further to $x = -5$.

Review Video: Solving Equations by Combining Like Terms
Visit mometrix.com/academy and enter code: 668506

Canceling Terms on Opposite Sides of an Equation

Two terms on opposite sides of an equation can be canceled if and only if they *exactly* match each other. They must have the same variable raised to the same power and the same coefficient. For example, in the equation $3x + 2x^2 + 6 = 2x^2 - 6$, $2x^2$ appears on both sides of the equation and can be canceled, leaving $3x + 6 = -6$. The 6 on each side of the equation *cannot* be canceled, because it is added on one side of the equation and subtracted on the other. While they cannot be canceled, however, the 6 and -6 are like terms and can be combined, yielding $3x = -12$, which simplifies further to $x = -4$.

It's also important to note that the terms to be canceled must be independent terms and cannot be part of a larger term. For example, consider the equation $2(x + 6) = 3(x + 4) + 1$. We cannot cancel the x's, because even though they match each other they are part of the larger terms $2(x + 6)$ and $3(x + 4)$. We must first distribute the 2 and 3, yielding $2x + 12 = 3x + 12 + 1$. Now we see that the terms with the x's do not match, but the 12s do, and can be canceled, leaving $2x = 3x + 1$, which simplifies to $x = -1$.

Process for Manipulating Equations

Isolating Variables

To **isolate a variable** means to manipulate the equation so that the variable appears by itself on one side of the equation, and does not appear at all on the other side. Generally, an equation or inequality is considered to be solved once the variable is isolated and the other side of the equation or inequality is simplified as much as possible. In the case of a two-variable equation or inequality, only one variable needs to be isolated; it will not usually be possible to simultaneously isolate both variables.

For a linear equation—an equation in which the variable only appears raised to the first power—isolating a variable can be done by first moving all the terms with the variable to one side of the equation and all other terms to the other side. (*Moving* a term really means adding the inverse of the term to both sides; when a term is *moved* to the other side of the equation its sign is flipped.) Then combine like terms on each side. Finally, divide both sides by the coefficient of the variable, if applicable. The steps need not necessarily be done in this order, but this order will always work.

Review Video: Solving One-Step Equations
Visit mometrix.com/academy and enter code: 777004

EQUATIONS WITH MORE THAN ONE SOLUTION

Some types of non-linear equations, such as equations involving squares of variables, may have more than one solution. For example, the equation $x^2 = 4$ has two solutions: 2 and –2. Equations with absolute values can also have multiple solutions: $|x| = 1$ has the solutions $x = 1$ and $x = -1$.

It is also possible for a linear equation to have more than one solution, but only if the equation is true regardless of the value of the variable. In this case, the equation is considered to have infinitely many solutions, because any possible value of the variable is a solution. We know a linear equation has infinitely many solutions if when we combine like terms the variables cancel, leaving a true statement. For example, consider the equation $2(3x + 5) = x + 5(x + 2)$. Distributing, we get $6x + 10 = x + 5x + 10$; combining like terms gives $6x + 10 = 6x + 10$, and the $6x$-terms cancel to leave $10 = 10$. This is clearly true, so the original equation is true for any value of x. We could also have canceled the 10s leaving $0 = 0$, but again this is clearly true—in general if both sides of the equation match exactly, it has infinitely many solutions.

EQUATIONS WITH NO SOLUTION

Some types of non-linear equations, such as equations involving squares of variables, may have no solution. For example, the equation $x^2 = -2$ has no solutions in the real numbers, because the square of any real number must be positive. Similarly, $|x| = -1$ has no solution, because the absolute value of a number is always positive.

It is also possible for an equation to have no solution even if does not involve any powers greater than one, absolute values, or other special functions. For example, the equation $2(x + 3) + x = 3x$ has no solution. We can see that if we try to solve it: first we distribute, leaving $2x + 6 + x = 3x$. But now if we try to combine all the terms with the variable, we find that they cancel: we have $3x$ on the left and $3x$ on the right, canceling to leave us with $6 = 0$. This is clearly false. In general, whenever the variable terms in an equation cancel leaving different constants on both sides, it means that the equation has no solution. (If we are left with the *same* constant on both sides, the equation has infinitely many solutions instead.)

FEATURES OF EQUATIONS THAT REQUIRE SPECIAL TREATMENT

LINEAR EQUATIONS

A linear equation is an equation in which variables only appear by themselves: not multiplied together, not with exponents other than one, and not inside absolute value signs or any other functions. For example, the equation $x + 1 - 3x = 5 - x$ is a linear equation; while x appears multiple times, it never appears with an exponent other than one, or inside any function. The two-variable equation $2x - 3y = 5 + 2x$ is also a linear equation. In contrast, the equation $x^2 - 5 = 3x$ is *not* a linear equation, because it involves the term x^2. $\sqrt{x} = 5$ is not a linear equation, because it involves a square root. $(x - 1)^2 = 4$ is not a linear equation because even though there's no exponent on the x directly, it appears as part of an expression that is squared. The two-variable equation $x + xy - y = 5$ is not a linear equation because it includes the term xy, where two variables are multiplied together.

Linear equations can always be solved (or shown to have no solution) by combining like terms and performing simple operations on both sides of the equation. Some non-linear equations can be solved by similar methods, but others may require more advanced methods of solution, if they can be solved analytically at all.

SOLVING EQUATIONS INVOLVING ROOTS

In an equation involving roots, the first step is to isolate the term with the root, if possible, and then raise both sides of the equation to the appropriate power to eliminate it. Consider an example equation, $2\sqrt{x+1} - 1 = 3$. In this case, begin by adding 1 to both sides, yielding $2\sqrt{x+1} = 4$, and then dividing both sides by 2, yielding $\sqrt{x+1} = 2$. Now square both sides, yielding $x + 1 = 4$. Finally, subtracting 1 from both sides yields $x = 3$.

Squaring both sides of an equation may, however, yield a spurious solution—a solution to the squared equation that is *not* a solution of the original equation. It's therefore necessary to plug the solution back into the original equation to make sure it works. In this case, it does: $2\sqrt{3+1} - 1 = 2\sqrt{4} - 1 = 2(2) - 1 = 4 - 1 = 3$.

The same procedure applies for other roots as well. For example, given the equation $3 + \sqrt[3]{2x} = 5$, we can first subtract 3 from both sides, yielding $\sqrt[3]{2x} = 2$ and isolating the root. Raising both sides to the third power yields $2x = 2^3$; i.e., $2x = 8$. We can now divide both sides by 2 to get $x = 4$.

Review Video: Solving Equations Involving Roots Visit mometrix.com/academy and enter code: 297670

SOLVING EQUATIONS WITH EXPONENTS

To solve an equation involving an exponent, the first step is to isolate the variable with the exponent. We can then take the appropriate root of both sides to eliminate the exponent. For instance, for the equation $2x^3 + 17 = 5x^3 - 7$, we can subtract $5x^3$ from both sides to get $-3x^3 + 17 = -7$, and then subtract 17 from both sides to get $-3x^3 = -24$. Finally, we can divide both sides by –3 to get $x^3 = 8$. Finally, we can take the cube root of both sides to get $x = \sqrt[3]{8} = 2$.

One important but often overlooked point is that equations with an exponent greater than 1 may have more than one answer. The solution to $x^2 = 9$ isn't simply $x = 3$; it's $x = \pm 3$ (that is, $x = 3$ or $x = -3$). For a slightly more complicated example, consider the equation $(x-1)^2 - 1 = 3$. Adding 1 to both sides yields $(x-1)^2 = 4$; taking the square root of both sides yields $x - 1 = 2$. We can then add 1 to both sides to get $x = 3$. However, there's a second solution. We also have the possibility that $x - 1 = -2$, in which case $x = -1$. Both $x = 3$ and $x = -1$ are valid solutions, as can be verified by substituting them both into the original equation.

Review Video: Solving Equations with Exponents Visit mometrix.com/academy and enter code: 514557

SOLVING EQUATIONS WITH ABSOLUTE VALUES

When solving an equation with an absolute value, the first step is to isolate the absolute value term. We then consider two possibilities: when the expression inside the absolute value is positive or when it is negative. In the former case, the expression in the absolute value equals the expression on the other side of the equation; in the latter, it equals the additive inverse of that expression—the expression times negative one. We consider each case separately and finally check for spurious solutions.

For instance, consider solving $|2x - 1| + x = 5$ for x. We can first isolate the absolute value by moving the x to the other side: $|2x - 1| = -x + 5$. Now, we have two possibilities. First, that $2x - 1$ is positive, and hence $2x - 1 = -x + 5$. Rearranging and combining like terms yields $3x = 6$, and hence $x = 2$. The other possibility is that $2x - 1$ is negative, and hence $2x - 1 = -(-x + 5) = x - 5$. In this case, rearranging and combining like terms yields $x = -4$. Substituting $x = 2$ and $x = -4$ back into the original equation, we see that they are both valid solutions.

Note that the absolute value of a sum or difference applies to the sum or difference as a whole, not to the individual terms; in general, $|2x - 1|$ is not equal to $|2x + 1|$ or to $|2x| - 1$.

Spurious Solutions

A **spurious solution** may arise when we square both sides of an equation as a step in solving it or under certain other operations on the equation. It is a solution to the squared or otherwise modified equation that is *not* a solution of the original equation. To identify a spurious solution, it's useful when you solve an equation involving roots or absolute values to plug the solution back into the original equation to make sure it's valid.

Choosing Which Variable to Isolate in Two-Variable Equations

Similar to methods for a one-variable equation, solving a two-variable equation involves isolating a variable: manipulating the equation so that a variable appears by itself on one side of the equation, and not at all on the other side. However, in a two-variable equation, you will usually only be able to isolate one of the variables; the other variable may appear on the other side along with constant terms, or with exponents or other functions.

Often one variable will be much more easily isolated than the other, and therefore that's the variable you should choose. If one variable appears with various exponents, and the other is only raised to the first power, the latter variable is the one to isolate: given the equation $a^2 + 2b = a^3 + b + 3$, the b only appears to the first power, whereas a appears squared and cubed, so b is the variable that can be solved for: combining like terms and isolating the b on the left side of the equation, we get $b = a^3 - a^2 + 3$. If both variables are equally easy to isolate, then it's best to isolate the dependent variable, if one is defined; if the two variables are x and y, the convention is that y is the dependent variable.

Review Video: Solving Equations with Variables on Both Sides
Visit mometrix.com/academy and enter code: 402497

Cross Multiplication

Finding an Unknown in Equivalent Expressions

It is often necessary to apply information given about a rate or proportion to a new scenario. For example, if you know that Jedha can run a marathon (26.2 miles) in 3 hours, how long would it take her to run 10 miles at the same pace? Start by setting up equivalent expressions:

$$\frac{26.2 \text{ mi}}{3 \text{ hr}} = \frac{10 \text{ mi}}{x \text{ hr}}$$

Now, cross multiply and solve for x:

$$26.2x = 30$$
$$x = \frac{30}{26.2} = \frac{15}{13.1}$$
$$x \approx 1.15 \text{ hrs } or \text{ } 1 \text{ hr } 9 \text{ min}$$

So, at this pace, Jedha could run 10 miles in about 1.15 hours or about 1 hour and 9 minutes.

Review Video: Cross Multiplying Fractions
Visit mometrix.com/academy and enter code: 893904

GRAPHING EQUATIONS

GRAPHICAL SOLUTIONS TO EQUATIONS

When equations are shown graphically, they are usually shown on a **Cartesian coordinate plane**. The Cartesian coordinate plane consists of two number lines placed perpendicular to each other and intersecting at the zero point, also known as the origin. The horizontal number line is known as the x-axis, with positive values to the right of the origin, and negative values to the left of the origin. The vertical number line is known as the y-axis, with positive values above the origin, and negative values below the origin. Any point on the plane can be identified by an ordered pair in the form (x, y), called coordinates. The x-value of the coordinate is called the abscissa, and the y-value of the coordinate is called the ordinate. The two number lines divide the plane into **four quadrants**: I, II, III, and IV.

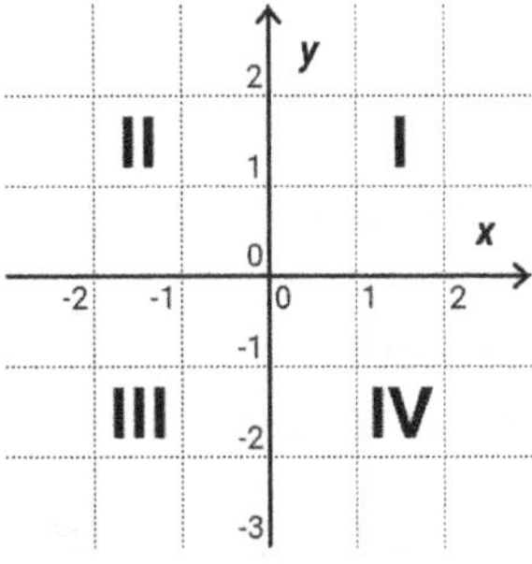

Note that in quadrant I $x > 0$ and $y > 0$, in quadrant II $x < 0$ and $y > 0$, in quadrant III $x < 0$ and $y < 0$, and in quadrant IV $x > 0$ and $y < 0$.

Recall that if the value of the slope of a line is positive, the line slopes upward from left to right. If the value of the slope is negative, the line slopes downward from left to right. If the y-coordinates are the same for two points on a line, the slope is 0 and the line is a **horizontal line**. If the x-coordinates are the same for two points on a line, there is no slope and the line is a **vertical line**. Two or more lines that have equivalent slopes are **parallel lines**. **Perpendicular lines** have slopes that are negative reciprocals of each other, such as $\frac{a}{b}$ and $\frac{-b}{a}$.

Review Video: Cartesian Coordinate Plane and Graphing
Visit mometrix.com/academy and enter code: 115173

GRAPHING EQUATIONS IN TWO VARIABLES

One way of graphing an equation in two variables is to plot enough points to get an idea for its shape and then draw the appropriate curve through those points. A point can be plotted by substituting in a value for one variable and solving for the other. If the equation is linear, we only need two points and can then draw a straight line between them.

For example, consider the equation $y = 2x - 1$. This is a linear equation—both variables only appear raised to the first power—so we only need two points. When $x = 0$, $y = 2(0) - 1 = -1$. When $x = 2$, $y = 2(2) - 1 = 3$. We can therefore choose the points $(0, -1)$ and $(2, 3)$, and draw a line between them:

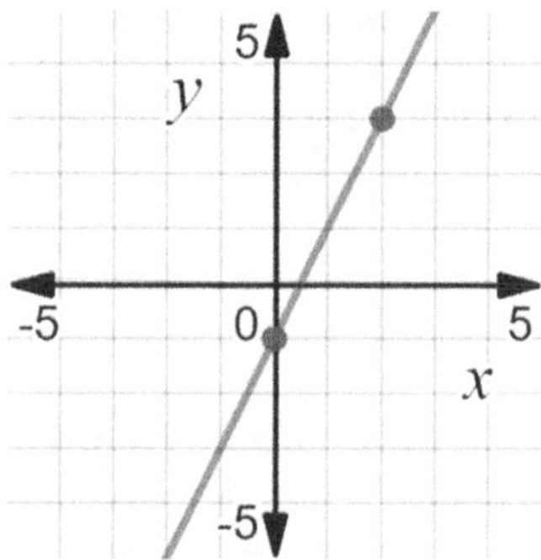

INEQUALITIES

WORKING WITH INEQUALITIES

Commonly in algebra and other upper-level fields of math you find yourself working with mathematical expressions that do not equal each other. The statement comparing such expressions with symbols such as $<$ (less than) or $>$ (greater than) is called an *inequality*. An example of an inequality is $7x > 5$. To solve for x, simply divide both sides by 7 and the solution is shown to be $x > \frac{5}{7}$. Graphs of the solution set of inequalities are represented on a number line. Open circles are used to show that an expression approaches a number but is never quite equal to that number.

Review Video: Solving Multi-Step Inequalities
Visit mometrix.com/academy and enter code: 347842

Review Video: Solving Inequalities Using All 4 Basic Operations
Visit mometrix.com/academy and enter code: 401111

Conditional inequalities are those with certain values for the variable that will make the condition true and other values for the variable where the condition will be false. **Absolute inequalities** can have any real number as the value for the variable to make the condition true, while there is no real number value for the variable that will make the condition false. Solving inequalities is done by following the same rules for solving equations with the exception that when multiplying or dividing by a negative number the direction of the inequality sign must be flipped or reversed. **Double inequalities** are situations where two inequality statements apply to the same variable expression. Example: $-c < ax + b < c$.

Review Video: Conditional and Absolute Inequalities
Visit mometrix.com/academy and enter code: 980164

DETERMINING SOLUTIONS TO INEQUALITIES

To determine whether a coordinate is a solution of an inequality, you can substitute the values of the coordinate into the inequality, simplify, and check whether the resulting statement holds true.

For instance, to determine whether $(-2,4)$ is a solution of the inequality $y \geq -2x + 3$, substitute the values into the inequality, $4 \geq -2(-2) + 3$. Simplify the right side of the inequality and the result is $4 \geq 7$, which is a false statement. Therefore, the coordinate is not a solution of the inequality. You can also use this method to determine which part of the graph of an inequality is shaded. The graph of $y \geq -2x + 3$ includes the solid line $y = -2x + 3$ and, since it excludes the point $(-2,4)$ to the left of the line, it is shaded to the right of the line.

Review Video: Graphing Linear Inequalities
Visit mometrix.com/academy and enter code: 439421

Flipping Inequality Signs

When given an inequality, we can always turn the entire inequality around, swapping the two sides of the inequality and changing the inequality sign. For instance, $x + 2 > 2x - 3$ is equivalent to $2x - 3 < x + 2$. Aside from that, normally the inequality does not change if we carry out the same operation on both sides of the inequality. There is, however, one principal exception: if we *multiply* or *divide* both sides of the inequality by a *negative number*, the inequality is flipped. For example, if we take the inequality $-2x < 6$ and divide both sides by –2, the inequality flips and we are left with $x > -3$. This *only* applies to multiplication and division, and only with negative numbers. Multiplying or dividing both sides by a positive number, or adding or subtracting any number regardless of sign, does not flip the inequality. Another special case that flips the inequality sign is when reciprocals are used. For instance, $3 > 2$ but the relation of the reciprocals is $\frac{1}{2} < \frac{1}{3}$.

Compound Inequalities

A **compound inequality** is an equality that consists of two inequalities combined with *and* or *or*. The two components of a proper compound inequality must be of opposite type: that is, one must be greater than (or greater than or equal to), the other less than (or less than or equal to). For instance, "$x + 1 < 2$ or $x + 1 > 3$" is a compound inequality, as is "$2x \geq 4$ and $2x \leq 6$." An *and* inequality can be written more compactly by having one inequality on each side of the common part: "$2x \geq 1$ and $2x \leq 6$," can also be written as $1 \leq 2x \leq 6$.

In order for the compound inequality to be meaningful, the two parts of an *and* inequality must overlap; otherwise, no numbers satisfy the inequality. On the other hand, if the two parts of an *or* inequality overlap, then *all* numbers satisfy the inequality and as such the inequality is usually not meaningful.

Solving a compound inequality requires solving each part separately. For example, given the compound inequality "$x + 1 < 2$ or $x + 1 > 3$," the first inequality, $x + 1 < 2$, reduces to $x < 1$, and the second part, $x + 1 > 3$, reduces to $x > 2$, so the whole compound inequality can be written as "$x < 1$ or $x > 2$." Similarly, $1 \leq 2x \leq 6$ can be solved by dividing each term by 2, yielding $\frac{1}{2} \leq x \leq 3$.

Review Video: Compound Inequalities
Visit mometrix.com/academy and enter code: 786318

Solving Inequalities Involving Absolute Values

To solve an inequality involving an absolute value, first isolate the term with the absolute value. Then proceed to treat the two cases separately as with an absolute value equation, but flipping the inequality in the case where the expression in the absolute value is negative (since that essentially involves multiplying both sides by –1.) The two cases are then combined into a compound inequality; if the absolute value is on the greater side of the inequality, then it is an *or* compound inequality, if on the lesser side, then it's an *and*.

Consider the inequality $2 + |x - 1| \geq 3$. We can isolate the absolute value term by subtracting 2 from both sides: $|x - 1| \geq 1$. Now, we're left with the two cases $x - 1 \geq 1$ or $x - 1 \leq -1$: note that in the latter, negative case, the inequality is flipped. $x - 1 \geq 1$ reduces to $x \geq 2$, and $x - 1 \leq -1$ reduces to $x \leq 0$. Since in the inequality $|x - 1| \geq 1$ the absolute value is on the greater side, the two cases combine into an *or* compound inequality, so the final, solved inequality is "$x \leq 0$ or $x \geq 2$."

Review Video: Solving Absolute Value Inequalities
Visit mometrix.com/academy and enter code: 997008

Solving Inequalities Involving Square Roots

Solving an inequality with a square root involves two parts. First, we solve the inequality as if it were an equation, isolating the square root and then squaring both sides of the equation. Second, we restrict the solution to the set of values of x for which the value inside the square root sign is non-negative.

For example, in the inequality, $\sqrt{x - 2} + 1 < 5$, we can isolate the square root by subtracting 1 from both sides, yielding $\sqrt{x - 2} < 4$. Squaring both sides of the inequality yields $x - 2 < 16$, so $x < 18$. Since we can't take the square root of a negative number, we also require the part inside the square root to be non-negative. In this case, that means $x - 2 \geq 0$. Adding 2 to both sides of the inequality yields $x \geq 2$. Our final answer is a compound inequality combining the two simple inequalities: $x \geq 2$ and $x < 18$, or $2 \leq x < 18$.

Note that we only get a compound inequality if the two simple inequalities are in opposite directions; otherwise, we take the one that is more restrictive.

The same technique can be used for other even roots, such as fourth roots. It is *not*, however, used for cube roots or other odd roots—negative numbers *do* have cube roots, so the condition that the quantity inside the root sign cannot be negative does not apply.

Review Video: Solving Inequalities Involving Square Roots
Visit mometrix.com/academy and enter code: 800288

Special Circumstances

Sometimes an inequality involving an absolute value or an even exponent is true for all values of x, and we don't need to do any further work to solve it. This is true if the inequality, once the absolute value or exponent term is isolated, says that term is greater than a negative number (or greater than or equal to zero). Since an absolute value or a number raised to an even exponent is *always* non-negative, this inequality is always true.

Graphical Solutions to Inequalities

Graphing Simple Inequalities

To graph a simple inequality, we first mark on the number line the value that signifies the end point of the inequality. If the inequality is strict (involves a less than or greater than), we use a hollow circle; if it is not strict (less than or equal to or greater than or equal to), we use a solid circle. We then fill in the part of the number line that satisfies the inequality: to the left of the marked point for less than (or less than or equal to), to the right for greater than (or greater than or equal to).

For example, we would graph the inequality $x < 5$ by putting a hollow circle at 5 and filling in the part of the line to the left:

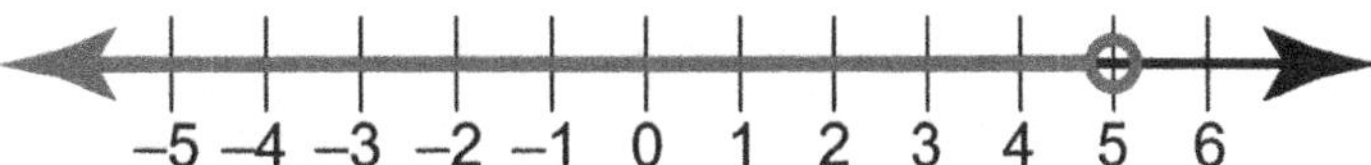

Graphing Compound Inequalities

To graph a compound inequality, we fill in both parts of the inequality for an *or* inequality, or the overlap between them for an *and* inequality. More specifically, we start by plotting the endpoints of each inequality on the number line. For an *or* inequality, we then fill in the appropriate side of the line for each inequality. Typically, the two component inequalities do not overlap, which means the shaded part is *outside* the two points. For an *and* inequality, we instead fill in the part of the line that meets both inequalities.

For the inequality "$x \leq -3$ or $x > 4$," we first put a solid circle at –3 and a hollow circle at 4. We then fill the parts of the line *outside* these circles:

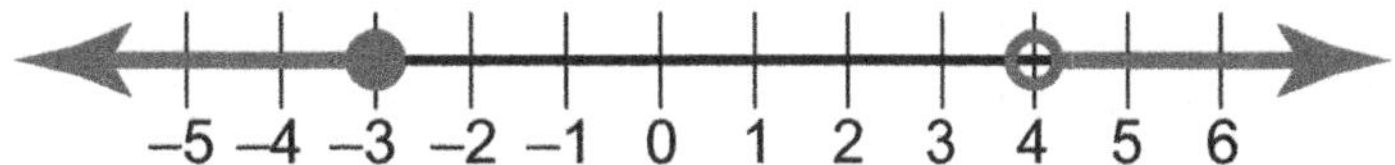

Graphing Inequalities Including Absolute Values

An inequality with an absolute value can be converted to a compound inequality. To graph the inequality, first convert it to a compound inequality, and then graph that normally. If the absolute value is on the greater side of the inequality, we end up with an *or* inequality; we plot the endpoints of the inequality on the number line and fill in the part of the line *outside* those points. If the absolute value is on the smaller side of the inequality, we end up with an *and* inequality; we plot the endpoints of the inequality on the number line and fill in the part of the line *between* those points.

For example, the inequality $|x + 1| \geq 4$ can be rewritten as $x \geq 3$ or $x \leq -5$. We place solid circles at the points 3 and –5 and fill in the part of the line *outside* them:

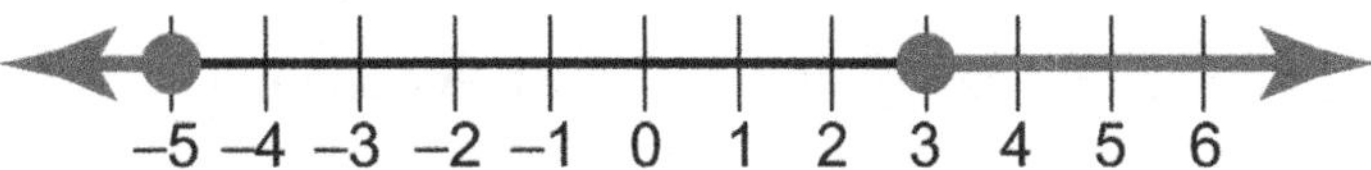

Graphing Inequalities in Two Variables

To graph an inequality in two variables, we first graph the border of the inequality. This means graphing the equation that we get if we replace the inequality sign with an equals sign. If the inequality is strict ($>$ or $<$), we graph the border with a dashed or dotted line; if it is not strict ($\geq$ or $\leq$), we use a solid line. We can then test any point not on the border to see if it satisfies the inequality. If it does, we shade in that side of the border; if not, we shade in the other side. As an example, consider $y > 2x + 2$. To graph this inequality, we first graph the border, $y = 2x + 2$. Since it is a strict inequality, we use a dashed line. Then, we choose a test point. This can be any point not on the border; in this case, we will choose the origin, (0,0). (This makes the calculation easy and is generally a good choice unless the border passes through the origin.) Putting this into the original inequality, we get $0 > 2(0) + 2$, i.e., $0 > 2$. This is *not* true, so we shade in the side of the border that does *not* include the point (0,0):

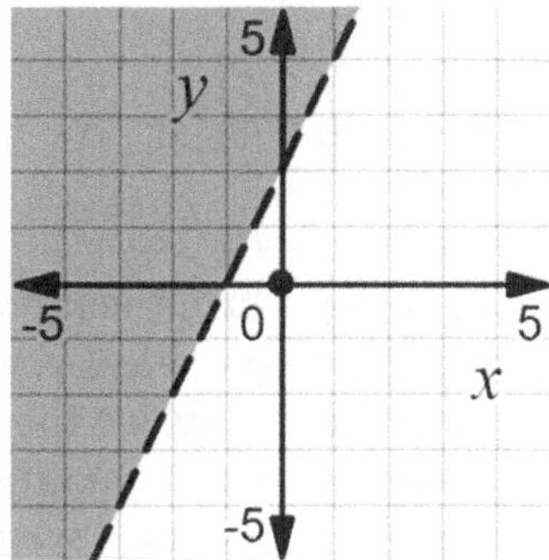

Graphing Compound Inequalities in Two Variables

One way to graph a compound inequality in two variables is to first graph each of the component inequalities. For an *and* inequality, we then shade in only the parts where the two graphs overlap; for an *or* inequality, we shade in any region that pertains to either of the individual inequalities.

Consider the graph of "$y \geq x - 1$ and $y \leq -x$":

We first shade in the individual inequalities:

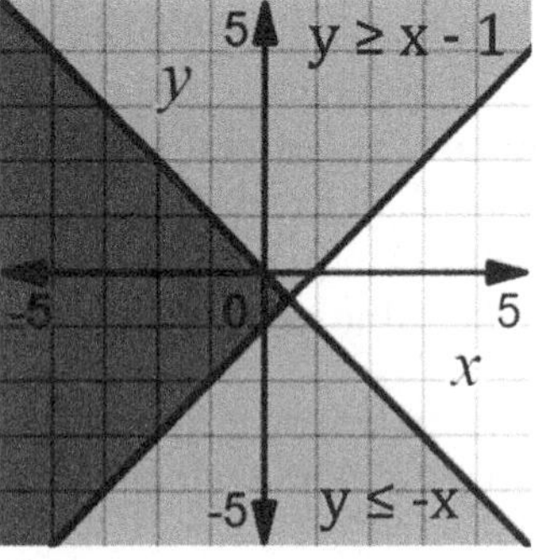

Now, since the compound inequality has an *and*, we only leave shaded the overlap—the part that pertains to *both* inequalities:

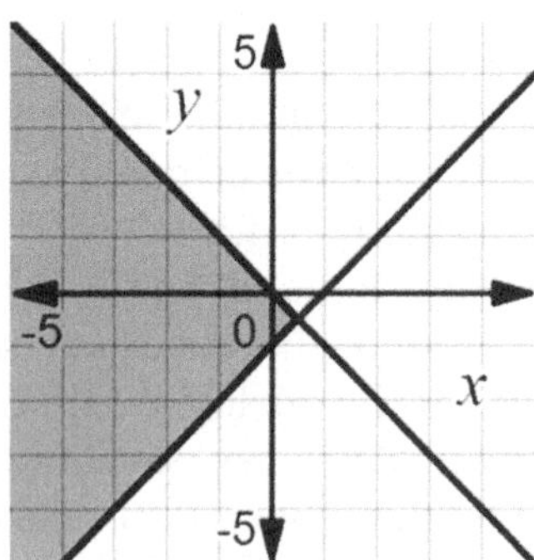

If instead the inequality had been "$y \geq x - 1$ or $y \leq -x$," our final graph would involve the *total* shaded area:

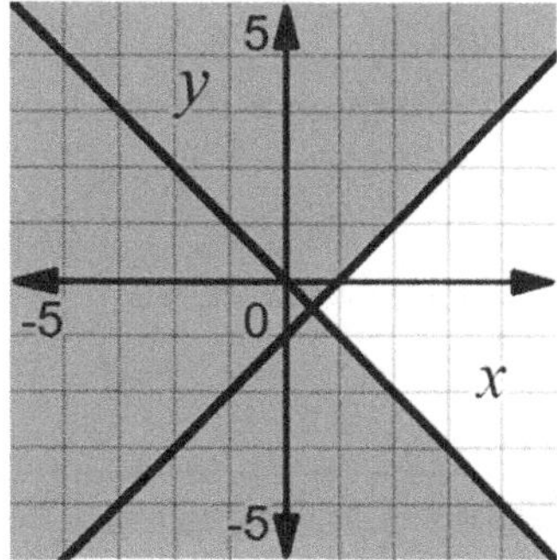

Review Video: Graphing Solutions to Inequalities
Visit mometrix.com/academy and enter code: 391281

Systems of Equations

Solving Systems of Equations

A **system of equations** is a set of simultaneous equations that all use the same variables. A solution to a system of equations must be true for each equation in the system. **Consistent systems** are those with at least one solution. **Inconsistent systems** are systems of equations that have no solution.

Review Video: Solving Systems of Linear Equations
Visit mometrix.com/academy and enter code: 746745

Substitution

To solve a system of linear equations by **substitution**, start with the easier equation and solve for one of the variables. Express this variable in terms of the other variable. Substitute this expression in the other equation and solve for the other variable. The solution should be expressed in the form (x, y). Substitute the values into both of the original equations to check your answer. Consider the following system of equations:

$$x + 6y = 15$$
$$3x - 12y = 18$$

Solving the first equation for x: $x = 15 - 6y$

Substitute this value in place of x in the second equation, and solve for y:

$$3(15 - 6y) - 12y = 18$$
$$45 - 18y - 12y = 18$$
$$30y = 27$$
$$y = \frac{27}{30} = \frac{9}{10} = 0.9$$

Plug this value for y back into the first equation to solve for x:

$$x = 15 - 6(0.9) = 15 - 5.4 = 9.6$$

Check both equations if you have time:

$$\begin{aligned} 9.6 + 6(0.9) &= 15 \\ 9.6 + 5.4 &= 15 \\ 15 &= 15 \end{aligned} \qquad \begin{aligned} 3(9.6) - 12(0.9) &= 18 \\ 28.8 - 10.8 &= 18 \\ 18 &= 18 \end{aligned}$$

Therefore, the solution is (9.6,0.9).

Review Video: The Substitution Method
Visit mometrix.com/academy and enter code: 565151

Review Video: Substitution and Elimination
Visit mometrix.com/academy and enter code: 958611

Elimination

To solve a system of equations using **elimination**, begin by rewriting both equations in standard form $Ax + By = C$. Check to see if the coefficients of one pair of like variables add to zero. If not, multiply one or both of the equations by a non-zero number to make one set of like variables add to zero. Add the two equations to solve for one of the variables. Substitute this value into one of the original equations to solve for the other variable. Check your work by substituting into the other equation. Now, let's look at solving the following system using the elimination method:

$$\begin{aligned} 5x + 6y &= 4 \\ x + 2y &= 4 \end{aligned}$$

If we multiply the second equation by -3, we can eliminate the y-terms:

$$\begin{aligned} 5x + 6y &= 4 \\ -3x - 6y &= -12 \end{aligned}$$

Add the equations together and solve for x:

$$\begin{aligned} 2x &= -8 \\ x &= \frac{-8}{2} = -4 \end{aligned}$$

Plug the value for x back in to either of the original equations and solve for y:

$$\begin{aligned} -4 + 2y &= 4 \\ y &= \frac{4+4}{2} = 4 \end{aligned}$$

Check both equations if you have time:

$$\begin{aligned} 5(-4) + 6(4) &= 4 \\ -20 + 24 &= 4 \\ 4 &= 4 \end{aligned} \qquad \begin{aligned} -4 + 2(4) &= 4 \\ -4 + 8 &= 4 \\ 4 &= 4 \end{aligned}$$

Therefore, the solution is $(-4,4)$.

Review Video: The Elimination Method
Visit mometrix.com/academy and enter code: 449121

GRAPHICALLY

To solve a system of linear equations **graphically**, plot both equations on the same graph. The solution of the equations is the point where both lines cross. If the lines do not cross (are parallel), then there is **no solution**.

For example, consider the following system of equations:

$$y = 2x + 7$$
$$y = -x + 1$$

Since these equations are given in slope-intercept form, they are easy to graph; the y-intercepts of the lines are (0,7) and (0,1). The respective slopes are 2 and –1, thus the graphs look like this:

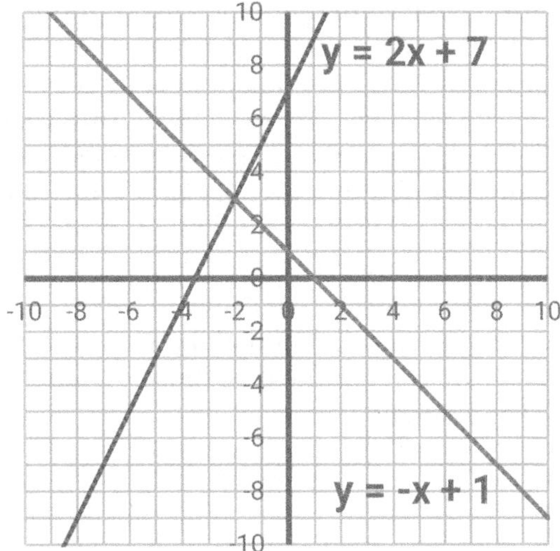

The two lines intersect at the point $(-2,3)$, thus this is the solution to the system of equations.

Solving a system graphically is generally only practical if both coordinates of the solution are integers; otherwise the intersection will lie between gridlines on the graph and the coordinates will be difficult or impossible to determine exactly. It also helps if, as in this example, the equations are in slope-intercept form or some other form that makes them easy to graph. Otherwise, another method of solution (by substitution or elimination) is likely to be more useful.

Review Video: Solving Systems by Graphing
Visit mometrix.com/academy and enter code: 634812

SOLVING SYSTEMS OF EQUATIONS USING THE TRACE FEATURE

Using the trace feature on a calculator requires that you rewrite each equation, isolating the y-variable on one side of the equal sign. Enter both equations in the graphing calculator and plot the graphs simultaneously. Use the trace cursor to find where the two lines cross. Use the zoom feature if necessary to obtain more accurate results. Always check your answer by substituting into the original equations. The trace method is likely to be less accurate than other methods due to the resolution of graphing calculators but is a useful tool to provide an approximate answer.

POLYNOMIALS

MONOMIALS AND POLYNOMIALS

A **monomial** is a single constant, variable, or product of constants and variables, such as 7, x, $2x$, or x^3y. There will never be addition or subtraction symbols in a monomial. Like monomials have like variables, but they may have different coefficients. **Polynomials** are algebraic expressions that use addition and subtraction to combine two or more monomials. Two terms make a **binomial**, three terms make a **trinomial**, etc. The **degree of a monomial** is the sum of the exponents of the variables. The **degree of a polynomial** is the highest degree of any individual term.

Review Video: Polynomials
Visit mometrix.com/academy and enter code: 305005

SIMPLIFYING POLYNOMIALS

Simplifying polynomials requires combining like terms. The like terms in a polynomial expression are those that have the same variable raised to the same power. It is often helpful to connect the like terms with arrows or lines in order to separate them from the other monomials. Once you have determined the like terms, you can rearrange the polynomial by placing them together. Remember to include the sign that is in front of each term. Once the like terms are placed together, you can apply each operation and simplify. When adding and subtracting polynomials, only add and subtract the **coefficient**, or the number part; the variable and exponent stay the same.

ADD POLYNOMIALS

To add polynomials, you need to add like terms. These terms have the same variable part. An example is $4x^2$ and $3x^2$ have x^2 terms. To find the sum of like terms, find the sum of the coefficients. Then, keep the same variable part. You can use the distributive property to distribute the plus sign to each term of the polynomial. For example:

$$(4x^2 - 5x + 7) + (3x^2 + 2x + 1) =$$
$$(4x^2 - 5x + 7) + 3x^2 + 2x + 1 =$$
$$(4x^2 + 3x^2) + (-5x + 2x) + (7 + 1) =$$
$$7x^2 - 3x + 8$$

SUBTRACT POLYNOMIALS

To subtract polynomials, you need to subtract like terms. To find the difference of like terms, find the difference of the coefficients. Then, keep the same variable part. You can use the distributive property to distribute the minus sign to each term of the polynomial. For example:

$$(-2x^2 - x + 5) - (3x^2 - 4x + 1) =$$
$$(-2x^2 - x + 5) - 3x^2 + 4x - 1 =$$
$$(-2x^2 - 3x^2) + (-x + 4x) + (5 - 1) =$$
$$-5x^2 + 3x + 4$$

Review Video: Adding and Subtracting Polynomials
Visit mometrix.com/academy and enter code: 124088

MULTIPLYING POLYNOMIALS

In general, multiplying polynomials is done by multiplying each term in one polynomial by each term in the other and adding the results. In the specific case for multiplying binomials, there is a useful acronym, FOIL, that can help you make sure to cover each combination of terms. The **FOIL method** for $(Ax + By)(Cx + Dy)$ would be:

F	Multiply the *first* terms of each binomial	$(\overbrace{Ax}^{first} + By)(\overbrace{Cx}^{first} + Dy)$	ACx^2
O	Multiply the *outer* terms	$(\overbrace{Ax}^{outer} + By)(Cx + \overbrace{Dy}^{outer})$	$ADxy$
I	Multiply the *inner* terms	$(Ax + \overbrace{By}^{inner})(\overbrace{Cx}^{inner} + Dy)$	$BCxy$
L	Multiply the *last* terms of each binomial	$(Ax + \overbrace{By}^{last})(Cx + \overbrace{Dy}^{last})$	BDy^2

Then, add up the result of each and combine like terms: $ACx^2 + (AD + BC)xy + BDy^2$.

For example, using the FOIL method on binomials $(x + 2)$ and $(x - 3)$:

$$\begin{aligned}
\text{First:} \quad & (\boxed{x} + 2)(\boxed{x} + (-3)) \rightarrow (x)(x) = x^2 \\
\text{Outer:} \quad & (\boxed{x} + 2)(x + \boxed{(-3)}) \rightarrow (x)(-3) = -3x \\
\text{Inner:} \quad & (x + \boxed{2})(\boxed{x} + (-3)) \rightarrow (2)(x) = 2x \\
\text{Last:} \quad & (x + \boxed{2})(x + \boxed{(-3)}) \rightarrow (2)(-3) = -6
\end{aligned}$$

This results in: $(x^2) + (-3x) + (2x) + (-6)$

Combine like terms: $x^2 + (-3 + 2)x + (-6) = x^2 - x - 6$

Review Video: Multiplying Terms Using the FOIL Method
Visit mometrix.com/academy and enter code: 854792

DIVIDING POLYNOMIALS

Use long division to divide a polynomial by either a monomial or another polynomial of equal or lesser degree.

When **dividing by a monomial**, divide each term of the polynomial by the monomial.

When **dividing by a polynomial**, begin by arranging the terms of each polynomial in order of one variable. You may arrange in ascending or descending order, but be consistent with both polynomials. To get the first term of the quotient, divide the first term of the dividend by the first term of the divisor. Multiply the first term of the quotient by the entire divisor and subtract that product from the dividend. Repeat for the second and successive terms until you either get a remainder of zero or a remainder whose degree is less than the degree of the divisor. If the quotient has a remainder, write the answer as a mixed expression in the form:

$$\text{quotient} + \frac{\text{remainder}}{\text{divisor}}$$

For example, we can evaluate the following expression in the same way as long division:

$$\frac{x^3 - 3x^2 - 2x + 5}{x - 5}$$

$$\begin{array}{r|l} & x^2 \quad + 2x \quad + 8 \\ \hline x - 5 & x^3 - 3x^2 \quad - 2x \quad + 5 \\ & -(x^3 - 5x^2) \\ & \qquad 2x^2 \quad - 2x \\ & \qquad -(2x^2 - 10x) \\ & \qquad\qquad 8x \quad + 5 \\ & \qquad\qquad -(8x - 40) \\ & \qquad\qquad\qquad 45 \end{array}$$

$$\frac{x^3 - 3x^2 - 2x + 5}{x - 5} = x^2 + 2x + 8 + \frac{45}{x - 5}$$

When **factoring** a polynomial, first check for a common monomial factor, that is, look to see if each coefficient has a common factor or if each term has an x in it. If the factor is a trinomial but not a perfect trinomial square, look for a factorable form, such as one of these:

$$x^2 + (a + b)x + ab = (x + a)(x + b)$$
$$(ac)x^2 + (ad + bc)x + bd = (ax + b)(cx + d)$$

For factors with four terms, look for groups to factor. Once you have found the factors, write the original polynomial as the product of all the factors. Make sure all of the polynomial factors are prime. Monomial factors may be *prime* or *composite*. Check your work by multiplying the factors to make sure you get the original polynomial.

Below are patterns of some special products to remember to help make factoring easier:

- Perfect trinomial squares: $x^2 + 2xy + y^2 = (x + y)^2$ or $x^2 - 2xy + y^2 = (x - y)^2$
- Difference between two squares: $x^2 - y^2 = (x + y)(x - y)$
- Sum of two cubes: $x^3 + y^3 = (x + y)(x^2 - xy + y^2)$
    - Note: the second factor is *not* the same as a perfect trinomial square, so do not try to factor it further.
- Difference between two cubes: $x^3 - y^3 = (x - y)(x^2 + xy + y^2)$
    - Again, the second factor is *not* the same as a perfect trinomial square.
- Perfect cubes: $x^3 + 3x^2y + 3xy^2 + y^3 = (x + y)^3$ and $x^3 - 3x^2y + 3xy^2 - y^3 = (x - y)^3$

Rational Expressions

Rational expressions are fractions with polynomials in both the numerator and the denominator; the value of the polynomial in the denominator cannot be equal to zero. Be sure to keep track of values that make the denominator of the original expression zero as the final result inherits the same restrictions. For example, a denominator of $x - 3$ indicates that the expression is not defined when $x = 3$ and, as such, regardless of any operations done to the expression, it remains undefined there.

To **add or subtract** rational expressions, first find the common denominator, then rewrite each fraction as an equivalent fraction with the common denominator. Finally, add or subtract the numerators to get the numerator of the answer, and keep the common denominator as the denominator of the answer.

When **multiplying** rational expressions, factor each polynomial and cancel like factors (a factor which appears in both the numerator and the denominator). Then, multiply all remaining factors in the numerator to get the numerator of the product, and multiply the remaining factors in the denominator to get the denominator of the product. Remember: cancel entire factors, not individual terms.

To **divide** rational expressions, take the reciprocal of the divisor (the rational expression you are dividing by) and multiply by the dividend.

Review Video: Rational Expressions
Visit mometrix.com/academy and enter code: 415183

Simplifying Rational Expressions

To simplify a rational expression, factor the numerator and denominator completely. Factors that are the same and appear in the numerator and denominator have a ratio of 1. For example, look at the following expression:

$$\frac{x-1}{1-x^2}$$

The denominator, $(1-x^2)$, is a difference of squares. It can be factored as $(1-x)(1+x)$. The factor $1-x$ and the numerator $x-1$ are opposites and have a ratio of -1. Rewrite the numerator as $-1(1-x)$. So, the rational expression can be simplified as follows:

$$\frac{x-1}{1-x^2}=\frac{-1(1-x)}{(1-x)(1+x)}=\frac{-1}{1+x}$$

Note that since the original expression is only defined for $x \neq \{-1,1\}$, the simplified expression has the same restrictions.

Review Video: Reducing Rational Expressions
Visit mometrix.com/academy and enter code: 788868

Quadratics

Solving Quadratic Equations

Quadratic equations are a special set of trinomials of the form $y = ax^2 + bx + c$ that occur commonly in math and real-world applications. The **roots** of a quadratic equation are the solutions that satisfy the equation when $y = 0$; in other words, where the graph touches the x-axis. There are several ways to determine these solutions including using the quadratic formula, factoring, completing the square, and graphing the function.

Review Video: Quadratic Equations Overview
Visit mometrix.com/academy and enter code: 476276

Review Video: Solutions of a Quadratic Equation on a Graph
Visit mometrix.com/academy and enter code: 328231

Quadratic Formula

The **quadratic formula** is used to solve quadratic equations when other methods are more difficult. To use the quadratic formula to solve a quadratic equation, begin by rewriting the equation in standard form $ax^2 + bx + c = 0$, where a, b, and c are coefficients. Once you have identified the values of the coefficients, substitute those values into the quadratic formula

$$x = \frac{-b \pm \sqrt{b^2 - 4ac}}{2a}$$

Evaluate the equation and simplify the expression. Again, check each root by substituting into the original equation. In the quadratic formula, the portion of the formula under the radical $(b^2 - 4ac)$ is called the **discriminant**. If the discriminant is zero, there is only one root: $-\frac{b}{2a}$. If the discriminant is positive, there are two different real roots. If the discriminant is negative, there are no real roots; you will instead find complex roots. Often these solutions don't make sense in context and are ignored.

Review Video: Using the Quadratic Formula
Visit mometrix.com/academy and enter code: 163102

Factoring

To solve a quadratic equation by factoring, begin by rewriting the equation in standard form, $x^2 + bx + c = 0$. Remember that the goal of factoring is to find numbers f and g such that $(x + f)(x + g) = x^2 + (f + g)x + fg$, in other words $(f + g) = b$ and $fg = c$. This can be a really useful method when b and c are integers. Determine the factors of c and look for pairs that could sum to b.

For example, consider finding the roots of $x^2 + 6x - 16 = 0$. The factors of -16 include, -4 and 4, -8 and 2, -2 and 8, -1 and 16, and 1 and -16. The factors that sum to 6 are -2 and 8. Write these factors as the product of two binomials, $0 = (x - 2)(x + 8)$. Finally, since these binomials multiply together to equal zero, set them each equal to zero and solve each for x. This results in $x - 2 = 0$, which simplifies to $x = 2$ and $x + 8 = 0$, which simplifies to $x = -8$. Therefore, the roots of the equation are 2 and -8.

Review Video: Factoring Quadratic Equations
Visit mometrix.com/academy and enter code: 336566

Completing the Square

One way to find the roots of a quadratic equation is to find a way to manipulate it such that it follows the form of a perfect square $(x^2 + 2px + p^2)$ by adding and subtracting a constant. This process is called **completing the square**. In other words, if you are given a quadratic that is not a perfect square, $x^2 + bx + c = 0$, you can find a constant d that could be added in to make it a perfect square:

$$x^2 + bx + c + (d - d) = 0; \ \{\text{Let } b = 2p \text{ and } c + d = p^2\}$$

then:

$$x^2 + 2px + p^2 - d = 0 \text{ and } d = \frac{b^2}{4} - c$$

Once you have completed the square you can find the roots of the resulting equation:

$$\begin{aligned} x^2 + 2px + p^2 - d &= 0 \\ (x + p)^2 &= d \\ x + p &= \pm\sqrt{d} \\ x &= -p \pm \sqrt{d} \end{aligned}$$

It is worth noting that substituting the original expressions into this solution gives the same result as the quadratic formula where $a = 1$:

$$x = -p \pm \sqrt{d} = -\frac{b}{2} \pm \sqrt{\frac{b^2}{4} - c} = -\frac{b}{2} \pm \frac{\sqrt{b^2 - 4c}}{2} = \frac{-b \pm \sqrt{b^2 - 4c}}{2}$$

Completing the square can be seen as arranging block representations of each of the terms to be as close to a square as possible and then filling in the gaps. For example, consider the quadratic expression $x^2 + 6x + 2$:

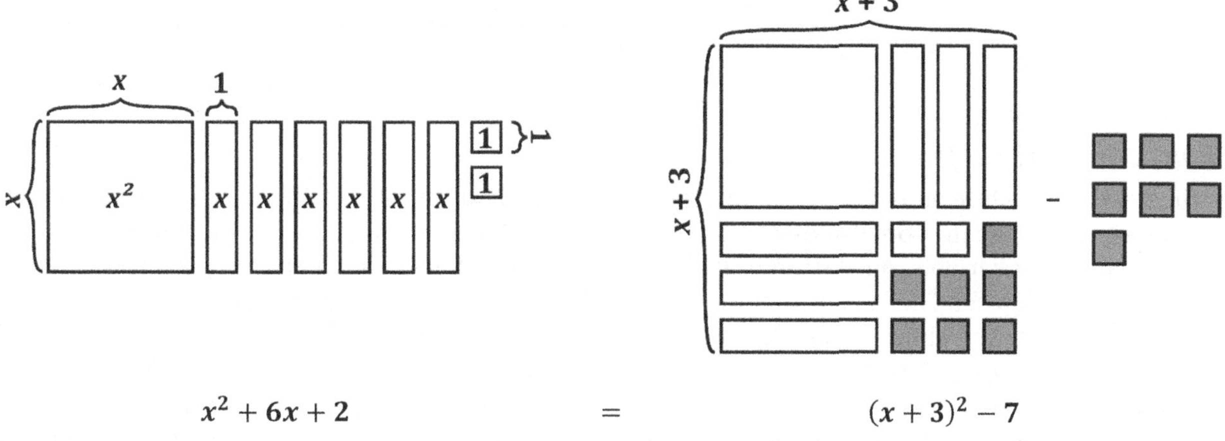

Review Video: Completing the Square
Visit mometrix.com/academy and enter code: 982479

Using Given Roots to Find Quadratic Equation

One way to find the roots of a quadratic equation is to factor the equation and use the **zero product property**, setting each factor of the equation equal to zero to find the corresponding root. We can use this technique in reverse to find an equation given its roots. Each root corresponds to a linear equation which in turn corresponds to a factor of the quadratic equation.

For example, we can find a quadratic equation whose roots are $x = 2$ and $x = -1$. The root $x = 2$ corresponds to the equation $x - 2 = 0$, and the root $x = -1$ corresponds to the equation $x + 1 = 0$.

These two equations correspond to the factors $(x - 2)$ and $(x + 1)$, from which we can derive the equation $(x - 2)(x + 1) = 0$, or $x^2 - x - 2 = 0$.

Any integer multiple of this entire equation will also yield the same roots, as the integer will simply cancel out when the equation is factored. For example, $2x^2 - 2x - 4 = 0$ factors as $2(x - 2)(x + 1) = 0$.

Parabolas

A **parabola** is the set of all points in a plane that are equidistant from a fixed line, called the **directrix**, and a fixed point not on the line, called the **focus**. The **axis** is the line perpendicular to the directrix that passes through the focus.

For parabolas that open up or down, the standard equation is $(x - h)^2 = 4c(y - k)$, where h, c, and k are coefficients. If c is positive, the parabola opens up. If c is negative, the parabola opens down. The vertex is the point (h, k). The directrix is the line having the equation $y = -c + k$, and the focus is the point $(h, c + k)$.

For parabolas that open left or right, the standard equation is $(y - k)^2 = 4c(x - h)$, where k, c, and h are coefficients. If c is positive, the parabola opens to the right. If c is negative, the parabola opens to the left. The vertex is the point (h, k). The directrix is the line having the equation $x = -c + h$, and the focus is the point $(c + h, k)$.

Review Video: Parabolas
Visit mometrix.com/academy and enter code: 129187

Review Video: Vertex of a Parabola
Visit mometrix.com/academy and enter code: 272300

Basic Functions

Function and Relation

When expressing functional relationships, the **variables** x and y are typically used. These values are often written as the **coordinates** (x, y). The x-value is the independent variable and the y-value is the dependent variable. A **relation** is a set of data in which there is not a unique y-value for each x-value in the dataset. This means that there can be two of the same x-values assigned to different y-values. A relation is simply a relationship between the x- and y-values in each coordinate but does not apply to the relationship between the values of x and y in the data set. A **function** is a relation where one quantity depends on the other. For example, the amount of money that you make depends on the number of hours that you work. In a function, each x-value in the data set has one unique y-value because the y-value depends on the x-value.

Functions

A function has exactly one value of **output variable** (dependent variable) for each value of the **input variable** (independent variable). The set of all values for the input variable (here assumed to be x) is the domain of the function, and the set of all corresponding values of the output variable (here assumed to be y) is the range of the function. When looking at a graph of an equation, the easiest way to determine if the equation is a function or not is to conduct the vertical line test. If a vertical line drawn through any value of x crosses the graph in more than one place, the equation is not a function.

Determining a Function

You can determine whether an equation is a **function** by substituting different values into the equation for x. You can display and organize these numbers in a data table. A **data table** contains the values for x and y, which you can also list as coordinates. In order for a function to exist, the table cannot contain any repeating x-values that correspond with different y-values. If each x-coordinate has a unique y-coordinate, the table contains a function. However, there can be repeating y-values that correspond with different x-values. An example of this is when the function contains an exponent. Example: if $x^2 = y$, $2^2 = 4$, and $(-2)^2 = 4$.

Review Video: Definition of a Function
Visit mometrix.com/academy and enter code: 784611

Finding the Domain and Range of a Function

The **domain** of a function $f(x)$ is the set of all input values for which the function is defined. The **range** of a function $f(x)$ is the set of all possible output values of the function—that is, of every possible value of $f(x)$, for any value of x in the function's domain. For a function expressed in a table, every input-output pair is given explicitly. To find the domain, we just list all the x-values and to find the range, we just list all the values of $f(x)$. Consider the following example:

x	-1	4	2	1	0	3	8	6
$f(x)$	3	0	3	-1	-1	2	4	6

In this case, the domain would be $\{-1, 4, 2, 1, 0, 3, 8, 6\}$ or, putting them in ascending order, $\{-1, 0, 1, 2, 3, 4, 6, 8\}$. (Putting the values in ascending order isn't strictly necessary, but generally makes the set easier to read.) The range would be $\{3, 0, 3, -1, -1, 2, 4, 6\}$. Note that some of these values appear more than once. This is entirely permissible for a function; while each value of x must be matched to a unique value of $f(x)$, the converse is not true. We don't need to list each value more than once, so eliminating duplicates, the range is $\{3, 0, -1, 2, 4, 6\}$, or, putting them in ascending order, $\{-1, 0, 2, 3, 4, 6\}$.

Note that by definition of a function, no input value can be matched to more than one output value. It is good to double-check to make sure that the data given follows this and is therefore actually a function.

Review Video: Domain and Range
Visit mometrix.com/academy and enter code: 778133

Review Video: Domain and Range of Quadratic Functions
Visit mometrix.com/academy and enter code: 331768

Writing a Function Rule Using a Table

If given a set of data, place the corresponding x- and y-values into a table and analyze the relationship between them. Consider what you can do to each x-value to obtain the corresponding y-value. Try adding or subtracting different numbers to and from x and then try multiplying or dividing different numbers to and from x. If none of these **operations** give you the y-value, try combining the operations. Once you find a rule that works for one pair, make sure to try it with each additional set of ordered pairs in the table. If the same operation or combination of operations satisfies each set of coordinates, then the table contains a function. The rule is then used to write the equation of the function in "$y = f(x)$" form.

Direct and Inverse Variations of Variables

Variables that vary directly are those that either both increase at the same rate or both decrease at the same rate. For example, in the functions $y = kx$ or $y = kx^n$, where k and n are positive, the value of y increases as the value of x increases and decreases as the value of x decreases.

Variables that vary inversely are those where one increases while the other decreases. For example, in the functions $y = \frac{k}{x}$ or $y = \frac{k}{x^n}$ where k and n are positive, the value of y increases as the value of x decreases and decreases as the value of x increases.

In both cases, k is the constant of variation.

Properties of Functions

There are many different ways to classify functions based on their structure or behavior. Important features of functions include:

- **End behavior**: the behavior of the function at extreme values ($f(x)$ as $x \to \pm\infty$)
- **y-intercept**: the value of the function at $f(0)$
- **Roots**: the values of x where the function equals zero ($f(x) = 0$)
- **Extrema**: minimum or maximum values of the function or where the function changes direction ($f(x) \geq k$ or $f(x) \leq k$)

Classification of Functions

An **invertible function** is defined as a function, $f(x)$, for which there is another function, $f^{-1}(x)$, such that $f^{-1}(f(x)) = x$. For example, if $f(x) = 3x - 2$ the inverse function, $f^{-1}(x)$, can be found:

$$x = 3(f^{-1}(x)) - 2$$

$$\frac{x+2}{3} = f^{-1}(x)$$

$$f^{-1}(f(x)) = \frac{3x - 2 + 2}{3}$$

$$= \frac{3x}{3}$$

$$= x$$

Note that $f^{-1}(x)$ is a valid function over all values of x.

In a **one-to-one function**, each value of x has exactly one value for y on the coordinate plane (this is the definition of a function) and each value of y has exactly one value for x. While the vertical line test will determine if a graph is that of a function, the horizontal line test will determine if a function is a one-to-one function. If a horizontal line drawn at any value of y intersects the graph in more than one place, the graph is not that of a one-to-one function. Do not make the mistake of using the horizontal line test exclusively in determining if a graph is that of a one-to-one function. A one-to-one function must pass both the vertical line test and the horizontal line test. As such, one-to-one functions are invertible functions.

A **many-to-one function** is a function whereby the relation is a function, but the inverse of the function is not a function. In other words, each element in the domain is mapped to one and only one element in the range. However, one or more elements in the range may be mapped to the same element in the domain. A graph of a many-to-one function would pass the vertical line test, but not the horizontal line test. This is why many-to-one functions are not invertible.

A **monotone function** is a function whose graph either constantly increases or constantly decreases. Examples include the functions $f(x) = x$, $f(x) = -x$, or $f(x) = x^3$.

An **even function** has a graph that is symmetric with respect to the y-axis and satisfies the equation $f(x) = f(-x)$. Examples include the functions $f(x) = x^2$ and $f(x) = ax^n$, where a is any real number and n is a positive even integer.

An **odd function** has a graph that is symmetric with respect to the origin and satisfies the equation $f(x) = -f(-x)$. Examples include the functions $f(x) = x^3$ and $f(x) = ax^n$, where a is any real number and n is a positive odd integer.

Review Video: Even and Odd Functions
Visit mometrix.com/academy and enter code: 278985

Constant functions are given by the equation $f(x) = b$, where b is a real number. There is no independent variable present in the equation, so the function has a constant value for all x. The graph of a constant function is a horizontal line of slope 0 that is positioned b units from the x-axis. If b is positive, the line is above the x-axis; if b is negative, the line is below the x-axis.

Identity functions are identified by the equation $f(x) = x$, where every value of the function is equal to its corresponding value of x. The only zero is the point (0,0). The graph is a line with a slope of 1.

In **linear functions**, the value of the function changes in direct proportion to x. The rate of change, represented by the slope on its graph, is constant throughout. The standard form of a linear equation is $ax + cy = d$, where a, c, and d are real numbers. As a function, this equation is commonly in the form $y = mx + b$ or $f(x) = mx + b$ where $m = -\frac{a}{c}$ and $b = \frac{d}{c}$. This is known as the slope-intercept form, because the coefficients give the slope of the graphed function (m) and its y-intercept (b). Solve the equation $mx + b = 0$ for x to get $x = -\frac{b}{m}$, which is the only zero of the function. The domain and range are both the set of all real numbers.

Review Video: Graphing Linear Functions
Visit mometrix.com/academy and enter code: 699478

Algebraic functions are those that exclusively use polynomials and roots. These would include polynomial functions, rational functions, square root functions, and all combinations of these functions, such as polynomials as the radicand. These combinations may be joined by addition, subtraction, multiplication, or division, but may not include variables as exponents.

Review Video: Common Functions
Visit mometrix.com/academy and enter code: 629798

Absolute Value Functions

An **absolute value function** is in the format $f(x) = |ax + b|$. Like other functions, the domain is the set of all real numbers. However, because absolute value indicates positive numbers, the range is limited to positive real numbers. To find the zero of an absolute value function, set the portion inside the absolute value sign equal to zero and solve for x. An absolute value function is also known as a piecewise function because it must be solved in pieces—one for if the value inside the absolute value sign is positive, and one for if the value is negative. The function can be expressed as:

$$f(x) = \begin{cases} ax + b \text{ if } ax + b \geq 0 \\ -(ax + b) \text{ if } ax + b < 0 \end{cases}$$

This will allow for an accurate statement of the range. The graph of an example absolute value function, $f(x) = |2x - 1|$, is below:

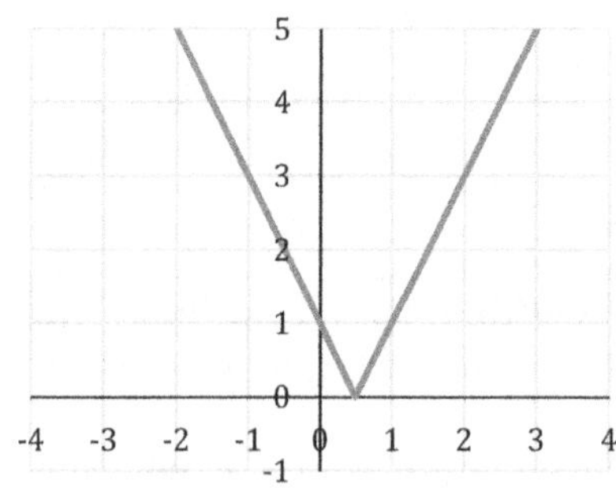

Piecewise Functions

A **piecewise function** is a function that has different definitions on two or more different intervals. The following, for instance, is one example of a piecewise-defined function:

$$f(x) = \begin{cases} x^2, & x < 0 \\ x, & 0 \le x \le 2 \\ (x-2)^2, & x > 2 \end{cases}$$

To graph this function, you would simply graph each part separately in the appropriate domain. The final graph would look like this:

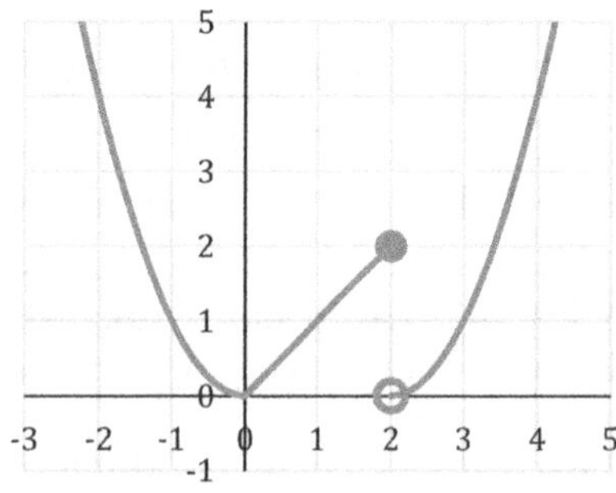

Note the filled and hollow dots at the discontinuity at $x = 2$. This is important to show which side of the graph that point corresponds to. Because $f(x) = x$ on the closed interval $0 \le x \le 2$, $f(2) = 2$. The point $(2, 2)$ is therefore marked with a filled circle, and the point $(2,0)$, which is the endpoint of the rightmost $(x - 2)^2$ part of the graph but *not actually part of the function*, is marked with a hollow dot to indicate this.

Review Video: Piecewise Functions
Visit mometrix.com/academy and enter code: 707921

Quadratic Functions

A **quadratic function** is a function in the form $y = ax^2 + bx + c$, where a does not equal 0. While a linear function forms a line, a quadratic function forms a **parabola**, which is a u-shaped figure that either opens upward or downward. A parabola that opens upward is said to be a **positive quadratic function,** and a parabola that opens downward is said to be a **negative quadratic function**. The shape of a parabola can differ, depending on the values of a, b, and c. All parabolas contain a **vertex**, which is the highest possible point, the **maximum**, or the lowest possible point, the **minimum**. This is the point where the graph begins moving in the opposite direction. A quadratic function can have zero, one, or two solutions, and therefore zero, one, or two x-intercepts. Recall that the x-intercepts are referred to as the zeros, or roots, of a function. A quadratic function will have only one y-intercept. Understanding the basic components of a quadratic function can give you an idea of the shape of its graph.

Example graph of a positive quadratic function, $x^2 + 2x - 3$:

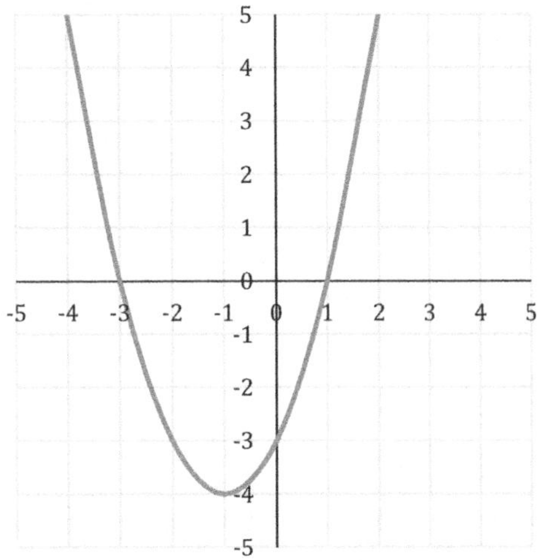

POLYNOMIAL FUNCTIONS

A **polynomial function** is a function with multiple terms and multiple powers of x, such as:

$$f(x) = a_n x^n + a_{n-1}x^{n-1} + a_{n-2}x^{n-2} + \cdots + a_1 x + a_0$$

where n is a non-negative integer that is the highest exponent in the polynomial and $a_n \neq 0$. The domain of a polynomial function is the set of all real numbers. If the greatest exponent in the polynomial is even, the polynomial is said to be of even degree and the range is the set of real numbers that satisfy the function. If the greatest exponent in the polynomial is odd, the polynomial is said to be odd and the range, like the domain, is the set of all real numbers.

RATIONAL FUNCTIONS

A **rational function** is a function that can be constructed as a ratio of two polynomial expressions: $f(x) = \frac{p(x)}{q(x)}$, where $p(x)$ and $q(x)$ are both polynomial expressions and $q(x) \neq 0$. The domain is the set of all real numbers, except any values for which $q(x) = 0$. The range is the set of real numbers that satisfies the function when the domain is applied. When you graph a rational function, you will have vertical asymptotes wherever $q(x) = 0$. If the polynomial in the numerator is of lesser degree than the polynomial in the denominator, the x-axis will also be a horizontal asymptote. If the numerator and denominator have equal degrees, there will be a horizontal asymptote not on the x-axis. If the degree of the numerator is exactly one greater than the degree of the denominator, the graph will have an oblique, or diagonal, asymptote. The asymptote will be along the line $y = \frac{p_n}{q_{n-1}}x + \frac{p_{n-1}}{q_{n-1}}$, where p_n and q_{n-1} are the coefficients of the highest degree terms in their respective polynomials.

SQUARE ROOT FUNCTIONS

A **square root function** is a function that contains a radical and is in the format $f(x) = \sqrt{ax + b}$. The domain is the set of all real numbers that yields a positive radicand or a radicand equal to zero. Because square root values are assumed to be positive unless otherwise identified, the range is all real numbers from zero to infinity. To find the zero of a square root function, set the radicand equal to zero and solve for x. The graph of a square root function is always to the right of the zero and always above the x-axis.

Example graph of a square root function, $f(x) = \sqrt{2x+1}$:

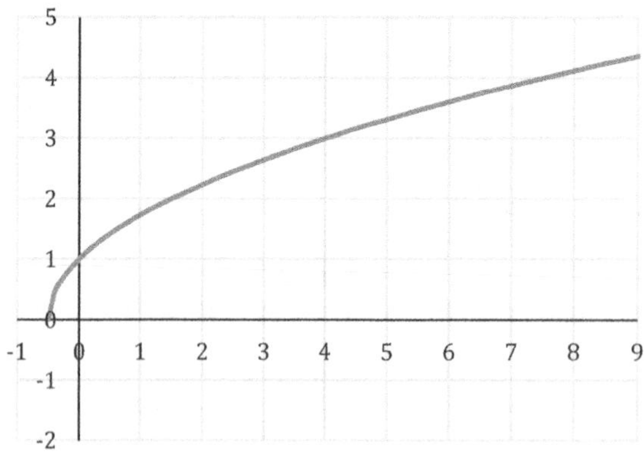

SEQUENCES

A **sequence** is an ordered set of numbers that continues in a defined pattern. The function that defines a sequence has a domain composed of the set of positive integers. Each member of the sequence is an element, or individual term. Each element is identified by the notation a_n, where a is the term of the sequence, and n is the integer identifying which term in the sequence a is.

There are two different ways to represent a sequence that contains the element a_n. The first is the simple notation $\{a_n\}$. The second is the expanded notation of a sequence: $a_1, a_2, a_3, \dots a_n, \dots$. Notice that the expanded form does not end with the nth term. There is no indication that the nth term is the last term in the sequence, only that the nth term is an element of the sequence.

ARITHMETIC SEQUENCES

An **arithmetic sequence**, or arithmetic progression, is a special kind of sequence in which a specific quantity, called the common difference, is added to each term to make the next term. The common difference may be positive or negative. The general form of an arithmetic sequence containing n terms is $a_1, a_1 + d, a_1 + 2d, \dots , a_1 + (n-1)d$, where d is the common difference. The general formula for any term of an arithmetic sequence is $a_n = a_1 + (n-1)d$, where a_n is the term you are looking for and d is the common difference. To find the sum of the first n terms of an arithmetic sequence, use the formula $s_n = \frac{n}{2}(a_1 + a_n)$.

Review Video: Arithmetic Sequence
Visit mometrix.com/academy and enter code: 676885

MONOTONIC SEQUENCES

A **monotonic sequence** is a sequence that is either nonincreasing or nondecreasing. A **nonincreasing** sequence is one whose terms either get progressively smaller in value or remain the same. Such a sequence is always bounded above, that is, all elements of the sequence must be less than some real number. A **nondecreasing** sequence is one whose terms either get progressively larger in value or remain the same. Such a sequence is always bounded below, that is, all elements of the sequence must be greater than some real number.

Recursive Sequences

When one element of a sequence is defined in terms of a previous element or elements of the sequence, the sequence is a **recursive sequence**. For example, given the recursive definition $a_1 = 1; a_2 = 1; a_n = a_{n-1} + a_{n-2}$ for all $n > 2$, you get the sequence 1,1,2,3,5,8, … . This is known as the Fibonacci sequence: a continuing sequence of numbers in which each number (after a_2) is the sum of the two previous numbers. The Fibonacci sequence can be defined as starting with either 1,1 or 0,1. Both definitions are considered correct in mathematics. Make sure you know which definition you are working with when dealing with Fibonacci numbers.

Sometimes in a recursive sequence, the terms can be found using a general formula that does not involve the previous terms of the sequence. Such a formula is called a **closed-form** expression for a recursive definition—an alternate formula that will generate the same sequence of numbers. However, not all sequences based on recursive definitions will have a closed-form expression. Some sequences will require the use of the recursive definition.

The Golden Ratio and the Fibonacci Sequence

The golden ratio is approximately 1.6180339887 and is often represented by the Greek letter phi, Φ. The exact value of Φ is $\frac{(1+\sqrt{5})}{2}$ and it is one of the solutions to $x - \frac{1}{x} = 1$. The golden ratio can be found using the Fibonacci sequence, since the ratio of a term to the previous term approaches Φ as the sequence approaches infinity:

n	a_n	a_{n-1}	$\frac{a_n}{a_{n-1}}$
3	2	1	2
4	3	2	1.5
5	5	3	$1.\overline{6}$
6	8	5	1.6
7	13	8	1.625
8	21	13	$1.\overline{615384}$
9	34	21	$1.\overline{619047}$
⋮	⋮	⋮	⋮
20	6,765	4,181	1.618033963 …

Geometric Sequences

A geometric sequence is a sequence in which each term is multiplied by a constant number (called the common ratio) to get the next term. Essentially, it's the same concept as an arithmetic sequence, but with multiplication instead of addition.

Consider the following example of a geometric sequence: Andy opens a savings account with $10. During each subsequent week, he plans to double the amount from the previous week.

Sequence: $10, 20, 40, 80, 160, \ldots$

Function: $a_n = 10 \times 2^{n-1}$

This is a geometric sequence with a common ratio of 2. All geometric sequences represent exponential functions. The nth term in any geometric sequence is $a_n = a_1 \times r^{n-1}$, where a_n represents the value of the nth term, a_1 is the initial term, r is the common ratio, and n is the number of terms. Thus, substituting the initial value of 10 and common ratio of 2 gives the function $a_n = 10 \times 2^{n-1}$.

Review Video: Geometric Sequences
Visit mometrix.com/academy and enter code: 140779

Geometry

Calculations Using Points

Sometimes you need to perform calculations using only points on a graph as input data. Using points, you can determine what the **midpoint** and **distance** are. If you know the equation for a line, you can calculate the distance between the line and the point.

To find the **midpoint** of two points (x_1, y_1) and (x_2, y_2), average the x-coordinates to get the x-coordinate of the midpoint, and average the y-coordinates to get the y-coordinate of the midpoint. The formula is: $\left(\frac{x_1+x_2}{2}, \frac{y_1+y_2}{2}\right)$.

The **distance** between two points is the same as the length of the hypotenuse of a right triangle with the two given points as endpoints, and the two sides of the right triangle parallel to the x-axis and y-axis, respectively. The length of the segment parallel to the x-axis is the difference between the x-coordinates of the two points. The length of the segment parallel to the y-axis is the difference between the y-coordinates of the two points. Use the Pythagorean theorem $a^2 + b^2 = c^2$ or $c = \sqrt{a^2 + b^2}$ to find the distance. The formula is $d = \sqrt{(x_2 - x_1)^2 + (y_2 - y_1)^2}$.

When a line is in the format $Ax + By + C = 0$, where A, B, and C are coefficients, you can use a point (x_1, y_1) not on the line and apply the formula $d = \frac{|Ax_1+By_1+C|}{\sqrt{A^2+B^2}}$ to find the distance between the line and the point (x_1, y_1).

Review Video: Calculations Using Points on a Graph
Visit mometrix.com/academy and enter code: 883228

Points, Lines, and Planes

Points and Lines

A **point** is a fixed location in space, has no size or dimensions, and is commonly represented by a dot. A **line** is a set of points that extends infinitely in two opposite directions. It has length, but no width or depth. A line can be defined by any two distinct points that it contains. A **line segment** is a portion of a line that has definite endpoints. A **ray** is a portion of a line that extends from a single point on that line in one direction along the line. It has a definite beginning, but no ending.

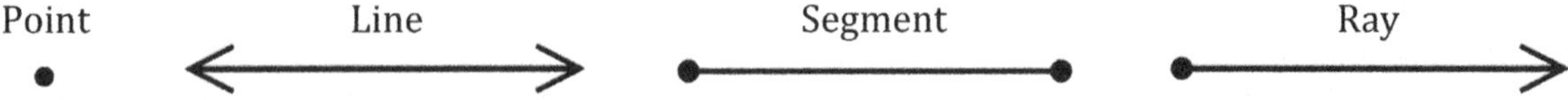

Interactions between Lines

Intersecting lines are lines that have exactly one point in common. **Concurrent lines** are multiple lines that intersect at a single point. **Perpendicular lines** are lines that intersect at right angles. They are represented by the symbol ⊥. The shortest distance from a line to a point not on the line is a perpendicular segment from the point to the line. **Parallel lines** are lines in the same plane that have no points in common and never meet. It is possible for lines to be in different planes, have no points in common, and never meet, but they are not parallel because they are in different planes.

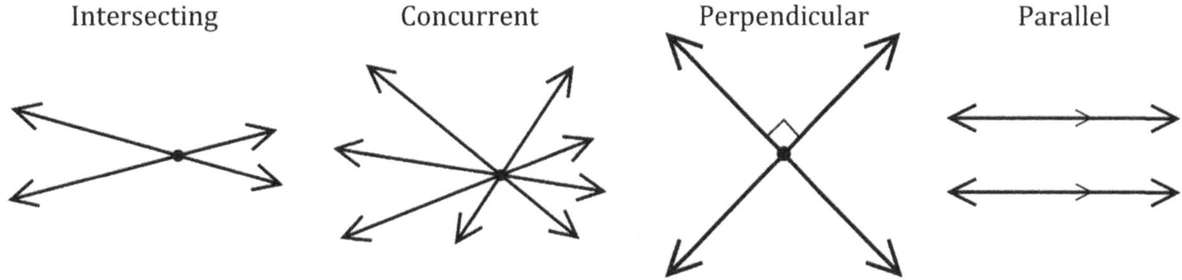

Review Video: Parallel and Perpendicular Lines
Visit mometrix.com/academy and enter code: 815923

A **transversal** is a line that intersects at least two other lines, which may or may not be parallel to one another. A transversal that intersects parallel lines is a common occurrence in geometry. A **bisector** is a line or line segment that divides another line segment into two equal lengths. A **perpendicular bisector** of a line segment is composed of points that are equidistant from the endpoints of the segment it is dividing.

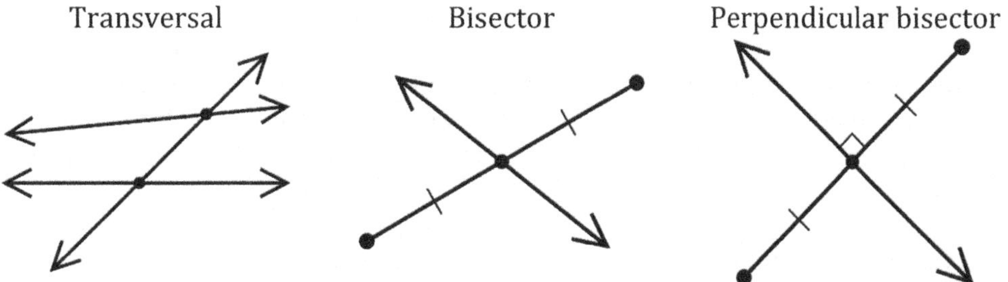

The **projection of a point on a line** is the point at which a perpendicular line drawn from the given point to the given line intersects the line. This is also the shortest distance from the given point to the line. The **projection of a segment on a line** is a segment whose endpoints are the points formed when perpendicular lines are drawn from the endpoints of the given segment to the given line. This is similar to the length a diagonal line appears to be when viewed from above.

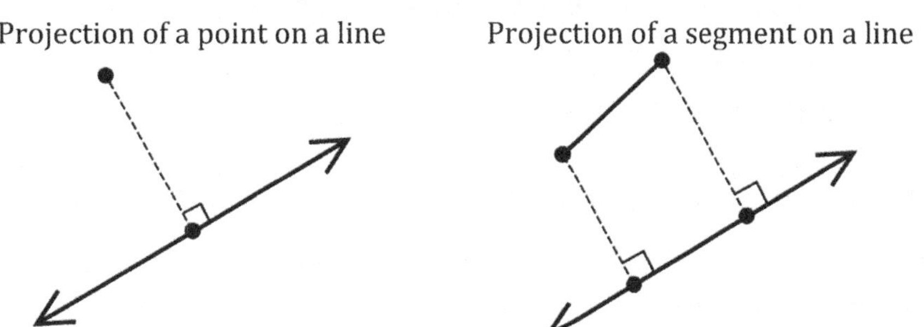

Planes

A **plane** is a two-dimensional flat surface defined by three non-collinear points. A plane extends an infinite distance in all directions in those two dimensions. It contains an infinite number of points, parallel lines and segments, intersecting lines and segments, as well as parallel or intersecting rays.

A plane will never contain a three-dimensional figure or skew lines, which are lines that don't intersect and are not parallel. Two given planes are either parallel or they intersect at a line. A plane may intersect a circular conic surface to form **conic sections**, such as a parabola, hyperbola, circle or ellipse.

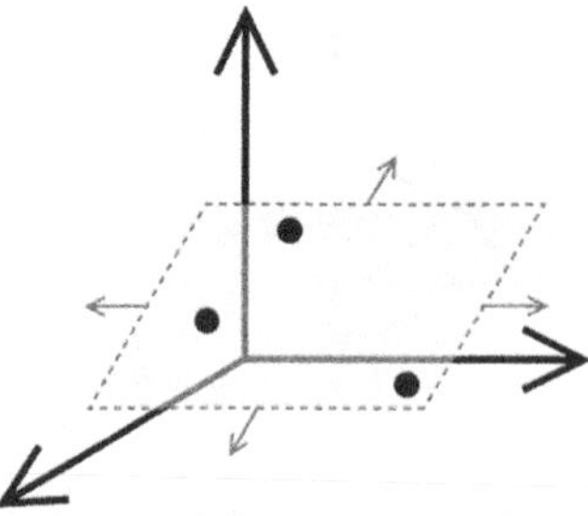

Review Video: Lines and Planes
Visit mometrix.com/academy and enter code: 554267

ANGLES

ANGLES AND VERTICES

An **angle** is formed when two lines or line segments meet at a common point. It may be a common starting point for a pair of segments or rays, or it may be the intersection of lines. Angles are represented by the symbol ∠.

The **vertex** is the point at which two segments or rays meet to form an angle. If the angle is formed by intersecting rays, lines, and/or line segments, the vertex is the point at which four angles are formed. The pairs of angles opposite one another are called vertical angles, and their measures are equal.

- An **acute** angle is an angle with a degree measure less than 90°.
- A **right** angle is an angle with a degree measure of exactly 90°.
- An **obtuse** angle is an angle with a degree measure greater than 90° but less than 180°.
- A **straight angle** is an angle with a degree measure of exactly 180°. This is also a semicircle.
- A **reflex angle** is an angle with a degree measure greater than 180° but less than 360°.
- A **full angle** is an angle with a degree measure of exactly 360°. This is also a circle.

Review Video: Angles
Visit mometrix.com/academy and enter code: 264624

RELATIONSHIPS BETWEEN ANGLES

Two angles whose sum is exactly 90° are said to be **complementary**. The two angles may or may not be adjacent. In a right triangle, the two acute angles are complementary.

Two angles whose sum is exactly 180° are said to be **supplementary**. The two angles may or may not be adjacent. Two intersecting lines always form two pairs of supplementary angles. Adjacent supplementary angles will always form a straight line.

Two angles that have the same vertex and share a side are said to be **adjacent**. Vertical angles are not adjacent because they share a vertex but no common side.

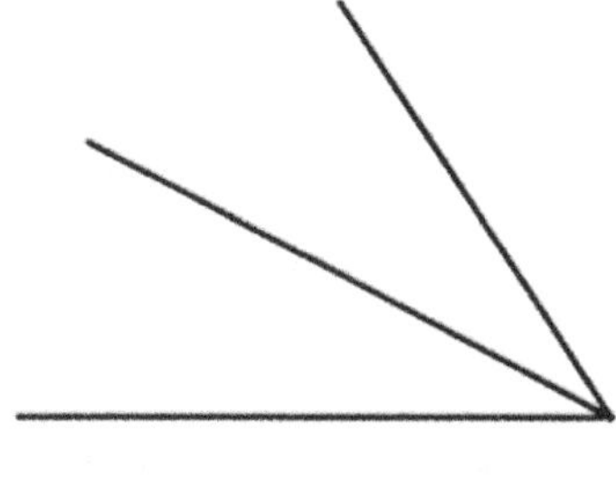

Adjacent
Share vertex and side

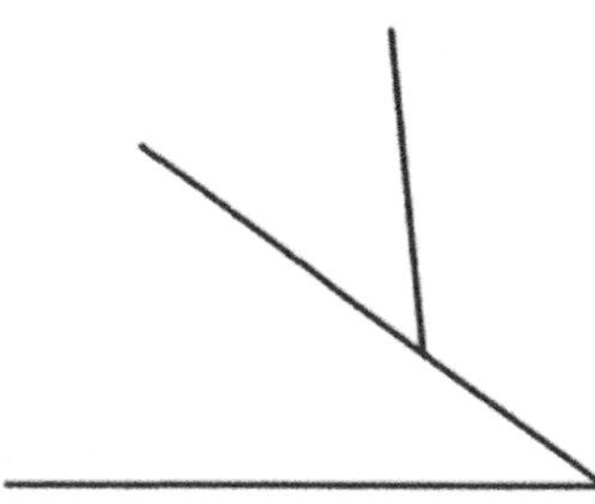

Not adjacent
Share part of a side, but not vertex

When two parallel lines are cut by a transversal, the angles that are between the two parallel lines are **interior angles**. In the diagram below, angles 3, 4, 5, and 6 are interior angles.

When two parallel lines are cut by a transversal, the angles that are outside the parallel lines are **exterior angles**. In the diagram below, angles 1, 2, 7, and 8 are exterior angles.

When two parallel lines are cut by a transversal, the angles that are in the same position relative to the transversal and a parallel line are **corresponding angles**. The diagram below has four pairs of corresponding angles: angles 1 and 5, angles 2 and 6, angles 3 and 7, and angles 4 and 8. Corresponding angles formed by parallel lines are congruent.

When two parallel lines are cut by a transversal, the two interior angles that are on opposite sides of the transversal are called **alternate interior angles**. In the diagram below, there are two pairs of alternate interior angles: angles 3 and 6, and angles 4 and 5. Alternate interior angles formed by parallel lines are congruent.

When two parallel lines are cut by a transversal, the two exterior angles that are on opposite sides of the transversal are called **alternate exterior angles**.

In the diagram below, there are two pairs of alternate exterior angles: angles 1 and 8, and angles 2 and 7. Alternate exterior angles formed by parallel lines are congruent.

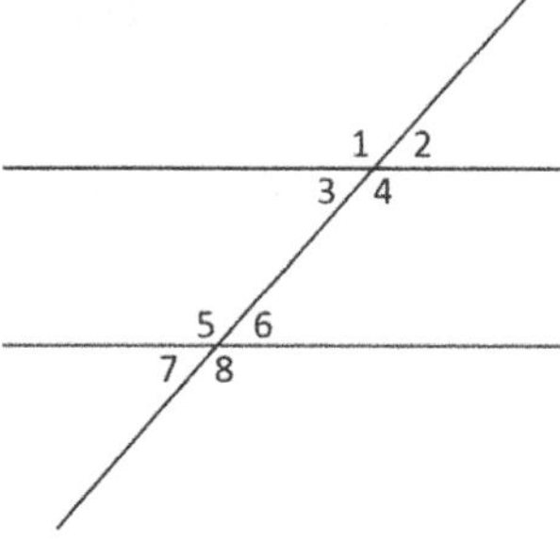

When two lines intersect, four angles are formed. The non-adjacent angles at this vertex are called vertical angles. Vertical angles are congruent. In the diagram, $\angle ABD \cong \angle CBE$ and $\angle ABC \cong \angle DBE$.

The other pairs of angles, $(\angle ABC, \angle CBE)$ and $(\angle ABD, \angle DBE)$, are supplementary, meaning the pairs sum to 180°.

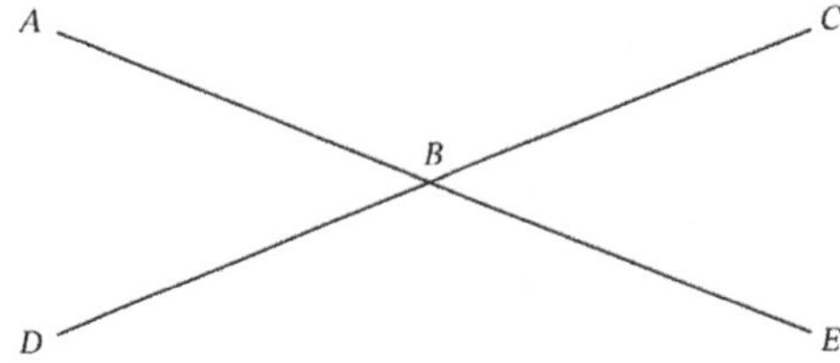

POLYGONS

A **polygon** is a closed, two-dimensional figure with three or more straight line segments called **sides**. The point at which two sides of a polygon intersect is called the **vertex**. In a polygon, the number of sides is always equal to the number of vertices. A polygon with all sides congruent and all angles equal is called a **regular polygon**. Common polygons are:

$$\begin{aligned} \text{Triangle} &= 3 \text{ sides} \\ \text{Quadrilateral} &= 4 \text{ sides} \\ \text{Pentagon} &= 5 \text{ sides} \\ \text{Hexagon} &= 6 \text{ sides} \\ \text{Heptagon} &= 7 \text{ sides} \\ \text{Octagon} &= 8 \text{ sides} \\ \text{Nonagon} &= 9 \text{ sides} \\ \text{Decagon} &= 10 \text{ sides} \\ \text{Dodecagon} &= 12 \text{ sides} \end{aligned}$$

More generally, an n-gon is a polygon that has n angles and n sides.

Review Video: Intro to Polygons Visit mometrix.com/academy and enter code: 271869

The sum of the interior angles of an n-sided polygon is $(n - 2) \times 180°$. For example, in a triangle $n = 3$. So the sum of the interior angles is $(3 - 2) \times 180° = 180°$. In a quadrilateral, $n = 4$, and the sum of the angles is $(4 - 2) \times 180° = 360°$.

Review Video: Sum of Interior Angles Visit mometrix.com/academy and enter code: 984991

CONVEX AND CONCAVE POLYGONS

A **convex polygon** is a polygon whose diagonals all lie within the interior of the polygon. A **concave polygon** is a polygon with a least one diagonal that is outside the polygon. In the diagram below, quadrilateral $ABCD$ is concave because diagonal $\overline{AC}$ lies outside the polygon and quadrilateral $EFGH$ is convex because both diagonals lie inside the polygon.

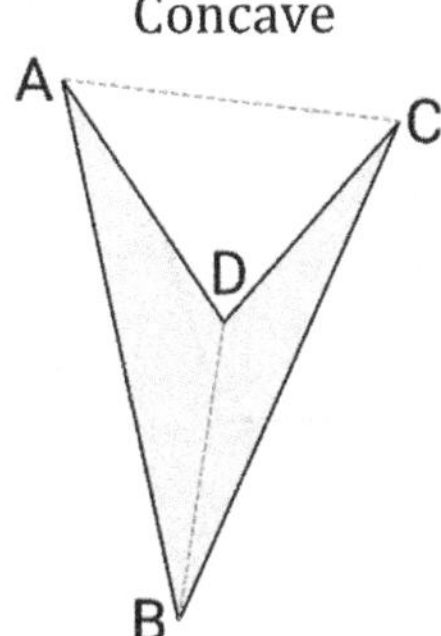

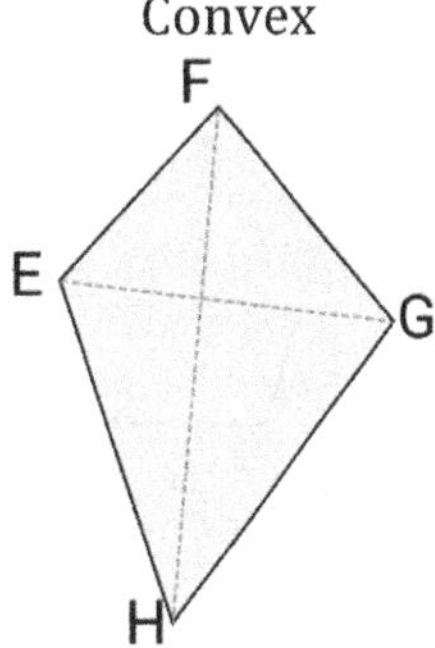

Apothem and Radius

A line segment from the center of a polygon that is perpendicular to a side of the polygon is called the **apothem**. A line segment from the center of a polygon to a vertex of the polygon is called a **radius**. In a regular polygon, the apothem can be used to find the area of the polygon using the formula $A = \frac{1}{2}ap$, where a is the apothem, and p is the perimeter.

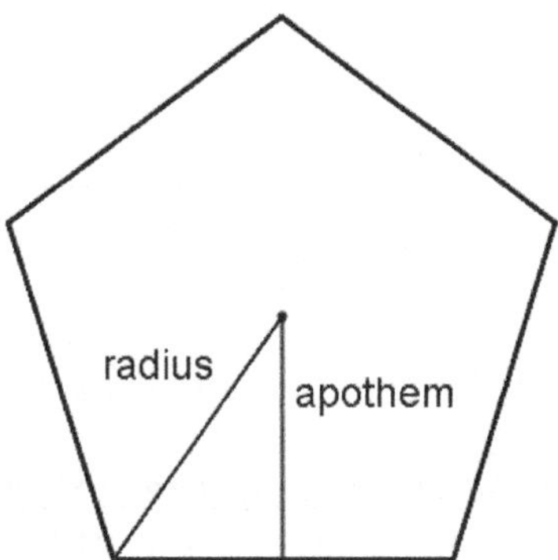

A **diagonal** is a line segment that joins two non-adjacent vertices of a polygon. The number of diagonals a polygon has can be found by using the formula:

$$\text{number of diagonals} = \frac{n(n-3)}{2}$$

Note that n is the number of sides in the polygon. This formula works for all polygons, not just regular polygons.

Congruence and Similarity

Congruent figures are geometric figures that have the same size and shape. All corresponding angles are equal, and all corresponding sides are equal. Congruence is indicated by the symbol $\cong$.

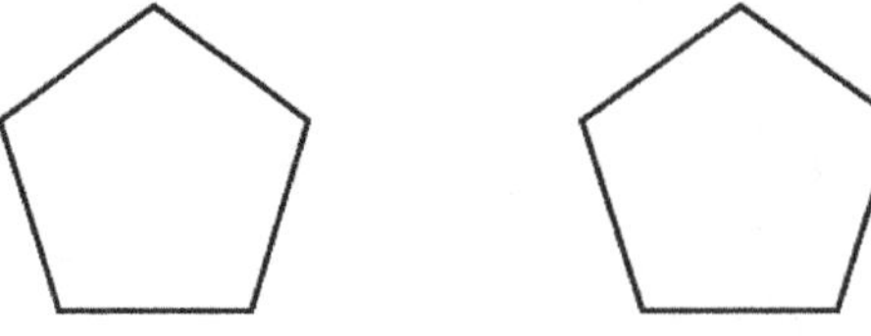

Congruent polygons

Similar figures are geometric figures that have the same shape, but do not necessarily have the same size. All corresponding angles are equal, and all corresponding sides are proportional, but they do not have to be equal. It is indicated by the symbol $\sim$.

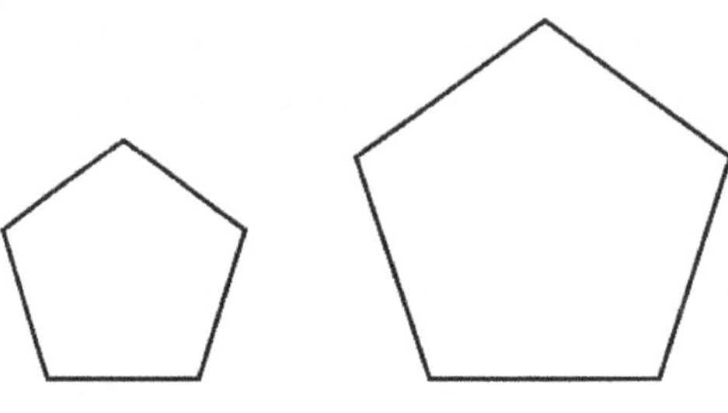

Similar polygons

Note that all congruent figures are also similar, but not all similar figures are congruent.

Review Video: Congruent Shapes
Visit mometrix.com/academy and enter code: 492281

Line of Symmetry

A line that divides a figure or object into congruent parts is called a **line of symmetry**. An object may have no lines of symmetry, one line of symmetry, or multiple (i.e., more than one) lines of symmetry.

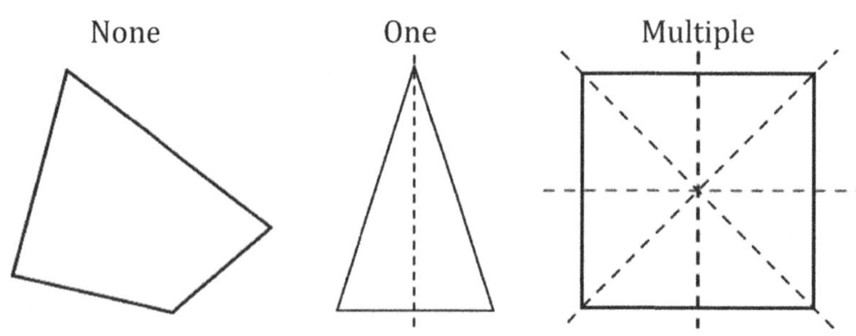

Review Video: Symmetry
Visit mometrix.com/academy and enter code: 528106

Triangles

A triangle is a three-sided figure with the sum of its interior angles being 180°. The **perimeter of any triangle** is found by summing the three side lengths; $P = a + b + c$. For an equilateral triangle, this is the same as $P = 3a$, where a is any side length, since all three sides are the same length.

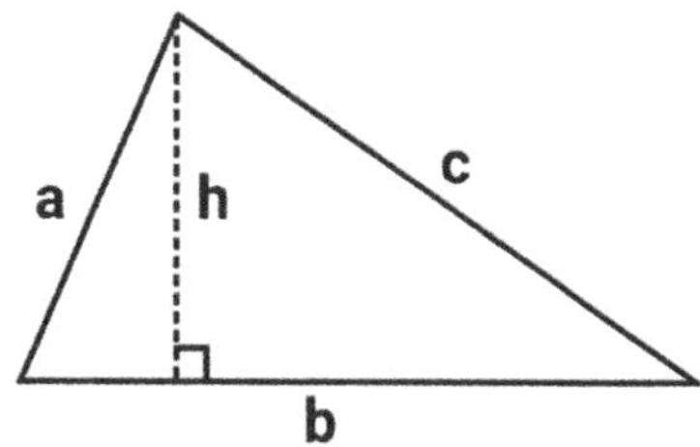

> **Review Video: Proof that a Triangle is 180 Degrees**
> Visit mometrix.com/academy and enter code: 687591
>
> **Review Video: Area and Perimeter of a Triangle**
> Visit mometrix.com/academy and enter code: 853779

The **area of any triangle** can be found by taking half the product of one side length referred to as the base, often given the variable b and the perpendicular distance from that side to the opposite vertex called the altitude or height and given the variable h. In equation form that is $A = \frac{1}{2}bh$. Another formula that works for any triangle is $A = \sqrt{s(s-a)(s-b)(s-c)}$, where s is the semiperimeter: $\frac{a+b+c}{2}$, and a, b, and c are the lengths of the three sides. Special cases include isosceles triangles, $A = \frac{1}{2}b\sqrt{a^2 - \frac{b^2}{4}}$, where b is the unique side and a is the length of one of the two congruent sides, and equilateral triangles, $A = \frac{\sqrt{3}}{4}a^2$, where a is the length of a side.

> **Review Video: Area of Any Triangle**
> Visit mometrix.com/academy and enter code: 138510

Parts of a Triangle

An **altitude** of a triangle is a line segment drawn from one vertex perpendicular to the opposite side. In the diagram that follows, $\overline{BE}$, $\overline{AD}$, and $\overline{CF}$ are altitudes. The length of an altitude is also called the height of the triangle. The three altitudes in a triangle are always concurrent. The point of concurrency of the altitudes of a triangle, O, is called the **orthocenter**. Note that in an obtuse triangle, the orthocenter will be outside the triangle, and in a right triangle, the orthocenter is the vertex of the right angle.

A **median** of a triangle is a line segment drawn from one vertex to the midpoint of the opposite side. In the diagram that follows, $\overline{BH}$, $\overline{AG}$, and $\overline{CI}$ are medians. This is not the same as the altitude, except the altitude to the base of an isosceles triangle and all three altitudes of an equilateral triangle. The point of concurrency of the medians of a triangle, T, is called the **centroid**. This is the same point as the orthocenter only in an equilateral triangle. Unlike the orthocenter, the centroid is always inside the triangle. The centroid can also be considered the exact center of the triangle. Any shape triangle can be perfectly balanced on a tip placed at the centroid. The centroid is also the point that is two-thirds the distance from the vertex to the opposite side.

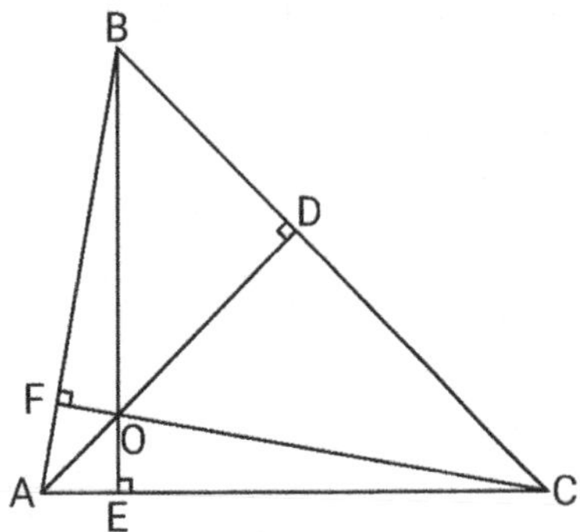

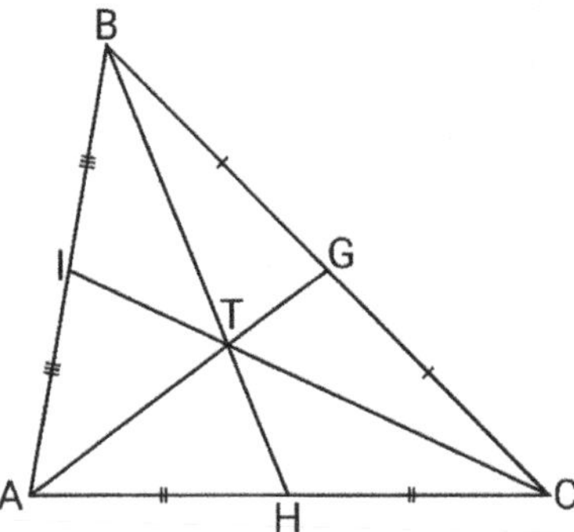

Review Video: Centroid, Incenter, Circumcenter, and Orthocenter
Visit mometrix.com/academy and enter code: 598260

Triangle Properties

Classifications of Triangles

A **scalene triangle** is a triangle with no congruent sides. A scalene triangle will also have three angles of different measures. The angle with the largest measure is opposite the longest side, and the angle with the smallest measure is opposite the shortest side. An **acute triangle** is a triangle whose three angles are all less than 90°. If two of the angles are equal, the acute triangle is also an **isosceles triangle**. An isosceles triangle will also have two congruent angles opposite the two congruent sides. If the three angles are all equal, the acute triangle is also an **equilateral triangle**. An equilateral triangle will also have three congruent angles, each 60°. All equilateral triangles are also acute triangles. An **obtuse triangle** is a triangle with exactly one angle greater than 90°. The other two angles may or may not be equal. If the two remaining angles are equal, the obtuse triangle is also an isosceles triangle. A **right triangle** is a triangle with exactly one angle equal to 90°. All right triangles follow the Pythagorean theorem. A right triangle can never be acute or obtuse.

The table below illustrates how each descriptor places a different restriction on the triangle:

Angles / Sides	**Acute:** All angles < 90°	**Obtuse:** One angle > 90°	**Right:** One angle = 90°
Scalene: No equal side lengths	$90° > \angle a > \angle b > \angle c$ $x > y > z$	$\angle a > 90° > \angle b > \angle c$ $x > y > z$	$90° = \angle a > \angle b > \angle c$ $x > y > z$
Isosceles: Two equal side lengths	$90° > \angle a, \angle b, or\ \angle c$ $\angle b = \angle c, \quad y = z$	$\angle a > 90° > \angle b = \angle c$ $x > y = z$	$\angle a = 90°$ $\angle b = \angle c = 45°$ $x > y = z$
Equilateral: Three equal side lengths	$60° = \angle a = \angle b = \angle c$ $x = y = z$		

Review Video: Introduction to Types of Triangles
Visit mometrix.com/academy and enter code: 511711

General Rules for Triangles

The **triangle inequality theorem** states that the sum of the measures of any two sides of a triangle is always greater than the measure of the third side. If the sum of the measures of two sides were equal to the third side, a triangle would be impossible because the two sides would lie flat across the third side and there would be no vertex. If the sum of the measures of two of the sides was less than the third side, a closed figure would be impossible because the two shortest sides would never meet. In other words, for a triangle with sides lengths A, B, and C: $A + B > C, B + C > A$, and $A + C > B$.

The sum of the measures of the interior angles of a triangle is always 180°. Therefore, a triangle can never have more than one angle greater than or equal to 90°.

In any triangle, the angles opposite congruent sides are congruent, and the sides opposite congruent angles are congruent. The largest angle is always opposite the longest side, and the smallest angle is always opposite the shortest side.

The line segment that joins the midpoints of any two sides of a triangle is always parallel to the third side and exactly half the length of the third side.

Review Video: General Rules (Triangle Inequality Theorem)
Visit mometrix.com/academy and enter code: 166488

Similarity and Congruence Rules

Similar triangles are triangles whose corresponding angles are equal and whose corresponding sides are proportional. Represented by AAA. Similar triangles whose corresponding sides are congruent are also congruent triangles.

Triangles can be shown to be **congruent** in 5 ways:

- **SSS**: Three sides of one triangle are congruent to the three corresponding sides of the second triangle.
- **SAS**: Two sides and the included angle (the angle formed by those two sides) of one triangle are congruent to the corresponding two sides and included angle of the second triangle.
- **ASA**: Two angles and the included side (the side that joins the two angles) of one triangle are congruent to the corresponding two angles and included side of the second triangle.
- **AAS**: Two angles and a non-included side of one triangle are congruent to the corresponding two angles and non-included side of the second triangle.
- **HL**: The hypotenuse and leg of one right triangle are congruent to the corresponding hypotenuse and leg of the second right triangle.

Review Video: Similar Triangles
Visit mometrix.com/academy and enter code: 398538

Transformations

Rotation

A **rotation** is a transformation that turns a figure around a point called the **center of rotation**, which can lie anywhere in the plane. If a line is drawn from a point on a figure to the center of rotation, and another line is drawn from the center to the rotated image of that point, the angle between the two lines is the **angle of rotation**. The vertex of the angle of rotation is the center of rotation.

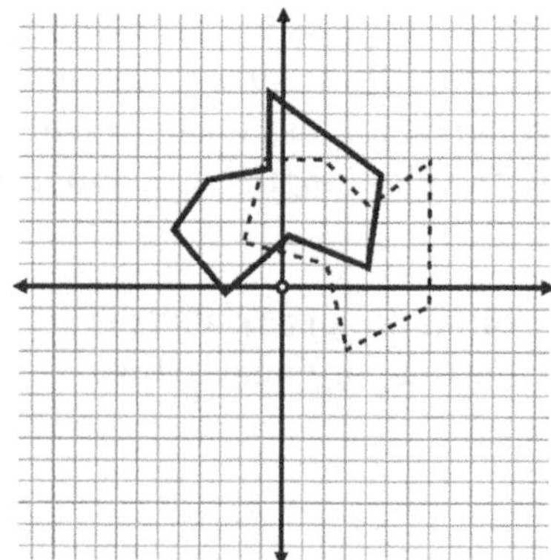

Review Video: Rotation
Visit mometrix.com/academy and enter code: 602600

Translation and Dilation

A **translation** is a transformation which slides a figure from one position in the plane to another position in the plane. The original figure and the translated figure have the same size, shape, and orientation. A **dilation** is a transformation which proportionally stretches or shrinks a figure by a **scale factor**. The dilated image is the same shape and orientation as the original image but a different size. A polygon and its dilated image are similar.

Translation

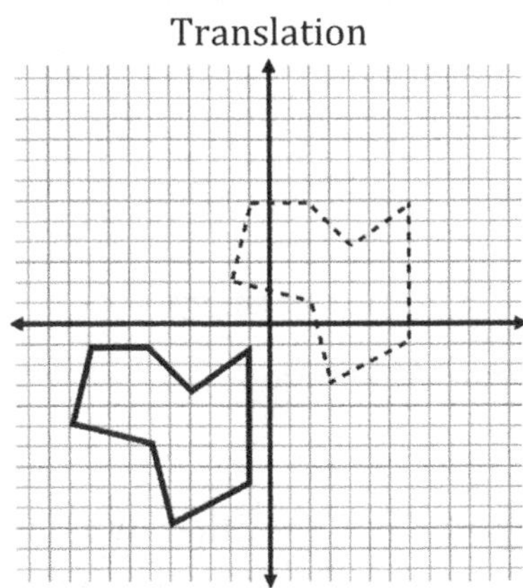

Dilation

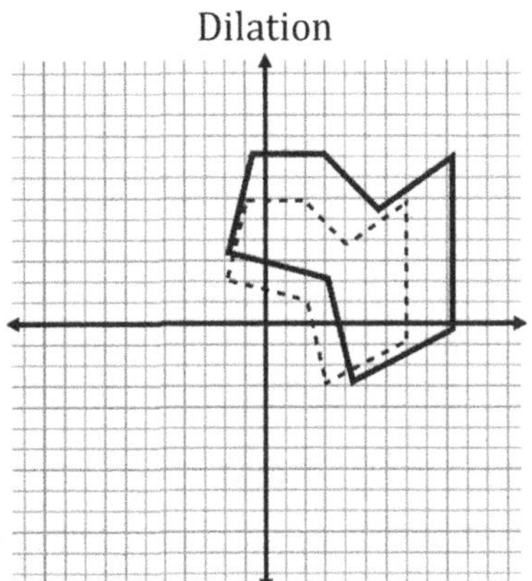

Review Video: Translation
Visit mometrix.com/academy and enter code: 718628

Review Video: Dilation
Visit mometrix.com/academy and enter code: 471630

A **reflection of a figure over a line** (a "flip") creates a congruent image that is the same distance from the line as the original figure but on the opposite side. The **line of reflection** is the perpendicular bisector of any line segment drawn from a point on the original figure to its reflected image (unless the point and its reflected image happen to be the same point, which happens when a figure is reflected over one of its own sides). A **reflection of a figure over a point** (an inversion) in two dimensions is the same as the rotation of the figure 180° about that point. The image of the figure is congruent to the original figure. The **point of reflection** is the midpoint of a line segment which connects a point in the figure to its image (unless the point and its reflected image happen to be the same point, which happens when a figure is reflected in one of its own points).

Reflection of a figure over a line

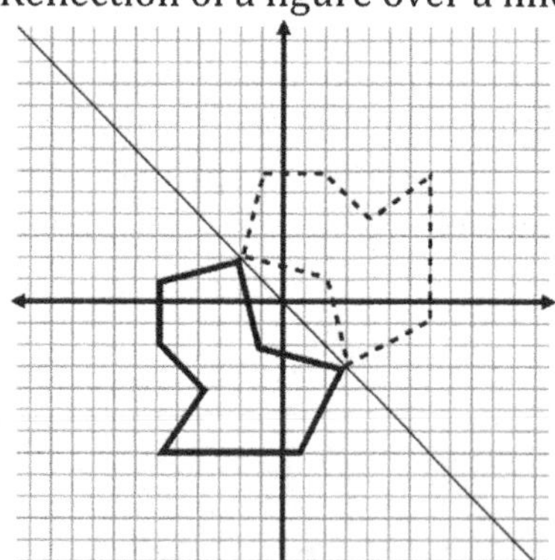

Reflection of a figure over a point

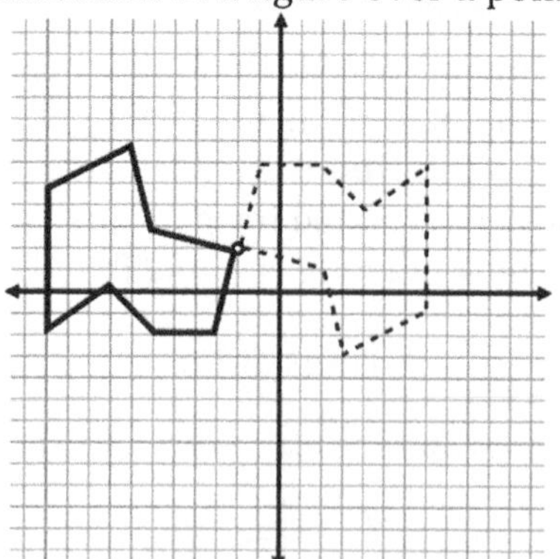

Review Video: Reflection
Visit mometrix.com/academy and enter code: 955068

PYTHAGOREAN THEOREM

The side of a triangle opposite the right angle is called the **hypotenuse**. The other two sides are called the legs. The Pythagorean theorem states a relationship among the legs and hypotenuse of a right triangle: ($a^2 + b^2 = c^2$), where a and b are the lengths of the legs of a right triangle, and c is the length of the hypotenuse. Note that this formula will only work with right triangles.

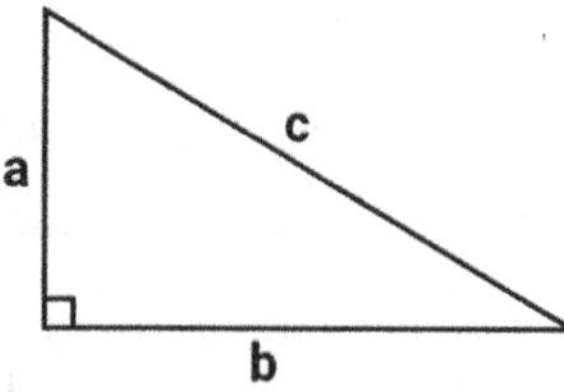

Review Video: Pythagorean Theorem
Visit mometrix.com/academy and enter code: 906576

TRIGONOMETRIC FORMULAS

In the diagram below, angle C is the right angle, and side c is the hypotenuse. Side a is the side opposite to angle A and side b is the side opposite to angle B. Using ratios of side lengths as a means to calculate the sine, cosine, and tangent of an acute angle only works for right triangles.

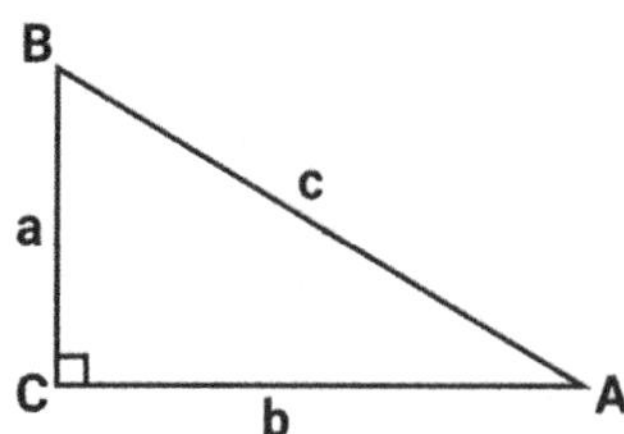

$$\sin A = \frac{\text{opposite side}}{\text{hypotenuse}} = \frac{a}{c} \qquad \csc A = \frac{1}{\sin A} = \frac{\text{hypotenuse}}{\text{opposite side}} = \frac{c}{a}$$

$$\cos A = \frac{\text{adjacent side}}{\text{hypotenuse}} = \frac{b}{c} \qquad \sec A = \frac{1}{\cos A} = \frac{\text{hypotenuse}}{\text{adjacent side}} = \frac{c}{b}$$

$$\tan A = \frac{\text{opposite side}}{\text{adjacent side}} = \frac{a}{b} \qquad \cot A = \frac{1}{\tan A} = \frac{\text{adjacent side}}{\text{opposite side}} = \frac{b}{a}$$

LAWS OF SINES AND COSINES

The **law of sines** states that $\frac{\sin A}{a} = \frac{\sin B}{b} = \frac{\sin C}{c}$, where A, B, and C are the angles of a triangle, and a, b, and c are the sides opposite their respective angles. This formula will work with all triangles, not just right triangles.

The **law of cosines** is given by the formula $c^2 = a^2 + b^2 - 2ab(\cos C)$, where a, b, and c are the sides of a triangle, and C is the angle opposite side c. This is a generalized form of the Pythagorean theorem that can be used on any triangle.

> **Review Video: Upper Level Trig: Law of Sines**
> Visit mometrix.com/academy and enter code: 206844
>
> **Review Video: Upper Level Trig: Law of Cosines**
> Visit mometrix.com/academy and enter code: 158911

QUADRILATERALS

A **quadrilateral** is a closed two-dimensional geometric figure that has four straight sides. The sum of the interior angles of any quadrilateral is 360°.

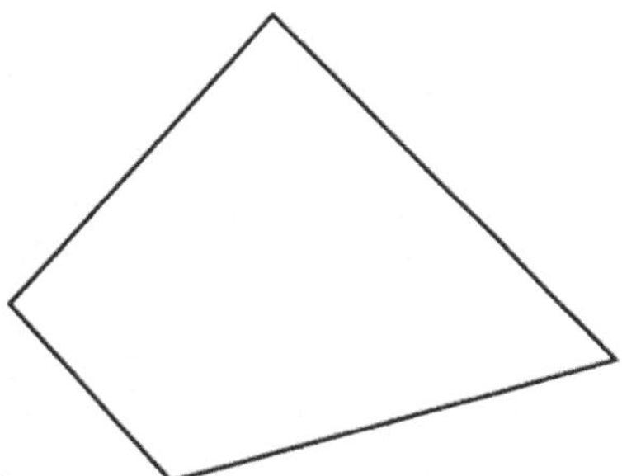

> **Review Video: Diagonals of Parallelograms, Rectangles, and Rhombi**
> Visit mometrix.com/academy and enter code: 320040

KITE

A **kite** is a quadrilateral with two pairs of adjacent sides that are congruent. A result of this is perpendicular diagonals. A kite can be concave or convex and has one line of symmetry.

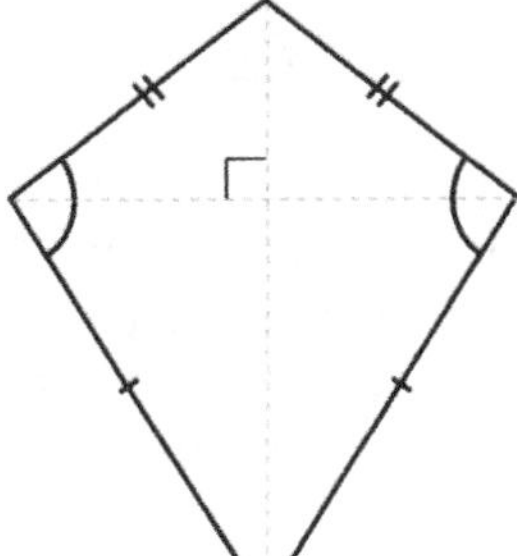

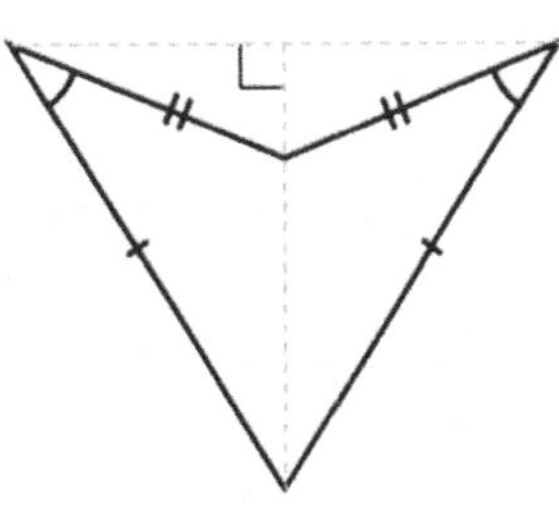

TRAPEZOID

Trapezoid: A trapezoid is defined as a quadrilateral that has at least one pair of parallel sides. There are no rules for the second pair of sides. So, there are no rules for the diagonals and no lines of symmetry for a trapezoid.

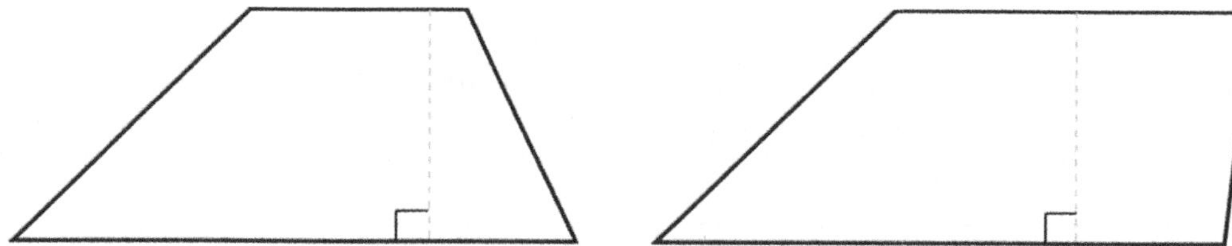

The **area of a trapezoid** is found by the formula $A = \frac{1}{2}h(b_1 + b_2)$, where h is the height (segment joining and perpendicular to the parallel bases), and b_1 and b_2 are the two parallel sides (bases). Do not use one of the other two sides as the height unless that side is also perpendicular to the parallel bases.

The **perimeter of a trapezoid** is found by the formula $P = a + b_1 + c + b_2$, where a, b_1, c, and b_2 are the four sides of the trapezoid.

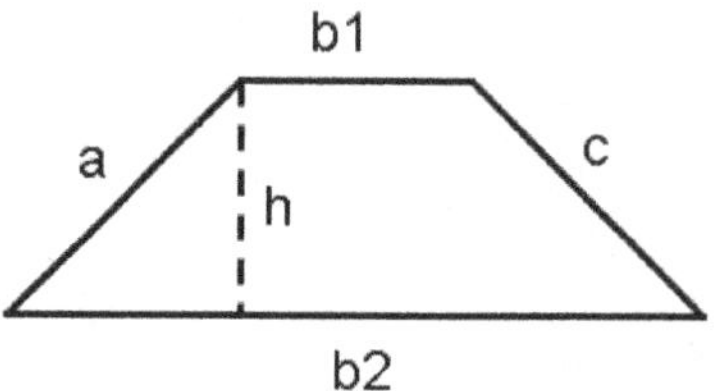

Review Video: Area and Perimeter of a Trapezoid
Visit mometrix.com/academy and enter code: 587523

Isosceles trapezoid: A trapezoid with equal base angles. This gives rise to other properties including: the two nonparallel sides have the same length, the two non-base angles are also equal, and there is one line of symmetry through the midpoints of the parallel sides.

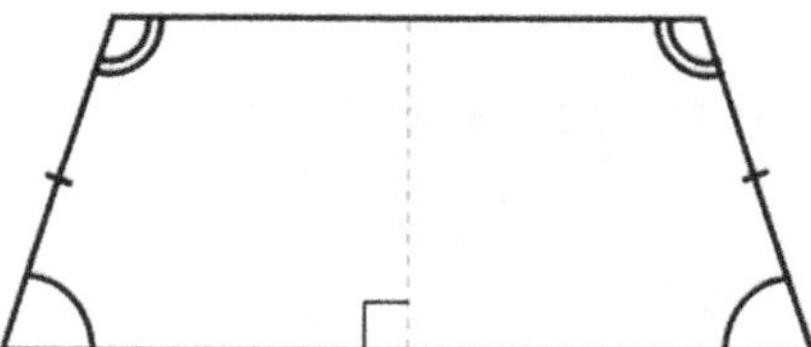

PARALLELOGRAM

A **parallelogram** is a quadrilateral that has two pairs of opposite parallel sides. As such it is a special type of trapezoid. The sides that are parallel are also congruent. The opposite interior angles are always congruent, and the consecutive interior angles are supplementary. The diagonals of a parallelogram divide each other. Each diagonal divides the parallelogram into two congruent triangles. A parallelogram has no line of symmetry, but does have 180-degree rotational symmetry about the midpoint.

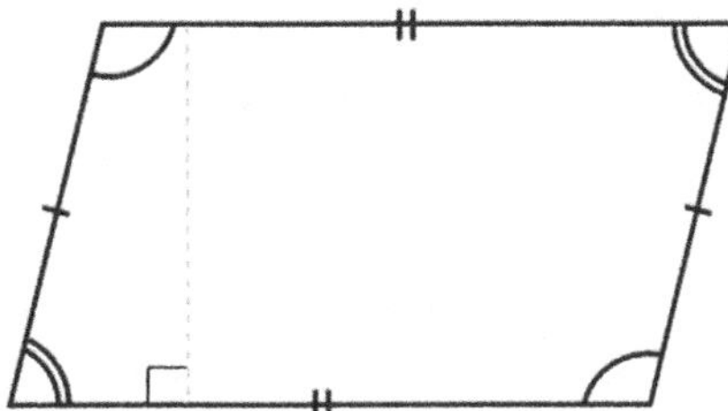

The **area of a parallelogram** is found by the formula $A = bh$, where b is the length of the base, and h is the height. Note that the base and height correspond to the length and width in a rectangle, so this formula would apply to rectangles as well. Do not confuse the height of a parallelogram with the length of the second side. The two are only the same measure in the case of a rectangle.

The **perimeter of a parallelogram** is found by the formula $P = 2a + 2b$ or $P = 2(a + b)$, where a and b are the lengths of the two sides.

Review Video: How to Find the Area and Perimeter of a Parallelogram
Visit mometrix.com/academy and enter code: 718313

Rectangle

A **rectangle** is a quadrilateral with four right angles. All rectangles are parallelograms and trapezoids, but not all parallelograms or trapezoids are rectangles. The diagonals of a rectangle are congruent. Rectangles have two lines of symmetry (through each pair of opposing midpoints) and 180-degree rotational symmetry about the midpoint.

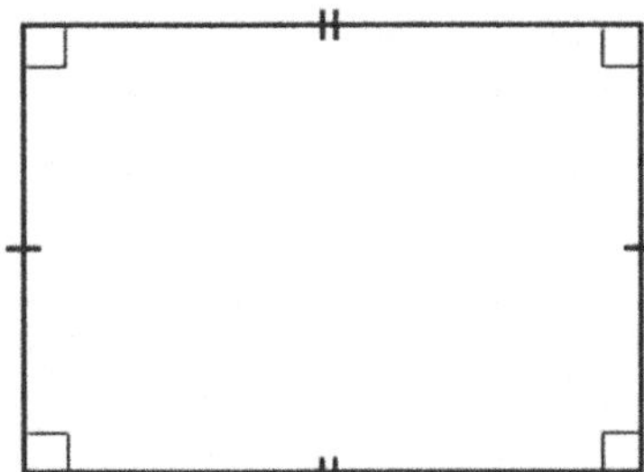

The **area of a rectangle** is found by the formula $A = lw$, where A is the area of the rectangle, l is the length (usually considered to be the longer side) and w is the width (usually considered to be the shorter side). The numbers for l and w are interchangeable.

The **perimeter of a rectangle** is found by the formula $P = 2l + 2w$ or $P = 2(l + w)$, where l is the length, and w is the width. It may be easier to add the length and width first and then double the result, as in the second formula.

Rhombus

A **rhombus** is a quadrilateral with four congruent sides. All rhombuses are parallelograms and kites; thus, they inherit all the properties of both types of quadrilaterals. The diagonals of a rhombus are perpendicular to each other. Rhombi have two lines of symmetry (along each of the diagonals) and 180° rotational symmetry. The **area of a rhombus** is half the product of the diagonals: $A = \frac{d_1 d_2}{2}$ and the perimeter of a rhombus is: $P = 2\sqrt{(d_1)^2 + (d_2)^2}$.

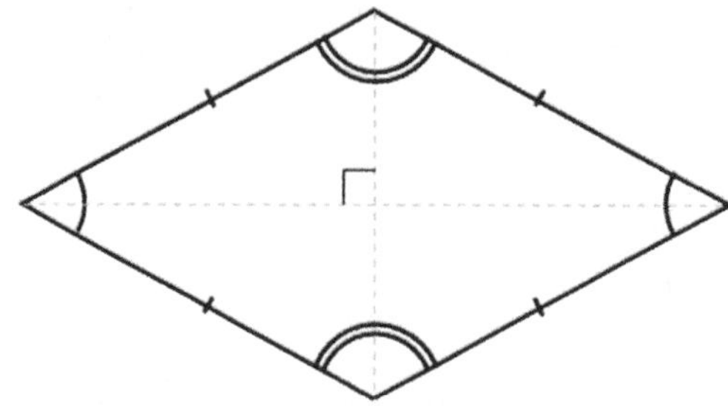

SQUARE

A **square** is a quadrilateral with four right angles and four congruent sides. Squares satisfy the criteria of all other types of quadrilaterals. The diagonals of a square are congruent and perpendicular to each other. Squares have four lines of symmetry (through each pair of opposing midpoints and along each of the diagonals) as well as 90° rotational symmetry about the midpoint.

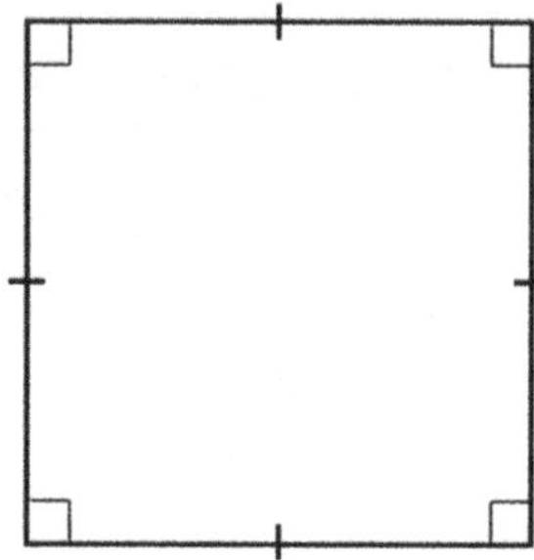

The **area of a square** is found by using the formula $A = s^2$, where s is the length of one side. The **perimeter of a square** is found by using the formula $P = 4s$, where s is the length of one side. Because all four sides are equal in a square, it is faster to multiply the length of one side by 4 than to add the same number four times. You could use the formulas for rectangles and get the same answer.

Review Video: Area and Perimeter of Rectangles and Squares
Visit mometrix.com/academy and enter code: 428109

Hierarchy of Quadrilaterals

The hierarchy of quadrilaterals is as follows:

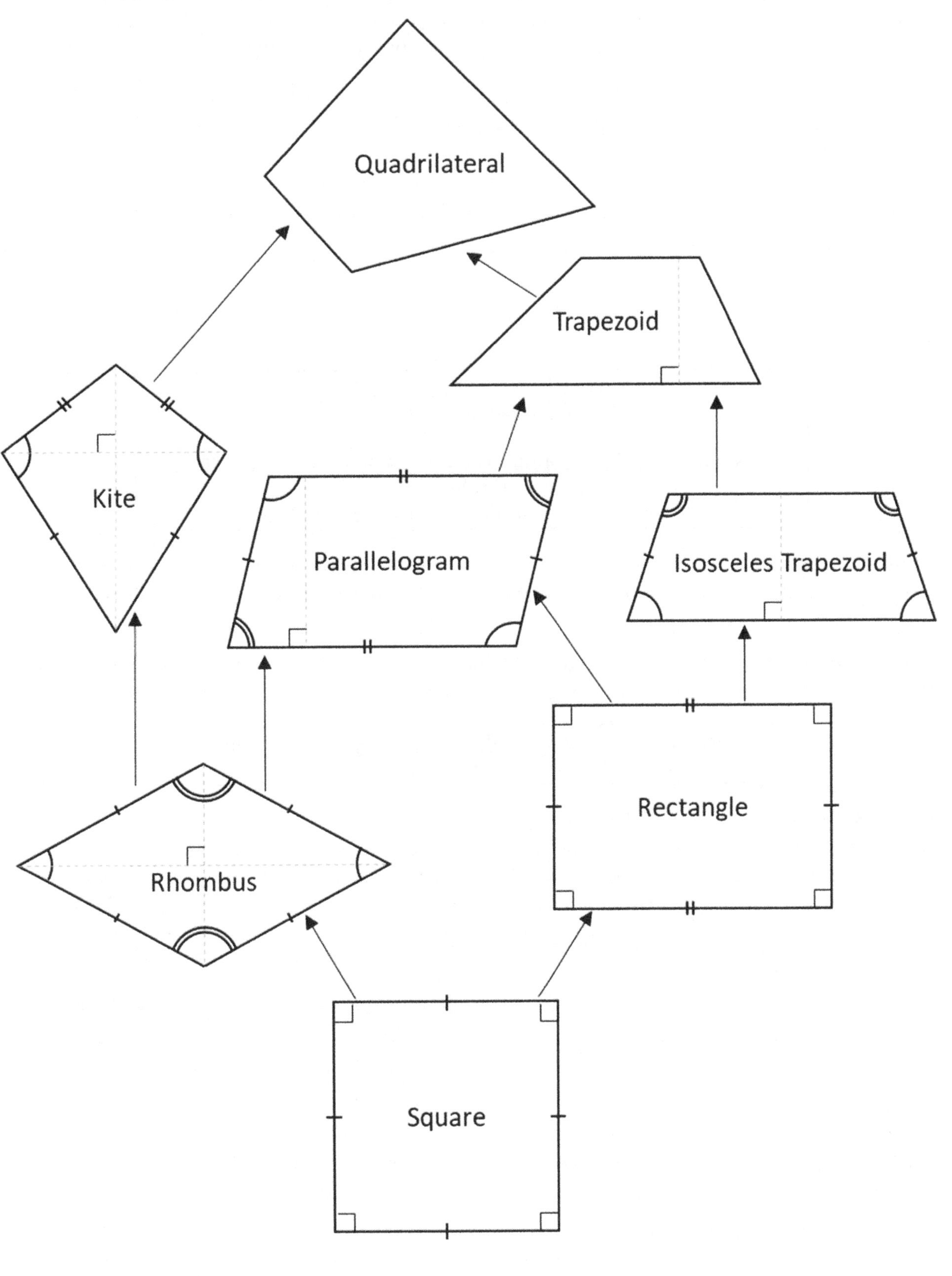

Circles

The **center** of a circle is the single point from which every point on the circle is **equidistant**. The **radius** is a line segment that joins the center of the circle and any one point on the circle. All radii of a circle are equal. Circles that have the same center but not the same length of radii are **concentric**. The **diameter** is a line segment that passes through the center of the circle and has both endpoints on the circle. The length of the diameter is exactly twice the length of the radius. Point O in the diagram below is the center of the circle, segments $\overline{OX}$, $\overline{OY}$, and $\overline{OZ}$ are radii; and segment $\overline{XZ}$ is a diameter.

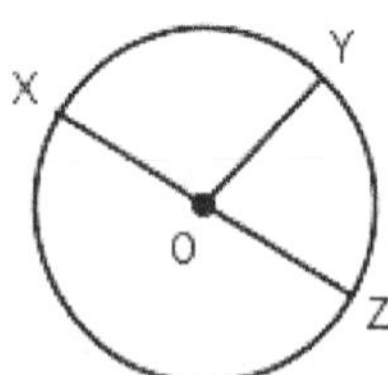

Review Video: Points of a Circle
Visit mometrix.com/academy and enter code: 420746

Review Video: The Diameter, Radius, and Circumference of Circles
Visit mometrix.com/academy and enter code: 448988

The **area of a circle** is found by the formula $A = \pi r^2$, where r is the length of the radius. If the diameter of the circle is given, remember to divide it in half to get the length of the radius before proceeding.

The **circumference** of a circle is found by the formula $C = 2\pi r$, where r is the radius. Again, remember to convert the diameter if you are given that measure rather than the radius.

Review Video: Area and Circumference of a Circle
Visit mometrix.com/academy and enter code: 243015

Inscribed and Circumscribed Figures

These terms can both be used to describe a given arrangement of figures, depending on perspective. If each of the vertices of figure A lie on figure B, then it can be said that figure A is **inscribed** in figure B, but it can also be said that figure B is **circumscribed** about figure A. The following table and examples help to illustrate the concept. Note that the figures cannot both be circles, as they would be completely overlapping and neither would be inscribed or circumscribed.

Given	Description	Equivalent Description	Figures
Each of the sides of a pentagon is tangent to a circle	The circle is inscribed in the pentagon	The pentagon is circumscribed about the circle	
Each of the vertices of a pentagon lie on a circle	The pentagon is inscribed in the circle	The circle is circumscribed about the pentagon	

Circle Properties

Arcs

An **arc** is a portion of a circle. Specifically, an arc is the set of points between and including two points on a circle. An arc does not contain any points inside the circle. When a segment is drawn from the endpoints of an arc to the center of the circle, a sector is formed. A **minor arc** is an arc that has a measure less than 180°. A **major arc** is an arc that has a measure of at least 180°. Every minor arc has a corresponding major arc that can be found by subtracting the measure of the minor arc from 360°. A **semicircle** is an arc whose endpoints are the endpoints of the diameter of a circle. A semicircle is exactly half of a circle.

Arc length is the length of that portion of the circumference between two points on the circle. The formula for arc length is $s = \frac{\pi r\theta}{180°}$, where s is the arc length, r is the length of the radius, and θ is the angular measure of the arc in degrees, or $s = r\theta$, where θ is the angular measure of the arc in radians (2π radians $=$ 360 degrees).

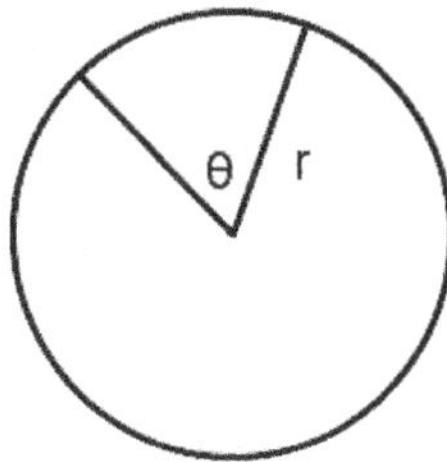

Angles of Circles

A **central angle** is an angle whose vertex is the center of a circle and whose legs intercept an arc of the circle. The measure of a central angle is equal to the measure of the minor arc it intercepts.

An **inscribed angle** is an angle whose vertex lies on a circle and whose legs contain chords of that circle. The portion of the circle intercepted by the legs of the angle is called the intercepted arc. The measure of the intercepted arc is exactly twice the measure of the inscribed angle. In the following diagram, angle ABC is an inscribed angle. $\widehat{AC} = 2(\text{m}\angle ABC)$.

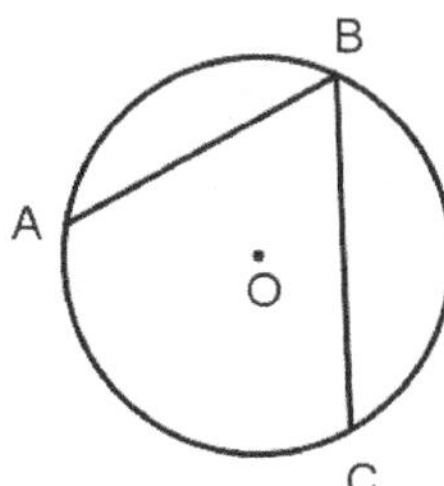

Any angle inscribed in a semicircle is a right angle. The intercepted arc is 180°, making the inscribed angle half that, or 90°. In the diagram below, angle ABC is inscribed in semicircle ABC, making angle ABC equal to 90°.

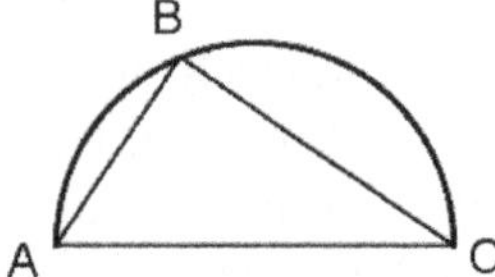

Review Video: Arcs and Angles of Circles
Visit mometrix.com/academy and enter code: 652838

Secants, Chords, and Tangents

A **secant** is a line that intersects a circle in two points. The segment of a secant line that is contained within the circle is called a **chord**. Two secants may intersect inside the circle, on the circle, or outside the circle. When the two secants intersect on the circle, an inscribed angle is formed. When two secants intersect inside a circle, the measure of each of two vertical angles is equal to half the sum of the two intercepted arcs. Consider the following diagram where $\text{m}\angle AEB = \frac{1}{2}(\widehat{AB} + \widehat{CD})$ and $\text{m}\angle BEC = \frac{1}{2}(\widehat{BC} + \widehat{AD})$.

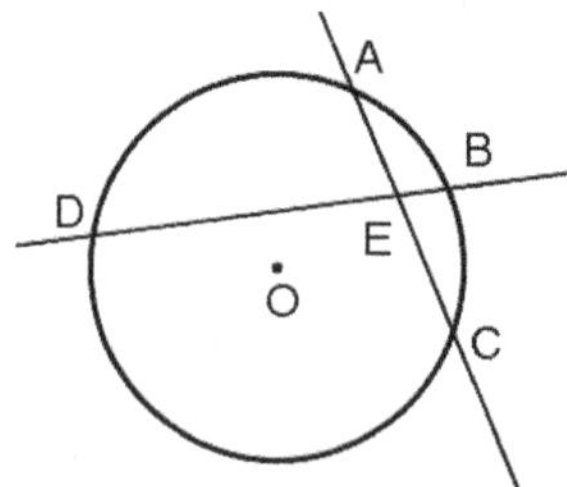

When two secants intersect outside a circle, the measure of the angle formed is equal to half the difference of the two arcs that lie between the two secants. In the diagram below, $\text{m}\angle AEB = \frac{1}{2}(\widehat{AB} - \widehat{CD})$.

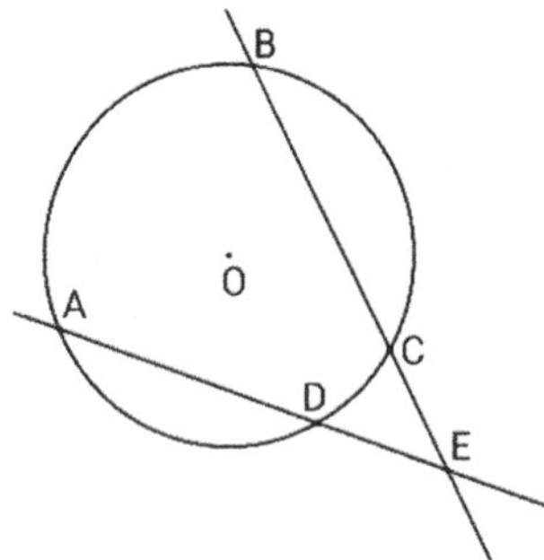

A **tangent** is a line in the same plane as a circle that touches the circle in exactly one point. The point at which a tangent touches a circle is called the **point of tangency**. While a line segment can be tangent to a circle as part of a line that is tangent, it is improper to say a tangent can be simply a line segment that touches the circle in exactly one point.

In the diagram below, $\overleftrightarrow{EB}$ is a secant and contains chord $\overline{EB}$, and $\overleftrightarrow{CD}$ is tangent to circle A. Notice that $\overline{FB}$ is not tangent to the circle. $\overline{FB}$ is a line segment that touches the circle in exactly one point, but if the segment were extended, it would touch the circle in a second point. In the diagram below, point B is the point of tangency.

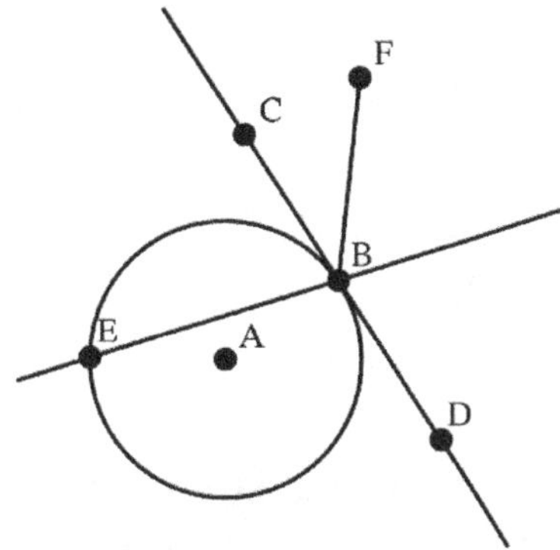

Review Video: Secants, Chords, and Tangents
Visit mometrix.com/academy and enter code: 258360

Review Video: Tangent Lines of a Circle
Visit mometrix.com/academy and enter code: 780167

Sectors

A **sector** is the portion of a circle formed by two radii and their intercepted arc. While the arc length is exclusively the points that are also on the circumference of the circle, the sector is the entire area bounded by the arc and the two radii.

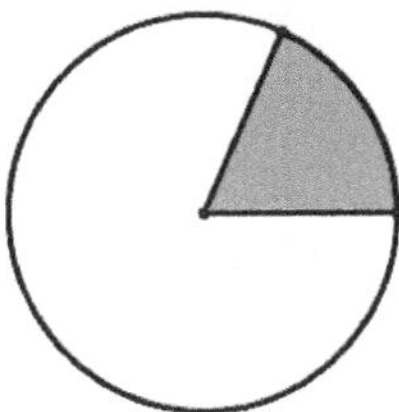

The **area of a sector** of a circle is found by the formula, $A = \frac{\theta r^2}{2}$, where A is the area, θ is the measure of the central angle in radians, and r is the radius. To find the area with the central angle in degrees, use the formula, $A = \frac{\theta \pi r^2}{360}$, where θ is the measure of the central angle and r is the radius.

3D Shapes

Solids

The **surface area of a solid object** is the area of all sides or exterior surfaces. For objects such as prisms and pyramids, a further distinction is made between base surface area (B) and lateral surface area (LA). For a prism, the total surface area (SA) is $SA = LA + 2B$. For a pyramid or cone, the total surface area is $SA = LA + B$.

The **surface area of a sphere** can be found by the formula $A = 4\pi r^2$, where r is the radius. The volume is given by the formula $V = \frac{4}{3}\pi r^3$, where r is the radius. Both quantities are generally given in terms of π.

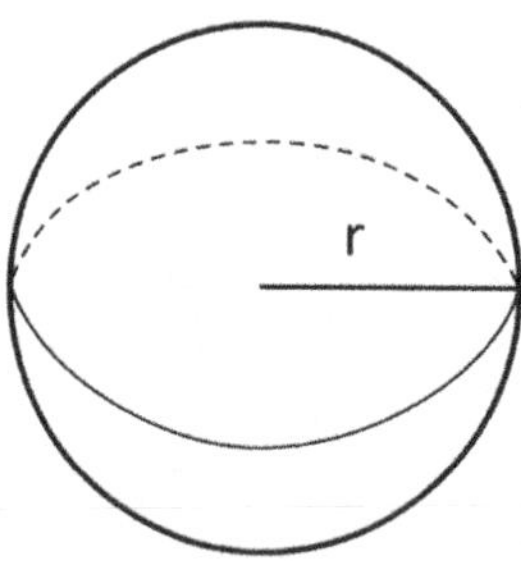

Review Video: Volume and Surface Area of a Sphere
Visit mometrix.com/academy and enter code: 786928

Review Video: How to Calculate the Volume of 3D Objects
Visit mometrix.com/academy and enter code: 163343

The **volume of any prism** is found by the formula $V = Bh$, where B is the area of the base, and h is the height (perpendicular distance between the bases). The surface area of any prism is the sum of the areas of both bases and all sides. It can be calculated as $SA = 2B + Ph$, where P is the perimeter of the base.

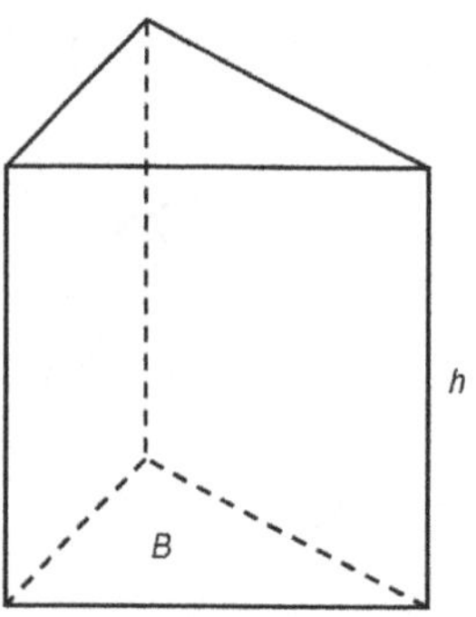

Review Video: Volume and Surface Area of a Prism
Visit mometrix.com/academy and enter code: 420158

For a **rectangular prism**, the volume can be found by the formula $V = lwh$, where V is the volume, l is the length, w is the width, and h is the height. The surface area can be calculated as $SA = 2lw + 2hl + 2wh$ or $SA = 2(lw + hl + wh)$.

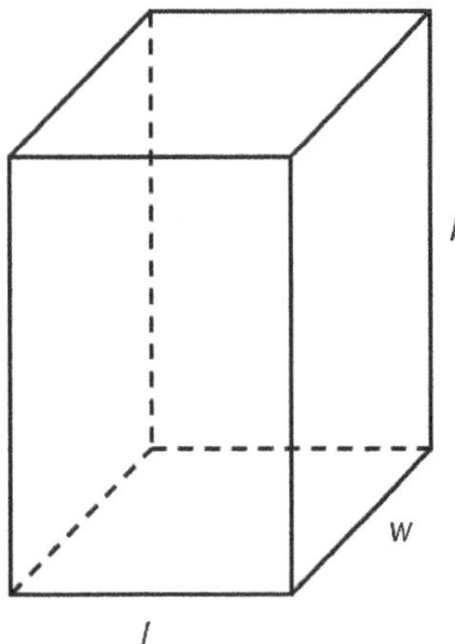

Review Video: Volume and Surface Area of a Rectangular Prism
Visit mometrix.com/academy and enter code: 282814

The **volume of a cube** can be found by the formula $V = s^3$, where s is the length of a side. The surface area of a cube is calculated as $SA = 6s^2$, where SA is the total surface area and s is the length of a side. These formulas are the same as the ones used for the volume and surface area of a rectangular prism, but simplified since all three quantities (length, width, and height) are the same.

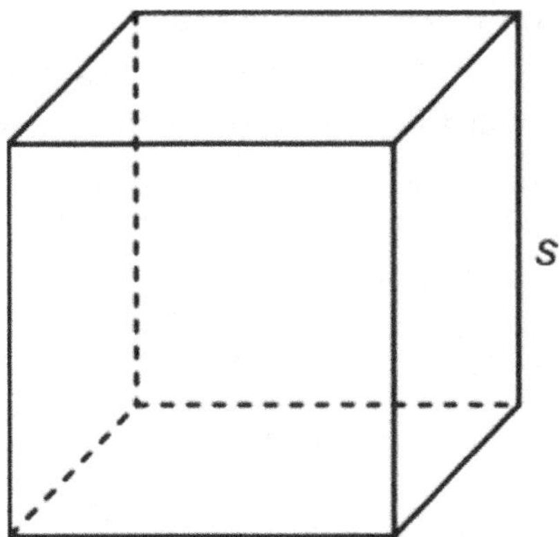

Review Video: Volume and Surface Area of a Cube
Visit mometrix.com/academy and enter code: 664455

The **volume of a cylinder** can be calculated by the formula $V = \pi r^2 h$, where r is the radius, and h is the height. The surface area of a cylinder can be found by the formula $SA = 2\pi r^2 + 2\pi rh$. The first term is the base area multiplied by two, and the second term is the perimeter of the base multiplied by the height.

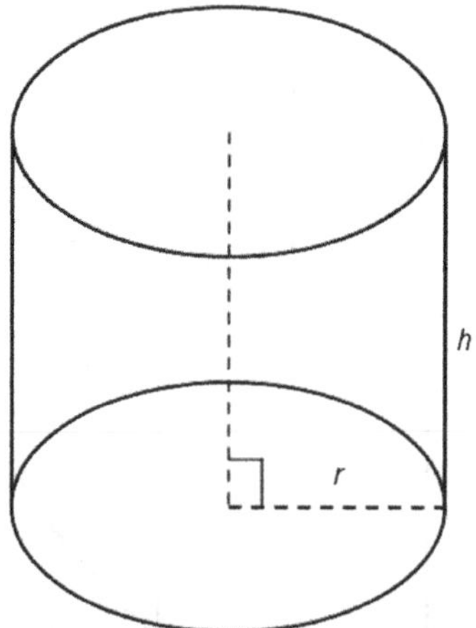

Review Video: Finding the Volume and Surface Area of a Right Circular Cylinder
Visit mometrix.com/academy and enter code: 226463

The **volume of a pyramid** is found by the formula $V = \frac{1}{3}Bh$, where B is the area of the base, and h is the height (perpendicular distance from the vertex to the base). Notice this formula is the same as $\frac{1}{3}$ times the volume of a prism. Like a prism, the base of a pyramid can be any shape.

Finding the **surface area of a pyramid** is not as simple as the other shapes we've looked at thus far. If the pyramid is a right pyramid, meaning the base is a regular polygon and the vertex is directly over the center of that polygon, the surface area can be calculated as $SA = B + \frac{1}{2}Ph_s$, where P is the perimeter of the base, and h_s is the slant height (distance from the vertex to the midpoint of one side of the base). If the pyramid is irregular, the area of each triangle side must be calculated individually and then summed, along with the base.

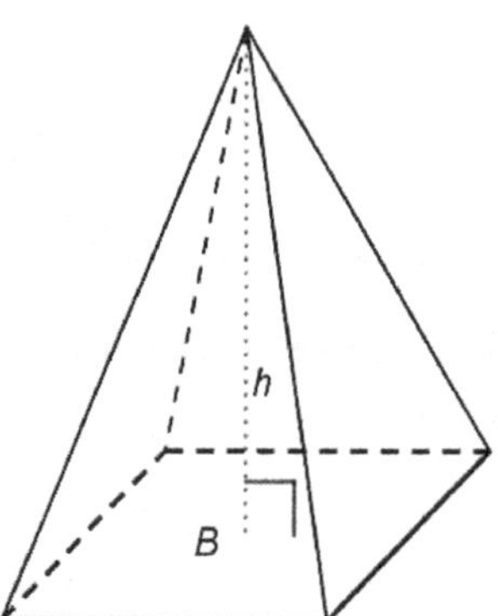

Review Video: Finding the Volume and Surface Area of a Pyramid
Visit mometrix.com/academy and enter code: 621932

The **volume of a cone** is found by the formula $V = \frac{1}{3}\pi r^2 h$, where r is the radius, and h is the height. Notice this is the same as $\frac{1}{3}$ times the volume of a cylinder. The surface area can be calculated as $SA = \pi r^2 + \pi rs$, where s is the slant height. The slant height can be calculated using the Pythagorean theorem to be $\sqrt{r^2 + h^2}$, so the surface area formula can also be written as $SA = \pi r^2 + \pi r\sqrt{r^2 + h^2}$.

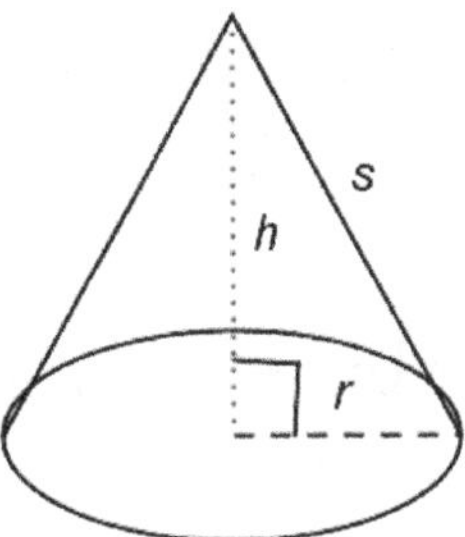

Review Video: Volume and Surface Area of a Right Circular Cone
Visit mometrix.com/academy and enter code: 573574

CLT Practice Test #1

Want to take this practice test in an online interactive format?
Check out the bonus page, which includes interactive practice questions and much more: **mometrix.com/bonus948/claslearntest**

Verbal Reasoning

Refer to the following for questions 1 - 10:

This passage is adapted from George Eliot's The Mill on the Floss, *originally published in 1860.*

Now, good Mr. Glegg himself was stingy in the most amiable manner; his neighbors called him "near," which always means that the person in question is a lovable skinflint. If you expressed a preference for cheese-parings, Mr. Glegg would remember to save them for you, with a good-natured delight in gratifying your palate, and he was given to pet all animals which required no appreciable keep.

There was no humbug or hypocrisy about Mr. Glegg; his eyes would have watered with true feeling over the sale of a widow's furniture, which a five-pound note from his side pocket would have prevented; but a donation of five pounds to a person "in a small way of life" would have seemed to him a mad kind of lavishness rather than "charity," which had always presented itself to him as a contribution of small aids, not a neutralizing of misfortune. And Mr. Glegg was just as fond of saving other people's money as his own; he would have ridden as far round to avoid a turnpike when his expenses were to be paid for him, as when they were to come out of his own pocket, and was quite zealous in trying to induce indifferent acquaintances to adopt a cheap substitute for blacking.

This inalienable habit of saving, as an end in itself, belonged to the industrious men of business of a former generation, who made their fortunes slowly, almost as the tracking of the fox belongs to the harrier,—it constituted them a "race," which is nearly lost in these days of rapid money-getting, when lavishness comes close on the back of want. In old-fashioned times an "independence" was hardly ever made without a little miserliness as a condition, and you would have found that quality in every provincial district, combined with characters as various as the fruits from which we can extract acid. The true Harpagons* were always marked and exceptional characters; not so the worthy tax-payers, who, having once pinched from real necessity, retained even in the midst of their comfortable retirement, with their wallfruit and wine-bins, the habit of regarding life as an ingenious process of nibbling out one's livelihood without leaving any perceptible deficit, and who would have been as immediately prompted to give up a newly taxed luxury when they had had their clear five hundred a year, as when they had only five hundred pounds of capital.

Mr. Glegg, being of a reflective turn, and no longer occupied with wool, had much wondering meditation on the peculiar constitution of the female mind as unfolded to him in his domestic life; and yet he thought Mrs. Glegg's household ways a model for her sex. It struck him as a pitiable irregularity in other women if they did not roll up their table-napkins with the same tightness and emphasis as Mrs. Glegg did, if their pastry had a less leathery consistence, and their damson cheese a less venerable hardness than hers; nay, even the peculiar combination of grocery and druglike odors in Mrs. Glegg's private cupboard impressed him as the only right thing in the way of cupboard smells. I am not sure that he would not have longed for the quarrelling again, if it had ceased for an entire week; and it is certain that an acquiescent, mild wife would have left his meditations comparatively jejune and barren of mystery.

*A reference to Moliere's play *The Miser*, in which Harpagon is devoted to accumulating money.

1. Which choice best describes the tone of the passage?

A) Carefully drawing a dark portrait of a selfish, morose man.
B) Humorously poking fun at a middle-aged man's eccentricities.
C) Romanticizing the thriftiness of a hard-working laborer.
D) Admiration of the longsuffering nature of a downtrodden husband.

2. The word "near" in Paragraph 1, Sentence 1 most nearly means

A) close by
B) dear
C) stingy
D) upcoming

3. What purpose does the hypothetical situation of the widow in Paragraph 2 serve?

A) To illustrate Mr. Glegg's ruling passion of frugality.
B) To give a glimpse of the community in which the Gleggs lived.
C) To show that the Gleggs were well-to-do.
D) To show the value of money in the time period in which the book is set.

4. Which of the following selections best illustrates Mr. Glegg's passion for frugality?

A) Paragraph 1, Sentence 1 ("good Mr. Glegg ... lovable skinflint")
B) Paragraph 2, Sentence 2 ("just as fond ... cheap substitute for blacking")
C) Paragraph 3, Sentence 2 ("In old-fashioned times ... as a condition")
D) Paragraph 4, Sentence 2 ("It struck him ... hardness than hers")

5. The examples in Paragraph 3 show which of the following views of men like Mr. Glegg?

A) Scorn at the quick and easy way they made their money.
B) Appreciation for the hard work that led to their wealth.
C) Disdain for the way they hoarded their fortunes.
D) Confusion at the variety of personalities that are drawn to be miserly.

6. The term "independence" in Paragraph 3, Sentence 2 refers to

A) political freedom
B) freedom from dependence on relatives
C) the state of making one's own decisions
D) sufficient savings to live on

7. What is the effect of using "pinched" instead of merely "saved" in Paragraph 3, Sentence 3?

A) To show the physical suffering required to save money.
B) To show the miserly attitude that gave pain to others in order to save.
C) To show that people often stole to be able to save money.
D) To show that saving money was difficult and required giving up comforts.

8. What can be deduced about Mr. Glegg's character from his opinion of his wife's cooking and cupboard, described in Paragraph 4?

A) His stinginess prevents him from appreciating any but the most economical housekeeping.
B) He has very fastidious tastes, and his wife has learned to cater to them specifically.
C) He finds comfort in the familiar, even when it would be considered unpleasant by others.
D) He is intimidated by his wife and has been brainwashed into thinking that everything she does is perfect.

9. Mr. Glegg : Harpagon ::

A) saving : hoarding
B) generosity : stinginess
C) adventure : security
D) training : relaxation

10. Mrs. Glegg's house : disorder ::

A) pig : mud
B) painter : creativity
C) flower : aroma
D) library : noise

Refer to the following for questions 11 - 20:

This passage is adapted from Karen Hao's "A Radical New Neural Network Design Could Overcome Big Challenges in AI," published in 2018 by MIT Technology Review.

An AI researcher at the University of Toronto, David Duvenaud wanted to build a deep-learning model that would predict a patient's health over time. But data from medical records is messy: throughout your life, you might visit the doctor at different times for different reasons, generating a smattering of measurements at arbitrary intervals. A traditional neural network struggles to handle this. Its design requires it to learn from data with clear stages of observation. Thus, it is a poor tool for modeling continuous processes, especially ones that are measured irregularly over time.

The challenge led Duvenaud and his collaborators to redesign neural networks as we know them. Neural nets are the core machinery that make deep learning so powerful. A traditional neural net is made up of stacked layers of simple computational nodes that work together to find patterns in data. The discrete layers are what keep it from effectively modeling continuous processes.

To understand this, we examine what the layers do in the first place. The most common process for training a neural network involves feeding it labeled data. Let's say you wanted to build a system that recognizes different animals. You'd feed a neural net animal pictures paired with corresponding animal names. Under the hood, it begins to solve a mathematical puzzle. It looks at all the picture-name pairs and figures out a formula that reliably turns one (the image) into the other (the category). Once it cracks that puzzle, it can reuse the formula again and again to correctly categorize new animal photos.

But finding a single formula to describe the entire picture-to-name transformation would be overly broad and result in a low-accuracy model. It would be like trying to use a single rule to differentiate cats and dogs. You could say dogs have floppy ears. But some dogs don't and some cats do, so you'd end up with a lot of false negatives and positives.

This is where a neural net's layers come in. They break up the transformation process into steps and let the network find a series of formulas that each describe a stage of the process. So the first layer might take in all the pixels and use a formula to pick out which ones are most relevant for cats versus dogs. Each subsequent layer would identify increasingly complex features of the animal, until the final layer decides "dog" on the basis of the accumulated calculations. This step-by-step breakdown of the process allows a neural net to build more sophisticated models—which in turn should lead to more accurate predictions.

The layer approach has served the AI field well—but it also has a drawback. If you want to model anything that transforms continuously over time, you also have to chunk it up into discrete steps. So, the best way to model reality as close as possible is to add more layers to increase the granularity. Taken to the extreme, this means the best neural network for this job would have an infinite number of layers to model infinitesimal step-changes.

If this is starting to sound familiar, that's because we have arrived at exactly the kind of problem that calculus was invented to solve. Calculus gives you equations for how to calculate a series of changes across infinitesimal steps—in other words, it saves you from the nightmare of modeling continuous change in discrete units.

The result is really not even a network anymore; there are no more nodes and connections, just one continuous slab of computation. Nonetheless, sticking with convention, the researchers named this design an "ODE net"—ODE for "ordinary differential equations."

Consider a continuous musical instrument like a violin, where you can slide your hand along the string to play any frequency you want; now consider a discrete one like a piano, where you have a distinct number of keys to play a limited number of frequencies. A traditional neural network is like a piano: try as you might, you won't be able to play a slide. Switching to an ODE net is like switching your piano to a violin.

Currently, the paper offers a proof of concept for the design, "but it's not ready for prime time yet," Duvenaud says. Like any initial technique proposed in the field, it still needs to fleshed out, experimented on, and improved until it can be put into production. But the method has the potential to shake up the field.

11. The main purpose of the passage is to

A) show the change in AI over the last few decades
B) encourage the reader to adopt a new technological trend
C) inform the reader of new developments in AI
D) express the current limitations of AI

12. Why is a traditional neural network insufficient for predicting patient health?

A) It computes too slowly, taking years to gather data and learn the individual needs of patients.
B) It needs clear data in regular steps, and most people's health history does not reflect that.
C) It requires more information than most people are comfortable sharing.
D) It is not able to handle the volume of information required for such predictions.

13. Why did Duvenaud seek to redesign neural networks?

A) They are not good at modeling continuous processes.
B) They have difficulty distinguishing between animals.
C) They take too long to accumulate the necessary data.
D) They cannot find patterns in data.

14. What does the author mean in Paragraph 3, Sentence 2 by "training" a neural network?

A) Feeding it images of animals until it learns what the different species look like.
B) Giving it a formula that enables it to discern patterns in data.
C) Teaching it to sort data into two categories with increasingly complex information.
D) Providing it with multiple data examples so that it can figure out patterns for categorization.

15. As used in Paragraph 4, Sentence 1, "broad" most nearly means

A) expansive
B) spacious
C) open-minded
D) general

16. Which of the following can be inferred about neural net layers?

A) There are an infinite number of layers in a neural net.
B) Each layer is more complex than the one before it.
C) The layers make it challenging to create accurate models.
D) The layers are more user-friendly than an ODE net.

17. Which selection provides the best evidence for the answer to the previous question?

A) Paragraph 1, Sentence 2 ("But data ... arbitrary intervals.")
B) Paragraph 2, Sentence 4 ("The discrete layers ... continuous processes.")
C) Paragraph 5, Sentence 2 ("They break up ... stage of the process.")
D) Paragraph 6, Sentence 3 ("So, the best ... increase the granularity.")

18. What is the main idea of the final paragraph?

A) The ODE net is only a design concept as yet and has to pass through significant testing and tweaking.
B) The ODE net is not ready for prime time.
C) The ODE net needs more work before it will be ready, but could make a large difference in the AI field.
D) The ODE net will revolutionize business in the AI sector.

19. traditional neural networks : continuous processes ::

A) calculator : equation
B) piano : violin
C) stopwatch : time intervals
D) dictionary : vocabulary words

20. computers : neural networks ::

A) mathematics : puzzles
B) dogs : floppy ears
C) brains : thinking
D) doctors : health records

Refer to the following for questions 21 - 30:

This passage is adapted from Aleksandr Solzhenitsyn's commencement address delivered at Harvard University on June 8, 1978, entitled "A World Split Apart".

Western society has given itself the organization best suited to its purposes, based, I would say, on the letter of the law. The limits of human rights and righteousness are determined by a system of laws; such limits are very broad. People in the West have acquired considerable skill in interpreting and manipulating law. Any conflict is solved according to the letter of the law and this is considered to be the supreme solution. If one is right from a legal point of view, nothing more is required. Nobody will mention that one could still not be entirely right, and urge self-restraint, a willingness to renounce such legal rights, sacrifice, and selfless risk. It would sound simply absurd. One almost never sees voluntary self-restraint. Everybody operates at the extreme limit of those legal frames.

I have spent all my life under a Communist regime and I will tell you that a society without any objective legal scale is a terrible one indeed. But a society with no other scale than the legal one is not quite worthy of man either. A society which is based on the letter of the law and never reaches any higher is taking very small advantage of the high level of human possibilities. The letter of the law is too cold and formal to have a beneficial influence on society. Whenever the tissue of life is woven of legalistic relations, there is an atmosphere of moral mediocrity, paralyzing man's noblest impulses. And it will be, simply, impossible to stand through the trials of this threatening century with only the support of a legalistic structure.

In today's Western society the inequality has been revealed [in] freedom for good deeds and freedom for evil deeds. A statesman who wants to achieve something important and highly constructive for his country has to move cautiously and even timidly. There are thousands of hasty and irresponsible critics around him; parliament and the press keep rebuffing him. As he moves ahead, he has to prove that each single step of his is well-founded and absolutely flawless. In fact, an outstanding and particularly gifted person who has unusual and unexpected initiatives in mind hardly gets a chance to assert himself; from the very beginning, dozens of traps will be set out for him. Thus mediocrity triumphs, with the excuse of restrictions imposed by democracy.

It is feasible and easy everywhere to undermine administrative power, and, indeed, it has been drastically weakened in all Western countries. The defense of individual rights has reached such extremes as to make society as a whole defenseless against certain individuals. It is time, in the West, to defend not so much human rights as human obligations.

21. Which choice best describes the tone of the passage?

A) wrathful condemnation of perversion of justice and lack of moral leadership
B) serious observations of past and present realities and possible eventualities
C) paranoid concerns regarding rapidly growing governmental power
D) scholarly critique of human nature and societal ills

22. Which sentence(s) in the passage provide(s) the best evidence in support of the answer to the previous question?

A) Paragraph 2, Sentences 5–6 ("Whenever the ... structure.")
B) Paragraph 2, Sentence 1("I have ... indeed.")
C) Paragraph 3, Sentence 1 ("In today's ... deeds.")
D) Paragraph 1, Sentences 3–5 ("People ... required.")

23. Which of the following is closest in meaning to the word "rebuffing" as it is used in Paragraph 3, Sentence 3?

A) to curtly deny or reject
B) to continuously pester or question
C) to speak poorly of without sufficient evidence
D) to mock or ridicule

24. Based on the passage, which of the following phrases would this author most likely agree with?

A) "Politicians and diapers must be changed often, and for the same reason."
B) "No law can give me the right to do what is wrong."
C) "Under capitalism, man exploits man. Under communism, it's just the opposite."
D) "Remember that life is neither pain nor pleasure; it is serious business, to be entered upon with courage and in a spirit of self-sacrifice."

25. It can be inferred from the passage that

A) the West may eventually turn into a communist regime.
B) the law is wholly sufficient to provide all forms of justice.
C) there is a lack of outstanding and gifted politicians in the West.
D) opposition may be strong, if not stronger, when one tries to do good.

26. Which of the following is closest in meaning to the phrase "high level of human possibilities" as used in Paragraph 2, Sentence 3?

A) the gathered collection of human knowledge
B) the greatest potential of mankind regarding beneficence
C) the apex of human logic
D) the collective capacity of human experience

27. In this passage, the author is primarily concerned with

A) establishing true and objective laws to be lived out for the betterment of mankind.
B) outlining the flaws of the communist system of which he was raised.
C) diminishing the rights of individuals through political action.
D) distinguishing between doing what is right and what is legal in regard to Western culture.

28. The author of the passage believes that

A) the West will not be able to endure into the future.
B) progress must be achieved by abolishing the law.
C) the press and politics can often stifle progress.
D) communism is the worst form of government.

29. individual : society ::

A) rung : ladder
B) race : contestant
C) employee : boss
D) lawyer : judge

30. statesman : country ::

A) team : coach
B) the press : politicians
C) judge : courtroom
D) manager : business

Refer to the following for questions 31 - 40:

Passage 1 is adapted from Dr. Martin Luther King Jr.'s "Letter from Birmingham Jail," written in April, 1963.

Passage 2 is an excerpt from Frederick Douglass' "Oration, Delivered in Corinthian Hall, Rochester," originally published on July 5, 1852.

Passage 1

I hope you are able to see the distinction I am trying to point out. In no sense do I advocate evading or defying the law, as would the rabid segregationist. That would lead to anarchy. One who breaks an unjust law must do so openly, lovingly, and with a willingness to accept the penalty. I submit that an individual who breaks a law that conscience tells him is unjust, and who willingly accepts the penalty of imprisonment in order to arouse the conscience of the community over its injustice, is in reality expressing the highest respect for the law.

Of course, there is nothing new about this kind of civil disobedience. It was evidenced sublimely in the refusal of Shadrach, Meshach and Abednego to obey the laws of Nebuchadnezzar, on the ground that a higher moral law was at stake. It was practiced superbly by the early Christians, who were willing to face hungry lions and the excruciating pain of chopping blocks rather than submit to certain unjust laws of the Roman Empire. To a degree, academic freedom is a reality today because Socrates practiced civil disobedience. In our own nation, the Boston Tea Party represented a massive act of civil disobedience.

We should never forget that everything Adolf Hitler did in Germany was "legal" and everything the Hungarian freedom fighters did in Hungary was "illegal." It was "illegal" to aid and comfort a Jew in Hitler's Germany. Even so, I am sure that, had I lived in Germany at the time, I would have aided and comforted my Jewish brothers. If today I lived in a Communist country where certain principles dear to the Christian faith are suppressed, I would openly advocate disobeying that country's antireligious laws.

Passage 2

Fellow Citizens, I am not wanting in respect for the fathers of this republic. The signers of the Declaration of Independence were brave men. They were great men too—great enough to give fame to a great age. It does not often happen to a nation to raise, at one time, such a number of truly great men. The point from which I am compelled to view them is not, certainly the most favorable; and yet I cannot contemplate their great deeds with less than admiration. They were statesmen, patriots and heroes, and for the good they did, and the principles they contended for, I will unite with you to honor their memory.

They loved their country better than their own private interests; and, though this is not the highest form of human excellence, all will concede that it is a rare virtue, and that when it is exhibited, it ought to command respect. He who will, intelligently, lay down his life for his country, is a man whom it is not in human nature to despise. Your fathers staked their lives, their fortunes, and their sacred honor, on the cause of their country. In their admiration of liberty, they lost sight of all other interests.

They were peace men; but they preferred revolution to peaceful submission to bondage. They were quiet men; but they did not shrink from agitating against oppression. They showed forbearance; but that they knew its limits. They believed in order; but not in the order of tyranny. With them, nothing was "settled" that was not right. With them, justice, liberty and humanity were "final"; not slavery and oppression. You may well cherish the memory of such men. They were great in their day and generation. Their solid manhood stands out the more as we contrast it with these degenerate times.

31. The author of Passage 1 believes that

A) breaking the law is justified if one is willing to accept the consequences.
B) as long as disobedience is civil, it is justified.
C) there may be occasions when breaking the law is justified and necessary.
D) only those who respect the law are willing to break it.

32. Which sentence in Passage 1 best summarizes the answer to the previous question?

A) Paragraph 1, Sentence 4 ("One who … the penalty.")
B) Paragraph 3, Sentence 1 ("We should … was 'illegal.'")
C) Paragraph 2, Sentence 5 ("In our own … civil disobedience.")
D) Paragraph 1, Sentence 5 ("I submit … the law.")

33. According to the author of Passage 1, those who break an unjust law should do so with

A) conviction and intolerance.
B) emotion and vigor.
C) confidence and resolve.
D) charity and accountability.

34. The author of Passage 2 believes that

A) order and tyranny are closely related.
B) to be willing to sacrifice one's life for a worthy cause is admirable.
C) revolution is only justified after it has already occurred.
D) to love others more than oneself is the highest form of virtue.

35. Which choice best describes the tone of Passage 2?

A) an elegiac reminder of forgotten men and the social climate of the time
B) a wistful reflection on the country's founding and its history since then
C) a detached exposition honoring deceased men and the principles for which they fought
D) a casual remembrance of fallen heroes and the memories they left behind

36. The authors of both passages would be likely to agree on which of the following ideas?

A) Governments are the largest source of injustice.
B) It is possible to commit injustice by doing nothing.
C) The truest patriots hate injustice in their own land more than anywhere else.
D) If there is no property there is no injustice.

37. How does the structure of each passage differ?

A) Passage 1 discusses the meaning of civil disobedience, whereas Passage 2 portrays a method of active rebellion.
B) Passage 1's intended audience is the oppressors, while Passage 2's intended audience is the oppressed.
C) Passage 1 is persuasive in nature, whereas Passage 2 is meant to call people to action.
D) Passage 1 depicts the necessity of civil disobedience, while Passage 2 expounds on the principles of a particular group of men.

38. Which of the following is closest in meaning to the phrase "solid manhood" as it is used in the final sentence of Passage 2?

A) unyielding strength of character
B) imposing stature
C) aggressive response to tyranny
D) willingness to do difficult things

39. Boston Tea Party : British tyranny ::

A) civil disobedience : laws of nature
B) Shadrach, Meshach, and Abednego's disobedience : laws of Nebuchadnezzar
C) Roman Empire : Christian martyrs
D) Socrates : academic freedom

40. country : private interests ::

A) liberty : fortunes
B) justice : humanity
C) oppression : manhood
D) order : forbearance

Grammar/Writing

Refer to the following for questions 41 - 50:

This passage is adapted from Education and the Good Life *by Bertrand Russell, first published in 1926.*

(41) To produce the habit of truthfulness should be one of the major aims of moral education. I do not mean truthfulness in speech only, but also in thought; indeed, of the two, the latter seems to me the more important. I prefer a person (42) who lies with full consciousness of what he is doing to a person who first subconsciously deceives himself and then imagines that he is being virtuous and truthful. Indeed, no man who thinks truthfully can believe that it is always wrong to speak untruthfully. Those who hold that a lie is always wrong have to supplement this view by a great deal of casuistry and considerable practice (43) on misplacing priorities, by means of which they deceive without admitting to themselves that they are lying. Nevertheless, I hold that the occasions when lying is justifiable are few—much fewer than would be inferred from the practice of high-minded men. And almost all the occasions which justify lying are occasions where power is being used (44) beneficially, or where people are engaged in some harmful activity such as war; therefore in a good social system they would be even rarer than they are now.

Untruthfulness, as a practice, is almost always a product of fear. The child brought up without fear will be truthful, not in virtue of a moral effort, but because it (45) has never occurred to him to be otherwise. The child who has been treated wisely and kindly has a frank look in the eyes, and a fearless demeanour even with strangers; whereas the child that has been subject to nagging or severity is in perpetual terror of incurring reproof, and terrified of having transgressed some rule whenever he has behaved in a natural manner. It does not at first occur to a young child that it is possible to lie. (46) Due to observation of grown-ups quickened by terror, the possibility of lying is a discovery. The child discovers that grown-ups lie to (47) him and that it is dangerous to tell them the truth: under these circumstances he takes to lying. Avoid these incentives, and he will not think of lying.

But in judging whether children are truthful, a certain caution is necessary. Children's memories are very (48) faulty; besides, they often do not know the answer to a question when grown-up people think they do. Their sense of time is very vague; a child under four will hardly distinguish between yesterday and a week ago, or between yesterday and six hours ago, or between a week ago and six hours ago. When they do not know the answer to a question, they tend to say yes or no according to the suggestion in your tone of voice. Again, (49) they are often talking in the dramatic character of some make-believe. (50) When they tell you solemnly that there is a lion in the back garden, this is obvious; but in many cases it is quite easy to mistake play for earnest. For all these reasons, a young child's statements are often objectively untrue, but without the slightest intention to deceive. Indeed, children tend, at first, to regard grown-ups as omniscient, and therefore incapable of being deceived.

41. To produce the habit of truthfulness should be one of the major aims of moral education.

A) NO CHANGE
B) To produce the habit of truthfulness is one of the major aims of moral education.
C) One of the major aims of moral education should be to produce the habit of truthfulness.
D) The habit of truthfulness should be one of the major aims of moral education to produce.

42. who lies with full consciousness of what he is doing to a person who first subconsciously deceives himself and

A) NO CHANGE
B) who lies, with full consciousness of what he is doing to a person, who first subconsciously deceives himself, and
C) who lies, with full consciousness of what he is doing; to a person who first subconsciously deceives himself, and
D) who lies with full consciousness, of what he is doing to a person who first subconsciously deceives himself, and

43. on misplacing priorities

A) NO CHANGE
B) in misplacing priorities
C) of misplacing priorities
D) at misplacing priorities

44. beneficially

A) NO CHANGE
B) tyrannically
C) effectively
D) foolishly

45. has never occurred

A) NO CHANGE
B) it will never occur
C) it never occurs
D) it is never occurring

46. Due to observation of grown-ups quickened by terror, the possibility of lying is a discovery.

A) NO CHANGE
B) Quickened by terror due to observation of grown-ups, the possibility of lying is a discovery.
C) Due to observation of grown-ups, the possibility of lying is a discovery quickened by terror.
D) By observing grown-ups quickened by terror, a child discovers the possibility of lying.

47. him and that it is dangerous to tell them the truth: under

A) NO CHANGE
B) him, and that it is dangerous to tell them the truth, under
C) him and that it is dangerous to tell them the truth: under
D) him, and that it is dangerous to tell them the truth; under

48. faulty; besides, they

A) NO CHANGE
B) faulty, but they
C) faulty, and they
D) faulty; similarly, they

49. they are often talking

A) NO CHANGE
B) they often talk
C) they often are talking
D) often they are talking

50. When they tell you solemnly that there is a lion in the back garden,

A) NO CHANGE
B) When, solemnly, they tell you that there is a lion in the back garden,
C) When a child tells you solemnly that there is a lion in the back garden,
D) When they tell you solemnly that the back garden has a lion in it,

Refer to the following for questions 51 - 60:

The following is adapted from Plutarch's The Life of Alexander, *a biography of Alexander the Great written around 200 AD.*

(51) Thus it was that at the age of twenty years Alexander received the kingdom, which was exposed to great jealousies, dire hatreds, and dangers on every hand. For the neighboring tribes of Barbarians would not tolerate their servitude, and longed for their (52) hereditary kingdoms; and as for Greece, although Philip had conquered her in the field, he had not had time enough to make her tame under his yoke, but had merely disturbed and changed the condition of affairs there, and then left them in a great surge and commotion, owing to the strangeness of the situation. The Macedonian counsellors of Alexander (53) had fears of the crisis, and thought he should give up the Greek states altogether and use no more compulsion there, and that he should call the revolting Barbarians back to their allegiance by mild measures and try to arrest the first symptoms of their revolutions. But he himself set out from opposite (54) palaces to win security and safety for his realm by boldness and a lofty spirit, assured that, were he seen to abate his dignity even but a little, all his enemies would set upon him. Accordingly, he put a speedy stop to the disturbances and wars among the Barbarians by overrunning (55) their territories with an army as far as to the river Danube, where he fought a great battle with Syrmus, the king of the Triballi, and defeated him. On learning that the Thebans had revolted and that the Athenians were in sympathy with them, he immediately led his forces through the pass of Thermopylae, (56) supposing that since Demosthenes had called him a boy while he was among the Illyrians and Triballians, and a stripling when he had reached Thessaly, he wished to show him that before the walls of Athens he was a man.

(57) Arrived before Thebes, and wishing to give her still a chance to repent of what she had done, he merely demanded the surrender of Phoenix and Prothytes, and proclaimed an amnesty for those who came over to his side. But the Thebans made a counter-demand that he should surrender to them Philotas and Antipater, and made a counter-proclamation that all (58) wished to help in setting Greece free should range themselves with them; and so Alexander set his Macedonians to the work of war. On the part of the Thebans, then, the struggle was carried on with a spirit and valour beyond their powers, since they were arrayed against an enemy who was many times more numerous than they; but when the Macedonian garrison also, leaving the citadel of the Cadmeia, fell upon them in the rear, most of them were surrounded, and fell in the battle itself, and their city was taken, plundered, and razed to the ground. This was done, in the main, because Alexander expected that the Greeks would be terrified by so great a disaster and cower down in quiet, but apart from this, he also (59) plumed himself on gratifying the complaints of his allies; for the Phocians and Plataeans had denounced the Thebans. So after separating out the priests, all who were guest-friends of the Macedonians, the descendants of Pindar, and those who had voted against the revolt, he sold the rest

into slavery, and they proved to be more than thirty thousand; those who had been slain were more than six thousand.

51. Thus it was that at the age of twenty years Alexander received the kingdom, which was exposed to great jealousies, dire hatreds, and dangers on every hand.

A) NO CHANGE
B) Thus, it was that at the age of twenty years Alexander received the kingdom, which was exposed to great jealousies, dire hatreds, and dangers on every hand.
C) Thus it was that, at the age of twenty years, Alexander received the kingdom, which was exposed to great jealousies, dire hatreds, and dangers on every hand.
D) Thus it was that at the age of twenty years Alexander received the kingdom, which was exposed to great jealousies, dire hatreds, and dangers, on every hand.

52. hereditary kingdoms; and as for Greece,

A) NO CHANGE
B) their hereditary kingdoms. As for Greece,
C) their hereditary kingdoms; as for Greece,
D) their hereditary kingdoms. And as for Greece,

53. had fears of the crisis, and thought

A) NO CHANGE
B) feared the crisis, and thought
C) feared the crisis and thought
D) had fears of the crisis and thought

54. palaces

A) NO CHANGE
B) principals
C) principalities
D) principles

55. their

A) NO CHANGE
B) It's
C) its
D) his

56. supposing

A) NO CHANGE
B) declaring
C) imagining
D) assuming

57. Arrived before Thebes,

A) NO CHANGE
B) He arrived before Thebes,
C) Arriving before Thebes,
D) I arrived before Thebes,

58. wished

A) NO CHANGE
B) wishing
C) who wished
D) who wishes

59. plumed

A) NO CHANGE
B) plumped
C) plumbed
D) primed

60. Which of the following is the best concluding sentence to add to the end of the passage?

A) No further conclusion should be added to the passage.
B) In the destruction of Thebes, Alexander's determination and strategic prowess marked the beginning of his journey as a conqueror and emperor of unparalleled ambition.
C) Thus, despite Alexander's young age and tendency to disregard counsel, Alexander was remarkably successful in governance and conquest.
D) This great event marks the tragic fall of Thebes, as its citizens were turned to slaves and refugees.

Refer to the following for questions 61 - 70:

Could the future of crops include planting without soil? The concept of hydroponics, or growing plants by directly exposing the roots to water and nutrients, (61) both conserving resources such as water and stimulating extra growth and food production.

While this concept sounds new and innovative—and (62) in fact has being extensively studied by NASA in recent years—the idea is not original to the past decade, or even the past century. (63) Books were published, as early as the 17th century, discussing the idea of growing plants without the traditional concept of planting them in the earth. The term "hydroponics" was first introduced in 1937 by William Gericke, who grew tomatoes in his back yard in a solution of minerals. Since this time, numerous experiments have been conducted and some large hydroponics farms have even been constructed.

Rather than soil, plants are grown in a variety of (64) substitutes; such as rockwool, clay pellets, pumice, wood fiber, or even packing peanuts. These allow the roots easy access to both the nutrient-rich water and to oxygen.

There are many advantages to hydroponic farming. Due to the controlled greenhouse environment, crops can be grown and no pesticides. There is also less waste of water because of no run-off. Furthermore, proponents of hydroponics claim that this method can lead to much greater yields. This is due not only to the better nutrition but (65) additionally to the protection from harsh weather conditions and pests. Additionally, hydroponics farmers are not limited to a single crop during the normal growing (66) season, they can produce year-round.

(67) In addition, hydroponics does have disadvantages. Before beginning, a farmer must have a greenhouse with proper growing stations and temperature control. Soil replacement, nutrients, and specialized lighting must also be purchased. Finally, removing exposure to the outdoor environment means that the farmer must (68) eliminate needs such as pollination. (69) The setup for growing without soil is costly.

Despite the disadvantages, hydroponics is likely to become more popular in coming years. Not only can crops be grown year-round, but plants can also be much closer together, or even grown (70) vertically, allowing for a much greater yield per acre. Additionally, hydroponics may have implications in other areas. For example, NASA has done research with hydroponics to mimic a Martian environment. (24) So while the work and expense of soil-less gardening is significant, this market, which is already in the hundreds of millions of dollars worldwide, may be a glimpse of the future of farming.

61. both conserving resources

A) NO CHANGE
B) allows farmers to both conserve resources
C) aids in both conserving resources
D) both conserves resources

62. in fact has being

A) NO CHANGE
B) has been
C) is been
D) having been

63. Books were published, as early as the 17th century,

A) NO CHANGE
B) Books, as early as the 17th century, were published:
C) As early as the 17th century, books were published
D) Books were published as early as the 17th century—

64. substitutes; such

A) NO CHANGE
B) substitutes, such
C) substitutes: like
D) substitutes, like

65. additionally to

A) NO CHANGE
B) in addition
C) even to
D) in also to

66. season, they

A) NO CHANGE
B) season, or they
C) season, then they
D) season; they

67. In addition

A) NO CHANGE
B) Comparatively
C) Moreover
D) However

68. eliminate

A) NO CHANGE
B) track
C) provide for
D) remove

69. What is the most logical place for this sentence?

The setup for growing without soil is costly.

A) NO CHANGE
B) after Paragraph 5, Sentence 1 ("In addition... disadvantages")
C) after Paragraph 5, Sentence 2 ("Before beginning...control")
D) after Paragraph 5, Sentence 3 ("Soil replacement...purchased")

70. vertically

A) NO CHANGE
B) in a vertical manner
C) vertical
D) horizontal

Refer to the following for questions 71 - 80:

This passage is adapted from Orthodoxy *by G.K. Chesterton, first published in 1908.*

(71) In the modern mind, materialism domineers because of one major mistaken assumption. It is supposed that if a thing goes on repeating itself it is probably dead; a piece of clockwork. People feel that if the universe was personal it would vary; if the sun were alive it would dance. This is a (72) fantasy even in relation to known fact. For the variation in human affairs is generally brought into them, not by life, but by death; by the dying down or breaking off of their strength or desire. A man varies his movements because of some slight element of failure or fatigue. (73) He will get into an omnibus because he is tired of walking; or he walks because he was tired of sitting still. But if his life and joy were so gigantic that he never tired of going to Islington, he might go to Islington as regularly as the Thames goes to Sheerness. The very speed and ecstacy of his life would have the stillness of death. The sun rises every morning. (74) I do not rise every morning, but my inaction is what varies, not my activity. Now, to put the matter in a popular phrase, it might be true that the sun rises regularly because he never gets tired of rising. His routine might be due, not to a lifelessness, but to a rush of life. The thing I mean can be seen, for instance, in children, when they find some game or joke that they specially enjoy. (75) A child kicks his legs in a steady rhythm because he is exceedingly lively. Because children have abounding vitality, because they are in spirit fierce and free, therefore they want things repeated and unchanged. They always (76) say, "Do it again"; and the grown-up person does it again until he is nearly dead. For grown-up people are not strong enough to (77) exult in monotony. But perhaps God is strong enough to exult in monotony. It is possible that God says every morning, "Do it again" to the sun; and every evening, "Do it again" to the moon. It may not be automatic necessity that makes all daisies alike; it may be that God makes every daisy separately, but has never got tired of making them. It may be that He has the eternal appetite of infancy; for we have sinned and grown old, and our Father is younger than we. The repetition in Nature may not be a mere recurrence; it may be a theatrical ENCORE. Heaven may ENCORE the bird who laid an egg. If the human being conceives and brings forth a human child instead of (78) having brought forth a fish, or a bat, or a griffin, the reason may not be that we are fixed in an animal fate without life or purpose. (79) It may be that our little tragedy has touched the gods and that they admire it from their starry galleries; and that at the end of every human drama man is called again and again before the curtain. Repetition may go on for millions of years, by mere choice, and at any instant it may stop. Man may stand on the earth generation after generation, and yet each birth be (80) his positively last appearance.

71. In the modern mind, materialism domineers because of one major mistaken assumption.

A) NO CHANGE
B) The modern mind is dominated by materialism based on one false assumption.
C) One false assumption is the cause of materialism's domination of the modern mind.
D) All the materialism that dominates the modern mind is ultimately because of one false assumption.

72. fantasy

A) NO CHANGE
B) fallacy
C) family
D) tapestry

73. He will get into an omnibus because he is tired of walking; or he walks because he was tired of sitting still.

A) NO CHANGE
B) He got into an omnibus because he is tired of walking; or he walks because he was tired of sitting still.
C) He gets into an omnibus because he tires of walking; or he is walking because he is tired of sitting still.
D) He gets into an omnibus because he is tired of walking; or he walks because he is tired of sitting still.

74. I do not rise every morning, but my inaction is what varies, not my activity.

A) NO CHANGE
B) I vary in my inaction, not in my activity, which is why I do not rise every morning.
C) I do not rise every morning; but the variation is due not to my activity, but to my inaction.
D) Variation in when I rise is not due to my activity, but to my inaction, so I do not rise every morning.

75. A child kicks his legs in a steady rhythm because he is exceedingly lively.

A) NO CHANGE
B) A child will kick his legs rhythmically through not absence, but instead an excess of life.
C) A child kicks his legs rhythmically through excess, not absence, of life.
D) A child rhythmically kicks his legs throughout an excess of life, not an absence of life.

76. say, "Do it again"; and

A) NO CHANGE
B) say, "Do it again," and
C) say "do it again" and
D) say "Do it again."; and

77. exult

A) NO CHANGE
B) exalt
C) suffer
D) exhale

78. having brought

A) NO CHANGE
B) brought
C) brings
D) bringing

79. It may be that our little tragedy has touched the gods and that they admire it from their starry galleries; and that at the end of every human drama man is called again and again before the curtain.

A) NO CHANGE
B) It may be that our little tragedy has touched the gods that they admire it from their starry galleries, and that at the end of every human drama man is called again, and again before the curtain.
C) It may be that our little tragedy has touched the gods, that they admire it from their starry galleries, and that at the end of every human drama man is called again and again before the curtain.
D) It may be, that our little tragedy has touched the gods, that they admire it from their starry galleries, and that at the end of every human drama, man is called again, and again before the curtain.

80. his

A) NO CHANGE
B) its
C) their
D) our

Quantitative Reasoning

81. Given the following system of equations, what is the value of y?

$$\begin{cases} 2x - 6y = 12 \\ -6x + 14y = 42 \end{cases}$$

A) –52.5
B) –19.5
C) –2.44
D) 6.56

82. Every person attending a meeting hands out a business card to every other person at the meeting. If a total of 30 cards are handed out, how many people are at the meeting?

A) 5 people
B) 6 people
C) 10 people
D) 15 people

83. Quinn deposits $250 from each quarterly paycheck into a savings account. How much will he have deposited in the account after 5 years?

A) $4,800
B) $5,000
C) $5,200
D) $5,400

84. Use the operation table to determine $(a * b) * (c * d)$.

*	a	b	c	d
a	d	a	b	c
b	a	b	c	d
c	b	c	d	a
d	c	d	a	b

A) a
B) b
C) c
D) d

85. Which of the following expressions is equal to $\sin\theta\tan\theta$?

A) $\cot\theta$
B) $\tan\theta$
C) $\csc\theta - \sin\theta$
D) $\sec\theta - \cos\theta$

86. Solve the inequality: $|x + 6| < 9$

A) $(-15, -3)$
B) $(-15, 3)$
C) $(3, -3)$
D) $(6, -9)$

87. Given the line $y = -\frac{3}{4}x + 1$, find the equation of a line perpendicular to that line that passes through the point $(0, 6)$.

A) $y = \frac{3}{4}x + 6$
B) $y = -\frac{3}{4}x + 6$
C) $y = -\frac{4}{3}x + 6$
D) $y = \frac{4}{3}x + 6$

88. Two even integers and one odd integer are multiplied together. Which of the following could be their product?

A) 3.75
B) 9
C) 16.2
D) 24

89. If $x^2 - 4 = 45$, then which of the following is a value of x?

A) 9
B) 5
C) 3
D) -7

90. If $x - 2$ is the least of three consecutive even integers, what is the sum of the three integers?

A) $3x - 3$
B) x
C) $3x$
D) $x - 3$

91. What is the perimeter of a 30-60-90 triangle if the short leg is 3 millimeters?

A) $\frac{9\sqrt{3}}{2}$ mm
B) $9\sqrt{3}$ mm
C) $(6 + 3\sqrt{3})$ mm
D) $(9 + 3\sqrt{3})$ mm

92. A recipe calls for 2 cups of water for every 6 cups of flour. Josie wants to make a smaller batch using only 2 cups of flour. How much water should she use?

A) $\frac{1}{2}$ cup
B) 2 cups
C) $\frac{2}{3}$ cup
D) 12 cups

93. What is the slope of a line that passes through the points $(4, 1)$ and $(-13, 8)$?

A) $\frac{7}{17}$
B) $-\frac{7}{17}$
C) $-\frac{17}{7}$
D) $\frac{17}{7}$

94. A commuter survey counts the people riding in cars on a highway in the morning. Each car contains only one man, only one woman, or both one man and one woman. Out of 25 cars, 13 contain a woman and 20 contain a man. How many contain both a man and a woman?

A) 0
B) 7
C) 8
D) 12

95. As shown below, four congruent isosceles trapezoids are positioned such that they form an arch. Find x for the indicated angle.

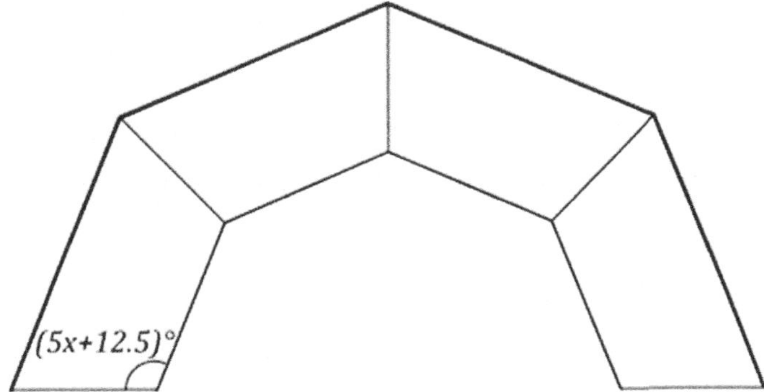

A) $x = 11$
B) $x = 20$
C) $x = 24.5$
D) The value of x cannot be determined from the information given.

96. What is the product of three consecutive odd integers, if the one in the middle is x?

A) $x^2 - 3x$
B) $x^2 - 5x$
C) $x^3 - x$
D) $x^3 - 4x$

97. The diagram shows two lines, l and m, with line n, a transversal, crossing them. Which of the following additional pieces of information would allow you to deduce that lines l and m are parallel to each other?

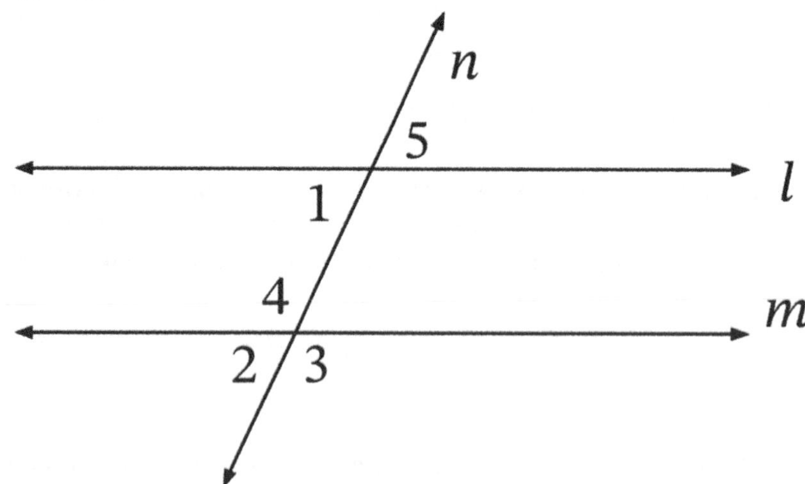

A) $m\angle 1 + m\angle 2 = 180°$
B) $m\angle 1 + m\angle 3 = 180°$
C) $\angle 1 \cong \angle 4$
D) $\angle 1 \cong \angle 5$

98. Put the following numbers in order from the least to greatest $2^3, 4^2, 6^0, 9, 10^1$.

A) $2^3, 4^2, 6^0, 9, 10^1$
B) $6^0, 9, 10^1, 2^3, 4^2$
C) $10^1, 2^3, 6^0, 9, 4^2$
D) $6^0, 2^3, 9, 10^1, 4^2$

99. The equation of a circle is shown below. What is the circle's diameter?

$$x^2 + y^2 - 4x + 2y = 4$$

A) 2
B) 3
C) 5
D) 6

100. A round table has six chairs, labeled H–M. If the chairs were set in a straight line in the same order that they have around the table, chair H would be on one end and chair K on the other. Chair J would be between chairs H and I, chair L would be between posts I and M, and chair M would be between chairs L and K. Which of these statements is (are) necessarily true?

I. The distance between chairs H and L is greater than the distance between chairs I and M.
II. Chair I is between chairs J and L.
III. The distance between chairs M and K is less than the distance between chairs H and L.

A) I, II, and III
B) I and III
C) II only
D) None of these is necessarily true

101. A survey of a random sample of 100 drivers asked them the color of their car. The results of the survey are presented in the table below.

Color of car	Number of drivers
Blue	26
Red	14
Yellow	36
Silver	24

If the parking lot at the local store is filled with 25 cars, how many yellow cars would be expected to be in the lot?

A) 6
B) 9
C) 11
D) 12

102. Find $[g \circ f]x$ when $f(x) = x + 2$ and $g(x) = 2x^2 - 4x + 2$.

A) $4x^2 + 10x + 6$
B) $2x^2 - 4x + 8$
C) $x^2 - 2$
D) $2x^2 + 4x + 2$

103. Which of the following lines is parallel to the line $y = 3x + 12$?

A) $3y - 9x = -36$
B) $y = -\frac{1}{3}x - 12$
C) $12y + 36x = 144$
D) $y + 3x + 12 = 0$

104. In ΔABC, if $\sin A = \cos 62°$, what is $\cos A$?

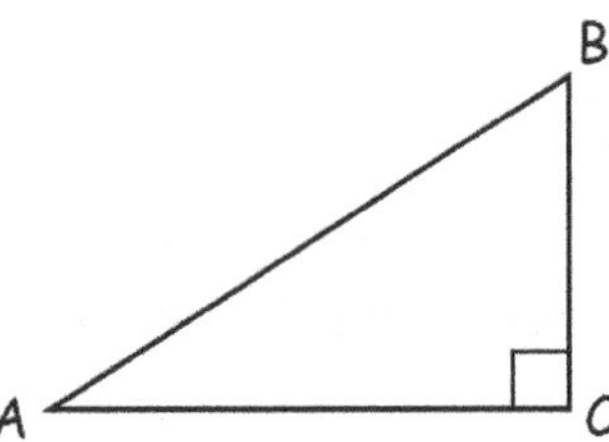

A) $\sin 28°$
B) $\sin 62°$
C) $\cos 62°$
D) $\sec 28°$

105. If an odd number is added to an even number, then which of the following must be true of the result?

A) It is odd
B) It is even
C) It is positive
D) It is zero

106. If a circle has a diameter of 12 cm, what is its approximate area? Use 3.14 for π.

A) 38 cm^2
B) 113 cm^2
C) 276 cm^2
D) 452 cm^2

107. If p and n are positive consecutive integers such that $p > n$, and $p + n = 15$, what is the value of n?

A) 5
B) 6
C) 7
D) 8

108. In a game played with toothpicks, players A and B take turns removing toothpicks from a row on a table. At each turn, each player must remove 1, 2, or 3 toothpicks from the row. The object is to force the other player to remove the last toothpick. If there are 6 toothpicks in the row, which of the following moves ensures a win?

A) Remove 1
B) Remove 2
C) Remove 3
D) Remove 1 or 2

109. What is $|x| + |x - 2|$ when $x = 1$?

A) 0
B) 1
C) 2
D) 3

110. Which of the following expressions is equal to $\cos\theta \cot\theta$?

A) $\sin\theta$
B) $\sec\theta \tan\theta$
C) $\csc\theta - \sin\theta$
D) $\sec\theta - \sin\theta$

111. Which of the following must be true about the product of two even numbers?

A) It is a prime number
B) It is an odd number
C) It is a fraction
D) It is an even number

112. Which of the following lines is perpendicular to the line $3x + 2y = 5$?

A) $y = -\frac{1}{3}x + 2$
B) $y = -\frac{2}{3}x + 5$
C) $y = \frac{1}{3}x - 5$
D) $y = \frac{2}{3}x - 7$

113. What is the area of a square that has a perimeter of 8 cm?

A) 2 cm^2
B) 4 cm^2
C) 32 cm^2
D) 64 cm^2

114. Sylvia, who is just over five feet tall, stands 195 feet away from the base of a tower and looks toward the top of the tower with a 45° angle of inclination. Approximately how tall is the tower?

A) 100 ft
B) 200 ft
C) 400 ft
D) $400\sqrt{3}$ ft

115. Simplify the expression $x^5 \times (2x)^3$.

A) $2x^8$
B) $2x^{15}$
C) $8x^8$
D) $8x^{15}$

116. The diagram shows a circle with center C and with points A, B, P, and Q lying on the circle. Which of the following statements is true?

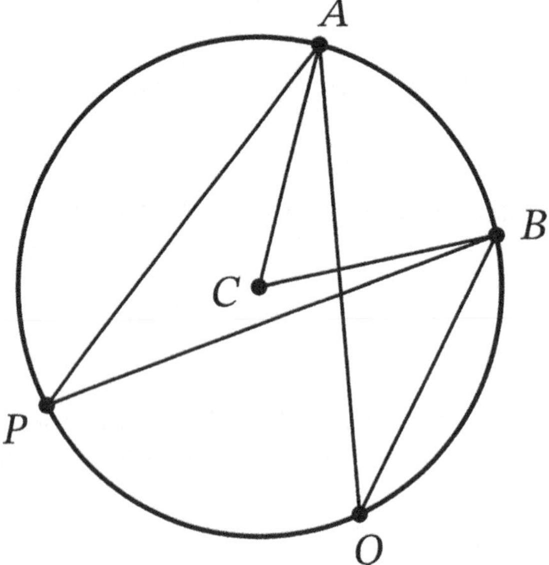

A) $m\angle APB + m\angle AQB < m\angle ACB$
B) $m\angle APB + m\angle AQB = m\angle ACB$
C) $m\angle APB + m\angle AQB > m\angle ACB$
D) The problem does not give enough information to determine how the values of $m\angle APB + m\angle AQB$ and $m\angle ACB$ compare.

117. What is the missing number in the sequence: 4, 6, 10, 18, ___, 66.

A) 22
B) 34
C) 45
D) 54

118. Students are asked to list pairs of terms that have a ratio of 5 : 4. Which of these pairs should not be on the list?

A) 25 and 20
B) 15 and 12
C) 35 and 24
D) 55 and 44

119. A case of canned corn has 2 layers. Each layer contains 4 rows of 6 cans. How many cans of corn does one case contain?

A) 12 cans
B) 20 cans
C) 36 cans
D) 48 cans

120. If the ratio of the measures of the three angles in a triangle are 2 : 6 : 10, what is the actual measure of the smallest angle?

A) 20 degrees
B) 40 degrees
C) 60 degrees
D) 80 degrees

Essay

1. Discuss the benefits of friendship and whether it is better to have a large circle of casual friends or a few very close friends. Be sure to explain your rationale with 2-3 main reasons.

Answer Key and Explanations

Verbal Reasoning

1. B: The tone of this passage is light-hearted as it describes Mr. Glegg's extreme thriftiness, to the point of absurdity. Along with thriftiness, the passage points out Mr. Glegg's view of his marriage—he is so used to the "leathery" pastry that he considers it the standard for cooking, and has come to expect frequent quarrels as a normal part of life. While his actions may be characterized at times as selfish or morose (A), the tone is not dark. And while Mr. Glegg is described as thrifty (C), the author does not romanticize his efforts. Finally, while he could possibly be considered downtrodden as a result of the quarrels and questionable housekeeping, the author writes with satire rather than admiration, to provoke laughter rather than sympathy.

2. C: The word "near" is used to describe Mr. Glegg's character as a miserly or stingy man. It is not the literal meaning of being physically close (A) or being "near and dear" (B), or of being about to appear on the scene (D).

3. A: The situation of the widow, in which Mr. Glegg expresses "true feeling" but is unwilling to make a small donation to help, shows that frugality is the ruling virtue of his life. The story does not give much insight into the Gleggs' community (B), as it is merely a hypothetical situation. It shows that the Gleggs have enough money to help a destitute widow, but does not give a clear picture of their monetary worth (C). And while we may gain some insight into the value of money at a time when five pounds would settle a widow's small debt, it does not give us an accurate idea of monetary value in this time period (D).

4. B: The anecdote in paragraph 2, in which Mr. Glegg not only tries to save his own money but is "quite zealous" in helping others live more cheaply, illustrates how passionate he is about frugality. Calling him a "lovable skinflint" (A) refers to his frugality but does not illustrate it. The selection from paragraph 3 (C) makes a general statement about miserliness but does not give a specific illustration of Mr. Glegg's frugality. His admiration for his wife's housekeeping (D) is not directly linked to frugality.

5. B: While the author pokes fun at Mr. Glegg for his eccentricities, in paragraph 3 she describes men like him as "industrious" and "marked and exceptional." She points out his lack of generosity in paragraph 2, but in this paragraph, she notes the hard work that went into slowly accumulating wealth by diligent industry and self-denial. The mention of quickly making money (A) is referring to a different set of people. The author does not show disdain (in this paragraph) for the hoarding of hard-won fortunes (C). And though she mentions the variety of characters that fall into this category, she does not appear to be confused by this (D).

6. D: Paragraph 3 is referring to those who carefully save to build up a sufficient amount to live comfortably, by their various standards. It is not referring to independence in a political or legal sense (A), or to being free from dependence on relatives (B), though that would be a natural side effect. Nor does it refer to independently making choices for oneself (C).

7. D: The use of "pinched" illustrates the challenges and self-denial involved in saving money. This could possibly have caused physical suffering with some of the sacrifices (A), but that is not the intended meaning. Pinched does not refer to pain caused to others by saving (B), though this doubtless happened on occasion, as in the hypothetical widow's situation in paragraph 2. The term "pinched" has been used as slang for "stole" (C), but that is not the intent here.

8. C: The entire selection shows that Mr. Glegg is a man of habit, whether of saving money or his household routine. The passage points out that although Mrs. Glegg's cooking is less than excellent (leathery pastry and hard damson cheese), Mr. Glegg prefers it to any other because he has grown accustomed to it. The passage does not state whether Mrs. Glegg's housekeeping is economical (A), nor does it give any indication that his wife tailors her cooking and housekeeping to Mr. Glegg's tastes (B). Finally, there is no evidence from this passage that Mr. Glegg has been brainwashed into thinking that his wife's housekeeping is perfect (D).

9. A: In the passage, Mr. Glegg is compared with industrious men of a former generation, characterized by the name Harpagon. These men are described in the third paragraph as having an "inalienable habit of saving," depicting a miserly obsession with money. Mr. Glegg is described as very interested in saving money for himself or for others and is much more moderate with saving, making an apt comparison between saving and hoarding.

10. D: In the passage, Mrs. Glegg is described as being extremely accomplished at cooking and keeping her house in order. The passage provides several examples of how excellent her work is. Mrs. Glegg's house is to disorder as a library is to noise.

11. C: The passage discusses the development of a new network design that has the potential to change the AI industry. It doesn't focus on how AI has changed (A), though it predicts change with the new development. It does not encourage the reader to adopt this trend (B), as it is not currently available. And while it mentions the current limitations of AI (D), the point is that a solution may have been found for these limitations.

12. B: The first paragraph states that a traditional neural network requires "data with clear stages of observation." Most people do not have enough regularly spaced, uniform doctor visits to meet this need. Years of data are needed, but the network itself does not take years to compute (A). There is no mention of sensitive information needed (C) or the inability to handle the amount of information available (D).

13. A: A traditional neural network is "a poor tool for modeling continuous processes," according to the first paragraph. While the third paragraph gives an example of distinguishing between animals (B), this is not the main problem. The networks themselves do not take too long to accumulate data (C), though it can be years before sufficient data is available for modeling. And they do find patterns in data (D), though the process needs improvement.

14. D: The author speaks of training a neural network by inputting labeled data, such as a picture of an animal along with the name of the animal (cat, dog, etc.). Because not all cats and dogs look alike, it is important to provide multiple examples so the network can figure out the patterns and create a formula to distinguish categories. The example given in the article is using images of animals (A), but a neural network can be used for much more than categorizing animals. The user does not give the formula to the network (B), but gives the network sufficient data to create its own formula. While the network does learn to sort data into categories (C), it is not limited to two, nor is the information necessarily increasing in complexity.

15. D: Paragraph 4 points out that using a single formula to classify data is too "broad." In other words, it is not specific or detailed enough to make accurate decisions. While "broad" can mean expansive (A), spacious (B), or open-minded (C) in different contexts, the emphasis here is that it is too general.

16. C: Duvenaud and his colleagues created the ODE net because the layers made it hard to use given data to model continuous processes. The number of layers in a neural net is not infinite (A); in fact, this is largely why they do not work smoothly. Paragraph 5 notes that each layer may identify a more complex feature (B) as it seeks to identify an animal, but does not say that the layers themselves become more complex as they go. The layers are not seen as more user-friendly than the ODE-net (D). Rather, the ODE-net eases the burden of creating multiple layers.

17. B: The answer to the previous question is C, "The layers make it challenging to create accurate models." The best evidence for this comes in Paragraph 2: "The discrete layers are what keep it from effectively modeling continuous processes." The sentence from Paragraph 1 (A) gives an example of why data collection is difficult, but does not specifically address the issue of layers. The sentence from Paragraph 5 (C) explains what the layers do, but not why they are a problem. The sentence from Paragraph 6 (D) explains that more layers are needed for better modeling, but still does not clearly state that the layers get in the way of accurate models.

18. C: The last paragraph makes two points: caution, because the ODE net is not ready for implementation and has several hurdles to clear first, and hope, because once it is ready it could "shake up" the AI field. Only answer choice C includes both of these points. Each of the other answer choices focuses on just one.

19. B: This passage directly provides this comparison. A piano has particular tones picked out and a tone that is not designated a key cannot be played on a piano. A violin, however, can play any note within its continuous range. Similarly, traditional neural networks have discrete layers and cannot operate outside of those layers. The new continuous processes of a newer neural network would not be limited in the way that discrete layers would provide, making an effective comparison between a discrete-toned instrument like a piano and a continuous-toned instrument like a violin.

20. D: The passage discusses how neural networks are made to simulate complex processes, just as brains are responsible for thinking through complex processes. The analogy correctly compares neural networks to thinking in a computer, though the passage presents advanced neural networks as being something of the future and not fully realized.

21. B: The author is highlighting contrasts between his personal observations throughout his life and the social atmosphere of the West at the time. He uses dry language to increase the weight of his words while providing no levity to break the tension. Answer choice A is incorrect because the author typically uses very measured and restrained language to offset his critiques without being condemnatory. For example, he says a legalistic society "not quite worthy of man" rather than condemning it outright. Choice C is incorrect because even though the author is intending to present a warning of possible eventualities, these efforts are not directed at accusing governmental powers of causing harm to him or the audience directly. Choice D is incorrect because all of the author's claims are personal observations rather than refutations of empirical data.

22. A: These sentences most directly support the author's attempt at drawing a serious warning concerning the future of society based on his personal observations. Answer choices B, C, and D are incorrect because they focus too directly on past or present observations without making any connections to the future.

23. A: The word "rebuff" means to deny or reject outright with little or no time spent in deliberation. The sentence indicates that his critics are both hasty and numerous, helping to describe a context in which all ideas are critiqued quickly and firmly with little room for persuasion. While choices C and D also suggest the idea of critiquing, it is the statesman's ideas that are being critiqued, not the statesman himself. Choice B misses the ideas of both rejection and haste.

24. B: The main moral of the passage is the idea that just because something is legal does not mean it is morally correct. Choice B supports this directly. Choice A is incorrect because the author does not give any direct indication that he dislikes politicians. (Though we might guess the author has some complaints that could be made to politicians, we must be careful and note that there is no evidence for the inference that he categorically dislikes them.) Choice C is incorrect because no negative sentiments or critiques of capitalism are expressed. Choice D is incorrect because the passage offers no inclination that the author believes that life is essentially serious, or that it is devoid of both pleasure and pain.

25. D: The third paragraph most explicitly presents the idea that even when a person has good ideas and intentions, there will almost always be resistance, and the good ideas and intentions may only mean increased resistance. Although the author makes direct references to communism, choice A is incorrect because no ideas directly express that the West is in danger of becoming such a regime. He simply illustrates that there are multiple roads to destruction. Choice B is a direct contradiction of the ideas expressed in Paragraphs 1 and 2. Choice C is incorrect because there are no references to a lack of qualified politicians, only to a surplus of critics.

26. B: This phrase is meant to instill a sense of moral understanding as established by the context of the paragraph it is placed in, i.e., it is not enough to be an upstanding citizen if one is not striving for a moral good that is beyond questions of legality. Choice B most accurately reflects the idea of leveraging mankind's potential to do what is morally good. Both Choices A and C miss the subtext of combining reason with compassion. Choice D is incorrect because it does not directly link experience with beneficence.

27. D: This idea is expressed most directly in the first paragraph and is then expounded on throughout the rest of the passage. Choice A is incorrect because the author makes no mention of any laws that he believes are particularly beneficial. Choice B is incorrect for a similar reason, in that the author spends no time elaborating on the conditions of his childhood, offering only a single and general critique. While the author does present the idea that hyper-individualism may in fact be detrimental to society in the long run, this is not his main focus, and thus, choice C is incorrect.

28. C: The author makes direct mention of the ability of both the parliament and the press to, through their criticisms and rejections, thwart the efforts of statesmen that have good intentions. While the author does reference a future in which the West does not endure, this is an outcome he believes is unavoidable only if strict legalism maintains its prevalence, which makes choice A incorrect. Choice B is incorrect because the author makes no mention of a desire to abolish the law, only of an obligation to understand what the law is for and not to let legalism be the sole guide for behavior. Communism is criticized by the author, but he makes no declaration of it being the worst form of government, meaning choice D is incorrect.

29. A: Individuals in a society are most analogous to rungs on a ladder. Each rung is part of the ladder, and together they make up a crucial aspect of the ladder's structure. Choice B is incorrect because the relationship between the two terms is reversed; a race is not part of a contestant, but a contestant is part of a race. Choices C and D are not correct because they illustrate hierarchical relationships rather than pieces of a collective system.

30. D: The relationship between a manager and a business most directly reflects the original analogy. A manager puts forth effort to help the business run as effectively as possible for the good of the business and all its employees. Choice A is incorrect because the terms are reversed, as coaches lead teams, and not the other way around. Choice B is incorrect because the press themselves are not politicians, though statesmen are citizens of their respective countries. While a judge is invested in the effectiveness of their courtroom, they are not attempting to improve and grow their courtroom. Furthermore, a courtroom cannot operate without a judge, though businesses can operate without managers, as countries can without statesmen. So this analogy is not parallel to the original, and choice C is incorrect.

31. C: The first paragraph of Passage 1 most directly substantiates this answer. If, as this paragraph implies, the law is meant to enforce morality and justice, then any laws that do not uphold this true purpose of the law should not be followed. Therefore, according to the first paragraph of Passage 1, sometimes breaking the law is not only warranted but in fact necessary. Choice A is incorrect because it does not define whether the law being broken is unjust, and the justness of the law is pivotal in Passage 1. Choice B fails in a similar vein of thought. Passage 1 focuses on civil disobedience as an obligation in the face of unjust laws. Disobedience of just laws is not supported by this reasoning, whether the disobedience is civil or not. Choice D presents a possible misunderstanding of the author's statement that civil disobedience is motivated by a higher form of respect for the law. This statement does not mean that one must respect the law in order to break it, only that tremendous respect for the law compels people to break unjust laws.

32. D: This sentence most distinctly summarizes why breaking the law may be justified. Choice A describes how one should break the law if the occasion calls for it. Choice B provides illustrative evidence to further support the assertion referred to in the previous question, but it is not itself a summary of that assertion. Choice C gives yet another example of civil disobedience, but it does summarize the idea referred to in the previous question.

33. D: "Accountability" and "charity" are the best words among those in the answer choices to describe the nature of the prescription given in Paragraph 1 of Passage 1: "One who breaks an unjust law must do so openly, lovingly, and with a willingness to accept the penalty." In other words, one must be accountable to others ("openly") and to authorities ("willingness to accept the penalty"), and one must have a spirit of charity ("lovingly"). Choice A is incorrect because intolerance contradicts the idea of being lovingly disobedient. Choice B is incorrect because it does not address the idea of being willing to accept punishment, only to break the law passionately. "Confidence" and "resolve" address the tenacity necessary to accept punishment in the eyes of a watching public, but they do not specifically reference doing so in a loving manner, making choice C incorrect.

34. B: This answer is most directly referenced in Paragraph 2 of Passage 2. The author believes that to be willing to sacrifice one's life for a worthy cause, such as for the sake of liberty, is honorable if done intelligently. Douglass remarks on both order and tyranny but makes a distinction between order and the order of tyranny, thus discrediting choice A. Choice C and D are incorrect because, while the author might agree with these sentiments, they are not supported by the passage and cannot reasonably be inferred.

35. C: The author's continual use of detached pronouns is purposefully used to demonstrate a distance that separates himself from the audience. He deliberately uses the terms "you" and "your fathers" to establish a divide that implies they are not his fathers. He also openly admits his view of them "is not, certainly the most favorable." And yet, he recognizes that "the principles they contended for" are worthy of honor and remembrance. Choice A is incorrect because "elegiac" would apply to a speech that was somber or mournful and poetic in nature. Also, the men are being explicitly remembered for their deeds; they have not been forgotten. Choice B falls short because his verbiage is not wistful and the passage does not go into detail about the country's founding or history. Choice D is incorrect because the passage continually gives honor and respect, so it cannot be labeled as casual.

36. B: Both passages recognize that there may come a time when, even though one desires peace, an injustice cannot be abided and action must be taken, because it would be a greater injustice to do nothing. Paragraph 1 of Passage 1 and Paragraph 3 of Passage 2 highlight this idea most explicitly. Neither of the authors makes any sort of claim to substantiate choice A. Even if they believed that governments were the source of the particular injustices they are discussing, there is no mention that governments are the largest source of injustice. Choice C is perhaps true, but the author of Passage 1 claims that if faced with similar injustices in other places, he would disobey all the same. This undermines the idea choice C presents, in that he is opposed to injustice anywhere because it is a threat to justice everywhere. Neither passage makes any reference to the idea that property or ownership is the root of injustice, making Choice D incorrect.

37. D: It most accurately reflects the nature of both passages in that Passage 1 is a generalized overview of the tenets of civil disobedience using several historical allusions to support his claims, and Passage 2 is essentially a eulogy for "patriots and heroes, and for the good they did." Choice A is incorrect because Passage 2 does not describe a methodology for how to rebel, only that the men mentioned had chosen to do so. While it may be possible to infer the authors' attitudes toward their intended audiences, nothing directly stated in the passages allows the reader to definitively determine the oppression status of the audiences, making Choice B incorrect. Choice C is incorrect because the author of Passage 2 does not call for any action to be taken on account of his words, only that the men being discussed are worthy of honor for their deeds.

38. A: The author uses this phrase at the end of a paragraph describing the resiliency and stalwart nature of these particular men. They were unmoving in their sense of justice and had the fortitude of will to bring their beliefs to fruition, even in the face of direct opposition. This makes "unyielding strength of character" the best answer. The author describes the men as both peaceful and quiet in the last paragraph, which directly contrasts the idea of "imposing stature." This makes choice B incorrect. Choice C misses the mark for a similar reason because the author is honoring the men for their willingness to fight against tyranny in spite of their peaceful nature. Although the men were certainly willing to do difficult things, this is too broad—many people are willing to do difficult things, but the passage specifically honors these men as brave and principled. Therefore, choice D is incorrect.

39. B: The author of Passage 1 explicitly uses the Boston Tea Party and the actions of Shadrach, Meshach, and Abednego as examples of civil disobedience, against British tyranny and the laws of Nebuchadnezzar respectively. Choice A is incorrect because the laws of nature are categorically different from the laws that the author advocates disobeying. Regardless of how one feels about gravity, no amount of resistance to it would change its status as a law of nature. Choice C is incorrect because the terms are reversed; Christian martyrs civilly disobeyed the Roman empire, and not the other way around. Choice D is incorrect because, according to Passage 1, "academic freedom" was the outcome of Socrates' resistance, not the object of it.

40. A: The men in Passage 2 were willing to forsake "their fortunes" for the sake of "liberty," which best coincides with the original terms. As the author says, "They loved their country better than their own private interests." Choice B is incorrect because the men did not give up their humanity in the pursuit of justice. Choice C is incorrect because oppression was not a goal they hoped to obtain, nor manhood something they had to give up to achieve it. Choice D is incorrect because, while the men did know the limits of forbearance (according to the passage), it was not a competing priority for the men, as private interests were.

Grammar/Writing

41. C: The original sentence is phrased in passive voice, as the object is in the first half of the sentence. Choice C effectively reorders the subject, verb, and object to improve clarity and make the voice active. Note that some authors write sentences in passive voice to slow the reader down and draw particular attention to ideas.

42. A: The original sentence is the best version available. Whereas this sentence is relatively long and contains many words describing that the subject ("I") prefers one person over another, all of the presented information is part of one long clause. All of the information given about the people whom the subject compares are parts of adverbial phrases and are not actually individual subjects of their own. The other options add unnecessary commas that disrupt the true meaning of the sentence.

43. C: The original sentence communicates the intended meaning well, but the preposition "of" does a better job of linking "practice" to misplacing in the same way that the sentence says "a great deal *of* casuistry." In addition to clarifying some of the meaning, it also helps to establish parallelism between the "great deal of casuistry" and the "considerable practice of misplacing priorities."

44. B: The context describes lying as something that should very rarely be justified and that is currently generally only justified by people who are "engaged in some harmful activity such as war." The parallelism between harmful activities and power being used tyrannically is the best fit for the context. Each of the choices matches grammatically, but disagree with the author's purpose for the sentence.

45. B: The original phrasing does not match the tense of the rest of the sentence. Both B and C communicate well and are likely correct, but choice B is best because it uses parallelism to connect the future tense of "will" to the "will be truthful" used in the first phrase.

46. D: The original sentence has several uncertain word choices and is written in passive voice, making the subject of the sentence unclear. By adding the subject ("child") in a more direct form, choice D clarifies the meaning while maintaining the passive voice chosen by the author.

47. D: In this sentence, the child discovers that adults lie and that acts as a cause, resulting in the child lying as well. Whereas the original sentence does use an independent clause before the colon appropriately, a colon is not the best way to signify cause and effect. The second half of the sentence is also a complete sentence on its own, so either a comma and a coordinating conjunction or a semicolon are necessary to connect the two ideas. There are no options using a coordinating conjunction, so the semicolon is the best available choice. Even better than this option would be to either separate the sentences and use a transitional word or connect the two ideas with a coordinating conjunction that describes how the two thoughts are related.

48. C: Choice C is the best available option because it appropriately uses a comma and a coordinating conjunction ("and") to connect the two complete clauses. These ideas are related and agree, so "but" does not fit the context as it would indicate that the two clauses are in opposition to one another. Choices A and D both use a semicolon alongside a coordinating conjunction. Semicolons are generally used to connect two thoughts when a coordinating conjunction is not desired.

49. B: Whereas the original sentence is grammatically correct, to say "they are often talking" puts the sentence into a passive voice. Choice B is a more active version and provides a minor improvement to clarity over the original. Note when editing a sentence like this one, it is helpful to pay attention to the sentence in light of the paragraph. The author began this sentence with the word "again" to point to the rest of his argument up to this point. A careless edit might introduce a change in meaning that affects the flow of the whole paragraph. Choices C and D introduce awkward phrasing that do not improve the clarity or flow of the sentence.

50. A: The original sentence is not improved by any of the available choices. Choice B slightly changes the meaning of the sentence while detracting from overall clarity. Choice C is nearly an improvement in that it clarifies who the subject of the sentence by replacing a pronoun with a noun, but the paragraph repeatedly uses plural pronouns to describe the actions of several children. Replacing the plural pronoun with a singular subject would harm the cohesion of the paragraph and change the meaning. Choice D is incorrect as it makes the phrase more passive.

51. C: The original is not incorrect, but adding the additional two commas separates out a non-essential phrase and helps to clarify the main point of the sentence. Often, the word "thus" functions as a transitional word, but it does not act as the full transition in this sentence. Choice D adds an unnecessary comma and harms the clarity and flow of the sentence.

52. B: The original sentence combines two related sentences in a reasonable way, but the length of the original sentence detracts from its readability. It is a good choice to separate the two thoughts into their own sentences, but the connection between the ideas needs to be preserved. The original semicolon, the word "and," and the words "as for" all act to establish a connection between two ideas. Ultimately, only one of these connection needs to be preserved to keep the meaning, so the most succinct and readable choice is to change the semicolon to a period and start a new sentence, dropping the word coordinating conjunction "and."

53. C: The phrase "had fears of" is written in passive voice and would be better if switched to active voice. The comma should be retained as it separates two independent clauses joined with a comma and a coordinating conjunction.

54. D: The term "principle" means a conviction or system of rules that someone follows, and it is the best choice for this context as the context describes Alexander having disagreements with the Macedonian counsellors. "Principal" means of highest priority or can be a person who is in charge of something, such as a school. A "principality" is a state that is ruled by a prince. A "palace" is a place in which a royal person lives.

55. A: The original word "their" fits the context best. "It's" is a contraction meaning "it is" and does not fit. The word "its" is a singular possessive pronoun and does not match the word "Barbarians" as a plural noun. "His" would correspond to Alexander and would change the meaning of the sentence to mean that Alexander was overrunning his own territories, which does not make sense.

56. B: The best choice for this sentence is the word "declaring" as it shows that Alexander was stating his reasoning for wanting to demonstrate to Demosthenes that he was a man, countering Demosthene's former criticism. This sentence would not work if Demosthenes' criticism was not real and was instead, supposed, imagined, or assumed.

57. B: Choice B is the best of the available options as it corrects the missing subject in the phrase "arrived before Thebes." Choices B and C both correct this error, but choice B makes a clearer connection between the subject (Alexander) and the verb. Choice C is contextually clear, but technically makes an unclear antecedent, which should be avoided for clarity's sake. Choice D uses the personal pronoun "I" in a passage that is largely not in first person. This does not fit the context.

58. C: Of the available options, "who wished" is the best match for the context. The original sentence is grammatically incorrect, making an unclear meaning. Choice B presents *wish* as a gerund, which implies that the Thebans currently wish to help as an ongoing action. The temporal feel of a gerund is not the clearest option available. Choice D has the same problem, acting as an ongoing wish. Choice C is the best option as it presents a time-bound choice for the Thebans to "range themselves with them" if they "wished" at that specific time.

59. D: A simple substitute to help answer the questions is that Alexander prided himself on gratifying the complaints of his allies. The word "plumed" is the best choice as pluming is derived from the way that birds have beautiful plumage, or feathers, and can mean to be very self-satisfied or self-impressed. Plumped is related to fattening, which would work better if the context said that Alexander was getting rich because of his victory instead of getting acknowledgement. Plumbed means that something has been measured or tested for verticality. Metaphorically, plumbed can be used to describe a person's moral uprightness as well, but that does not fit the context well either. Finally, primed does not fit as primed describes being ready or motivated to do something. The context suggests that Alexander had another primary meaning and that the "complaints of his allies" was a secondary reason.

60. B: The original passage would be improved by the addition of a summary, as it ends abruptly and does not resolve. Choice B acts as the best summary and concluding sentence for the passage as it ties together all of the main ideas from the passage. The story tells of Alexander's beginnings and an early conquest showing strategic ability. The other choices do not represent the main ideas of the passage.

61. C: This clause needs a present-tense verb for the sentence to be complete. Answer choice A is incorrect because it does not include a present-tense verb ("conserving" and "stimulating" are participles). Choices B and D are incorrect because they change the participle "conserving" to the present-tense verb "conserve(s)" without adjusting "stimulating," so the parts of speech do not match. Choice C correctly adds a verb (aids) and leaves "conserving" to match "stimulating."

62. B: The correct present perfect phrase is "has been." To use "being" (A), the verb needs to be "is" instead of "has" (although this would not fit logically with the sentence, referring to past research rather than an ongoing process). "Is been" (C) incorrectly combines present tense and present perfect. "Having been" (D) is a correct pairing but does not flow logically with this clause because of the "and" before the underlined portion.

63. C: Answer choice C is both straightforward and clear. Choice A places the clauses in a less clear order and adds unnecessary commas. Choice B also creates an awkward order and adds an incorrect colon, since the part of the sentence after the colon does not define the first or give a list. Choice D removes the unnecessary commas but adds an incorrect em-dash, since it does not set off a parenthetical statement or provide a necessary pause.

64. B: The phrase "such as" begins a nonrestrictive clause (a clause that can be removed from the sentence without altering the meaning). Nonrestrictive clauses must be preceded by commas. Using a semicolon (A) is incorrect. Changing "such" to "like" (C, D) is incorrect because this causes the sentence to read "like as," which is incorrect.

65. A: This sentence uses a form of "not only ... but also," substituting "additionally" for "also." To use "in addition" (B) is incorrect because it lacks the "to." "Even to" (C) is incorrect because it does not go with "not only." "In also to" (D) is incorrect because of the added "in."

66. D: Both the part of the sentence before the punctuation and after it are independent clauses (stand-alone sentences). They can either be separated with a period or joined by a semicolon. Joining them with a comma (A) creates a comma-splice sentence. Using a conjunction such as "and" would be grammatically correct with a comma, but "or" (B) does not make sense. Adding "then" (C) creates another independent clause, again needing a semicolon or period rather than a comma.

67. D: This paragraph is written in contrast to the previous one, showing the disadvantages rather than the advantages. So, the introduction needs to reflect that. Choices A, B, and C each use a term that shows agreement rather than contrast.

68. C: Because the plants are not exposed to the open air, they are not pollinated by insects (unless introduced by the farmer). It is the farmer's responsibility to provide for these needs. He/she cannot eliminate (A) or remove (D) natural needs, and simply tracking them (B) is not sufficient.

69. B: This sentence gives an introduction to the subject of cost, which is discussed in sentences 16 and 17. So the best place for this sentence would be immediately preceding them. After sentence 16 or 17 (C, D) would be awkward positioning. Finally, its current position (A) is incorrect because it does not summarize the entire set of disadvantages, but only some of them.

70. A: The term is modifying the verb "grown" so it must be an adverb. Although "in a vertical manner" (B) is technically correct, it is unnecessarily verbose and therefore not the best answer. Answer choices C and D are adjectives rather than adverbs.

71. D: In the original sentence and in choice B, the sentence structure is unclear and makes it difficult to find the meaning of the cause-and-effect relationship. Choice C is passive and changes the emphasis intended by the author. Choice D does a good job of maintaining the author's style, establishes a clear cause-and-effect relationship, and places the emphasis on "assumption," setting up for the rest of his argument.

72. B: The sentence requires noun that means that something is false as an antonym to "facts." The word "fantasy" does contrast with "facts," but it refers to imagination, not a status of being false. Choice C is not relevant to the topic. Choice D sounds somewhat like "fallacy," but refers to a textile product commonly hung on walls.

73. D: The two clauses of this sentence should be parallel in structure, including verb tense. The original sentence mixes future, present, and past tenses. Choice B mixes present and past tenses. Choice C mixes simple present tense with continuous present tense.

74. C: Choice C is the clearest of the available options and places a clear emphasis on the cause-and-effect relationship between the author's inaction and his variation. Choice B subtly changes the meaning of the sentence.

75. C: Choice C is the most concise and clear of the available options and places the correct emphasis on the reason that a child kicks his legs. The original sentence does not communicate as clearly because it omits the comparison. Choice B introduces minor grammatical errors and choice D is unnecessarily repetitive.

76. B: The correct way to punctuate a direct quote is to follow the word "say" with a comma, then start the quote with a capital letter. If the quote is a statement and is followed by a dependent clause, close the quote with a comma and then quotation marks. The original sentence incorrectly uses a semicolon after the quote. Choice C omits the commas and does not capitalize the quote.

Choice D incorrectly omits the first comma, replaces the second comma with a period, and has an extraneous semicolon.

77. A: Earlier sentences described children as bursting with life and wanting things to be "repeated and unchanged" and grown-ups as tiring of repeating behavior until they are "nearly dead." This sentence further describes grown-ups as unable to take joy in monotony. The original sentence uses the word "exult," which means to be in the state of happiness or joy over something and is a good fit for the sentence. To exalt means to give high regard to someone or something. To suffer is to be in pain or sorrow. To exhale means to breathe out. None of the other options are suitable replacements for "exult."

78. D: The hypothetical situation that the author poses is set in future tense, so the verb tense "bringing" is the best fit for the sentence as it matches the tense for "conceives" and "brings." The author could have chosen a past tense construction to equal effect, but the verbs would still need to agree.

79. C: The sentence contains two independent clauses. In place of the semicolon, there needs to be a comma before the conjunctive adverbial phrase "and that." Choices B and D also introduce an error by adding the comma in "again and again" at the end of the sentence.

80. A: Prounouns must match their antecedents in both number and gender. Even though "man" is used here to refer to all humans, it is a gendered singular noun, so it takes the pronoun "his."

Quantitative Reasoning

81. B: To solve for a variable using a system of equations, one of the variables must be canceled out. To eliminate x from these equations, use the elimination method. Start by multiplying the top equation by 3.

$$3(2x - 6y = 12)$$
$$6x - 18y = 36$$

Then, add the two equations to eliminate x.

$$\begin{array}{r} 6x - 18y = 36 \\ \underline{+\ (-6x + 14y = 42)} \\ -4y = 78 \end{array}$$

Solve for y by dividing both sides by -4.

$$\frac{-4y}{-4} = \frac{78}{-4}$$
$$y = -19.5$$

Therefore, the value of y is -19.5.

82. B: Call the number of people present at the meeting x. If each person hands out a card to every other person (that is, every person besides himself), then each person hands out $x - 1$ cards. The total number of cards handed out is therefore $x(x - 1)$. Since we are told there are a total of 30 cards handed out, we have the equation $x(x - 1) = 30$, which we can rewrite as the quadratic equation $x^2 - x - 30 = 0$. We can solve this equation by factoring the quadratic expression. One way to do this is to find two numbers that add up to the coefficient of x (in this case, -1) and that multiply to the constant term (in this case, –30). Those two numbers are 5 and –6. Our factored equation is therefore $(x+5)(x-6)=0$. To make the equation true, one or both of the factors must be zero: either $x+5=0$, in which case $x=-5$, or $x-6=0$, in which case $x=6$. Obviously, the number of people at the meeting cannot be negative, so the second solution, $x=6$, must be correct. There are 6 people at the meeting.

83. B: There are 60 months in 5 years. Since a quarter is 3 months, the following proportion may be written.

$$\frac{250}{3}=\frac{x}{60}$$

We solve by first cross-multiplying.

$$3x=15{,}000$$

Then, divide both sides of the equation by 3.

$$x=5{,}000$$

Therefore, Quinn will have deposited $5,000 into the account after 5 years.

84. D: First, use the table to determine the values of $(a*b)$ and $(c*d)$. Since $(a*b)=a$ and $(c*d)=a$, that means $(a*b)*(c*d)=a*a$, which is equal to d.

$*$	a	b	c	d
a	d	a	b	c
b	a	b	c	d
c	b	c	d	a
d	c	d	a	b

85. D: Use trigonometric equalities and identities to rewrite the expression. First, convert $\tan\theta$ to $\frac{\sin\theta}{\cos\theta}$.

$$\sin\theta\tan\theta$$

$$\sin\theta\times\frac{\sin\theta}{\cos\theta}$$

From here, multiply the two values.

$$\frac{\sin^2\theta}{\cos\theta}$$

Use the trigonometric identity $\sin^2\theta=1-\cos^2\theta$.

$$\frac{1-\cos^2\theta}{\cos\theta}$$

Then, separate the fractions into two separate fractions.

$$\frac{1}{\cos\theta}-\frac{\cos^2\theta}{\cos\theta}$$

$$\frac{1}{\cos\theta} - \cos\theta$$

Finally, convert $\frac{1}{\cos\theta}$ to $\sec\theta$.

$$\sec\theta - \cos\theta$$

86. B: The inequality is solved by writing a double inequality equivalent to the given inequality but without the absolute value bars.

$$-9 < x + 6 < 9$$

Solve the double inequality by subtracting 6 from all three parts.

$$-15 < x < 3$$

The solution set can be written using interval notation.

$$(-15,3)$$

87. D: The slope of the original line is $m = -\frac{3}{4}$. Since the new line needs to be perpendicular, the new slope needs to be the negative reciprocal of the original slope. The negative reciprocal of $-\frac{3}{4}$ is $\frac{4}{3}$. The given point is (0,6), which is equivalent to (x_1, y_1) in the point-slope equation of $y - y_1 = m(x - x_1)$. Substitute in the new slope and given point, and solve for y.

$$y - 6 = \frac{4}{3}(x - 0)$$
$$y - 6 = \frac{4}{3}x$$
$$y = \frac{4}{3}x + 6$$

Therefore, the equation of a line perpendicular to $y = -\frac{3}{4}x + 1$ that passes through the point (0,6) is $y = \frac{4}{3}x + 6$.

88. D: The integers consist of all positive and negative whole numbers and the number zero. The product of three integers must be an integer, so you can eliminate any answer choice that is not an integer. The product of two even integers is even. The product of an even and odd integer is even. The only even choice is 24, and in fact we can see that $2 \times 4 \times 3 = 24$.

89. D: Start by solving the equation as you typically would until you isolate the x^2 on one side.

$$x^2 - 4 = 45$$

$$x^2 = 49$$

When you take the square root of a number, the answer is the positive and negative values of the root. Therefore, $x = 7$ and $x = -7$. Since only -7 is an answer choice, that is the correct answer.

90. C: Consecutive even integers increase by 2. So if the first integer is $x - 2$, the second is $x - 2 + 2 = x$, and the third is $x + 2$. Adding the three integers together yields: $x - 2 + x + x + 2 = 3x$.

91. D: In a 30-60-90 triangle, the hypotenuse is twice the short leg and the long leg is equal to the short leg multiplied by $\sqrt{3}$. So if the short leg is 3 mm, the hypotenuse is 3 mm $\times$ 2 = 6 mm and the long leg is $3\sqrt{3}$ mm. The perimeter is found by adding the three sides together.

$$3 + 6 + 3\sqrt{3} = 9 + 3\sqrt{3}$$

Therefore, the perimeter of the triangle is $(9 + 3\sqrt{3})$ mm.

92. C: To start, we can write our ratio in fractional form as $\frac{2\text{ cups of water}}{6\text{ cups of flour}}$. We know Josie wants to lessen the flour to only 2 cups, making our proportion $\frac{2\text{ cups of water}}{6\text{ cups of flour}} = \frac{x\text{ cups of water}}{2\text{ cups of flour}}$. To find the value of x, we can cross multiply the two diagonal values we know, 2 and 2, and divide their product by the remaining value, 6. $2 \times 2 = 4$, and $4 \div 6 = \frac{4}{6}$, which simplifies to $\frac{2}{3}$. This means Josie should use $\frac{2}{3}$ of a cup of water for every 2 cups of flour.

93. B: The slope of a line can be calculated using the following equation.

$$m = \frac{y_2 - y_1}{x_2 - x_1}$$

Substitute (4,1) for (x_1, y_1) and (−13,8) for (x_2, y_2).

$$m = \frac{1 - 8}{4 - (-13)} = \frac{1 - 8}{4 + 13} = -\frac{7}{17}$$

Therefore, the slope of the line is $-\frac{7}{17}$.

94. C: The total number of people mentioned is $20 + 13 = 33$, but there are only 25 cars. Therefore, $33 - 25$, or 8 cars must have both a man and a woman inside.

95. B: If the touching edges of the trapezoids are extended, they meet at a point on the horizontal. Using this information and the following geometric relationships, solve for x:

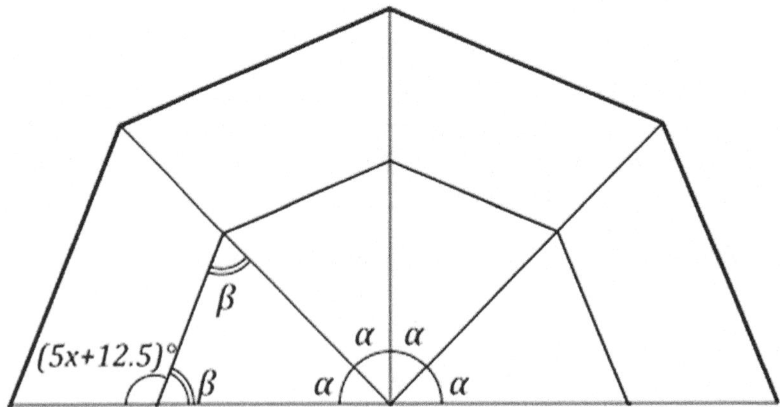

$$4\alpha = 180^\circ \quad \alpha + 2\beta = 180^\circ \quad (5x + 12.5)^\circ + \beta = 180^\circ$$
$$\alpha = 45^\circ \quad \beta = \frac{135^\circ}{2} \quad (5x + 12.5)^\circ = 112.5^\circ$$
$$\beta = 67.5^\circ \quad 5x = 100$$
$$x = 20$$

96. D: The difference between any two consecutive odd integers is 2. Therefore, if there are three consecutive odd integers and the middle number is x, then the other two integers must be $x - 2$ and $x + 2$. This results in the following expression.

$$x(x - 2)(x + 2)$$

Since $(a - b)(a + b) = a^2 - b^2$, the expression can be simplified as shown below.

$$x(x^2 - 4)$$

$$x^3 - 4x$$

97. B: Suppose it is true that $m\angle 1 + m\angle 3 = 180°$. We note that $\angle 3 \cong \angle 4$ since they are vertical angles, and thus $m\angle 3 = m\angle 4$ since congruent angles have the same measure. By substitution, then, we have $m\angle 1 + m\angle 4 = 180°$. This makes consecutive interior angles $\angle 1$ and $\angle 4$ supplementary. That is, they sum to 180°. This demonstrates that lines l and m are parallel.

98. D: When a number is raised to a power, you multiply the number by itself by the number of times of the power. For example, $2^3 = 2 \times 2 \times 2 = 8$. A number raised to the power of 0 is always equal to 1. So, 6^0 is the smallest number shown. Similarly, for the other numbers:

$$9 = 9;\ 10^1 = 10;\ 4^2 = 4 \times 4 = 16$$

Since $1 < 8 < 9 < 10 < 16$, we can write the order as $6^0, 2^3, 9, 10^1, 4^2$.

99. D: The equation of a circle is $(x - h)^2 + (y - k)^2 = r^2$, where r is the radius. We need to put the equation in this form to solve for r. First, we separate the x- and y-terms and then we complete the square.

$$(x^2 - 4x) + (y^2 + 2y) = 4$$

$$(x^2 - 4x + 4) - 4 + (y^2 + 2y + 1) - 1 = 4$$

$$(x - 2)^2 + (y + 1)^2 - 5 = 4$$

$$(x - 2)^2 + (y + 1)^2 = 9$$

$$(x - 2)^2 + (y + 1)^2 = 3^2$$

Thus, we can see that the radius is 3 (be careful not to mistakenly choose answer choice B). Since the diameter is twice the radius, we multiply 3 by 2 to obtain 6.

100. C: The problem does not give any information about the size of the table or the spacing between any of the chairs. Nevertheless, creating a simple illustration that shows the order of the chairs will help when approaching this problem. The line below shows the row of chairs and possible positions based on the parameters.

H	J	I	L	M	K

Statements I and III seem to be true from the drawing, but since we are not given any information about the spacing between chairs, we cannot say definitively that H and L are farther apart than I and M, or that M and K are closer together than H and L. However, we do know that chair I is between chairs J and L, so the only statement that is necessarily true is statement II.

101. B: There are 36 out of 100 yellow cars in the sample. Since the parking lot has $\frac{1}{4}$ as many cars as the sample, $\frac{1}{4}$ as many yellow cars should be expected.

$$36 \times \frac{1}{4} = 9$$

Therefore, 9 yellow cars are expected to be in the lot.

102. D: Substitute $x + 2$ for x in the function $g(x)$ and simplify.

$$\begin{aligned}[g \circ f\,]x &= g\big(f(x)\big) \\ &= g(x+2) \\ &= 2(x+2)^2 - 4(x+2) + 2 \\ &= 2(x^2 + 4x + 4) - 4(x+2) + 2 \\ &= 2x^2 + 8x + 8 - 4x - 8 + 2 \\ &= 2x^2 + 4x + 2\end{aligned}$$

103. A: Parallel lines have the same slope. We are given $y = 3x + 12$. This form is known as slope-intercept or $y = mx + b$, where m is slope and b is the y-intercept. In this case the slope is 3. To answer the question, we must find the slope for each option. In other words, we need to solve for y.

Given	Slope-Intercept Form	Slope
$3y - 9x = -36$	$y = 3x - 12$	3
$y = -\frac{1}{3}x - 12$	$y = -\frac{1}{3}x - 12$	$-\frac{1}{3}$
$12y + 36x = 144$	$y = -3x + 12$	-3
$y + 3x + 12 = 0$	$y = -3x - 12$	-3

Since parallel lines have the same slope, the correct choice is $3y - 9x = -36$.

104. B: The sine function is represented by the ratio $\frac{\text{opposite leg}}{\text{hypotenuse}}$. So, the sine of angle A can be written as $\frac{BC}{AB}$. The cosine function is represented by the ratio $\frac{\text{adjacent leg}}{\text{hypotenuse}}$. In ΔABC, $\cos B$ can also be written as $\frac{BC}{AB}$. We can also determine that angle B is 62°. Since the two acute angles of a right triangle are complementary, we can find that angle A is $90 - 62 = 28°$. Since we can see that the sine of angle A is equal to the cosine of angle B, we know that the cosine of angle A will also be equal to the sine of angle B. So $\cos A = \sin B = \sin 62°$.

105. A: An odd number can be considered as an even number N plus 1. Two even numbers added together produce an even number, so the result of adding an odd and an even number must be an even number plus 1, which is odd. For example, $4 + 3 = 7$, and 7 is odd.

106. B: The formula for the area of a circle is πr^2. The diameter of a circle is equal to twice its radius. Therefore, to find the radius, divide the diameter by 2.

$$12 \div 2 = 6$$

Therefore, the radius of the circle is 6 cm. Then, use the formula to find the area of the circle.

$$A = \pi r^2$$

$$A = (3.14)(6)^2$$

$$A = 113.04$$

The circle has an area approximately equal to 113 cm^2.

107. C: This can be solved as two equations with two unknowns. Since the integers are consecutive with $p > n$, we have $p - n = 1$, so that $p = 1 + n$. Substituting this value into $p + n = 15$ gives $1 + 2n = 15$, or $n = \frac{14}{2} = 7$.

108. A: Since a player cannot remove fewer than 1 or more than 3 toothpicks per turn, it follows that leaving 2, 3, or 4 toothpicks in a row allows a winning response, and that leaving 5 toothpicks forces the next player to leave 2, 3, or 4. Therefore, you should start by removing 1 toothpick.

109. C: Substitute 1 for x in the expression and solve.

$$\begin{aligned} |x| + |x - 2| &= |1| + |1 - 2| \\ &= |1| + |-1| \\ &= 1 + 1 \\ &= 2 \end{aligned}$$

110. C: Use trigonometric identities to simplify.

$\cos\theta \cot\theta$	Write out the original expression.
$\cos\theta \times \frac{\cos\theta}{\sin\theta}$	Convert $\cot\theta$ to its identity $\frac{\cos\theta}{\sin\theta}$.
$\frac{\cos^2\theta}{\sin\theta}$	Multiply the two terms.
$\frac{1 - \sin^2\theta}{\sin\theta}$	Convert $\cos^2\theta$ to its identity $1 - \sin^2\theta$.
$\frac{1}{\sin\theta} - \frac{\sin^2\theta}{\sin\theta}$	Split the fraction into two separate fractions.
$\frac{1}{\sin\theta} - \sin\theta$	Simplify the second term by dividing.
$\csc\theta - \sin\theta$	Convert $\frac{1}{\sin\theta}$ to $\csc\theta$.

111. D: Even numbers must be integers, so the result cannot be a fraction. Only one even number, 2, is prime, so the result cannot be prime. The product of any number and an even number must be even, so the result cannot be odd, and choice D must be correct.

112. D: Perpendicular lines have negative reciprocal slopes. The answer choices are all in slope-intercept form, in which the slope is simply the coefficient of x. The slopes of the lines in the choices are, respectively, $-\frac{1}{3}$, $-\frac{2}{3}$, $\frac{1}{3}$, and $\frac{2}{3}$. The given line, $3x + 2y = 5$, is not in slope-intercept form but in standard form. To find its slope, we can convert the equation to slope-intercept form and determine the coefficient of x.

$$\begin{aligned} 3x + 2y &= 5 \\ 2y &= -3x + 5 \\ y &= -\frac{3}{2}x + \frac{5}{2} \end{aligned}$$

The slope of this line is $-\frac{3}{2}$. Its negative reciprocal is $\frac{2}{3}$. This matches the slope of $y = \frac{2}{3}x - 7$, which is therefore perpendicular to the given line.

113. B: First, we must calculate the length of one side of the square. Since we know the perimeter is 8 cm, and that a square has 4 equal sides, the length of each side can be calculated by dividing the perimeter (8 cm) by 4.

$$8 \div 4 = 2$$

The length of one side of the square is 2 cm. The formula for the area of a square is length squared.

$$A = 2^2 = 4$$

Therefore, the area of the square is 4 cm^2.

114. B: From the given information, we can sketch the following figure (not to scale).

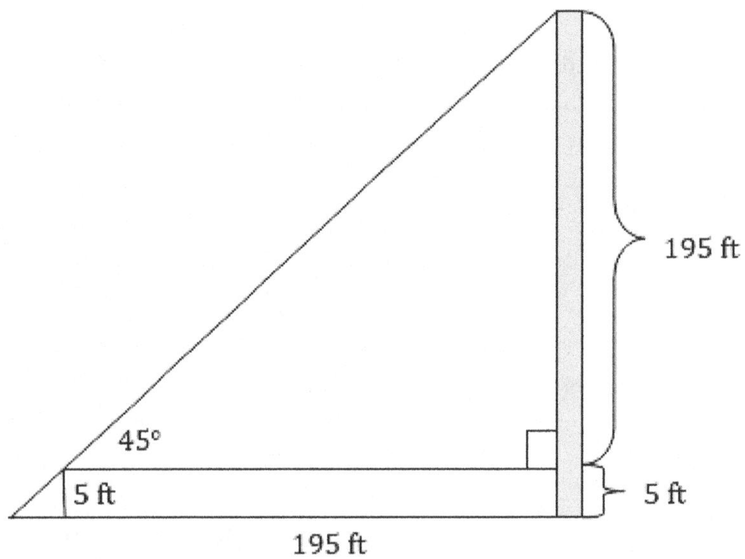

The legs of a 45°–45°–90° triangle are congruent; therefore, the vertical distance from the top of the tower to Sylvia's horizontal line of sight is the same as the distance Sylvia stands from the tower, 195 feet. Since Sylvia is approximately 5 feet tall, the height of the tower is approximately 195 ft + 5 ft = 200 ft.

115. C: To simplify the expression, first simplify the expression with parentheses. To raise $2x$ to the third power, raise both 2 and x to the third power separately.

$$\begin{aligned} x^5 \times (2x)^3 &= x^5 \times 2^3 \times x^3 \\ &= x^5 \times 8x^3 \end{aligned}$$

Next, multiply the terms. Since they have the same base and are being multiplied together, add the exponents to the like base.

$$\begin{aligned} x^5 \times 8x^3 &= 8x^{5+3} \\ &= 8x^8 \end{aligned}$$

116. B: Since the points P and Q lie on the circle, the angles $\angle APB$ and $\angle AQB$ are inscribed angles. The degree measure of an inscribed angle is half the measure of the arc that subtends it, so $m\angle APB = m\angle AQB = \frac{1}{2} m\,\widehat{AB}$. Since point C is the center of the circle, the angle $\angle ACB$ is a central angle. The degree measure of a central angle equals the degree measure of the arc that subtends it, so $m\angle ACB = \frac{1}{2} m\,\widehat{AB}$. Putting these equations together gives us $m\angle APB + m\angle AQB = \frac{1}{2} m\,\widehat{AB} + \frac{1}{2} m\,\widehat{AB} = m\,\widehat{AB} = m\angle ACB$.

117. B: Double the number that is added to the previous number. So, 4+2=6, 6+4=10, 10+8=18, 18+16=34, and 34+32=66.

118. C: 35 and 24 should not be on this list because they do not have a ratio of 5 : 4. The ratio of 35 to 24 cannot be simplified. Pairs of numbers will only have the correct ratio if they can be produced by multiplying 5 and 4 by the same numbers. For instance, 25 and 20 are produced by multiplying 5 and 4 by 5. 15 and 12 are produced by multiplying 5 and 4 by 3. 55 and 44 are produced by multiplying 5 and 4 by 11.

119. D: The number of cans in a case is equal to the product of the number of cans in a layer and the number of layers. Each layer contains 4 rows of 6 cans, or 24 cans ($4 \times 6 = 24$). The case contains two layers, so it has a total of 2×24 or 48 cans.

120. A: The sum of the measures of the three angles of any triangle is 180 degrees. The equation for the sum of the angles of this triangle can be written as $2x + 6x + 10x = 180$, or $18x = 180$. Therefore, $x = 10$. We multiply 2 by 10 to find that the measure of the smallest angle is 20 degrees.

Essay

1. Your Classic Learning Test essay is not included in your final score, but it does provide an opportunity to demonstrate your unfiltered writing skills to the colleges that receive your score. There is no official rubric or length requirement to meet. That said, it is a great opportunity to distinguish your essay with good organization and strong arguments. Longer is not always better, but your essay should be long enough to demonstrate your ability to make a logical argument with good evidence.

Essay question graders commonly look for the following elements in a strong response: strong content knowledge, clear organization, and effective arguments or examples. Language and usage are not usually strictly graded, but can make a big impact on the clarity of your ideas.

Please use the provided rubric to make sure your response meets these common criteria. Try to have a friend or family member grade your response for you or take a break after writing your response and return to grade it with fresh eyes.

CONSTRUCTED RESPONSE RUBRIC

Domain	Description
Content Knowledge	• The response directly addresses every part of the prompt. • The response demonstrates independent knowledge of the topic. • The response discusses the topic at an appropriate depth.
Organization	• The response introduces the topic, usually with a thesis statement or by restating the prompt. • The response directly addresses the prompt by providing a clear and concise answer or solution. • The answer or solution is supported by logical arguments or evidence. • The response restates the main idea in the conclusion.
Arguments and Examples	• The response provides a reasonable answer to the prompt. • The answer is supported by strong reasoning or evidence. • The response develops ideas logically and connects ideas to one another. • The reasoning and evidence provided act to support a unified main idea.
Language and Usage	• The response demonstrates effective use of grammar and uses varied sentence structure throughout the response. • The response demonstrates correct use of spelling, punctuation, and capitalization. • The response demonstrates strong and varied use of vocabulary relevant to the topic and appropriate for the intended audience.

CLT Practice Test #2

Verbal Reasoning

Refer to the following for questions 1 - 10:

The following passage is an excerpt from Emma *by Jane Austen, originally published in 1815.*

Emma Woodhouse, handsome, clever, and rich, with a comfortable home and happy disposition, seemed to unite some of the best blessings of existence; and had lived nearly twenty-one years in the world with very little to distress or vex her.

She was the youngest of the two daughters of a most affectionate, indulgent father; and had, in consequence of her sister's marriage, been mistress of his house from a very early period. Her mother had died too long ago for her to have more than an indistinct remembrance of her caresses; and her place had been supplied by an excellent woman as governess, who had fallen little short of a mother in affection.

Sixteen years had Miss Taylor been in Mr. Woodhouse's family, less as a governess than a friend, very fond of both daughters, but particularly of Emma. Between them it was more the intimacy of sisters. Even before Miss Taylor had ceased to hold the nominal office of governess, the mildness of her temper had hardly allowed her to impose any restraint; and the shadow of authority being now long passed away, they had been living together as friend and friend very mutually attached, and Emma doing just what she liked; highly esteeming Miss Taylor's judgment, but directed chiefly by her own.

The real evils, indeed, of Emma's situation were the power of having rather too much her own way, and a disposition to think a little too well of herself; these were the disadvantages which threatened her many enjoyments. The danger, however, was at present so unperceived, that they did not by any means rank as misfortunes with her.

Sorrow came—a gentle sorrow—but not at all in the shape of any disagreeable consciousness—Miss Taylor married. It was Miss Taylor's loss which first brought grief. It was on the wedding-day of this beloved friend that Emma first sat in mournful thought of any continuance. The wedding over, and the bride-people gone, her father and herself were left to dine together, with no prospect of a third to cheer a long evening. Her father composed himself to sleep after dinner, as usual, and she had then only to sit and think of what she had lost.

The event had every promise of happiness for her friend. Mr. Weston was a man of unexceptionable character, easy fortune, suitable age, and pleasant manners; and there was some satisfaction in considering with what self-denying, generous friendship she had always wished and promoted the match; but it was a black morning's work for her. The want of Miss Taylor would be felt every hour of every day. She recalled her past kindness—the kindness, the affection of sixteen years—how she had taught and how she had played with her from five years old—how she had devoted all her powers to attach and amuse her in health—and how nursed her through the various illnesses of childhood. A large debt of gratitude was owing here...the equal footing and perfect unreserve which had soon followed Isabella's marriage, on their being left to each other, was yet a dearer, tenderer recollection. She had been a friend and companion such as few possessed: intelligent, well-informed, useful, gentle, knowing all the ways of the family, interested in all its concerns, and peculiarly interested in herself, in every pleasure, every scheme of hers—one to whom she could speak every thought as it arose, and who had such an affection for her as could never find fault.

How was she to bear the change?—It was true that her friend was going only half a mile from them; but Emma was aware that great must be the difference between a Mrs. Weston, only half a mile from them, and a Miss Taylor in the house; and with all her advantages, natural and domestic, she was now in great danger of suffering from intellectual solitude. She dearly loved her father, but he was no companion for her. He could not meet her in conversation, rational or playful.

The evil of the actual disparity in their ages (and Mr. Woodhouse had not married early) was much increased by his constitution and habits; for having been a valetudinarian all his life, without activity of mind or body, he was a much older man in ways than in years; and though everywhere beloved for the friendliness of his heart and his amiable temper, his talents could not have recommended him at any time.

Her sister, though comparatively but little removed by matrimony, being settled in London, only sixteen miles off, was much beyond her daily reach; and many a long October and November evening must be struggled through at Hartfield, before Christmas brought the next visit from Isabella and her husband, and their little children, to fill the house, and give her pleasant society again.

1. Based on this excerpt, Emma can be described as:

A) Unfortunate
B) Devious
C) Selfish
D) Studious

2. How does Miss Taylor's marriage affect Emma?

A) Miss Taylor's marriage disrupts the comfort Emma had enjoyed all her life.
B) Emma is happy her friend is marrying a wonderful man.
C) Emma regards the change as a challenge and opportunity for intellectual growth.
D) Miss Taylor's marriage makes Emma think about getting married herself.

3. Which of the following lines provides the best support to the answer of the previous question?

A) Paragraph 6, Sentence 1: ("The event...for her friend.")
B) Paragraph 6, Sentence 3 ("The want of...every day.")
C) Paragraph 7, Sentence 4 ("He could...rational or playful.")
D) Paragraph 4, Sentence 1 ("The real evils...many enjoyments.")

4. As used in the first paragraph, what does the word *vex* mean?

A) Interest
B) Fulfill
C) Support
D) Displease

5. How do themes of class and maturity interact in this excerpt?

A) Emma's upper-class background gives her greater access to education, thereby making her more interested in intellectual stimulation than a less mature person might be.
B) The privilege that comes with an upper-class background can prevent a person from having the necessary skills for dealing with change in a mature way.
C) Emma's first twenty-one years were so happy because she enjoyed a privileged, upper-class lifestyle, and that happiness made her a more mature person.
D) Having people constantly take care of her has prevented Emma from developing feelings of kindness and love for others.

6. Why does the author describe Miss Taylor's wedding as a "black morning's work"?

A) Emma has to work to pretend she is happy about the wedding.
B) The day of Miss Taylor's wedding is a bad day for Emma.
C) Emma worked hard to organize the wedding.
D) The wedding party dresses in black.

7. Which of the following best matches the meaning of the word "valetudinarian" as used in paragraph 9 of the passage?

A) A doctor who works with elderly patients.
B) A person who enjoys traveling for leisure.
C) A person who is frequently concerned with their health.
D) A close friend who offers support during emotionally challenging times.

8. Which of the following best describes the tone of the passage?

A) Celebratory
B) Melancholic
C) Anxious
D) Lighthearted

9. Emma : lonely ::

A) Mr. Woodhouse : active
B) Emma's sister : cold
C) Mrs. Weston : available
D) Miss Taylor : familial

10. Emma : enthusiastic ::

A) Emma's father : affectionate
B) Emma's mother : compassionate
C) Miss Taylor : controlling
D) Isabella : quarrelsome

Refer to the following for questions 11 - 20:

This passage is adapted from Christine A. Scheller, "Health Researchers Urge New Focus on Ancestry, Social Struggles," originally published in 2019 by American Association for the Advancement of Science.

When medical professionals make appearance-based assumptions about patients without respect to genetic variation, it can lead to serious health consequences, said National Institutes of Health genetic epidemiologist Charles Rotimi at an 18 December 2018 discussion held at the American Association for the Advancement of Science headquarters, sponsored by the AAAS Dialogue on Science, Ethics, and Religion.

Rotimi said that 97.3% of people have mixed genetic ancestry. "At the genome level, trying to use genetics to define what we call 'race' is like slicing soup," Rotimi said. "You can cut wherever you want, but the soup stays mixed. The ubiquity of mixed ancestry emphasizes the importance of accounting for ancestry in history, forensics, and health including drug labeling."

Rotimi described a "critically important" example from a 1996 study: An eight-year-old European boy was scheduled for unnecessary surgery because doctors failed to diagnose him with sickle cell anemia. His parents were from Grenada and of Indian, northern European, and Mediterranean ancestry. Rotimi noted that Greece has a higher population of sickle cell carriers than South Africa.

"If we trace our ancestry far back enough, we're going to end up somewhere on the continent of Africa," said Rotimi, who is director of the Center for Research on Genomics and Global Health at the NIH. "This common history is the reason why we share so much of our genetic inheritance," he said.

The human genome looks like a history book that captures the experiences of our ancestors, Rotimi said. For instance, there is a high rate of kidney failure among African-Americans. Although they are 13% of the US population, African Americans make up 32% of patients with kidney failure. Genetic variations associated with increased kidney disease risk likely rose to high population frequency in Africa because they confer resistance to trypanosomal parasite infection and protect against the lethal form of African sleeping sickness, which was historically a bigger threat than kidney failure, Rotimi said.

"Individuals who don't look like Africans but have African ancestry carry this variant. So, you cannot use the concept of black or white to describe it," Rotimi said. "Ancestry is critically important, especially when talking about precision medicine or treating individuals. It's a whole lot more important than the way we see ourselves."

For these reasons, improving the lack of diversity in genomic research has long been Rotimi's passion. Although Rotimi said that the driving force behind health disparities is social structures, not genetics, he concluded, "The fact that we're not engaging different populations can actually lead us to wrong decisions."

Medical anthropologist Lesley Jo Weaver expanded on this idea, describing her research on how structural inequalities shape the health outcomes of women with Type 2 Diabetes in northern India.

"Racial legacies of colonialism underpin many of the health inequalities that we see today in India and beyond," said Weaver, an assistant professor of international studies at the University of Oregon.

Weaver told the story of a New Delhi woman who found it difficult to properly manage her diabetes because her low caste, dark skin, and lack of education severely limited her opportunities.

India has the second highest Type 2 Diabetes rate in the world, with 60 million people across all castes suffering from the condition, Weaver said. Systematic inequality is layered on top of systematic inequality to reinforce health disparities in the population, she said. "This is something that public health practitioners rarely think about."

The women in Weaver's study who used religious practice as a coping mechanism along with biomedical interventions were more successful at managing the stresses associated with their diabetes than were women who used biomedical interventions alone, but the best health outcomes were found among those who implemented both approaches, she said.

"There is something in our cultural and spiritual heritage that is relevant for scientists and other researchers doing precision medicine and analyzing the human genome," said Gay Byron, professor at the Howard University School of Divinity.

Byron suggested, "It is only in telling our stories in the fullness of their particularity that we can begin to appreciate the full tapestry of health."

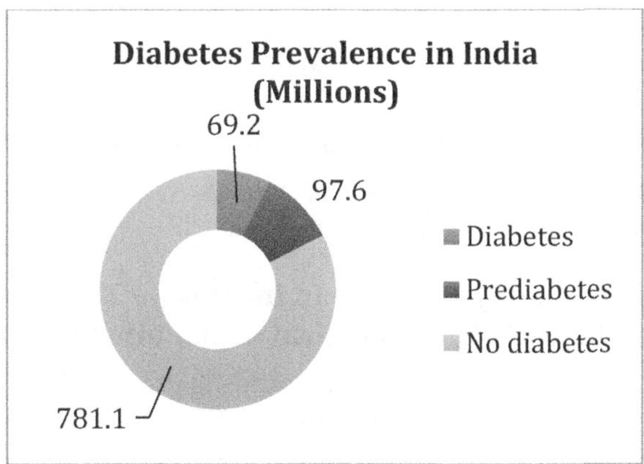

Data taken from hindustantimes.com.

11. As used in Paragraph 4, Sentence 2, "inheritance" most nearly means

A) a parent's estate, left in a will to offspring.
B) a parent's genetics.
C) the health habits that are passed down through the generations.
D) the genetic combination of one's ancestors.

12. What does the "critically important" example in paragraph 3 indicate to support the author's premise?

A) Mixed ancestry makes it more challenging to understand one's health tapestry.
B) Sickle cell anemia is difficult to diagnose without knowledge of where one's ancestors lived.
C) Knowing one's genetic background is critical to obtaining proper healthcare.
D) Too many doctors are unaware of how to glean health information from one's family background.

13. The main purpose of the passage is to

A) bring to light the difficulties of underprivileged people in obtaining healthcare.
B) show the importance of race in one's health.
C) describe the role of genetics and social background in health.
D) show the differences in Eastern and Western medical practice.

14. The passage implies that

A) with better understanding of genetic backgrounds, doctors can provide better treatment.
B) as people understand their ancestry better, they can improve their health.
C) combining spiritual and physical practices can be instrumental in finding a cure for disease.
D) diabetes could be eliminated with proper study of genetics.

15. Which of the following choices best supports the answer to the previous question?

A) Paragraph 3, Sentence 1 ("Rotimi described ... cell anemia.")
B) Paragraph 6, Sentence 3 ("Ancestry is ... treating individuals.")
C) Paragraph 13, Sentence 1 ("The women ... interventions alone.")
D) Paragraph 13, Sentence 1 ("There is ... human genome.")

16. As used in the final paragraph, "tapestry" most nearly means

A) a colorful textile.
B) a depiction of how health is like a beautiful, intricate blanket.
C) a picture made of multiple interwoven components.
D) a combination of everything that leads to good health.

17. Paragraph 11 states that 60 million people in India have Type 2 diabetes, while the chart shows 69.2 million with diabetes. What is a logical explanation for this discrepancy?

A) The author of the passage could have been rounding down for simplicity.
B) The passage refers to Type 2 diabetes, while the chart could include Type 1 as well.
C) The passage could have been referring to just the country of India, while the chart could have included small, surrounding nations.
D) Either the passage or the chart could have used incorrect information.

18. Which of the following statements is best supported by the data in the chart?

A) While nearly 70 million people in India currently have diabetes, an even greater number have prediabetes and may not even know it.
B) The nation of India is in crisis, with nearly half of the country either diabetic or prediabetic.
C) Despite the prevalence of diabetes in India, the outlook is improving due to a lower number with prediabetes.
D) India's diabetes problem is poised to worsen, as the number of those with prediabetes is nearly double the number of those currently diagnosed with diabetes.

19. human genome : medical professionals ::

A) history book : historians
B) recipe : chef
C) law : police officers
D) map : geologist

20. knife : soup ::

A) sickle-cell anemia : India
B) genetics : race
C) colonialism : diversity
D) religious practices : health outcomes

Refer to the following for questions 21 - 30:

This passage is an excerpt from The Consolation of Philosophy *by Boethius, translated here by H.R. James in 1897.*

1 'First, then, wilt thou suffer me by a few questions to make some attempt to test the state of thy mind, that I may learn in what way to set about thy cure?'

2 'Ask what thou wilt,' said I, 'for I will answer whatever questions thou choosest to put.'

3 Then said she: 'This world of ours—thinkest thou it is governed haphazard and fortuitously, or believest thou that there is in it any rational guidance?'

4 'Nay,' said I, 'in no wise may I deem that such fixed motions can be determined by random hazard, but I know that God, the Creator, presideth over His work, nor will the day ever come that shall drive me from holding fast the truth of this belief.'

5 'Yes,' said she; 'thou didst even but now affirm it in song, lamenting that men alone had no portion in the divine care. As to the rest, thou wert unshaken in the belief that they were ruled by reason. Yet I marvel exceedingly how, in spite of thy firm hold on this opinion, thou art fallen into sickness. But let us probe more deeply: something or other is missing, I think. Now, tell me, since thou doubtest not that God governs the world, dost thou perceive by what means He rules it?'

6 'I scarcely understand what thou meanest,' I said, 'much less can I answer thy question.'

7 'Did I not say truly that something is missing, whereby, as through a breach in the ramparts, disease hath crept in to disturb thy mind? But, tell me, dost thou remember the universal end towards which the aim of all nature is directed?'

8 'I once heard,' said I, 'but sorrow hath dulled my recollection.'

9 'And yet thou knowest whence all things have proceeded.'

10 'Yes, that I know,' said I, 'and have answered that it is from God.'

11 'Yet how is it possible that thou knowest not what is the end of existence, when thou dost understand its source and origin? However, these disturbances of mind have force to shake a man's position, but cannot pluck him up and root him altogether out of himself. But answer this also, I pray thee: rememberest thou that thou art a man?'

12 'How should I not?' said I.

13 'Then, canst thou say what man is?'

14 'Is this thy question: Whether I know myself for a being endowed with reason and subject to death? Surely I do acknowledge myself such.'

15 Then she: 'Dost know nothing else that thou art?'

16 'Nothing.'

17 'Now,' said she, 'I know another cause of thy disease, one, too, of grave moment. Thou hast ceased to know thy own nature. So, then, I have made full discovery both of the causes of thy sickness and the means of restoring thy health. It is because forgetfulness of thyself hath bewildered thy mind that thou hast bewailed thee as an

exile, as one stripped of the blessings that were his; it is because thou knowest not the end of existence that thou deemest abominable and wicked men to be happy and powerful; while, because thou hast forgotten by what means the earth is governed, thou deemest that fortune's changes ebb and flow without the restraint of a guiding hand.

18 These are serious enough to cause not sickness only, but even death; but, thanks be to the Author of our health, the light of nature hath not yet left thee utterly. In thy true judgment concerning the world's government, in that thou believest it subject, not to the random drift of chance, but to divine reason, we have the divine spark from which thy recovery may be hoped. Have, then, no fear; from these weak embers the vital heat shall once more be kindled within thee. But seeing that it is not yet time for strong remedies, and that the mind is manifestly so constituted that when it casts off true opinions it straightway puts on false, wherefrom arises a cloud of confusion that disturbs its true vision, I will now try and disperse these mists by mild and soothing application, that so the darkness of misleading passion may be scattered, and thou mayst come to discern the splendour of the true light.'

21. According to Boethius, what are the defining characteristics of being human?

A) reason and sickness
B) sickness and mortality
C) sickness and fear
D) mortality and reason

22. Which sentence(s) in the passage provide(s) the best evidence in support of the answer to the previous question?

A) Paragraph 18, Sentence 1 ("These are ... utterly.")
B) Paragraph 14, Sentences 1–2("Is this ... myself such.")
C) Paragraph 5, Sentences 1–2 ("'Yes,' said she ... by reason.")
D) Paragraph 17, Sentence 4 ("It is because ... guiding hand.")

23. According to the passage, why has the narrator fallen into such a pitiful state?

A) He has been ravaged by mental sickness.
B) Wicked men have exercised their power over him and those he cares about.
C) He was in the wrong place at the wrong time.
D) His situation has made him question his philosophical foundations.

24. Which of the following is closest in meaning to the word "bewailed" as it is used in Paragraph 17, Sentence 4?

A) to yell in frustration
B) to forget
C) to lament
D) to identify with

25. Which choice best describes the tone of the passage?

A) an apathetic exposition on suffering and the search for meaning behind it
B) a contemplative dialogue regarding the order of the universe prompted by suffering
C) a schizophrenic discourse of a man in the throes of despair
D) a cynical rumination regarding man's inability to avoid suffering

26. Which of the following is closest in meaning to the phrase "true light" as it is used in the last sentence of the passage?

A) unrestrained radiant positivity
B) the brilliance of the soul
C) illuminative truth that provides peace of mind
D) brightness of disposition that yields regained mental health

27. In this passage, the narrator is primarily concerned with

A) condemning the chaotic nature of the world.
B) exposing the injustice that is perpetrated against innocent people.
C) expressing inner turmoil through poetic dialogue.
D) highlighting present struggles and making peace with what is to come.

28. It can be inferred that the woman in the passage is

A) the narrator's memory of his wife.
B) another outcast trying to help the narrator.
C) an imaginary representation based on a former teacher of the narrator.
D) the personification of philosophy trying to lift the narrator's spirits with reason.

29. the narrator : philosophy

A) patient : nurse
B) nurse : doctor
C) darkness : light
D) humanity : God

30. sickness : disease

A) depression : despair
B) truth : falsehood
C) imprisonment : banishment
D) sorrow : medicine

Refer to the following for questions 31 - 40:

Passage 1 is adapted from Edmund Burke's Reflections on the Revolution in France, *originally published 1790.*

Passage 2 is adapted from Thomas Paine's Rights of Man, *originally published 1791. Paine's work was written in response to Burke's, regarding the French Revolution.*

Passage 1

When I see the spirit of liberty in action, I see a strong principle at work; and this, for a while, is all I can possibly know of it. The wild gas, the fixed air, is plainly broke loose; but we ought to suspend our judgment until the first effervescence is a little subsided, till the liquor is cleared, and until we see something deeper than the agitation of a troubled and frothy surface. I must be tolerably sure, before I venture publicly to congratulate men upon a blessing, that they have really received one.

Flattery corrupts both the receiver and the giver, and adulation is not of more service to the people than to kings. I should, therefore, suspend my congratulations on the new liberty of France until I was informed how it had been combined with government, with public force, with the discipline and obedience of armies, with the collection of an effective and well-distributed revenue, with morality and religion, with the solidity of property, with peace and order, with civil and social manners. All these (in their way) are good things, too, and without them liberty is not a benefit whilst it lasts, and is not likely to continue long.

The effect of liberty to individuals is that they may do what they please; we ought to see what it will please them to do, before we risk congratulations which may be soon turned into complaints. Prudence would dictate this in the case of separate, insulated, private men, but liberty, when men act in bodies, is power. Considerate people, before they declare themselves, will observe the use which is made of power and particularly of so trying a thing as new power in new persons of whose principles, tempers, and dispositions they have little or no experience, and in situations where those who appear the most stirring in the scene may possibly not be the real movers.

Passage 2

It was not against Louis XVI, but against the despotic principles of the Government, that the nation revolted. These principles had not their origin in him, but in the original establishment, many centuries back: and they were become too deeply rooted to be removed, and the Augean stables of parasites and plunderers too abominably filthy to be cleansed by anything short of a complete and universal Revolution.

When it becomes necessary to do anything, the whole heart and soul should go into the measure, or not attempt it. That crisis was then arrived, and there remained no choice but to act with determined vigor, or not to act at all. The king was known to be the friend of the nation, and this circumstance was favorable to the enterprise. Perhaps no man bred up in the style of an absolute king, ever possessed a heart so little disposed to the exercise of that species of power as the present King of France.

But the principles of the Government itself still remained the same. The Monarch and the Monarchy were distinct and separate things; and it was against the established despotism of the latter, and not against the person or principles of the former, that the revolt commenced, and the Revolution has been carried.

Mr. Burke does not attend to the distinction between men and principles, and, therefore, he does not see that a revolt may take place against the despotism of the latter, while there lies no charge of despotism against the former....

What Mr. Burke considers as a reproach to the French Revolution (that of bringing it forward under a reign more mild than the preceding ones) is one of its highest honors. The Revolutions that have taken place in other European countries, have been excited by personal hatred. The rage was against the man, and he became the victim. But, in the instance of France we see a Revolution generated in the rational contemplation of the Rights of Man, and distinguishing from the beginning between persons and principles. Lay then the axe to the root, and teach governments humanity.

31. In Passage 1, Burke indicates that it is important to

A) admire the strong principle of liberty.
B) wait to rejoice in freedom until it is certain that it will be good for the people.
C) congratulate those who have received liberty on their blessing.
D) avoid judging other cultures on their preferred freedoms until they are fully understood.

32. In the first paragraph of Passage 2, how did Paine justify the French Revolution?

A) The government had been corrupted beyond salvaging, and the only solution was a complete change.
B) The aristocracy was a parasite that was sucking the life out of its people, and the nation would not survive without changing government.
C) Louis XVI's rule was crippling the country and he needed to be replaced immediately with no chance of reinstatement.
D) The laws were centuries old and were inappropriate for governing the French people.

33. Paine feels that Burke does not understand that

A) liberty should be obtained at any cost.
B) revolting against corrupt principles is not the same as rebelling against the rulers.
C) the king of France actually loved his people.
D) the nation of France was in crisis, and it was necessary to act decisively before it was too late.

34. How would Burke most likely have responded to Paine's statement in the last paragraph of Passage 2 that the revolution was "generated in the rational contemplation of the Rights of Man"?

A) He would contend that human rights were actually violated by the revolution, not supported.
B) He would point out that human rights cannot be rationally contemplated because they cannot be defined.
C) He would argue that the revolution was not considered rationally, but emotionally.
D) He would state that the people doing the contemplation were not the real movers, and thus their results were invalid.

35. As used in Paragraph 5, Sentence 2 of Passage 2, "excited" most nearly means

A) giddy.
B) instigated.
C) enraged.
D) invented.

36. Paine and Burke would most likely agree that

A) liberty is the highest gift a person can be given.
B) while the king may love his people, he cannot change centuries of law and tradition.
C) it is important to weigh options carefully before seeking freedom from a government.
D) the original French government was corrupt, and some kind of action was necessary.

37. As used in Paragraph 1, Sentence 2 of Passage 1, "liquor" most nearly means

A) strong drink.
B) celebratory champagne.
C) obscuring darkness.
D) haze of excitement.

38. Which of the following choices from Passage 1 provides the best evidence to answer the previous question?

A) Paragraph 1, Sentence 2 ("The wild gas ... frothy surface.")
B) Paragraph 1, Sentence 3 ("I must ... received one.")
C) Paragraph 2, Sentence 3 ("All these ... continue long.")
D) Paragraph 3, Sentence 2 ("Prudence would ... is power.")

39. Paine : confident ::

A) France : defeated
B) Burke : hesitant
C) monarchy : absolute
D) Louis XVI : dismissive

40. Paine : revolution ::

A) baker : baking familiar recipes
B) gardener : planting seeds
C) surgeon : amputating a leg
D) editor : removed unnecessary words

Grammar/Writing

Refer to the following for questions 41 - 50:

This passage is adapted from Utilitarianism *by John Stuart Mill, originally published in 1879.*

On the present occasion, I shall, without further discussion of the other theories, attempt to contribute something towards the understanding and appreciation of the Utilitarian or Happiness theory, and towards such proof as it is susceptible of. (41) It is evident that this cannot be proof in the ordinary and popular meaning of the term. Questions of ultimate ends are not amenable to direct proof. (42) Whatever can be proved to be good, must be so by being shown to be a means to something admitted to be good without proof. The medical art is proved to be good, by its conducing to health; but how is it possible to prove that health is good? (43) The art of music is good, for the reason, among others, that it produces pleasure; but what proof is it possible to give that it is good? If, then, it is asserted that there is a comprehensive formula, including all things which are in themselves good, and that whatever else is good, is not so as an end, but as a mean, the formula may be accepted or rejected, but is not a subject of what is commonly understood by proof. We are not, (44) in like manner, to infer that its acceptance or rejection must depend on blind impulse, or arbitrary choice. There is a larger meaning of the word (45) proof, in which this question is as amenable to it as any other of the disputed questions of philosophy. The subject is within the (46) cognition of the rational faculty; and neither does that faculty deal with it solely in the way of intuition. Considerations may be presented capable of determining the intellect either to give or withhold (47) its assent to the doctrine; and this is equivalent to proof.

We shall examine presently of what nature are these (48) considerations; in what manner they apply to the case, and what rational grounds, therefore, can be given for accepting or rejecting the utilitarian formula. But it is a preliminary condition of rational acceptance or rejection, that the formula should be correctly understood. I believe that the very imperfect notion ordinarily formed of its meaning, is the chief obstacle which impedes its reception, and that could it be cleared, even from only the grosser misconceptions, the question would be greatly simplified, and a large proportion of its difficulties removed. (49) Before I attempt to enter into the philosophical grounds which can be given for assenting to the utilitarian standard, I shall therefore offer some illustrations of the doctrine itself, with the view of showing more clearly what it is, distinguishing it from what it is not, and disposing of such of the practical objections to it as either originate in, or are closely connected with, mistaken interpretations of its meaning. (50) With that out of the way, I will be able to show why utilitarianism is a superior philosophical theory.

41. It is evident that this cannot be proof in the ordinary and popular meaning of the term.

A) NO CHANGE
B) Obviously, this can't be the usual kind of proof.
C) It is clear that the common understanding of the word "proof" does not apply here.
D) The kind of proof I can provide is not the kind most people are used to.

42. Whatever can be proved to be good, must be so by being shown to be a means to something admitted to be good without proof.

A) NO CHANGE
B) A thing must be shown to be a means to something good without proof for it to be proven as good.
C) For something to be considered proved to be good, we must show that it leads to something that can be considered good without proof.
D) Whatever can be proved to be good must be a means to something that is accepted as good without proof.

43. The art of music is good, for the reason, among others, that it produces pleasure; but what proof is it possible to give that it is good?

A) NO CHANGE
B) The art of music is good, for the reason, among others, that the art of music produces pleasure; but what proof is it possible to give that pleasure is good?
C) The art of music is good, for the reason, among others, that it produces pleasure; but what proof is it possible to give that pleasure is good?
D) It is good, for the reason, among others, that the art of music produces pleasure; but what proof is it possible to give that it is good?

44. in like manner

A) NO CHANGE
B) for that reason
C) at the present time
D) however

45. proof, in

A) NO CHANGE
B) "proof," in
C) "proof", in
D) "proof" in

46. cognition

A) NO CHANGE
B) cognizant
C) cognizance
D) cognitive

47. its assent to the doctrine; and this is

A) NO CHANGE
B) their assent to the doctrine; and this is
C) its assent to the doctrine; and they are
D) their assent to the doctrine; and they are

48. considerations; in what manner they apply to the case, and what rational grounds, therefore, can

A) NO CHANGE
B) considerations; in what manner they apply to the case; and what rational grounds, therefore, can
C) considerations, in what manner they apply to the case, and what rational grounds, therefore, can
D) considerations in what manner they apply to the case; and what rational grounds therefore can

49. Before I attempt to enter into the philosophical grounds which can be given for assenting to the utilitarian standard, I shall therefore offer some illustrations of the doctrine itself

A) NO CHANGE
B) Before, therefore, I attempt to enter into the philosophical grounds which can be given for assenting to the utilitarian standard, I shall offer some illustrations of the doctrine itself
C) Before I attempt to enter into the philosophical grounds which can be given for assenting to the utilitarian standard, therefore I shall offer some illustrations of the doctrine itself
D) Before I therefore attempt to enter into the philosophical grounds which can be given for assenting to the utilitarian standard, I shall offer some illustrations of the doctrine itself

50. With that out of the way, I will be able to show why utilitarianism is a superior philosophical theory.

A) NO CHANGE
B) Having thus prepared the ground, I shall afterwards endeavor to throw such light as I can upon the question, considered as one of philosophical theory.
C) After I set up the background, I will attempt to explain why everyone should be a utilitarian.
D) Having done that, I shall undertake the task of illustrating this question of philosophical theory.

Refer to the following for questions 51 - 60:

Archimedes was born around 287 BC in Syracuse, (51) that was a Greek city-state in Sicily. Throughout his life, he contributed to various fields including mathematics, physics, and engineering, providing many concepts and devices still used today. Archimedes came from a family of scholars and mathematicians. We do not know much about his early life, (52) but we have known that he received a comprehensive education in philosophy, mathematics, and science. It is believed that Archimedes studied in Alexandria, Egypt, which was a Greek center of study. (53) Alexandria was founded by Alexander the Great during his incredible expansion of Greece across the known world.

Archimedes is best known for his contributions to mathematics. In his works "On the Sphere and Cylinder" and (54) "Measurement of a Circle," he was able to use geometry to approximate the value of pi, the exact value of which is famously elusive even to this day. He is also credited with advancements in number theory and methods for calculating values in geometry, which became the foundation for calculus.

Archimedes' contributions to physics could be considered of equal weight. He defined some of the principles of statics and (55) hydrostatics, helping to pave the way for fluid mechanics. He is the eponym for the term "Archimedes' Principle," which states that an object submerged in a fluid experiences a buoyant force equal to the weight of the displaced fluid. Though ships had made use of buoyancy long before Archimedes, the improved understanding of the underlying forces revolutionized the design and efficiency of watercraft.

In addition to his contributions to theoretical (56) understandings of mathematics and physics Archimedes was himself an inventor. He invented and built various machines, often manipulating common machines like screws and pulleys (57) for great effect. One of his inventions that is still in use today is his screw pump, which consists of a simple screw inside of a cylinder. (58) The fluids on one end of the pump are pulled to the other end as the screw is turned, allowing for active pumping of fluids in irrigation and drainage systems. Archimedes also created many war machines to help defend the city of Syracuse from Roman invaders. Among these were the "Claw of Archimedes" and the "Archimedes Death Ray," which were intended to be used against naval invaders.

One popular story associated with Archimedes is his "eureka moment." Archimedes was given the seemingly impossible (59) task, to determine whether a crown produced for the king was made of pure gold or if it was an alloy. According to legend, Archimedes was soaking in a bath, he noticed that his body caused the water level to rise, and he realized that he could use the principle of displacement to measure the mass of the crown and find out what it was made of. He was so excited that he shouted "eureka," which is the Greek term for "I have found it!" This story and the associated term "eureka" have become commonplace in pop culture, demonstrating the lasting impact of Archimedes' innovations.

As Archimedes lived in a time of great wars, his life was not all centered around peaceful discovery. In 212 BC, Syracuse was attacked by Rome. Archimedes was supposedly entranced by a geometric equation when the city was overtaken. Instead of stopping his work to hide or fight, he continued to work and (60) employed a Roman soldier to not disturb his circles. The soldier did not recognize Archimedes and killed him for resisting. Archimedes' tragic death serves as a powerful symbol of his unwavering devotion to his work. Archimedes' contributions to science and mathematics have served as an incredible legacy and foundation for future scientists and mathematicians, including Sir Isaac Newton and Carl Friedrich Gauss.

51. that was

A) NO CHANGE
B) which was
C) that is
D) that are

52. but we have known

A) NO CHANGE
B) but we are learning
C) but we do know
D) but we will know

53. What change, if any, should be made to the following sentence?

Alexandria was founded by Alexander the Great during his incredible expansion of Greece across the known world.

A) NO CHANGE
B) Move it to the end of paragraph 3.
C) Move it to the beginning of paragraph 6.
D) Remove it.

54. "Measurement of a Circle," he was

A) NO CHANGE
B) "Measurement of a Circle;" he was
C) "Measurement of a Circle." He was
D) "Measurement of a Circle:" he was

55. hydrostatics, helping

A) NO CHANGE
B) hydrostatics, which helped
C) hydrostatics, and this helped
D) hydrostatics, which helped him

56. understandings of mathematics and physics Archimedes was himself an inventor.

A) NO CHANGE
B) understandings of mathematics and physics, Archimedes was himself an inventor.
C) understandings, of mathematics and physics, Archimedes was himself an inventor.
D) understandings of mathematics and physics Archimedes was, himself, an inventor.

57. for

A) NO CHANGE
B) in
C) to
D) at

58. The fluids on one end of the pump are pulled to the other end as the screw is turned, allowing for active pumping of fluids in irrigation and drainage systems.

A) NO CHANGE
B) As the screw is turned, the fluids on one end of the pump are pulled to the other end, allowing for active pumping of fluids in irrigation and drainage systems.
C) Allowing for active pumping of fluids in irrigation and drainage systems, the fluids on one end of the pump are pulled to the other end as the screw is turned.
D) As the screw is turned, active pumping of fluids in irrigation and drainage systems are allowed for, as the fluids on one end of the pump are pulled to the other end.

59. task, to

A) NO CHANGE
B) task to
C) task; to
D) task: to

60. employed

A) NO CHANGE
B) assured
C) adjured
D) adored

Refer to the following for questions 61 - 70:

One of a person's most unique characteristics is eye color. Eyes come in a variety of shades, (61) depends on the DNA of one's parents. While most children have the color of one (or both) of their parents, some actually have a completely different hue.

While eye color (62) were something that is determined by a variety of genes, the shade depends largely on the concentration of melanin in the iris. (63) Range of pigment from light brown to black, the iris shade is based on the amount of melanin. The greater the concentration of melanin, the darker the eye color. The most common eye color in the world—brown—is caused by high levels of melanin. Melanin is produced in the body by being exposed to light, so babies are often born with blue-gray eyes because they have very low levels of melanin.

All lighter (64) eyes, such as blue and green, have low concentrations of melanin. In reality, eyes aren't actually blue or green. They only appear so because of the way light is scattered in the upper layer of the iris (the stroma). This is called Tyndall scattering, (65) but is similar to the way we see the sky as blue during the day even though it isn't. Blue eyes are generally considered recessive, but this is determined by several genes, (66) which is why children can have different eye colors than both parents and why siblings can also have different eye colors.

While some European nations have as much as 90% of the population with blue eyes, this color comprises only 8% of the world's population. By far the most common color is brown, particularly in Asia and Africa. Early humans were most likely (67) brown-eyed, a genetic mutation at some point resulted in lighter eyes.

(68) Although blue eyes are less common than brown, they are now becoming even more rare. As various nationalities intermarry, the recessive blue is decreasing. (69) Blue eyes can potentially see better at night. Blue eyes are unlikely to completely disappear since the genes will remain even when others are dominant. They will simply become less common.

Other comparatively (70) common colors such as green (2% of the world population) and hazel (5%) come from different genes. Green eyes are also a genetic mutation, but have more melanin than blue. Hazel eyes have the most melanin aside from brown. The back layer of the iris of a hazel eye has the same amount of melanin as a brown eye, but the front layer, or stroma, has much less.

While eye color patterns are shifting worldwide, each person's shade remains a unique part of his or her identity and a sign of his or her genetics.

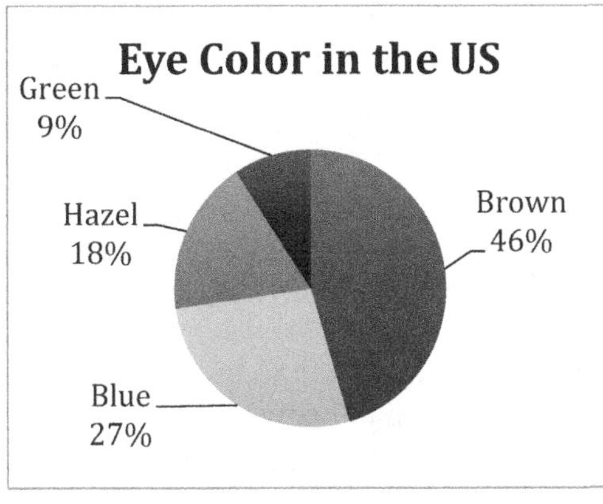

61. depends

A) NO CHANGE
B) depended
C) depending
D) it depends

62. were

A) NO CHANGE
B) has been
C) was
D) is

63. Range of pigment from light brown to black

A) NO CHANGE
B) Ranging, from light brown to black, in pigment
C) The pigment ranges from light brown to black
D) With pigment ranging from light brown to black

64. eyes, such

A) NO CHANGE
B) eyes: such
C) eyes—like
D) eyes; like

65. but

A) NO CHANGE
B) yet
C) and
D) even

66. which is why

A) NO CHANGE
B) the reason being that
C) such as how
D) because

67. brown-eyed, a

A) NO CHANGE
B) brown-eyed, then a
C) brown-eyed; a
D) brown-eyed: until a

68. Although blue eyes are less common than brown,

A) NO CHANGE
B) While blue eyes are already less common than brown
C) Despite blue eyes are less common than brown
D) However blue eyes are much less common than brown

69. What is the most logical place for this sentence?

Blue eyes can potentially see better at night.

A) NO CHANGE
B) After Paragraph 5, Sentence 1
C) After Paragraph 5, Sentence 5
D) Remove from selection

70. common

A) NO CHANGE
B) normal
C) familiar
D) rare

Refer to the following for questions 71 - 80:

This passage is adapted from an excerpt of the speech given by President Lydon B. Johnson on July 1, 1968 about the Nuclear Non-Proliferation Treaty.

As one of the nations (71) having nuclear weapons, the United States—all through these years—has borne an awesome responsibility. And this treaty increases that responsibility, for we have pledged that we shall use our weapons only in conformity with the Charter of the United Nations.

(72) Furthermore, we have made clear to the United Nations Security Council what I would like to repeat today: if a state which has accepted this treaty does not have weapons and is a victim of aggression, or is subject to a threat of aggression, involving nuclear weapons, the United States shall be prepared to ask immediate Security Council action to provide assistance in accordance with the Charter.

In welcoming the treaty that prevents the spread of nuclear weapons, I should like to repeat the (73) United States commitment to honor all of our obligations under existing treaties of mutual security. Such agreements have added greatly, we think, to the security of our Nation and the nations with which such agreements exist. They have created a degree of stability in a sometimes unstable world.

And this treaty is a very important security measure. But it also lays an indispensable foundation (74) for expanded cooperation in the peaceful application of nuclear energy; for additional measures to halt the nuclear arms race.

And we will cooperate fully to bring the treaty safeguards into being. And we shall thus help provide the basis (75) of confidence that's necessary for increased cooperation in the peaceful nuclear field. After the treaty has come into force we will permit the International Atomic Energy Agency to apply its safeguards to all nuclear activities in the United States—excluding only those with direct national security significance. (76) Thus, the United States is not asking any country to accept any safeguards that we are not willing to accept ourselves.

(77) As the treaty requires we shall also engage in the fullest possible exchange of equipment, and materials, and scientific and technological information for the peaceful uses of nuclear energy. And the needs of the developing nations will be given especially particular attention.

We shall make ready available to the nonnuclear treaty partners the benefits of nuclear explosions for peaceful purposes. And we shall do so without delay and under the treaty's provisions.

Now at this moment of achievement and great hope, I am gratified to be able to report and announce to the world a significant agreement—an agreement that we have actively sought and worked for since January 1964.

Agreement has been reached between the Governments of the Union of Socialist Republics and the United States to enter in the nearest future into discussions on the limitation and the reduction of both offensive strategic nuclear weapons delivery systems and systems of defense against ballistic missiles.

Discussion of this most complex subject will not be easy. (78) We have no allusions that it will be. I know the stubborn, patient persistence that it has required to come this far. And we do not underestimate the difficulties that may lie ahead. (79) I know the fears, and the suspicions, and the anxieties that you shall have to overcome. (80) But we do believe that the same spirit of accommodation that is reflected in the negotiation of the present treaty can bring us to a good and fruitful result.

Man can still shape his destiny in the nuclear age—and learn to live as brothers.

71. having

A) NO CHANGE
B) that will have
C) that has
D) that have

72. Furthermore, we have made clear to the United Nations Security Council what I would like to repeat today:

A) NO CHANGE
B) I would like to repeat what we have made clear to the United Nations Security Council:
C) We made it clear to the United Nations Security Council, and I would like to repeat it today:
D) Furthermore, as I told the United Nations Security Council:

73. United States

A) NO CHANGE
B) United States's
C) United States'
D) United State'

74. for expanded cooperation in the peaceful application of nuclear energy; for

A) NO CHANGE
B) for expanded cooperation into the peaceful application of nuclear energy, and it lays an indispensable foundation for additional
C) for: expanded cooperation into the peaceful application of nuclear energy, and for: additional
D) for expanded cooperation into the peaceful application of nuclear energy, and for additional

75. of confidence that's

A) NO CHANGE
B) of confidence is
C) of the confidence that is
D) of the confidence which is

76. Thus

A) NO CHANGE
B) Nevertheless
C) Furthermore
D) Henceforth

77. As the treaty requires we shall also engage in the fullest possible exchange of equipment, and materials, and scientific and technological information for the peaceful uses of nuclear energy.

A) NO CHANGE
B) As the treaty requires we shall also engage in the fullest possible exchange of: equipment, and materials, and scientific and technological information for the peaceful uses of nuclear energy.
C) As the treaty requires, we shall also engage in the fullest possible exchange of equipment, and materials, and scientific and technological information for the peaceful uses of nuclear energy.
D) As the treaty requires, we shall also engage in the fullest possible exchange of: equipment and materials, and scientific and technological information for the peaceful uses of nuclear energy.

78. allusions

A) NO CHANGE
B) illusions
C) delusions
D) disillusions

79. I know the fears, and the suspicions, and the anxieties that you shall have to overcome.

A) NO CHANGE
B) We know the fears, and the suspicions, and the anxieties that we shall have to overcome.
C) We know the fears, and the suspicions, and the anxieties that you shall have to overcome.
D) I know the fears, and the suspicions, and the anxieties that we shall have to overcome.

80. But we do believe that the same spirit of accommodation that is reflected in the negotiation of the present treaty can bring us to a good and fruitful result.

A) NO CHANGE
B) But I do believe that the same spirit of accommodation that is reflected in the negotiation of the present treaty can bring us to a good and fruitful result.
C) But we do believe that the same spirit of accommodation that is reflected in the negotiation of the present treaty can bring me to a good and fruitful result.
D) But we do believe that the same spirit of accommodation that is reflected in the negotiation of our present treaty can bring us to a good and fruitful result.

Quantitative Reasoning

81. Which number comes next in the sequence?

16, 24, 34, 46, 60

A) 56
B) 72
C) 74
D) 76

82. Mr. Carver is teaching his students about deductive reasoning and states the premises listed below. Which of these students has reached a valid conclusion?

Premise 1	All primates are mammals.
Premise 2	All lemurs are primates.

A) Mia states, "All primates are lemurs."
B) Carlos states, "All lemurs are mammals."
C) Xavier states, "All whales are mammals."
D) Gavin states, "All monkeys are primates."

83. If $2x = 5x - 30$, what is the value of x?

A) -10
B) -4.3
C) 4.3
D) 10

84. The total perimeter of an L-shaped field is 800 feet. The longest side is 300 feet, and the longest width is 100 feet. The shorter sides are 50 feet and 50 feet respectively. What is the total area of the field?

A) 17,500 square feet
B) 22,500 square feet
C) 30,000 square feet
D) 45,000 square feet

85. The rectangle below has an area of 245 inches^2. What is the length of the longest side of the rectangle?

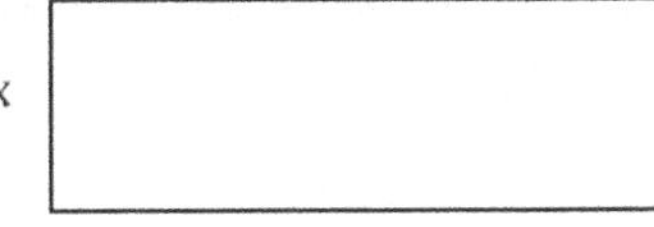

A) 25 inches
B) 30 inches
C) 35 inches
D) 40 inches

86. On a coordinate plane, what is the distance between the points $(4, 9)$ and $(15, 18)$?

A) 9
B) $\sqrt{11}$
C) 202
D) $\sqrt{202}$

87. In the following inequality, solve for x.

$$-4x + 8 \geq 48$$

A) $x \geq 10$
B) $x \geq -10$
C) $x \leq 10$
D) $x \leq -10$

88. Two odd integers, one positive and one negative, are multiplied. Which of the following statements is true?

A) The product must be odd and positive.
B) The product must be even and negative.
C) The product must be odd and negative.
D) The product must be even and positive.

89. Archie's gas tank is $\frac{1}{3}$ full. If Archie adds 3 gallons of gas to the tank, it will be $\frac{1}{2}$ full. What is the capacity of Archie's tank?

A) 12 gallons
B) 18 gallons
C) 20 gallons
D) 28 gallons

90. The perimeter of a square is 160 m. What is the area?

A) 400 m^2
B) 1,200 m^2
C) 1,400 m^2
D) 1,600 m^2

91. An odd number is multiplied by an even number, and the result is multiplied by another odd number. Which of the following must be true about the final result?

A) It is odd
B) It is even
C) It is negative
D) It is positive

92. A classroom has 15 boys and 13 girls. If 10 more girls join the class, what is the ratio of girls to boys?

A) 15 : 23
B) 13 : 15
C) 10 : 15
D) 23 : 15

93. If a, b, and c are even integers and $3a^2 + 9b^3 = c$, which of these is the largest number which must be factor of c?

A) 2
B) 3
C) 6
D) 12

94. What is the perimeter of a 45-45-90 triangle if the hypotenuse is 4 inches?

A) 4 inches
B) 8 inches
C) $4 + 4\sqrt{2}$ inches
D) $4 + 2\sqrt{2}$ inches

95. Solve the system of equations.

$$3x + 4y = 2$$
$$2x + 6y = -2$$

A) $\left(0, \frac{1}{2}\right)$
B) $\left(\frac{2}{5}, \frac{1}{5}\right)$
C) $(2, -1)$
D) $\left(-1, \frac{5}{4}\right)$

96. If $6q + 3 = 8q - 7$, what is q?

A) -7
B) $-\frac{5}{7}$
C) $\frac{5}{7}$
D) 5

97. Which of the following lines is perpendicular to the line $y = -5x + 27$?

A) $y = 5x + 27$
B) $y = -\frac{x}{5} + 27$
C) $y = \frac{x}{5} + 27$
D) $y = -\frac{x}{5} - 27$

98. A large rectangular-prism-shaped tank at the zoo is 8 feet wide and 5 feet high. How long is the tank if it holds a volume of 200 cubic feet of water?

A) 5 feet
B) 6 feet
C) 8 feet
D) 13 feet

99. Which of the following expressions is equal to x^3x^5?

A) x^2
B) x^8
C) $2x^8$
D) x^{15}

100. Which of the following is the solution to $3 - 2x < 5$?

A) $x < 1$
B) $x > 1$
C) $x < -1$
D) $x > -1$

101. Given the line $y = -\frac{5}{2}x + 2$, what is the equation of a line parallel to that line that passes through the point $(2, 3)$?

A) $5x + 2y = 16$
B) $-2x + 5y = 11$
C) $-5x + 2y = -4$
D) $2x + 5y = 19$

102. The two triangles shown below are similar. What is the measurement of x?

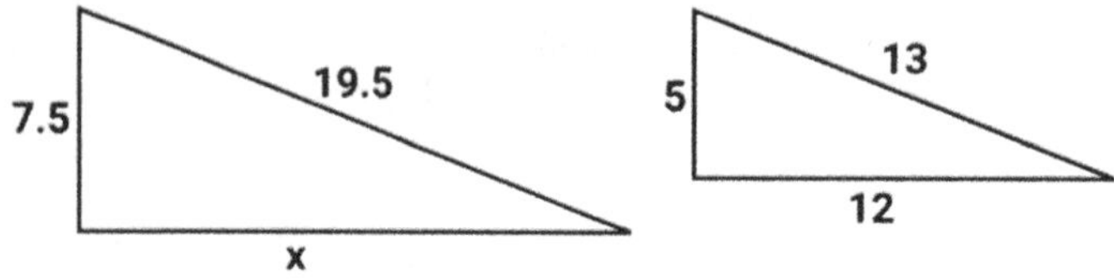

A) 12.5
B) 18
C) 21.25
D) 24

103. Annette read that out of 20 televisions sold in her state last year, 3 were Brand V. If a furniture store near her home sold 360 televisions last year, about how many should Annette expect to be Brand V?

A) 18
B) 54
C) 1,080
D) 2,400

104. Which of the following expressions is equal to $\sin\theta \sec\theta$?

A) $\cot\theta$
B) $\tan\theta$
C) $\csc\theta$
D) $\sec\theta - 1$

105. Ride Service A charges a flat rate of \$10 for the first 10 miles, plus 25 cents per mile for anything over 10 miles. Ride Service B charges 40 cents per mile. Both services charge the same for a trip that is how long?

A) 40 miles
B) 45 miles
C) 50 miles
D) 55 miles

106. In a town, the ratio of men to women is 2 : 1. If the number of women in the town is doubled, what will be the new ratio of men to women?

A) 1 : 2
B) 1 : 1
C) 2 : 1
D) 3 : 1

107. Elena counted the number of birds that came to her bird bath one afternoon. While she watched, 20 sparrows, 16 finches, 4 wrens, and 10 jays came to the bird bath. Which ratio, in simplest form, compares the number of finches that Elena counted to the number of sparrows?

A) 4 : 5
B) 4 : 9
C) 16 : 20
D) 20 : 36

108. The two prisms shown below are similar. What is the measurement of x?

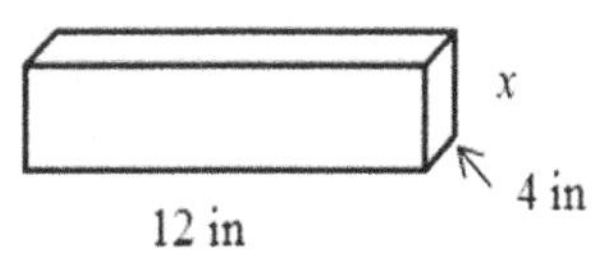

A) $4\frac{3}{4}$ in
B) $5\frac{1}{3}$ in
C) $5\frac{2}{3}$ in
D) $5\frac{3}{4}$ in

109. Harold learned that 6 out of 10 students at his school live within two miles of the school. If 240 students attend Grade 6 at his school, about how many of these students should Harold expect to live within two miles of the school?

A) 24
B) 40
C) 144
D) 180

110. What is the midpoint of a line segment that runs from the point (6, 20) to the point (10, 40)?

A) (30,8)
B) (16,60)
C) (8,30)
D) (7,15)

111. A circular cattle pen includes 12 posts, labeled A–L. The fence is located between posts C and D. If the fence was stretched out into a straight line, post A would be between posts B and C, post B would be between posts A and E, and post E would be between posts B and D. Posts F–L would be between posts E and D. Which of these statements is (are) necessarily true?

I. The distance between posts A and E is less than the distance between posts C and D.
II. Post G is between posts B and D.
III. The distance between posts E and D is greater than the distance between posts A and E.

A) I, II, and III
B) II and III only
C) I and II only
D) II only

112. What is the slope of the line described by the equation $5 - 3y = 2x + 8$?

A) $-\frac{2}{3}$
B) -1
C) $\frac{2}{3}$
D) 2

113. Equal numbers of dimes and pennies are placed in a single row on a table. Which of the following must be true?

A) Every dime will be next to a penny.
B) If there are two dimes at one end of the row, two pennies must be next to one another.
C) If there is a dime at one end of the row, there must be a penny at the other end.
D) If there are two pennies together anywhere in the row, there must be dimes at both ends.

114. Which of the following equations describes a line that is parallel to the x-axis?

A) $y = 3$
B) $y = 2x$
C) $(x + y) = 0$
D) $y = -3x$

115. A square flower garden has an area of 81 feet. What is the length of one side of the garden?

A) 9 feet
B) 20.25 feet
C) 40.5 feet
D) 324 feet

116. What is the distance on a coordinate plane from $(-8, 6)$ to $(4, 3)$?

A) $\sqrt{139}$
B) $\sqrt{147}$
C) $\sqrt{153}$
D) $\sqrt{161}$

117. A cafeteria requires 3 workers for every 24 students. How many workers will be needed for a school with 136 students?

A) 8
B) 13
C) 17
D) 24

118. What is the sum of all values of x that satisfy the following equation?

$$3x^2 - 3x - 34 = 2$$

A) -3
B) 0
C) 1
D) 4

119. A circle has an area equal to 36π. What is its diameter?

A) 4
B) 6
C) 12
D) 4π

120. If Leonard bought 2 packs of batteries for x dollars, how many packs of batteries could he purchase for $5.00 at the same rate?

A) $10x$
B) $\frac{2}{x}$
C) $2x$
D) $\frac{10}{x}$

Essay

1. Is it ever acceptable to lie? If so, explain the circumstances in which lying is justified, and what types of falsehoods can be told in those circumstances. If not, explain why not and how one should handle a situation in which the truth might be very difficult to state or accept.

Answer Key and Explanations

Verbal Reasoning

1. C: The author states that Emma possessed the "power of having rather too much her own way," and instead of feeling happy for her recently married friend, she feels sorry for herself. These descriptions characterize Emma as selfish. Emma may consider herself unfortunate following Miss Taylor's marriage, but a lifetime of privilege and having her own way hardly makes her an unfortunate character. While Emma may indeed prove to be devious, this excerpt offers no evidence of deviousness. Although Emma seems to value intellectual interaction, nothing in the excerpt implies that she is particularly studious.

2. A: Emma's life had been marked by the comfort of consistency, a close relationship with Miss Taylor, and the knowledge she tended to get her own way. Miss Taylor's marriage upsets that comfort and consistency because a major aspect of Emma's life will change. Emma is afraid her intellect will be stifled without Miss Taylor, so she does not approach the change as an opportunity for possible intellectual growth.

3. D: The following quote from the passage describes in further detail how Emma felt "mournful" and lonely after Miss Taylor was married.

"It was on the wedding-day of this beloved friend that Emma first sat in mournful thought of any continuance. The wedding over, and the bride-people gone, her father and herself were left to dine together, with no prospect of a third to cheer a long evening."

These lines demonstrate how Miss Taylor's marriage disrupted the usual companionship and comfort that Emma had enjoyed with her friend, leaving Emma feeling lonely and mournful.

4. D: The author uses words such as *comfortable* and *happy* to describe Emma's first twenty-one years. During this time, little vexed her. Based on this context, you can conclude that *vex* has the opposite meaning of words such as *comfortable* and *happy*. The answer choice most different from these positive words is *displease*.

5. B: A product of upper-class privilege, Emma has grown accustomed to always getting her way. When Miss Taylor's marriage disrupts this aspect of her life, Emma cannot deal with the situation in a mature fashion and instead sinks into self-pity and sorrow. Although Emma cannot enjoy Miss Taylor's happiness at her wedding because Emma is so wrapped up in her own feelings, this does not mean she feels neither kindness nor love for her friend.

6. B: The color black is often used figuratively to suggest badness. Emma is sad about Miss Taylor's wedding, and enduring the event has become nothing more than "black work" to her. Perhaps she pretends she is happy about the wedding, but no evidence in this excerpt suggests this conclusion. In addition, no evidence in the excerpt suggests that Emma organized the wedding. The author does not use *black* as a literal color in this excerpt, and no evidence in the excerpt suggests the wedding party wears black clothing.

7. C: The passage describes Mr. Woodhouse as a valetudinarian while referring to his overt caution regarding what he engages in. Due to his consistution and concerns for his health, he is both mentally and physically inactive.

8. B: The passage discusses events that are happy, but which cause sadness for the main character, providing a bittersweet, or melancholic tone. Emma experiences the feeling of loss when her governess and close friend, Miss Taylor, is married and leaves Emma's home. To reinforce the thoughtful and somber attitude, the passage explores loss in Emma's past and her solitude in light of other members of her family.

9. D: In this passage, Emma is described as having a familial bond, similar to sisterhood with Miss Taylor. They spend nearly every day together until Miss Taylor is married and becomes Mrs. Weston. After marriage, Mrs. Weston (Miss Taylor) is no longer available. Mr. Woodhouse is described as being "without activity of mind or body," indicating that he is an inactive person. The passage does not provide much information about Emma's sister and never indicates that they have a cold relationship, but instead, describes Emma's sister as living at a distance such that they cannot frequently see each other.

10. D: In the first paragraph, Emma is described as being "handsome, clever, and rich, with a comfortable home and happy disposition." Later, she is described as being willful as well. These ideas synthesize to depict Emma as a generally enthusiastic person. The answer choices compare Emma's enthusiasm with that of other characters in the story. Emma's father is depicted with many character traits with language such as pleasant, generous, indulgent, and affectionate.

11. D: The author is referring to a person's genetic makeup that has been combined and passed down over generations. It is not referring to a legal inheritance (A) or simply one parent's genetics (B). It is referring to physical makeup rather than adapted health habits (C).

12. C: The author uses the example of the young boy whose doctors failed to diagnose sickle cell disease to show how one's genetic background can hold valuable clues regarding healthcare. The boy's mixed ancestry may have made it more challenging (A), but that was not the author's point. Sickle cell anemia may be more easily diagnosed with knowledge of where one's ancestors lived (B), but this is only the illustration, not the main point. The author decries the fact that doctors do not take genetic background into account, but does not indicate that they are unaware (D).

13. C: The passage highlights how one's genetic makeup can affect health, along with one's social background (hint: a glance at the article title often helps to deduce the main idea). It mentions the difficulties of underprivileged people (A), but that is not the main point. The article discusses race, but mentions that it's not a matter of "black or white," but the complex genetic makeup that matters. The passage does discuss health practices in India, but does not use this article to contrast Eastern and Western practices.

14. A: The passage implies that if doctors were aware of the genetic backgrounds of their patients, they would be better able to give treatment tailored to their specific needs. It does not state that the patients themselves could improve their health through knowledge of their ancestry (B). The passage mentions combining religious practices and biomedical interventions (C) to cope with stress, but does not claim that this can cure disease. Nor does the passage claim that greater knowledge of genetics could be used to eliminate diabetes (D), but rather to provide better treatment.

15. B: The answer to the previous question is that with better understanding of genetic backgrounds, doctors can provide better treatment. Paragraph 6 gives the best evidence for this: "Ancestry is critically important, especially when talking about precision medicine or treating individuals." The sentence from paragraph 3 (B) gives an example that the author uses to show the importance of genetics, but does not clearly state the idea. Paragraph 12 (C) is about diabetes and could also be linked to an incorrect answer choice from the previous question. Paragraph 13 (D) discusses the importance of cultural and spiritual heritage, not genetics, and could be used as evidence for one of the incorrect answer choices from the previous question.

16. C: The author uses the word "tapestry" in the final sentence as an illustration of how a person's health is affected by genetic makeup, social setting, and religious practices, all woven together into a single picture. She is not referring to a literal tapestry (A), nor is she calling health a blanket (B). While "tapestry" is a combination of health-related topics, it is not only the parts that lead to good health (D).

17. B: The most likely explanation is that the chart includes both Type 1 and Type 2, since it does not specify. While the author could have rounded the number, it is very unlikely that she would have rounded down from 69.2 to 60, rather than up to 70, so answer choice A is incorrect. There is no reason to believe that the chart includes data from countries outside India, so answer choice C is incorrect. There is always a possibility of misinformation, but it is unwise to presume this, with no other evidence, when finding a discrepancy, so answer choice D is incorrect.

18. A: The chart shows that 69.2 million people in India have diabetes and 97.6 million have prediabetes. Since 97.6 million is greater than 69.2, answer choice A is supported. Answer choice B states that nearly half of India's population is either diabetic or prediabetic, but it is clear from the chart that these two categories take up much less than half of the doughnut chart, so this answer choice is incorrect. The number of those with prediabetes is greater than the number with diabetes, so answer choice C is incorrect because it states the opposite. And while the number with prediabetes is larger than the number with diabetes, it is not close to double the number, so answer choice D is incorrect.

19. D: The passage describes the human genome as being like a history book that captures the experiences of our ancestors, explaining that the history, or ancestry, plays a big role in understanding how disease prevalence exists in different people groups. The passage also describes some instances in which the medical professionals ignored the genetics of their patients, leading to misdiagnoses that were catastrophic as a result.

20. B: The author makes the comparison that using genetics to categorize race is like using a knife to cut soup, arguing that "you can cut wherever you want, but the soup stays mixed." The author uses this point to say that race is somewhat arbitrary and unhelpful in medical diagnosis as ancestry is extremely complicated. The author goes on to argue that no matter where someone is from, their ancestry is traceable to unexpected places, solidifying the point that true genetics, and not visual appearance, should be considered when treating a patient.

21. D: This answer is a paraphrase of Paragraph 14, which states that man is "a being endowed with reason and subject to death," making choice D the correct answer. None of the other choices contain these two qualities without introducing other ideas, such as sickness and fear.

22. B: As referenced above, Paragraph 14, Sentences 1–2 are the lines that directly address the answer to the previous question, making choice B correct.

23. D: Paragraph 17 most definitively illustrates why the narrator is in the state he is. He is struggling to reconcile his apparently dire circumstances with a God who is supposed to run an orderly universe. When evil has seemingly won the day, the author must wrestle with the meaning of suffering and the order of the universe. Therefore, choice D is the best option. Choice A is incorrect because, while his mind is faltering with a "sickness," it is only a part of the total problem, rather than a full summation. Choice B provides a summary of events that we can infer are likely, but it is incorrect because, again, this is only a part of the whole problem. The passage also does not give any insight as to others that may have been impacted. Nothing is stated directly in the passage to offer the idea that his circumstances are a result of unfortunate timing or position, so choice C is incorrect.

24. C: The word "bewailed" most directly means to regretfully mourn or lament poor circumstances. There are mentions of lost blessings and the vacillation of fortune in the paragraph that provide contextual clues. The root of the word is "wail," which carries a deep sense of loss and sadness that goes beyond the idea of mere yelling, making choice A incorrect. Though forgetfulness is mentioned, it is not that the narrator has forgotten that his apparent exile, but that he has forgotten the foundations upon which he has built his life. This has led him into lamentation, which makes choice B incorrect. Choice D is incorrect because, although he must now identify as an exile, this word does not convey any of the sadness that "bewailed" is used to describe.

25. B: The narrator is revealing an intimate look within his psyche through contemplative dialogue with a personified Philosophy. He is contemplating the structure and order of the universe as he deals with the suffering he now endures personally. While he is searching for meaning in his suffering, he is certainly not apathetic in his exposition, which invalidates choice A. Although the narrator is indeed having an imagined conversation with the personified form of Philosophy, the conversation serves to structure his turmoil into easily understood dialogue, and it does not seem like a disjointed or schizophrenic delusion, so choice C is incorrect. The narrator is not cynical in his approach to the events that have unfurled, nor is his suffering described as something inevitable, so choice D is incorrect.

26. C: The phrase "true light" is meant to draw a direct contrast to the "darkness of misleading passion" and the "cloud of confusion" referenced earlier in the paragraph. Because misleading passion is considered a darkness, it logically follows that something that provides light would not be misleading, but something that could be trusted. Thus, "illuminative truth that provides peace of mind" is the most apt description. While choices A and B both have adjectives describing the idea of light, there is no mention of positivity or the soul in the passage to justify either of these answers. Choice D also uses light-related imagery, but disposition is the outcome of regained mental health, not the source of it.

27. C: This is the only choice that describes the nature of the passage as a dialogue hoping to determine the root cause of the man's "sickness" and a potential cure for his state of mind. Although the narrator and Philosophy discuss whether the world is ordered or chaotic, the passage does not serve to condemn any chaos in the world, so choice A is incorrect. In a similar fashion, the narrator laments the injustice perpetrated against him, but the idea that the narrator wishes to expose this injustice in the hope of some sort of vindication is not substantiated in the passage, invalidating choice B. Choice D is incorrect because the whole passage focuses on making peace with what has already occurred; it deals with the future only in the sense that Philosophy proposes to cure the narrator of his confusion.

28. D: The most direct explanation for this choice can be ascertained from the title of the passage, but the woman's words throughout the passage reveal a context wherein she is determined to understand the man's philosophical assumptions in order to produce a diagnosis and cure. She continuously dissects the man's worldview to point out inconsistencies in his reasoning in the hopes of mitigating the force of his sorrow. The passage offers nothing to suggest nor substantiate any of the other choices.

29. A: The entirety of the passage is Philosophy's attempt to "cure" the man of his "sickness," thus making the patient and nurse relationship readily identifiable. Choice B is incorrect because a nurse and a doctor work together to cure patients, not diagnosing or attempting to cure one another. Although "true light" is referenced as the cure for the "darkness of misleading passion," the woman in the passage makes no claim to be the cure for the man's ills, only to be able to diagnose and offer remedies, making choice C incorrect. Although God would typically be a reasonable analog in this situation, the woman refers to the divine in the third person in the final paragraph, implying that she is not God and invalidating choice D.

30. A: The relationship between the terms "depression" and "despair" most directly parallels the relationship of the original terms, especially as referenced throughout the passage. "Sickness" and "disease" are used interchangeably throughout the entirety of the passage, so the terms in the correct answer would need to be very closely synonymous as well. Neither choice B nor D has synonymous terms. Although imprisonment and banishment are both forms of punishment, these words are not synonymous in the typical sense, eliminating choice C.

31. B: In the opening paragraph, Burke cautions the reader to wait to congratulate people on their freedom until he or she can see beyond the turmoil and emotions and judge whether this freedom is actually "a blessing." While he does call liberty a strong principle, he advises caution on admiring it. He also advises caution in congratulating those who have just found liberty. His reference to avoiding judgment was not in reference to different cultures and their preferred freedoms, but a general statement about understanding what newly won freedom really was.

32. A: Paine advocates the overthrow of the government rather than its reform, claiming that its despotic principles were "too deeply rooted to be removed" except by revolution. Paine does not claim that the nation would not survive without change. Paine specifically states that the revolution is **not** against Louis XVI. Paine refers to the principles that are centuries old but makes no reference to laws that may be inappropriate for the current generation of French people.

33. B: In paragraph 4 of Passage 2, Paine states that Burke does not "attend to the distinction between men and principles." In other words, he does not understand that revolting against a corrupt government is not synonymous with rejecting a king. Paine does not argue that liberty should be obtained at any cost; rather, he comments that many other revolutions were inspired by hatred instead of good motives. Paine does refer to the king's regard for his people but does not indicate that Burke is unaware of this. And while Paine does urge acting "with determined vigor" in the crisis, he again does not indicate that Burke is unaware.

34. C: Burke argues in the first paragraph of Passage 1 that the emotions of the revolution make it difficult to judge rationally. He does not make any mention of human rights. He mentions that the real movers are not always the ones who "appear the most stirring" but does not imply that those who contemplated the revolution were not the movers.

35. B: Paine uses the word "excited" to describe how hatred has instigated revolutions in many countries. He is not referring to feelings of excitement or giddiness. Though he is discussing rage, it would not be correct to say that the revolutions themselves were enraged. "Invented" does not give the correct connotation; revolutions were encouraged by hatred, but hatred did not invent them.

36. C: Burke spends the entire passage warning against revolting without a clear idea of what victory would look like, and Paine also mentions the importance of careful forethought rather than being led by emotions. Neither indicates that liberty is the highest gift a person can be given, though Paine does consider it very important. Paine makes the point that the king may love his people while the laws are still corrupt, but Burke makes no mention of this. Paine also indicates that the French government was corrupt and action was necessary, but Burke does not concede that anything was necessary other than caution before action.

37. D: Burke uses the analogy of liquor to explain how people could not think rationally in the early excitement of liberty. He was not referring to literal liquor (A, B). While it did have the connotation of obscuring the truth, there is no reference to darkness (C).

38. A: The answer to the previous question is C. The best evidence to support Burke's idea of using emotions over rational thought is in paragraph 1, where he likens the heightened emotions associated with the revolution to drinking alcohol, making it difficult to think clearly. In answer choice B, Burke cautions people on rejoicing over liberty before they are sure it will be for the best. In answer choice C, Burke warns that liberty will not last without the structure of government. In answer choice D, Burke explains that liberty is power, when people act together. None of these statements address the idea of rationale and emotions.

39. B: The two passages describe different responses to the excitement taking place in France after a great revolution. The French government, headed by Louis XVI, was overthrown. Burke sees this revolution in a light of uncertainty. He does not want to celebrate too soon and so wants to hesitate to make sure that the newly earned freedom is good and is also secure. Paine argues against Burke's hesitation and vigorously celebrates the revolt against a tyrranical government. Pain is confident, where Burke is hesitant.

40. C: In the second passage, Paine describes the process of revolutions against tyrranical governments as something warranted and something that should not be mild, but something to be fought for with passion. In the final paragraph, Paine recommends lying "the axe to the root" so as to destroy the old system at its root. This is similar to the way a surgeon might want to amputate a leg if the leg is the source of disease that can only be cured by completely eradicating it, even if the necessary action is drastic.

Grammar/Writing

41. A: The original sentence does not contain any noteworthy grammatical issues, although it does contain some passive language. The other available options all change the tone, detracting from the overall feel of the passage. In this case, the original is better than the alternatives because it maintains the most appropriate tone for the passage.

42. D: The original sentence is excessively wordy, and the awkward phrase "must be so by being shown to be a means to something" makes it difficult to follow. Choice A and choice C are similarly difficult to follow. Choice D also respects and keeps some of the more particular wording from the original.

43. C: In the original sentence, the antecedent for the last "it" could be either "the art of music" or "pleasure," which makes the sentence confusing. Choice B is clear, but repeating the phrase "the art of music" is awkward, and using the pronoun "it" would be clear and concise. Choice D twice uses the pronoun "it" with no clear antecedent. Choice C makes a clear connection between the pronoun "it" and the antecedent, "pleasure," helping with overall clarity.

44. D: The previous sentence stated that the process of proving something to be good does not involve following a simple formula. In this sentence, Mill starts with the words "we are not," indicating that this sentence is in opposition to the previous sentence. Mill advises against making an arbitrary choice based on a simple formula. The words "in like manner" suggest agreement between the two ideas, so it is incorrect. Choice B implies that not following a formula is the reason to not rely on impulse, and choice C implies that basing judgement of goodness on impulse will be appropriate at a later time. Choice D, the word "however," correctly coordinates the two ideas by showing that they disagree.

45. B: When a word is referred to as for a definition, it should be set apart from the rest of the sentence in some way, unlike in the original sentence. While there are numerous ways to do this, the available options all use quotation marks. In this case, the word "proof" must be followed by a comma to offset the next phrase, and the correct way to do this is to put the comma inside the quotation marks. Note that there is a broad range of ways to set off words for definitions including italics, bolding, or the use of a colon, but the use of quotation marks is one of the more common methods.

46. C: The sentence requires the use of a noun that fits a state of being. The original word, cognition, refers to the process of thinking or acquiring knowledge. Whereas the original term can work, there is room for improvement. Cognizance means "awareness" or "the state of knowing," and better fits the use. Choices B and D are both adjectives and do not fit grammatically.

47. A: Pronouns must be singular or plural in agreement with their antecedents. In the original sentence, "it" refers to "intellect" and "this is" refers to the entire phrase "considerations may be presented ..." Choice B incorrectly uses the plural "their" to refer to "intellect," choice C incorrectly uses the plural "they are" to refer to the first part of the sentence, and choice D uses the incorrect plural forms in both places.

48. C: The original sentence incorrectly uses a semicolon to separate a dependent clause from an independent clause. Choice B incorrectly treats the sentence as a list, with complex items separated by semicolons. Choice D incorrectly uses a semicolon where it should use a comma and does not use commas at all.

49. A: Out of the available choices, the original maintains the best sentence structure. The word "therefore" could still be improved by setting it off with commas or by eliminating it altogether, but it should not be moved to the beginning, as in choices B and D. Choice C introduces awkward wording that disagrees with the introductory phrase. Whereas the original is still not perfect, it is the best choice.

50. B: While all of the available choices convey the same idea, only choice B fits with the author's writing style. The original phrasing seems less formal than it should. Choice D also seems curt and informal. Choice C uses future tense in the introductory phrase, when it should be in past tense.

51. B: The second half of the sentence contains information that is non-essential to the primary clause. When describing essential information, the word "that" is appropriate, but when adding optional information, the word "which" should be used. This sentence also appropriately uses the word "was," indicating a past-tense application of the information. Syracuse might still exist, but in this case, changing the word from "was" to "are" changes the meaning and would introduce a factual error.

52. C: The original sentence uses past perfect tense, which means that an action took place at some point in the past. To "have known" something means that it was learned at some point in the past and that knowledge continues today. This sentence technically communicates a logical and grammatically-correct idea, but it is unusual and not as clear or contextually appropriate as the simple affirmative that "we do know." The other options do not make sense in light of the context.

53. D: This sentence does not pertain to the main idea of the story and should be removed to minimize unnecessary information. If the sentence were to be left in the story, it would not be better in a different location, as its current location is the only place in which the city of Alexandria is mentioned. Nevertheless, the information adds no relevant information and acts as a distractor from the main idea of the paragraph and the passage as a whole.

54. A: The first part of the sentence is an introductory phrase and cannot stand alone, so it needs to be a single sentence. A comma is the most appropriate choice to use to connect the introductory phrase to the primary clause. Colons are used to introduce a list or a subsequent idea and is only used when following an independent clause. A semicolon is used in place of a conjunction to connect two independent clauses. Since the first phrase does not contain a verb, it cannot be joined to the rest of the sentence with a semicolon.

55. B: The original sentence is grammatically acceptable, but the revised sentence does a better job of clarifying the specific meaning that the principles that Archimedes defined are doing the action in the sentence and not Archimedes himself. Whereas the original sentence is acceptable for most applications and the meaning does not substantially change, the revision is more grammatically precise.

56. B: The original sentence was missing an essential comma separating the introductory phrase from the independent clause. The phrase "In addition to his contributions to theoretical understandings of mathematics and physics" cannot stand alone and must be subordinated to the primary clause "Archimedes was himself an inventor."

57. C: The original sentence is incorrect because the word "for" implies purpose or result. It is not clear from the context that Archimedes would build machines for the purpose of "great effect." The meaning of the sentence is largely clear no matter what word is inserted at this point, but the most accurate preposition to use in this context is "to." In and at are usually used as directional or temporal prepositions. The word "to" is appropriate in this context because it helps to connect manipulation of common machines to the result of achieving a great effect.

58. B: The sentence conveys several pieces of information including explaining how a screw pump works and the cause-and-effect relationship between screw pumps and irrigation and drainage systems. All of the information from the original sentence needs to be preserved, but the organization can be changed to help with voice and clarity. The original is written in a slightly passive voice and does not demonstrate the dual cause-and-effect relationship as well as choice B does. The organizations of information found in choices C and D are more confusing as the causes and effects are not presented in a logical order.

59. D: Several of these choices are grammatically acceptable but detract from the pacing of the information. Out of the options, choice D does the best job of placing appropriate emphasis on the second half of the sentence, which serves to set up the importance of what Archimedes had to do. The other choices try to make the second half of the sentence either equal or subordinate, making the details seem less important than they should be. By using the colon, the author sets the reader up to want to know what was so difficult about Archimedes' task.

60. C: The best fitting word is "adjured," which means to beg or implore someone to do something. The original word, "employed," does not fit the context as the soldier was clearly a stranger and an enemy. To assure someone is to reinforce their actions or thoughts, which is the opposite of Archimedes' intentions. The word "adore" means to love or care for someone or something and does not fit the context.

61. C: This clause needs a participle for the sentence to be complete. Answer choice A is incorrect because it is a present-tense verb. Choice B is incorrect because it is a past-tense verb. Choice D is incorrect because this clause is introduced with a comma, so adding a new subject makes it a comma-splice (it would need a semicolon instead). Choice C correctly uses the participle "depending."

62. D: From the rest of the sentence, we can see that it is in present tense. Only answer choice D fits this. Answer choices A and C are past tense, and answer choice B is past perfect.

63. D: Answer choice D is both straightforward and clear. Choice A is grammatically incorrect because the first clause lacks a preposition (such as "With a range..."). Choice B is awkward and confusing because of how the words are arranged. Choice C creates a comma-splice, since it changes the opening clause into an independent clause, capable of being a complete sentence on its own.

64. A: The phrase "such as" begins a nonrestrictive clause (a clause that can be removed from the sentence without altering the meaning). Nonrestrictive clauses must be preceded by commas. Using a colon (B), dash (C), or semicolon (D) is incorrect. Additionally, changing "such" to "like" (C, D) is incorrect because this causes the sentence to read "like as," which is incorrect.

65. C: The two parts of the sentence are agreeing with one another—the second adds information to the first. So a contrast word such as "but" (A) or "yet" (B) does not fit. Choice D is incorrect because "even" does not fit grammatically, as it is missing a conjunction.

66. A: The first part of the sentence makes a statement, and the second part draws a conclusion from this statement. Choice B indicates the opposite: that the first part sets up the conclusion and the second part gives the reasoning. Choice C is incorrect because "such as" indicates sharing an example of the preceding noun ("genes"). Choice D is incorrect because like choice B, it indicates that the first part of the sentence is the example and the second part is the reason, instead of vice versa.

67. C: Both the part of the sentence before the punctuation and after it are independent clauses (stand-alone sentences). They can either be separated with a period or joined by a semicolon. Joining them with a comma (A) creates a comma-splice sentence. Adding "then" (B) creates another independent clause, again needing a semicolon or period rather than a comma. A colon (D) is incorrect here because the clause after the punctuation is not a list or a definition of the previous clause.

68. B: The first part of the sentence makes a statement, and the second takes it a step further. This is not a contrast, so answer choice A is incorrect (along with C and D). Answer choice B adds "already," which provides the needed connection with "now" rather than contrast. Choice C is incorrect because "Despite" needs a phrase like "the fact that." Choice D is incorrect because "However" needs to be followed by a comma.

69. D: This sentence gives an interesting fact about blue eyes, but the theme of this paragraph is about how blue eyes are becoming less common, so this factoid does not fit as it does not support the main idea.

70. D: This sentence is comparing green and hazel eyes to blue, stating that each of these colors is fairly uncommon (as can be seen by the percentages). Only "rare" fits this description; each of the other terms implies the opposite.

71. C: The original sentence is technically correct, but "having" is a form of participle, in which a verb is used as an adjective, making the sentence more passive than other options. Choice B is in future tense and does not match the rest of the sentence. Choice D matches the tense, but it introduces subject-verb agreement issues as have is a plural verb that is paired with "the United States," which is a singular noun. Choice C matches the tense and does not introduce any agreement issues, making it the best choice.

72. B: Choice B is the clearest and most concise form of the sentence, maintaining the original meaning. The original phrase acted as an introductory phrase, but included a redundant transition word, "furthermore." Choice C correctly eliminates some of the redundancy but does not communicate concisely. Furthermore, choice C changes the tense, reducing some of the accuracy of the wording. Choice D also introduces a tense shift, possibly changing the meaning of the sentence.

73. C: The sentence requires that "United States" be a possessive form. Choice B is an informal way of writing the possessive form of a word ending in "-s" and choice D omits the last letter incorrectly. Choice C correctly applies the possessive form of the collective noun "United States."

74. D: The original sentence incorrectly uses a semicolon to connect two unequal clauses to one another. Choice D is the best option, as it uses a comma and a coordinating conjunction to help the reader understand how the ideas relate to one another. Choices B and C introduce redundancy and make the overall meaning less clear.

75. C: Choice C provides several improvements to the original sentence. First, the word "the" is added, which acts as a determiner to clarify the meaning of the word "confidence." Secondly, the contraction "that's" is informal and should be avoided in formal usage. Choice D incorrectly uses the word "which," changing the meaning slightly and making the phrase "necessary for increased cooperation in the peaceful nuclear field" into a non-essential phrase. Whereas that is a grammatically correct choice, it changes the meaning and makes the sentence less direct.

76. A: The original sentence uses the most appropriate transitional adverb for the context. The word "thus" communicates a result or conclusion agreeing with evidence that has already been presented. "Nevertheless" indicates that a conclusion is in spite of something previously discussed. "Furthermore" indicates that the writer is continuing an argument, not concluding it. "Henceforth" is a temporal transitional word, indicating that something is changing 'from this time forward' or 'from now on.' None of these other options fit the context.

77. C: Choice C provides the best phrasing and use of punctuation. Firstly, there needs to be a comma after "as the treaty requires" to set off the introductory phrase.

Secondly, the list of equipment, materials, and scientific and technological information needs to be handled appropriately. There are more than one way to organize this list in a grammatically accurate way, but the meaning changes slightly, depending on the organization of ideas.

Either of the following are appropriate:

Compound lists:

List 1 — List 2

...equipment and materials and scientific and technological information ...

Simple List with one compound point:

$\underbrace{\text{...equipment}}_{}$ — Item 1, Item 2, Item 3 (compound)

...equipment, materials, and scientific and technological information...

Choice C is the only choice that addresses all of the issues.

78. B: The term "allusions" means a reference to something else and is incorrect in this sentence. The term that fits best is "illusion," which is a false perception or belief. By saying "we have no illusions," Johnson is indicating that they have a clear understanding that the road ahead is not easy. Choice C is similar in meaning to "illusions," but is not a word that would be used in this context. A "disillusion" is when someone feels disappointed or let down by a belief and no longer agrees with it. This word carries complex meanings that would confuse and disagree with what the author intends to say.

79. D: Throughout the speech, President Johnson used "we" to refer to both the United States government and its people as a whole. He also referred to himself as the person who is reporting the information, as well as his personal understanding of how Americans feel about the possibility of nuclear proliferation. He portrays the burden of dealing with the difficulties of living in the nuclear age as something falling on all Americans, himself included.

80. A: The sentence does not need to change and has good pronoun agreement overall. Choice B would also work, but changes the subject to "I" and changes the meaning. This change is not preferred because it alters how the sentence functions in light of the rest of the paragraph, which is largely focused on a "we" mindset.

Quantitative Reasoning

81. D: The numbers in this sequence progress according to a pattern. Each progressing number can be expressed by the equation $x + 2 = n$, where x is the difference between the previous two numbers and n is the number added to the previous number to yield the progressing number. For instance, the difference in 24 and 16 is 8. By adding 2 to 8, you know that you must add 10 to 24 in order to yield 34. In the next part of the sequence, $x = 10$ and $n = 12$. $34 + 12 = 46$, the next number in the sequence. Therefore, by following this pattern, you would add 16 to 60, which results in 76.

82. B: If all primates are mammals, and all lemurs are primates, then all lemurs are mammals. All primates are not lemurs. Since neither whales nor monkeys are mentioned in the premises, they cannot be included in the conclusion. The conclusion can only be based on the information given in the premises. Therefore, the correct answer is choice B.

83. D: First, subtract $5x$ from both sides to get the variable to one side of the equation.

$$2x = 5x - 30$$
$$2x - 5x = 5x - 30 - 5x$$
$$-3x = -30$$

Then, divide both sides by –3 to solve for x.

$$\frac{-3x}{-3} = \frac{-30}{-3}$$
$$x = 10$$

84. A: This may be solved in a few different ways, each of which involves calculating the area of two rectangular sections whose areas can be calculated directly. The area of the L can be split into two pieces, a 300 ft by 50 ft section and a 50 ft by 50 ft section or a 250 ft by 50 ft section and a 100 ft by 50 ft section. In either case, the areas are calculated directly and then summed. The alternative is to view the L as a larger rectangle that has had a smaller rectangle removed from it. In this method, the large rectangle is a 300 ft by 100 ft section, and the smaller rectangle is a 250 ft by 50 ft section. These areas can be calculated and the smaller subtracted from the larger. In both methods, the area comes out to 17,500 square feet.

85. C: A rectangle's area is found by multiplying length by width. Here, length is $5x$ and width is x.

$$245 \text{ in}^2 = x \cdot 5x$$
$$245 \text{ in}^2 = 5x^2$$
$$49 \text{ in}^2 = x^2$$
$$7 \text{ in} = x$$

Therefore, the longest side is $5 \times 7 \text{ in} = 35 \text{ in}$.

86. D: The distance between two points (x_1, y_1) and (x_2, y_2) can be found with the following formula.

$$\text{distance} = \sqrt{(x_2 - x_1)^2 + (y_2 - y_1)^2}$$

Substitute the given points.

$$\text{distance} = \sqrt{(15-4)^2 + (18-9)^2}$$
$$= \sqrt{(11)^2 + (9)^2}$$
$$= \sqrt{121 + 81}$$
$$= \sqrt{202}$$

The distance between the two points is $\sqrt{202}$.

87. D: To solve for x, first isolate the variable by subtracting 8 from both sides.

$$-4x + 8 \geq 48$$

$$-4x \geq 40$$

Then, divide both sides by –4 to solve for x. When an inequality is divided by a negative number, the sign must change directions.

$$\frac{-4x}{-4} \geq \frac{40}{-4}$$

$$x \leq -10$$

88. C: The product of two odd numbers must be odd. The product of a positive number and a negative number must be negative. Therefore, this product is odd and negative.

89. B: This problem can be solved with the following equation, in which x is the total capacity of the tank.

$$\frac{1}{2}x = \frac{1}{3}x + 3$$
$$\left(\frac{1}{2} - \frac{1}{3}\right)x = 3$$
$$\left(\frac{3}{6} - \frac{2}{6}\right)x = 3$$
$$\frac{1}{6}x = 3$$
$$x = 18$$

Therefore, Archie's tank can hold 18 gallons of gas.

90. D: The area of a square is the length of one side squared, so first calculate the side. The perimeter of a square is 4 times the length of the side, so the length of one side for this square is $\frac{160}{4} = 40$ m. to obtain the area, square this number, getting the result $40 \times 40 = 1{,}600\text{ m}^2$.

91. B: The product of any number and an even number must be even. Therefore, the first product will be even. The second multiplication produces the product of this even number and an odd number, which must also be even. Therefore, the final result must be even.

92. D: First, calculate how many girls there will be after 10 more join the class.

$$13 + 10 = 23$$

Then, express the number of girls compared to boys as a ratio.

$$23 : 15$$

93. D: Since a and b are even integers, each can be expressed as the product of 2 and an integer. So, if we let $a = 2x$ and $b = 2y$, then $3(2x)^2 + 9(2y)^3 = c$.

$$3(4x^2) + 9(8y^3) = c$$
$$12x^2 + 72y^3 = c$$
$$12(x^2 + 6y^3) = c$$

Since c is the product of 12 and some other integer, 12 must be a factor of c. Incidentally, the numbers 2, 3, and 6 must also be factors of c since each is also a factor of 12.

94. C: In a 45-45-90 triangle, the legs can be found by dividing the hypotenuse by $\sqrt{2}$, so one leg is $\frac{4}{\sqrt{2}}$. We simplify $\frac{4}{\sqrt{2}}$ by multiplying by $\frac{\sqrt{2}}{\sqrt{2}}$.

$$\frac{4\sqrt{2}}{\sqrt{2}\sqrt{2}} = \frac{4\sqrt{2}}{2} = 2\sqrt{2}$$

Therefore, the three sides of the triangle are $2\sqrt{2}$, $2\sqrt{2}$, and 4. We add these sides together to obtain the perimeter: $4 + 4\sqrt{2}$.

Answer choice A is incorrect because it is the area rather than the perimeter. Answer choice B is incorrect because it is the area without the last step of dividing by 2. Answer choice D is incorrect because it is only two of the three sides.

95. C: A system of linear equations can be solved by using matrices or by using the graphing, substitution, or elimination (also called linear combination) method. The elimination method is shown here:

$$3x + 4y = 2$$
$$2x + 6y = -2$$

In order to eliminate x by linear combination, multiply the top equation by 2 and the bottom equation by –3 so that the coefficients of the x-terms will be additive inverses.

$$2(3x + 4y = 2)$$
$$-3(2x + 6y = -2)$$

Then, add the two equations and solve for y.

$$\begin{aligned} 6x + 8y &= 4 \\ \underline{-6x - 18y} &\underline{= 6} \\ -10y &= 10 \\ y &= -1 \end{aligned}$$

Substitute –1 for y in either of the given equations and solve for x.

$$\begin{aligned} 3x + 4y &= 2 \\ 3x + 4(-1) &= 2 \\ 3x - 4 &= 2 \\ 3x &= 6 \\ x &= 2 \end{aligned}$$

The solution to the system of equations is $(2, -1)$.

96. D: Rearrange the equation to isolate q. First, subtract $6q$ from both sides.

$$6q + 3 = 8q - 7$$

$$3 = 2q - 7$$

Then, add 7 to both sides.

$$10 = 2q$$

Finally, divide both sides by 2.

$$5 = q$$

97. C: Lines that are perpendicular to each other have negative reciprocal slopes. The slope of the original equation is $-5x$. The negative reciprocal of this is $\frac{x}{5}$. The value of the y-intercept is not important for the purpose of answering this question. The only equation with a slope of $\frac{x}{5}$ is $y = \frac{x}{5} + 27$, so this is the correct answer.

98. A: Use the volume of a rectangular prism formula, $V = l \times w \times h$, to determine the length of the tank. Substitute the known values and solve for l.

$$200 = l \times (8) \times (5)$$
$$200 = 40l$$
$$5 = l$$

Therefore, the length of the tank is 5 feet.

99. B: To multiply two powers that have the same base, you need to add their exponents. This is represented by the property $x^m \cdot x^n = x^{m+n}$. So, $x^3x^5 = x^{3+5} = x^8$.

100. D: To solve the inequality $3 - 2x < 5$, we can first subtract 3 from both sides to get $-2x < 2$. Now we can divide both sides of the inequality by -2. When an inequality is multiplied or divided by a negative number, its direction changes ($<$ becomes $>$, $\leq$ becomes $\geq$, and vice versa). So $-2x < 2$ becomes $\frac{-2x}{-2} > \frac{2}{-2}$, or $x > -1$.

101. A: The slope of the original line is $m = -\frac{5}{2}$. Since the new line needs to be parallel, the new slope needs to be the same as the original slope. The given point is (2,3), which is equivalent to (x_1, y_1) in the point-slope equation of $y - y_1 = m(x - x_1)$. Substitute in the new slope and given point.

$$y - 3 = -\frac{5}{2}(x - 2)$$

Distribute on the right side of the equation.

$$y - 3 = -\frac{5}{2}x + 5$$

Add 3 to both sides of the equation.

$$y = -\frac{5}{2}x + 8$$

Multiply through by 2 and move the x-value to the left to get the answer in standard form.

$$5x + 2y = 16$$

Therefore, the equation of a line parallel to $y = -\frac{5}{2}x + 2$ that passes through the point (2,3) is $5x + 2y = 16$.

102. B: Since the figures are similar, the following proportion may be written and solved for x.

$$\frac{5}{7.5} = \frac{12}{x}$$

$$5x = 90$$

$$x = 18$$

Therefore, the missing side length is 18.

103. B: One method that can be used to answer this question is to write and solve the proportion $\frac{3}{20} = \frac{V}{360}$, where V stands for the number of Brand V televisions that were sold at the furniture store. To solve the proportion, we can cross multiply.

$$20V = 1{,}080$$

We solve this equation by dividing both sides of the equation by 20.

$$V = 54$$

Therefore, she should expect 54 of the televisions sold to be Brand V.

104. B: Use trigonometric identities to simplify. First, convert $\sec\theta$ to $\frac{1}{\cos\theta}$.

$$\sin\theta\sec\theta$$

$$\sin\theta \times \frac{1}{\cos\theta}$$

Then, multiply the two values.

$$\frac{\sin\theta}{\cos\theta}$$

Remember, $\frac{\sin\theta}{\cos\theta} = \tan\theta$, so the simplified form of the expression is $\tan\theta$.

105. C: The expression representing the charge for Ride Service A is $\$10 + \$0.25(m - 10)$, where m is the number of miles. Set this expression equal to the charge for Ride Service B, which is $\$0.40m$. Solve for m to find the number of miles the two companies charge the same amount.

$$\begin{aligned} \$10 + \$0.25(m - 10) &= \$0.40m \\ \$10 + \$0.25m - \$2.50 &= \$0.40m \\ \$7.50 &= \$0.15m \\ m &= 50 \end{aligned}$$

So, the cost of the two services would be the same for a 50-mile ride.

106. B: Currently, there are two men for every woman. If the number of women is doubled, then the new ratio is 2 : 2. This is equivalent to 1 : 1.

107. A: The ratio asked for is the number of finches compared to the number of sparrows. This compares is the ratio 16 : 20, but the ratio can be written in simpler form by dividing both numbers in the ratio by 4. This gives the ratio 4 : 5. It is important to notice the order of the ratio. Since the number of finches is written before the number of sparrows, the ratio must be 16 to 20 and not 20 to 16. Also, note that the number of wrens or jays does not matter here.

108. B: Since the figures are similar, the following proportion may be written and solved for x.

$$\frac{6}{4} = \frac{8}{x}$$
$$6x = 4 \times 8$$
$$6x = 32$$
$$x = \frac{32}{6} = 5\frac{2}{6} = 5\frac{1}{3}$$

Therefore, the measure of x is $5\frac{1}{3}$ in.

109. C: One way to find this answer is to set up a proportion: $\frac{6}{10} = \frac{G}{240}$, in which G represents the number of Grade 6 students living within two miles of the school. To solve the proportion, cross-multiply.

$$10G = 1{,}440$$

To solve the equation, divide both sides of the equation by 10.

$$G = 144$$

Therefore, Harold should expect 144 students to live within two miles of the school.

110. C: To calculate the midpoint of a line segment, use the midpoint formula.

$$\text{midpoint} = \left(\frac{x_1 + x_2}{2}, \frac{y_1 + y_2}{2}\right)$$

Substitute (6,20) for (x_1, y_1) and (10,40) for (x_2, y_2).

$$\text{midpoint} = \left(\frac{6 + 10}{2}, \frac{20 + 40}{2}\right)$$
$$\text{midpoint} = \left(\frac{16}{2}, \frac{60}{2}\right)$$
$$\text{midpoint} = (8{,}30)$$

Therefore, the midpoint is (8,30).

111. C: The problem does not give any information about the size of the pen or the spacing between any of the posts. Nevertheless, creating a simple illustration that shows the order of the posts will help when approaching this problem. The line below shows the stretched-out fence and possible positions of the posts based on the parameters.

C A B E F-L D

From the drawing above, we can see that statements I and II are true. Statement III appears to be true, but since we are not given any information about the spacing between posts, we cannot say definitively that E and D are farther apart than A and E.

112. A: The slope is the variable in front of the x when the equation is in the following form: $y = mx + b$. We rewrite the equation $5 - 3y = 2x + 8$ by first subtracting 5 from both sides.

$$-3y = 2x + 8$$

Then, divide both sides by -3.

$$y = -\frac{2}{3}x - 1$$

The slope is the number in front of the x, which is $-\frac{2}{3}$.

113. B: Since there are equal numbers of each coin in the row, if two of one type are next to each other, two of the other type must also be next to each other someplace within the row, or else at each end of the row. Since the two dimes take up one end of the row, the two pennies must be together.

114. A: For the line to be parallel to the x-axis, the slope must be 0. This condition is met for all equations $y = a$, where a is any constant.

115. A: Use the area formula for a square: $A = s^2$. Substitute the known information into the equation and solve for s.

$$81 = s^2$$
$$s = \pm 9$$

Since the side of the garden is a length, it must be positive. Therefore, the length of one side of the garden is 9 feet.

116. C: The distance may be calculated using the distance formula, $d = \sqrt{(x_2 - x_1)^2 + (y_2 - y_1)^2}$. Substitute the given coordinates into the formula.

$$d = \sqrt{(4 - (-8))^2 + (3 - 6)^2}$$
$$d = \sqrt{(12)^2 + (-3)^2}$$
$$d = \sqrt{144 + 9}$$
$$d = \sqrt{153}$$

Therefore, the distance between the two points is $\sqrt{153}$.

117. C: First, calculate how many students one worker could serve by dividing 24 by 3.

$$24 \div 3 = 8$$

One worker can serve 8 students. Now, divide the total number of students by the number each worker could serve.

$$136 \div 8 = 17$$

Therefore, 17 workers will be needed for a school with 136 students.

118. C: We need to simplify the equation so we can factor it. First, we subtract 2 from each side.

$$3x^2 - 3x - 36 = 0$$

Then we can divide each term by 3.

$$x^2 - x - 12 = 0$$

Finally, we can factor.

$$(x + 3)(x - 4) = 0$$

Setting each factored term equal to 0 yields $x + 3 = 0$ and $x - 4 = 0$, or $x = -3$ and $x = 4$. The sum of -3 and 4 is 1.

119. C: The area of a circle is equal to πr^2, where r is the radius. Therefore, $\pi r^2 = 36\pi$, and $r = \sqrt{36} = 6$. Since the diameter is twice the radius, it is equal to 12.

120. D: First set the relationship up. Then, solve for the number of packs by cross multiplying.

$$\frac{x}{2} = \frac{5}{\text{packs}}$$

$$x(\text{packs}) = 10$$

$$\text{packs} = \frac{10}{x}$$

Therefore, Leaonard can buy $\frac{10}{x}$ packs for \$5.00.

Essay

1. Your Classic Learning Test essay is not included in your final score, but it does provide an opportunity to demonstrate your unfiltered writing skills to the colleges that receive your score. There is no official rubric or length requirement to meet. That said, it is a great opportunity to distinguish your essay with good organization and strong arguments. Longer is not always better, but your essay should be long enough to demonstrate your ability to make a logical argument with good evidence.

Essay question graders commonly look for the following elements in a strong response: strong content knowledge, clear organization, and effective arguments or examples. Language and usage are not usually strictly graded, but can make a big impact on the clarity of your ideas.

Please use the provided rubric to make sure your response meets these common criteria. Try to have a friend or family member grade your response for you or take a break after writing your response and return to grade it with fresh eyes.

Constructed Response Rubric

Domain	Description
Content Knowledge	• The response directly addresses every part of the prompt. • The response demonstrates independent knowledge of the topic. • The response discusses the topic at an appropriate depth.
Organization	• The response introduces the topic, usually with a thesis statement or by restating the prompt. • The response directly addresses the prompt by providing a clear and concise answer or solution. • The answer or solution is supported by logical arguments or evidence. • The response restates the main idea in the conclusion.
Arguments and Examples	• The response provides a reasonable answer to the prompt. • The answer is supported by strong reasoning or evidence. • The response develops ideas logically and connects ideas to one another. • The reasoning and evidence provided act to support a unified main idea.
Language and Usage	• The response demonstrates effective use of grammar and uses varied sentence structure throughout the response. • The response demonstrates correct use of spelling, punctuation, and capitalization. • The response demonstrates strong and varied use of vocabulary relevant to the topic and appropriate for the intended audience.

How to Overcome Test Anxiety

Just the thought of taking a test is enough to make most people a little nervous. A test is an important event that can have a long-term impact on your future, so it's important to take it seriously and it's natural to feel anxious about performing well. But just because anxiety is normal, that doesn't mean that it's helpful in test taking, or that you should simply accept it as part of your life. Anxiety can have a variety of effects. These effects can be mild, like making you feel slightly nervous, or severe, like blocking your ability to focus or remember even a simple detail.

If you experience test anxiety—whether severe or mild—it's important to know how to beat it. To discover this, first you need to understand what causes test anxiety.

Causes of Test Anxiety

While we often think of anxiety as an uncontrollable emotional state, it can actually be caused by simple, practical things. One of the most common causes of test anxiety is that a person does not feel adequately prepared for their test. This feeling can be the result of many different issues such as poor study habits or lack of organization, but the most common culprit is time management. Starting to study too late, failing to organize your study time to cover all of the material, or being distracted while you study will mean that you're not well prepared for the test. This may lead to cramming the night before, which will cause you to be physically and mentally exhausted for the test. Poor time management also contributes to feelings of stress, fear, and hopelessness as you realize you are not well prepared but don't know what to do about it.

Other times, test anxiety is not related to your preparation for the test but comes from unresolved fear. This may be a past failure on a test, or poor performance on tests in general. It may come from comparing yourself to others who seem to be performing better or from the stress of living up to expectations. Anxiety may be driven by fears of the future—how failure on this test would affect your educational and career goals. These fears are often completely irrational, but they can still negatively impact your test performance.

Elements of Test Anxiety

As mentioned earlier, test anxiety is considered to be an emotional state, but it has physical and mental components as well. Sometimes you may not even realize that you are suffering from test anxiety until you notice the physical symptoms. These can include trembling hands, rapid heartbeat, sweating, nausea, and tense muscles. Extreme anxiety may lead to fainting or vomiting. Obviously, any of these symptoms can have a negative impact on testing. It is important to recognize them as soon as they begin to occur so that you can address the problem before it damages your performance.

The mental components of test anxiety include trouble focusing and inability to remember learned information. During a test, your mind is on high alert, which can help you recall information and stay focused for an extended period of time. However, anxiety interferes with your mind's natural processes, causing you to blank out, even on the questions you know well. The strain of testing during anxiety makes it difficult to stay focused, especially on a test that may take several hours. Extreme anxiety can take a huge mental toll, making it difficult not only to recall test information but even to understand the test questions or pull your thoughts together.

Effects of Test Anxiety

Test anxiety is like a disease—if left untreated, it will get progressively worse. Anxiety leads to poor performance, and this reinforces the feelings of fear and failure, which in turn lead to poor performances on subsequent tests. It can grow from a mild nervousness to a crippling condition. If allowed to progress, test anxiety can have a big impact on your schooling, and consequently on your future.

Test anxiety can spread to other parts of your life. Anxiety on tests can become anxiety in any stressful situation, and blanking on a test can turn into panicking in a job situation. But fortunately, you don't have to let anxiety rule your testing and determine your grades. There are a number of relatively simple steps you can take to move past anxiety and function normally on a test and in the rest of life.

Physical Steps for Beating Test Anxiety

While test anxiety is a serious problem, the good news is that it can be overcome. It doesn't have to control your ability to think and remember information. While it may take time, you can begin taking steps today to beat anxiety.

Just as your first hint that you may be struggling with anxiety comes from the physical symptoms, the first step to treating it is also physical. Rest is crucial for having a clear, strong mind. If you are tired, it is much easier to give in to anxiety. But if you establish good sleep habits, your body and mind will be ready to perform optimally, without the strain of exhaustion. Additionally, sleeping well helps you to retain information better, so you're more likely to recall the answers when you see the test questions.

Getting good sleep means more than going to bed on time. It's important to allow your brain time to relax. Take study breaks from time to time so it doesn't get overworked, and don't study right before bed. Take time to rest your mind before trying to rest your body, or you may find it difficult to fall asleep.

Along with sleep, other aspects of physical health are important in preparing for a test. Good nutrition is vital for good brain function. Sugary foods and drinks may give a burst of energy but this burst is followed by a crash, both physically and emotionally. Instead, fuel your body with protein and vitamin-rich foods.

Also, drink plenty of water. Dehydration can lead to headaches and exhaustion, especially if your brain is already under stress from the rigors of the test. Particularly if your test is a long one, drink water during the breaks. And if possible, take an energy-boosting snack to eat between sections.

Along with sleep and diet, a third important part of physical health is exercise. Maintaining a steady workout schedule is helpful, but even taking 5-minute study breaks to walk can help get your blood pumping faster and clear your head. Exercise also releases endorphins, which contribute to a positive feeling and can help combat test anxiety.

When you nurture your physical health, you are also contributing to your mental health. If your body is healthy, your mind is much more likely to be healthy as well. So take time to rest, nourish your body with healthy food and water, and get moving as much as possible. Taking these physical steps will make you stronger and more able to take the mental steps necessary to overcome test anxiety.

Mental Steps for Beating Test Anxiety

Working on the mental side of test anxiety can be more challenging, but as with the physical side, there are clear steps you can take to overcome it. As mentioned earlier, test anxiety often stems from lack of preparation, so the obvious solution is to prepare for the test. Effective studying may be the most important weapon you have for beating test anxiety, but you can and should employ several other mental tools to combat fear.

First, boost your confidence by reminding yourself of past success—tests or projects that you aced. If you're putting as much effort into preparing for this test as you did for those, there's no reason you should expect to fail here. Work hard to prepare; then trust your preparation.

Second, surround yourself with encouraging people. It can be helpful to find a study group, but be sure that the people you're around will encourage a positive attitude. If you spend time with others who are anxious or cynical, this will only contribute to your own anxiety. Look for others who are motivated to study hard from a desire to succeed, not from a fear of failure.

Third, reward yourself. A test is physically and mentally tiring, even without anxiety, and it can be helpful to have something to look forward to. Plan an activity following the test, regardless of the outcome, such as going to a movie or getting ice cream.

When you are taking the test, if you find yourself beginning to feel anxious, remind yourself that you know the material. Visualize successfully completing the test. Then take a few deep, relaxing breaths and return to it. Work through the questions carefully but with confidence, knowing that you are capable of succeeding.

Developing a healthy mental approach to test taking will also aid in other areas of life. Test anxiety affects more than just the actual test—it can be damaging to your mental health and even contribute to depression. It's important to beat test anxiety before it becomes a problem for more than testing.

Study Strategy

Being prepared for the test is necessary to combat anxiety, but what does being prepared look like? You may study for hours on end and still not feel prepared. What you need is a strategy for test prep. The next few pages outline our recommended steps to help you plan out and conquer the challenge of preparation.

Step 1: Scope Out the Test

Learn everything you can about the format (multiple choice, essay, etc.) and what will be on the test. Gather any study materials, course outlines, or sample exams that may be available. Not only will this help you to prepare, but knowing what to expect can help to alleviate test anxiety.

Step 2: Map Out the Material

Look through the textbook or study guide and make note of how many chapters or sections it has. Then divide these over the time you have. For example, if a book has 15 chapters and you have five days to study, you need to cover three chapters each day. Even better, if you have the time, leave an extra day at the end for overall review after you have gone through the material in depth.

If time is limited, you may need to prioritize the material. Look through it and make note of which sections you think you already have a good grasp on, and which need review. While you are studying, skim quickly through the familiar sections and take more time on the challenging parts.

Write out your plan so you don't get lost as you go. Having a written plan also helps you feel more in control of the study, so anxiety is less likely to arise from feeling overwhelmed at the amount to cover.

Step 3: Gather Your Tools

Decide what study method works best for you. Do you prefer to highlight in the book as you study and then go back over the highlighted portions? Or do you type out notes of the important information? Or is it helpful to make flashcards that you can carry with you? Assemble the pens, index cards, highlighters, post-it notes, and any other materials you may need so you won't be distracted by getting up to find things while you study.

If you're having a hard time retaining the information or organizing your notes, experiment with different methods. For example, try color-coding by subject with colored pens, highlighters, or post-it notes. If you learn better by hearing, try recording yourself reading your notes so you can listen while in the car, working out, or simply sitting at your desk. Ask a friend to quiz you from your flashcards, or try teaching someone the material to solidify it in your mind.

Step 4: Create Your Environment

It's important to avoid distractions while you study. This includes both the obvious distractions like visitors and the subtle distractions like an uncomfortable chair (or a too-comfortable couch that makes you want to fall asleep). Set up the best study environment possible: good lighting and a comfortable work area. If background music helps you focus, you may want to turn it on, but otherwise keep the room quiet. If you are using a computer to take notes, be sure you don't have any other windows open, especially applications like social media, games, or anything else that could distract you. Silence your phone and turn off notifications. Be sure to keep water close by so you stay hydrated while you study (but avoid unhealthy drinks and snacks).

Also, take into account the best time of day to study. Are you freshest first thing in the morning? Try to set aside some time then to work through the material. Is your mind clearer in the afternoon or evening? Schedule your study session then. Another method is to study at the same time of day that you will take the test, so that your brain gets used to working on the material at that time and will be ready to focus at test time.

Step 5: Study!

Once you have done all the study preparation, it's time to settle into the actual studying. Sit down, take a few moments to settle your mind so you can focus, and begin to follow your study plan. Don't give in to distractions or let yourself procrastinate. This is your time to prepare so you'll be ready to fearlessly approach the test. Make the most of the time and stay focused.

Of course, you don't want to burn out. If you study too long you may find that you're not retaining the information very well. Take regular study breaks. For example, taking five minutes out of every hour to walk briskly, breathing deeply and swinging your arms, can help your mind stay fresh.

As you get to the end of each chapter or section, it's a good idea to do a quick review. Remind yourself of what you learned and work on any difficult parts. When you feel that you've mastered the material, move on to the next part. At the end of your study session, briefly skim through your notes again.

But while review is helpful, cramming last minute is NOT. If at all possible, work ahead so that you won't need to fit all your study into the last day. Cramming overloads your brain with more information than it can process and retain, and your tired mind may struggle to recall even previously learned information when it is overwhelmed with last-minute study. Also, the urgent nature of cramming and the stress placed on your brain contribute to anxiety. You'll be more likely to go to the test feeling unprepared and having trouble thinking clearly.

So don't cram, and don't stay up late before the test, even just to review your notes at a leisurely pace. Your brain needs rest more than it needs to go over the information again. In fact, plan to finish your studies by noon or early afternoon the day before the test. Give your brain the rest of the day to relax or focus on other things, and get a good night's sleep. Then you will be fresh for the test and better able to recall what you've studied.

Step 6: Take a Practice Test

Many courses offer sample tests, either online or in the study materials. This is an excellent resource to check whether you have mastered the material, as well as to prepare for the test format and environment.

Check the test format ahead of time: the number of questions, the type (multiple choice, free response, etc.), and the time limit. Then create a plan for working through them. For example, if you have 30 minutes to take a 60-question test, your limit is 30 seconds per question. Spend less time on the questions you know well so that you can take more time on the difficult ones.

If you have time to take several practice tests, take the first one open book, with no time limit. Work through the questions at your own pace and make sure you fully understand them. Gradually work up to taking a test under test conditions: sit at a desk with all study materials put away and set a timer. Pace yourself to make sure you finish the test with time to spare and go back to check your answers if you have time.

After each test, check your answers. On the questions you missed, be sure you understand why you missed them. Did you misread the question (tests can use tricky wording)? Did you forget the information? Or was it something you hadn't learned? Go back and study any shaky areas that the practice tests reveal.

Taking these tests not only helps with your grade, but also aids in combating test anxiety. If you're already used to the test conditions, you're less likely to worry about it, and working through tests until you're scoring well gives you a confidence boost. Go through the practice tests until you feel comfortable, and then you can go into the test knowing that you're ready for it.

Test Tips

On test day, you should be confident, knowing that you've prepared well and are ready to answer the questions. But aside from preparation, there are several test day strategies you can employ to maximize your performance.

First, as stated before, get a good night's sleep the night before the test (and for several nights before that, if possible). Go into the test with a fresh, alert mind rather than staying up late to study.

Try not to change too much about your normal routine on the day of the test. It's important to eat a nutritious breakfast, but if you normally don't eat breakfast at all, consider eating just a protein bar. If you're a coffee drinker, go ahead and have your normal coffee. Just make sure you time it so that the caffeine doesn't wear off right in the middle of your test. Avoid sugary beverages, and drink enough water to stay hydrated but not so much that you need a restroom break 10 minutes into the test. If your test isn't first thing in the morning, consider going for a walk or doing a light workout before the test to get your blood flowing.

Allow yourself enough time to get ready, and leave for the test with plenty of time to spare so you won't have the anxiety of scrambling to arrive in time. Another reason to be early is to select a good seat. It's helpful to sit away from doors and windows, which can be distracting. Find a good seat, get out your supplies, and settle your mind before the test begins.

When the test begins, start by going over the instructions carefully, even if you already know what to expect. Make sure you avoid any careless mistakes by following the directions.

Then begin working through the questions, pacing yourself as you've practiced. If you're not sure on an answer, don't spend too much time on it, and don't let it shake your confidence. Either skip it and come back later, or eliminate as many wrong answers as possible and guess among the remaining ones. Don't dwell on these questions as you continue—put them out of your mind and focus on what lies ahead.

Be sure to read all of the answer choices, even if you're sure the first one is the right answer. Sometimes you'll find a better one if you keep reading. But don't second-guess yourself if you do immediately know the answer. Your gut instinct is usually right. Don't let test anxiety rob you of the information you know.

If you have time at the end of the test (and if the test format allows), go back and review your answers. Be cautious about changing any, since your first instinct tends to be correct, but make sure you didn't misread any of the questions or accidentally mark the wrong answer choice. Look over any you skipped and make an educated guess.

At the end, leave the test feeling confident. You've done your best, so don't waste time worrying about your performance or wishing you could change anything. Instead, celebrate the successful completion of this test. And finally, use this test to learn how to deal with anxiety even better next time.

Review Video: Test Anxiety
Visit mometrix.com/academy and enter code: 100340

Important Qualification

Not all anxiety is created equal. If your test anxiety is causing major issues in your life beyond the classroom or testing center, or if you are experiencing troubling physical symptoms related to your anxiety, it may be a sign of a serious physiological or psychological condition. If this sounds like your situation, we strongly encourage you to seek professional help.

Additional Bonus Material

Due to our efforts to try to keep this book to a manageable length, we've created a link that will give you access to all of your additional bonus material:

mometrix.com/bonus948/claslearntest

Made in the USA
Las Vegas, NV
01 March 2024